The ARTS
OF DEMOCRACY

The ARTS
OF DEMOCRACY
ART, PUBLIC CULTURE, AND THE STATE

Edited by CASEY NELSON BLAKE

WOODROW WILSON CENTER PRESS
Washington, D.C.

UNIVERSITY OF PENNSYLVANIA PRESS
Philadelphia

EDITORIAL OFFICES
Woodrow Wilson Center Press
Woodrow Wilson International Center for Scholars
One Woodrow Wilson Plaza
1300 Pennsylvania Avenue, N.W.
Washington, D.C. 20004-3027
Telephone: 202-691-4010
www.wilsoncenter.org

ORDER FROM
University of Pennsylvania Press
P.O. Box 50370
Baltimore, Maryland 21211-4370
www.upenn.edu/pennpress
Telephone: 1-800-537-5487
(Hopkins Fulfillment Services)

2 4 6 8 9 7 5 3 1

Library of Congress Cataloging-in-Publication Data

The arts of democracy : art, public culture, and the state / edited by
  Casey Nelson Blake.
       p.   cm.
    Includes bibliographical references and index.
    ISBN-13: 978-0-8122-4029-0 (hardcover : alk. paper)
    ISBN-10: 0-8122-4029-4 (hardcover : alk. paper)
    1. Arts and society—United States.   2. Art and state—United States.
  3. Democracy and the arts—United States.   I. Blake, Casey Nelson
  NX180.S3A785 2008
  700.1′030973—dc22
                                                        2007037149

The Woodrow Wilson International Center for Scholars, established by Congress in 1968 and headquartered in Washington, D.C., is a living national memorial to President Wilson. The Center's mission is to commemorate the ideals and concerns of Woodrow Wilson by providing a link between the worlds of ideas and policy, while fostering research, study, discussion and collaboration among a broad spectrum of individuals concerned with policy and scholarship in national and international affairs. Supported by public and private funds, the Center is a nonpartisan institution. It establishes and maintains a neutral forum for free, open and informed dialogue. Conclusions or opinions expressed in Center publications and programs are those of the authors and speakers and do not necessarily reflect the views of the Center staff, fellows, trustees, advisory groups, or any individuals or organizations that provide financial support to the Center.

The Center is the publisher of *The Wilson Quarterly* and home of Woodrow Wilson Center Press, *dialogue* radio and television, and the monthly newsletter "Centerpoint." For more information about the Center's activities and publications, please visit us on the Web at www.wilsoncenter.org.

To the memory of Kenneth Cmiel

Contents

List of Figures   xi
Acknowledgments   xiii

Editor's Introduction: Public Culture Reconsidered   1

PART I COMMERCIAL CULTURE AS PUBLIC CULTURE

1 Festival Culture, American Style   11
   Neil Harris

2 Norman Rockwell, Public Artist   31
   Michele H. Bogart

PART II CULTURAL POLICY AND THE STATE

3 Culture and the State in America   69
   Michael Kammen

4 The Happy Few—en Masse: Franco-American
   Comparisons in Cultural Democratization   97
   Vera L. Zolberg

5 Exporting America: The U.S. Propaganda Offensive,
   1945–1959   123
   Laura A. Belmonte

6 The Goodwill Ambassador: Duke Ellington and
   Black Worldliness   151
   Penny M. Von Eschen

7   A Modernist Vision: The Origins and Early Years of the
    National Endowment for the Arts' Visual Arts Program   171
    Donna M. Binkiewicz

8   Between Civics and Politics: The Modernist Moment
    in Federal Public Art   197
    Casey Nelson Blake

PART III THE ARTS AND CIVIC CULTURE AFTER MODERNISM

9   The Swirl of Image and Sound: On the Latest Version
    of Antirealism   223
    Kenneth Cmiel

10 Public Attitudes toward Cultural Authority and Cultural
    Diversity in Higher Education and the Arts   243
    Paul DiMaggio and Bethany Bryson

11 "Subtle, Intangible, and Non-Quantifiable": Aesthetics,
    Law, and Speech in Public Space   275
    Leslie Prosterman

12 The Public Display of Religion   305
    Sally M. Promey

Contributors   343
Index   347

List of Figures

2.1   Norman Rockwell, *Pipe and Bowl Sign Painter*   37
2.2   Norman Rockwell, *Sign Painter, Billboard Painter*   39
2.3   Norman Rockwell, *Boy Gazing at Glamour Stars*   41
2.4   Norman Rockwell, *The Deadline*   42
2.5   Norman Rockwell, *Shuffleton's Barber Shop*   44
2.6   Norman Rockwell, *The Art Critic*   45
2.7   Norman Rockwell, *Triple Self-Portrait*   46
2.8   Norman Rockwell, *The Connoisseur*   48
5.1   U.S. information officials highlight the loving nature of
      American family relations   128
5.2   A woman visiting the National Gallery of Art scrutinizes
      Benvenuto Cellini's *Salt Cellar*   129
5.3   U.S. Information Agency photograph paints a bleak
      portrait of Soviet daily life   137
7.1   President Lyndon Baines Johnson swearing in the first
      members of the National Council on the Arts, Washington   174
7.2   David Smith, *Cubi XII*, Washington   178
7.3   Richard Diebenkorn, *Berkeley No. 22*, Washington   179
7.4   Alexander Calder, *La Grande Vitesse*, Grand Rapids   182
7.5   Robert Goodnough, *Movement of Horses B*, Washington   185
7.6   Mark di Suvero, *Are Years What? (For Marianne Moore)*,
      Washington   190
8.1   Dedication ceremonies for Alexander Calder's *La Grande
      Vitesse*, Grand Rapids   198
8.2   Alexander Calder, *Flamingo*, Chicago   199

8.3	Richard Serra, *Tilted Arc*, Lower Manhattan	201
8.4	George Sugarman, *Baltimore Federal*, Baltimore	209
8.5	Guy Dill, *Hoe Down*, Huron, South Dakota	213
8.6	Nizette Brennan, *Knoxville Flag*, Knoxville	215
9.1	Frank Gehry, Gehry residence, Santa Monica, California	227
9.2	Frank Gehry, Nationale-Nederlanden Building, Prague	228
9.3	Frank Gehry, American Center, Paris	229
9.4	Frank Gehry, California Aerospace Museum, Los Angeles	230
11.1	The annual Smithsonian Folklife Festival on the National Mall, Washington	277
11.2	The 1963 Civil Rights March on Washington	281
11.3	Demonstrators on the grounds of the Lincoln Memorial during the 1963 March on Washington	282
11.4	Middle Eastern students marching in Lafayette Park, in front of the White House, Washington	299
12.1	Memorial in Union Square by candlelight, New York City	307
12.2	Ten Commandments yard sign, Louisville, Ohio	308
12.3	Jesse Treviño, *Spirit of Healing*, Santa Rosa Children's Hospital, San Antonio	311
12.4	*Billings Gazette* menorah, Billings, Montana	316
12.5	Frédéric Brenner, *Citizens Protesting Anti-Semitic Acts, Billings, Montana, 1994*	317
12.6	Chimayo Holy Chiles, Chimayo, New Mexico	319
12.7	Cambodian Buddhist temple, Colesville, Maryland	320
12.8	Consecration ceremony, Our Lady of Vietnam Catholic Church, Silver Spring, Maryland	322
12.9	The Reverend George Stallings performing a Good Friday iconoclastic ritual, Washington	323
12.10	"Only One Judge" tattoo, based on Albrecht Dürer's *Praying Hands*	325
12.11	The Washington Temple, Church of Jesus Christ of Latter-Day Saints	326
12.12	"Surrender Dorthy" [sic] graffito on a railway overpass approaching the Washington Temple, Church of Jesus Christ of Latter-Day Saints	327
12.13	Adolph Weinman, east end of the north frieze, including a figure of Muhammad, Courtroom, U.S. Supreme Court, Washington	330
12.14	Intersection of New Hampshire Avenue and Norwood Road, Montgomery County, Maryland	335

Acknowledgments

This volume would not have been possible without the patience, persistence, and steadfast support of Susan Nugent, program assistant for the Division of United States Studies at the Woodrow Wilson International Center for Scholars. In fact, the Woodrow Wilson Center served as a home of sorts for the project from the outset. Michael Lacey, the inspired former director of the Division of United States Studies, was an ally and promoter. James Morris, formerly the director of the Historical, Cultural, and Literary Studies Program at the Woodrow Wilson Center, sponsored a conference that was the initial inspiration for this project. Herman Lebovics was an important contributor and colleague in the planning of that conference.

Robert Lockhart at the University of Pennsylvania Press was everything one could hope for in an editor: smart, committed, and humane, he expertly guided this book to publication. His assistant Chris Hu offered indispensable help with illustrations and permissions. Thanks also to Christopher Bell and Sandra Haviland at Penn Press for their hard work on publicity. Joe Brinley and Yamile Kahn at the Woodrow Wilson Center Press stepped in at crucial moments in the early and final stages of this project, offering support and close readings of the manuscript.

Daniel Horowitz and Charles McGovern provided characteristically insightful commentary on an early version of this book. We thank them both for their invaluable assistance.

As this book was going to press, we received the heartbreaking news that our colleague and fellow contributor Ken Cmiel had died. Ken's scholarship on public speech, aesthetics, social welfare, and human rights addressed the big questions at the heart of this volume with wisdom and eloquence that few of us can hope to match. We dedicate the collection to his memory.

The ARTS
OF DEMOCRACY

Editor's Introduction:
Public Culture Reconsidered

The most deadly terrorist attacks in the history of the United States provoked a wave of art making remarkable for its intensity and public engagement. Particularly in New York City, the site of the greatest devastation, the events of September 11, 2001, unleashed wave after wave of aesthetic expression and debate about the place of the arts in public life that have still not run their course six years later. In the days and weeks after the killings, impromptu memorials, graffiti murals, musical performances, poetry readings, and hastily organized oral history projects claimed urban spaces for rites of mourning and expressions of patriotism. Residents of the city who asked after their neighbors' safety—"Are you all right? Is your family all right?"—joined with people they did not know in expressions of grief and fellow feeling that immediately took artistic form. Their shared experience of trauma and solidarity lives on in the fascination with the rebuilding of the World Trade Center site and the design of a memorial to the dead.

The artistic reckoning with the terrible events of that day is a reminder, if any were necessary, of humans' need for symbolic representations of the lives they share with others—and of the private loss and pain that haunt their loneliest hours. The art making and art talk that followed the attacks likewise revealed with unusual clarity the complex convergence of imperatives that characterize public culture in a democracy. Informal acts of commemoration and small-scale responses to unfathomable tragedy clashed quickly in New York with the desire of local authorities to normalize public spaces in time for the lucrative holiday season. Those intrepid tourists who came to the city for Christmas 2001 found American flags and slick postings by charities and government agencies requesting donations for victims' families, not the heartbreaking "missing" posters, prayer cards, melted candles, and political slogans that had filled the streets only weeks before. Free spaces like the city's Union Square—which offered visitors a mesmerizing collage of religious, political, and artistic responses to mass murder—were sanitized by Thanksgiving, their artifacts hauled off to archives, as the World Trade Center site itself became a backdrop to photo opportunities for politicians. The local and international meanings of the tragedy—this was after all a *world* commercial center, located in lower Manhattan—quickly gave way to patriotic images that set the Twin Towers alongside the Statue of Liberty and Old Glory. Postcards depicting the missing towers as two enormous vertical flags are now staples in the city's tourist shops. Such images recast a visual landscape that had resonated with a multitude of emotions and opinions as a place of nationalist fervor, a launching pad for war.

By the time of the fourth anniversary of the attacks, the familiar dynamic of the cultural wars had extinguished any hope for the rebuilt World Trade Center as an open, public space. Conservative relatives of the victims and their political and media allies mobilized to banish a proposed "Freedom Center" for the site on the grounds that it might dishonor the dead. New York's Governor George Pataki, weighing a possible presidential race in 2008, insisted in the summer of 2005 that Ground Zero was no place for "debate" or "dissension." "We will not tolerate anything on that site that denigrates America, denigrates New York or freedom, or denigrates the sacrifice and courage that the heroes showed on September 11."[1] By the fall of that year, the museum and a smaller gallery for drawing were scrapped. Security concerns led to a major redesign of the so-called Freedom Tower as a hulking fortress, an eerie symbol of a civic imagination depleted by fear and a seemingly endless "war on terror."

Art and Democracy

The essays collected in this volume do not address the 9/11 tragedy and its aftermath, or the ongoing debates about how best to commemorate its victims, but they do illuminate the often contradictory impulses that have shaped the relationship between the arts and public life in modern America. The competing claims of commerce and democracy, of artists and patrons, of the nation-state and its citizens, of religion and politics, and of the ideal of a shared, democratic public sphere and the demands of diverse social groups—these are the recurrent themes of an emerging body of scholarship that unites art historians, historians of culture, politics, and diplomacy, ethnographers, sociologists, interpreters of public memory and commemoration, legal theorists, and scholars working in American studies, cultural studies and cultural policy, and religious studies, among many other fields. The essays collected here, which reflect the influence of two decades of debates inside and outside the academy about the arts, politics, and public life, represent the coming of age of one of the liveliest fields in contemporary scholarship.

Vigorous argument about the public life of artistic experience has a long pedigree in the United States and elsewhere. The earliest debates about the need for a distinctive American aesthetic appropriate to the conditions of a new, democratic nation themselves drew on a long tradition of republican aesthetics dating back to the ancient world, which saw in classical and neo-classical forms a public language appropriate to civic-humanist ideals. In more recent times, progressives, pragmatists, and radicals in the orbit of twentieth-century artistic movements—to name only a few, the Constructivists in the Soviet Union; the Bauhaus in Weimar Germany; and John Dewey, John Cotton Dana, Lewis Mumford, Holger Cahill, and Stuart Davis in the United States—expanded on these precedents in efforts to identify the artistic prerequisites of a more expansive participatory public life that still informs contemporary discussions in the arts. They were joined by leaders of the twentieth-century avant-garde—including dadaists, surrealists, Marxist advocates of the "alienation effect" in theater and the destruction of the sacralized "aura" surrounding fine art, and Situationists—all of whom sought to banish artificial distinctions between art and "real life." Within the realm of cultural history alone, the early work of Raymond Williams in Britain and of American Neil Harris (the contributor of chapter 1 in this volume) established a vital tradition of inquiry into the social history and public possibilities of artistic expression. This volume is indebted to such pioneers even as it expands their analysis into new realms of public life.[2]

In its concern with the role of the arts in enabling a democratic way of life, this collection also responds to a rich literature on public culture and the public sphere. Theorists of the liberal public sphere and democracy—from Dewey to Hannah Arendt, Jürgen Habermas, and Robert Putnam—have influenced a wider consideration of the symbolic environment conducive to civic engagement. Critics have charged such theorists with a homogeneous vision of politics that marginalizes difference and conflict in the name of a phantom public sphere; they offer instead a politics of contending "publics" and "counterpublics." Though many of the contributors to this collection acknowledge and indeed emphasize the competing claims that different groups have made on the ideal of the public, on balance this volume upholds the notion of a democratic public sphere as a regulative ideal and a resource for political criticism. At its best, the aesthetic fashioning and refashioning of a common public world is a project resonant with civic meanings and democratic aspirations.[3]

The essays that make up this volume also offer a rough road map of the history of the arts and public culture in the modern United States, tracing the shift from a historical moment at the turn of the last century when the market nurtured expressions of civic identity to a variety of state-sponsored cultural projects associated with the triumph of liberalism and modernism in the postwar period. The concluding essays of the collection detail the collapse of that liberal-modernist synthesis and the resulting pluralism of expressive languages and politics that mark our conflicted, postmodern public culture. Though not a systematic narrative, the volume's chapters lay the groundwork for future scholarship on the complex, interwoven histories of artistic expression, values, ideology, statecraft, and democratic aspiration.

Overview of the Book

This book is organized as follows. Part I includes chapters by Neil Harris and Michele Bogart on, respectively, turn-of-the-century musical festivals and the painting of Norman Rockwell, which confound the assumption that a private art market is necessarily hostile to the expression of civic identity. Music festivals at the turn of the nineteenth and twentieth centuries, Harris explains in chapter 1, "anticipated, with surprising precision, flash points of contemporary controversy." Their promiscuous mixing of high and low, commercial and public-spirited, national and international musical traditions likewise anticipated the long career of the twentieth-century artist and commercial illustrator Norman Rockwell, whom Bogart interprets in chapter 2 as a public artist of an idealized liberal America. Her chapter challenges the notion that public art is limited to monuments and murals in traditional civic spaces. Drawing on letters from Rockwell's admirers and critics, she charts the movement across the boundaries of refined and amateur tastes, and of the public and the profitable, that gave his work its national resonance and popular appeal. Like Harris, whose chapter examines the patrons and audiences for local music festivals, Bogart sets Rockwell's art in a cultural field made up of multiple actors, including commercial publishing, art markets, popular audiences, the mass media, and—of course—the artist himself. Together, these two chapters nicely represent a multiperspectival approach to the history of art and culture that inspires all the work in this collection.

The chapters in part II address the role of state cultural agencies in the middle years of the twentieth century. As chapter 3, Michael Kammen's now-classic essay on culture and the state charts the unique history of government-sponsored art and cultural work in the United States. In chapter 4, Vera Zolberg's examination of American and French approaches to national cultural policy compares the relatively limited U.S. experiments in this area with the more robust, centralized approach of the French state. This international perspective on American state policy informs chapter 5 by Laura Belmonte and chapter 6 by Penny Von Eschen on U.S. cultural initiatives abroad during the Cold War. Belmonte describes the efforts of the United States Information Agency to broadcast a distinctive "American way of life" around the globe, whereas Von Eschen's chapter reveals how Duke Ellington and other African-American jazz musicians made use of State Department–sponsored tours to promote the civil rights movement at home and liberation movements in postcolonial Africa.

Cold War imperatives deeply shaped the ideology of the architects of the National Endowment for the Arts in the early 1960s, according to Donna Binkiewicz, who demonstrates in chapter 7 that its oft-condemned "politicization" long predated the so-called art wars of the 1980s and 1990s. Indeed, Binkiewicz's chapter reminds us that the federal government's promotion of American art at midcentury was a political enterprise from the very start—

one meant to advance the national goals of Cold War policymakers even as it heralded American cultural freedom and the country's coming of age as an artistic power. In chapter 8, Casey Blake describes the rise and fall of a liberal-modernist project in federally sponsored public art, thus taking this story to its conclusion. Popular resistance to elite cultural policy after the 1960s combined hostility to modernist aesthetics with disgust at the failed promises of urban liberalism. In the aftermath of the local protests of art installations of the 1970s and 1980s, public artists and their allies have sharply divided between a radical "community arts" movement and a conservative campaign to revive patriotic and neotraditionalist iconography for public spaces. In both instances, the original commitment of liberal modernists to a shared public culture among Americans of diverse backgrounds has evaporated.

What unites the chapters in part II is both a nuanced understanding of the many historical groups and individuals that shaped arts policy during a period of confident liberal state building and their authors' refusal to see the audiences for government-sponsored art as passive recipients, let alone victims, of an elite cultural enterprise. Instead, as Von Eschen and Blake argue, liberal cultural policy had unintended consequences in the postwar period, enabling the expression of popular grievances that challenged many of the guiding assumptions of government authorities and art administrators. Despite initial limits on public participation, the midcentury experiment in state-sponsored art created opportunities for democratic debate and cultural innovation that, like the civil rights movement of the same period, marked both the apogee of liberal civic culture and its transcendence.

In part III, the chapters by Kenneth Cmiel, Paul DiMaggio and Bethany Bryson, Leslie Prosterman, and Sally Promey map a postliberal, postmodernist landscape in which competing artistic and civic languages frustrate hopes for a shared public life. Cmiel's examination of the "disconnect" of postmodern aesthetics and our media-oriented politics from the lived experience of ordinary citizens in chapter 9 finds an echo in DiMaggio and Bryson's analysis of survey research on the culture wars in chapter 10. In both cases, educated elites willfully ignore the commonsense judgments that people exercise in everyday life, impeding the creation of a more inclusive democratic culture. Whether in the early architecture of Frank Gehry, the magical realism of recent film and fiction, or the cynical political and cultural campaigns that dominate the media, the fragmentation of public experience represents Americans' multiple visions of a good life in ways that rule out the very possibility of a common conversation between citizens.

The chapters by Leslie Prosterman and Sally Promey bring the book to a close by examining the clash between an often chaotic public culture with liberal assumptions of a rational and resolutely secular public sphere. In chapter 11, Prosterman's treatment of federal regulations of protests on the National Mall, and her parallel discussion of court cases and legal precedents limiting artistic expressions, indicate the extent to which the nation-state's conception of appropriate public conduct has narrowed our imagination of the vigorous pluralism that a space like the Mall enables. In chapter 12, Promey's analysis of the "public display" of contemporary religious beliefs and practices in American life probes the limits of a liberal conception of public life cleansed of pluralistic contention. Mindful of the potential for intolerance and exclusions inherent in public expressions of faith, and of the historic needs that resulted in strict understandings of separation of church and state, Promey nonetheless makes a compelling case for the contributions of artistic expressions of religious commitment to a democratic public sphere.

If the chapters in part III chart the cacophony of voices and images that have fractured public discourse and aesthetic experience, their authors hold out the possibility for richer, more inclusive expressions of what holds us together as citizens and human beings. That hope animates this collection as a whole. From the music festivals of the late nineteenth century to the activism of jazz musicians in the middle years of the twentieth century to the religious display of the twenty-first century, the history chronicled here is less fitful than it may first appear. Continuities emerge in the reworking of artistic traditions, defiance of conventions of high and low, creative uses of commercial and public venues, fights over aesthetics and artistic practice, and the collision of state cultural policy and the popular imagination that have unleashed the cultural vitality and political innovation of the last century. Even in an age of global crusades, mass fear, and terrorist violence, such practices remain indispensable conditions for the arts of democracy.

Notes

1. Patrick D. Healy, "Pataki Warns Cultural Groups for Museum at Ground Zero," *New York Times*, June 25, 2005.
2. The literature on modernist and avant-garde efforts to erase the boundaries between art and everyday life is too enormous to cite here. The best theoretical introduction to the subject remains Peter Burger, *Theory of the Avant-Garde* (Minneapolis: University of Minnesota Press, 1984). On the pragmatist and broadly social-democratic efforts in the United States to rethink the arts as a public good, the central texts are John Dewey, *Art as Experience* (New York: Minton, Balch, and Co., 1934) and Lewis Mumford's classics from the 1930s, *Technics and Civilization* (New York: Harcourt, Brace, 1934), and *The Culture of Cities* (New York: Harcourt, Brace, 1938). For historical treatments of the intellectual and cultural milieu that Dewey and Mumford shared with other critics and many artists, see Casey Nelson Blake, *Beloved Community: The Cultural Criticism of Randolph Bourne, Van Wyck Brooks, Waldo Frank, and Lewis Mumford* (Chapel Hill: University of North Carolina Press, 1990); and A. Joan Saab, *Art for the Millions: American Art and Culture between the Wars* (Philadelphia: University of Pennsylvania Press, 2004). Richard Shusterman carries on the Deweyan tradition of aesthetic speculation in his *Pragmatist Aesthetics: Living Beauty,*

Rethinking Art (Lanham, Md.: Rowman & Littlefield, 2000). The tradition in cultural history that has influenced most of the contributors in this volume is represented, above all, by Raymond Williams, *Culture and Society, 1780–1950* (New York: Columbia University Press, 1958); and Raymond Williams, *The Long Revolution* (New York: Columbia University Press, 1961); as well as by the work of the contributor to this volume, Neil Harris, notably *The Artist in American Society: The Formative Years, 1790–1860* (New York: Braziller, 1966), and *Cultural Excursions: Marketing Appetites and Cultural Tastes in Modern America* (Chicago: University of Chicago Press, 1990).

3. The modern tradition of inquiry into the history and contemporary possibilities of the public sphere is best charted in the following classics: John Dewey, *The Public and Its Problems* (New York: H. Holt and Company, 1927); Hannah Arendt, *The Human Condition* (Chicago: University of Chicago Press, 1958); Jürgen Habermas, *The Structural Transformation of the Public Sphere: An Inquiry into a Category of Bourgeois Society* (Cambridge, Mass.: MIT Press, 1989); and Robert Putnam, *Bowling Alone: The Collapse and Revival of American Community* (New York: Simon & Schuster, 2000). Dewey's lifelong quest to expand the boundaries of democratic public life is the subject of Robert B. Westbrook, *John Dewey and American Democracy* (Ithaca, N.Y.: Cornell University Press, 1991). An excellent introduction to the debates surrounding Habermas's theory of the public sphere, including examples of critics who argue instead for a theory of multiple publics and counterpublics, is Craig Calhoun, ed., *Habermas and the Public Sphere* (Cambridge, Mass.: MIT Press, 1992).

PART ONE

Commercial Culture
as Public Culture

CHAPTER 1

Festival Culture, American Style

NEIL HARRIS

Of the making of festivals there is apparently no end. They flourish on both sides of the Atlantic as well as along the Pacific Rim. Hosted by small towns and large cities alike, ranging from a day or two to several months in length, they stretch across a considerable portion of every year, admittedly with special summer concentrations. Numerous enough to support imposing bibliographic guides, they are organized in festival handbooks by location, season, and theme.[1] And, in keeping with contemporary usage, the Web site Festivals.com offers online guidance for Internet users to more than 1,500 "merriment possibilities," which range from Native American powwows to monster-truck extravaganzas.[2]

Thematic divisions are probably the most problematic for any analyst to sustain, because American varieties challenge easy categorization.[3] Some appear historically oriented—Indian festivals, Spanish festivals, Wild West festivals. Others are athletic and/or agricultural—Logger's Jubilee (Morton, Wash.), Tulip Time (Holland, Mich., et al.), Carrot Festival (Holtville, Calif.), Cotton Carnival (Memphis). Still others possess a culinary basis—Pancake Festival (Glenn, Mich.), Maple Syrup Festival (Saint Albans, Vt.), Wild Rice Festival (Deer River, Minn.), Lobster and Seafood Festival (Rockland, Maine). But quite a few straddle any distinctive classification: Husking Bee (Kent, Conn.), Red Flannel Days (Cedar Springs, Mich.), Wizard of Oz Festival (Chesterton, Ind.). What almost all these share, along with their European counterparts, is a strong promotional bias, oriented toward maximizing the impact of tourist dollars. Alongside these are other organized events—county and state fairs, pageants, sporting championships—that share many features of the festival, lacking only the festival title or some near synonym.[4]

The apparent limitlessness and weightlessness of today's festival label, as well its candid commercial character and extraordinary amorphousness, have tended to trivialize its historic functions. Festivals devoted to the performance arts, especially to music, constitute a surprisingly neglected channel of cultural transfer and international exchange.[5] Music forms a suggestive typology for other areas of cultural migration, because, simultaneously, it constitutes a universal language and reflects distinctive national practices and affiliations. This chapter concentrates on the music festival, arguing that the early deployment of regularized, highly repetitive, and occasionally competitive celebrations played a major role in structuring and defining American high culture at the end of the nineteenth century. At the same time, principally for marketing reasons, music festivals also encouraged a more promiscuous performance tradition in America, mingling categories and levels of sophistication that resisted the formalizing, sacralizing trends that usually followed upon institutionalization.

Festivals were crucial channels for the importation and nurturing of a European-defined canon of artistic masterpieces, identifying communities of admirers. But they also managed to challenge and qualify this heritage. Begun often as popular enterprises, or drawing at least upon broadly inclusive civic ideals, festivals ironically helped stimulate the foundation of American orchestral and operatic organizations that often distanced themselves from popular audiences. But at a later point in the mid–twentieth century, in another reversal, they would be turned to as repopularizing instruments, devices for broader engagement. And even more recently, festivals have legitimated and exported back to Europe vernacular artistic accomplishments on their own. Thus festivals have serviced both conservative and insurgent agendas. While doing this, they have raised significant questions about relationships between high and popular culture, and the identification of audiences for both. The apparently endless proliferation of festival events today may testify to the internationalization of leisure and the power of tourist needs, as well as the allure of tourist dollars. But the festival form itself demonstrates the longevity of many contemporary debates about art patronage, national taste, and commercialization. Thus it has anticipated, with surprising precision, flash points of contemporary controversy, even while serving as a dedicated international transmission channel for culture.

English Precursors of American Festivals

Festivals of one kind or another have been around for thousands of years. Religious texts abound with references to them.[6] Modern festival histories acknowledge their antiquity by invoking, summarizing, and then quickly abandoning these ancient rites. Necessarily, I will do the same. Collective rituals associated with worship, merriment, pageantry, and performance have their origins, some anthropologists argue, in efforts to influence or propitiate nature with magical interventions.[7] They are linked to the agricultural calendar, along with a number of other religious holidays and celebrations.

Cultural festivals began to emerge with separate identities as political leaders deployed them to solidify power, dignify status, affect international relations, and curry favor with the masses. Festival timing and management increasingly came to have political significance. Dynastic ambitions during the Renaissance, particularly in France, Italy, and England, were crucial to festival music, processional art, and dramatic masques. The artists, musicians, composers, and dramatists who honored the birthdays, state visits, engagements, weddings, and triumphal entries of monarchs and other rulers, epitomized the most creative talent of their eras.[8] They provided specially commissioned statements of fealty and artistic imagination. In this sense, performance festivals, up through the seventeenth century—and beyond, if one acknowledges the immense set of festivals associated with the French and Russian revolutions—were important moments for the exercise of patronage and the presentation of new works. They were not yet what they would primarily become in the nineteenth century: restatements of canonized classics or popular favorites whose power rested on their honored familiarity.

Significant models for the modern musical festival—critically esteemed works performed by well-known artists, highly publicized and linked to special occasions—developed most clearly in eighteenth-century England.[9] It is here that the origins of this formal system of transatlantic transmission lie. Some precedents existed, but the English festival tradition flourished largely because of the popularity of George Frederick Handel. Handel's composing heyday lay in the reigns of George I and George II, but true adulation for his work developed while their successor, George III, sat on the throne.

Both in London and the provinces, Handel commemorations and oratorio festivals attracted huge audiences in the late eighteenth century. Their ramifications went far beyond simple pleasure in Handel's music. Historians have found them to be at one and the same time occasions bringing Anglicans and dissenters together, celebrations of civil comity and political tolerance, demonstrations of loyalty to the Hanoverian crown, parades of aristocratic lineage and pretension, displays of urban self-esteem, and finally, centerpieces for elaborate sets of social interactions. Thus their political meaning was complex and served various kinds of itineraries. But with their many social and political functions, these festivals seemed to possess a fundamentally religious character. Accounts by spectators and participants alike testify to rapturous mass emotions, almost unparalleled in their intensity. Though certainly there were other venues in England for musical performances, those events calling themselves festivals presumed that contemporaries would understand their heavily commemorative role.

Such events took place even during Handel's lifetime. One was the Three Choirs Festival, a gathering of singers and musicians first at Worcester and then alternating at Gloucester and Hereford. Lasting only one day, at first, and featuring collections taken up for the widows and orphans of clergymen and choir members, as the years passed it was extended in duration and repertory. Morning concerts in the cathedral were followed by evening concerts, all dominated by Handel oratorios. Other provincial towns also held periodic performances of Handel oratorios in the late eighteenth century, among them Winchester, Derby, Bristol, Leicester, Nottingham, and Salisbury. Some historians associate them with a long-term gentrifying process, particularly in the North of England. These concert clusters went under the name of festivals by reason of size; reliance upon visiting performers; and, with some frequency, anticipated recurrence—although a number of festivals were unique events, dedicating organs, for example, or accompanying official installations in office.

There were also specific religious encouragements to festival activity. During Lent, for example, because of prohibitions on dramatic performances, London theaters presented multiple and competing performances of Handel's music, known as festivals. The period's taste for Handel climaxed with the 1784 centennial commemoration of his birth, celebrated at Westminster Abbey and the Pantheon, an observance that galvanized general attention. So "extraordinary a spectacle, we believe, never before solicited the public notice," declared one journal.[10] Coming just after a series of political and constitutional crises, including the American Revolution, it became "the expression of hope for a harmonious new order," William Weber has written, "a ritual that . . . dramatized the reunion of Tory and Whig within a new political community."[11]

The passion for Handel festivals was even more closely identified with triennial events held in the city of Birmingham.[12] Lasting for almost 150 years, the Birmingham observances ended only with the coming of World War I. These musical extravaganzas, and extravaganzas they soon became, were linked originally to philanthropic purposes: in Birmingham's case, to raising money to build a general hospital. But the musical performances soon became their own reason for being. They featured soloists, often Italian singers, commanding large fees, and imported stars would eventually become a modern festival tradition. However, choir members and instrumentalists usually worked without any wages; indeed, in many instances they had to pay for their own transport and lodging. As a rule, they were members of choral societies in other cities, and they sang and played because of musical enthusiasm and social gregariousness. Because most festivals were not annual and lasted only two or three days, the costs they assumed were not enormous.

The scale of performance, however, was indeed enormous. By the 1840s and 1850s, what had been substantial but relatively modest gatherings now achieved truly gargantuan proportions. Choruses of two or three thousand, orchestras of five hundred or more, these became hallmarks of festival events. And the notion of a festival was becoming synonymous not only with large scale choral and instrumental performances but with expressly chosen pieces.

Festival programs were highly repetitive, dominated by specific Handel works: *The Messiah*, the *Dettingen Te Deum, Israel in Egypt, Judas Maccabeus,* and occasional extracts from other sacred oratorios. During the nineteenth century, sacred compositions by contemporary composers were often added.

Another festival tradition, which would be exported to America, was the construction of special buildings. The size of these great ensembles taxed existing facilities. Thus Birmingham built its famous Town Hall specifically for the triennial festival. It was for this auditorium that composers like Gounod, Elgar, Dvorak, and Sir Arthur Sullivan conducted or prepared specially commissioned music. In 1840 Mendelssohn led the premiere of what would become one of the most popular of all Victorian compositions—both in Britain and America—his sacred oratorio *Elijah.* In London, starting in the 1850s huge festival orchestras and choruses found a home in the much enlarged and reconstructed Crystal Palace, moved, after the Great Exhibition had ended, from Hyde Park to Sydenham. Triennially, starting in 1862, Handel Festivals were held here that, with some interruptions, survived until the 1920s. Lasting several days each triennium, the performances attracted as many as 25,000 people.[13] Mounted at a time when the American impresario P. T. Barnum was achieving an international reputation for the colossal and the overstated, the British festivals demonstrated that elaborate advertising and an emphasis on scale, sound level, and associated spectacle effects was as much a European development as it was an American invention.

But the spirit of the festivals, even when not linked to specific charitable purposes, continued to be overwhelmingly religious, or at least devout. Covering one of the triennial Handel Festivals at the Crystal Palace in 1868, Moncure D. Conway, a former radical abolitionist and now a London pastor, stressed the piety of the crowds, calling the setting one of the great "churches of the middle classes."[14] This particular festival increased the chorus to more than 4,000 for the opening performance, and Conway himself worried that the fireworks demonstrations meant to enhance the occasion were in danger of overwhelming the music. Showmanship, in short, was becoming a dominant festival force and was already a source of concern to high culture enthusiasts. Such tension would constitute a long-running theme in festival management.

Festivals Come to America

The English festivals had a direct American influence, both in form and substance. They were engines in the transmission of the musical repertory that continues to dominate American concert performances. The clearest link lay in Boston's Handel and Haydn Society, an organization whose 1815 foundation makes it one of the oldest continuously operating musical societies in the country.[15] On one level at least, the Boston society's existence testified to the same American delight with the oratorios that had captured England. Tastes traveled across the ocean along with immigrants. The society's early activities were decidedly modest, although it held oratorio festivals, on a reduced scale from the British model, in 1857 and 1865.[16] Influenced also by British precedent, the city of Worcester, Massachusetts, hosted musical meetings that became festivals in the 1850s. There were also, in this era, occasional visits to New York by European conductors and "jumbo" ensembles, like Jullien's famed "Musical Congress" of 1854, that did everything but claim the festival title.[17]

But (with just a few anticipations) it was not until the late 1860s that anything like British enormity appeared. Then it did so with a vengeance and a somewhat less single-minded focus. Irish-born Patrick Gilmore was a band conductor with grand ambitions. His promotional talents surfaced on a number of occasions during the 1850s, 1860s, and 1870s, including a set of giant concerts organized for occupied New Orleans during the Civil War.[18] Gilmore was a serious musician who would revolutionize American band practices, but he was most celebrated (or notorious) for two great musical festivals he led in Boston in 1869 and 1872. These events were the products of a vision Gilmore claimed to have received by divine transmission. The first was labeled a National Jubilee; the second, a World Jubilee. Both were held in temporary structures built for the occasion, each bearing the name Coliseum. Despite its imposing name, the first Coliseum was destroyed by a storm after the jubilee had concluded.

Tens of thousands of New Englanders flocked to Boston for these performed pastiches of classical music, marches, arias, hymns, and popular tunes. The blend of repertory was far wider than it had been at the English festivals, and the scale was exceeded. These were, in fact, truly popular events, moving far beyond the ambitions of a few decades earlier. Spectators at both jubilees were joined by President Ulysses Grant and members of his Cabinet. Concerts almost invariably began and ended with hymns, some of which were sung by the audience, sustaining the sense of piety that lingered around the British festivals. Mingling the popular and the classic, Gilmore had a shrewd sense of what public taste permitted; for his second jubilee, he imported several European concert bands to play for the crowds, as well as the composer-conductor Johann Strauss Jr., who scored a personal triumph.

The number of musicians and choristers was huge. Gilmore doubled the performers from one jubilee to the next. After having 10,000 voices in 1869, he aimed for 20,000 in 1872, using a combination of speaking tubes and telegraph keys to control the immense ensemble. Again, the scale of the English festivals—smaller than Gilmore's but quite considerable on their own—had also dictated novel (and not invariably successful) methods to coordinate such performances. The highlights of the first jubilee, or the lowlights—according to the critic and novelist William Dean Howells, just launching his career in 1869 and transfixed by the immensities he encountered—were performances of the "Anvil Chorus" from Verdi's *Il Trovatore* featuring hundreds of local firemen, backed up by cannon firings and church bells.[19]

Such pyrotechnics were not absolutely novel. By contrast with the visiting French conductor Jullien, who complemented his New York presentation of the "Fireman's Quadrille" in the 1850s with a fire alarm and a brigade of uniformed firemen entering the hall, Gilmore might have seemed a model of restraint.[20] But his love of anvils, bells, and accompanying artillery produced some waves of shame from the musical establishment in Boston and torrents of criticism from various New York observers. Writing in the *Century*, William Foster Apthorp complained about the expense, the interruption of "more legitimate business," the "unpleasant air of charlatanry or vulgarity," and most of all, creation of "an unnatural and perverted appetite for what is merely big, rather than for what is great and good."[21] This was the festival as a vulgarized, crowd-pleasing, simpleminded exercise in excess. Not everyone agreed with Apthorp. The New Yorker George William Curtis insisted that it was "certainly a good thing to hear the famous orchestras and singers and players without going to Europe."[22] Making money and exaggeration were not the exclusive property of New England, Curtis informed his fellow New Yorkers; Gotham had its share of both.

The popularity and apparent vulgarity of Gilmore's efforts placed some festival enthusiasts in an embarrassing position, because the core of the festival form was size, and Gilmore was merely lifting this feature to ever higher levels. Gilmore himself appeared to repent; after a final bow to gargantuanism in Chicago in 1873, celebrating the city's recovery from its fire, he turned his attention to renovating the concert band, and he managed to take his troupe of trained musicians on a tour of Europe. Though he made no fortune from this trip, Gilmore scored a string of artistic successes, surprising Europeans with his playing of music by Liszt and Wagner. The Gilmore tour was an early reversal of cultural flow, an indication that American musical organizations could export their skills as well as import them.

The balance of trade, however, was still in deficit. The major reason that Americans did not have to visit Europe to hear high-quality musical ensembles and distinguished soloists was that so many performers had already come to America, particularly from Germany. The English festival tradition had created precedents and expectations for musical celebrations and established a foothold for a traditional repertory. But more influential in the long run would be the presence of German émigrés and their own custom of organizing musical societies and holding choral festivals.

The German Americans' Role

German singing societies were organized in American cities throughout the nineteenth century—some places literally containing dozens of them. Competitive zeal and a delight in camaraderie led to periodic gatherings known as Saengerfests (singing festivals), starting in the 1850s.[23] Cities with substantial German American populations, like St. Louis, Louisville, Cincinnati, Cleveland, and Chicago, were soon hosting Saengerfests. Such meetings bore some relationship to the English music festivals, except that the repertory tended to be less ambitious, the audiences much smaller, and the beer-drinking socializing more formidable. For a time confined to the ethnic community itself, they broke out of it partly because of the national standing of certain German American musicians, and partly because specific U.S. cities sought to elevate their accomplishments in the interests of local ambitions. An 1870 Saengerfest in Cincinnati, for example, and the construction of a special Saenger Hall, demonstrated the presence of a substantial audience for music and the possibility for more permanent musical structures.

Most notable among the musical transplants was the celebrated German-born conductor Theodore Thomas, who had emigrated to the United States as a young man, and who proceeded to revolutionize American musical appreciation and the orchestral world. Serious to a point of caricature, charismatic, and imbued with a missionary spirit, Thomas transformed the musical life of several cities, including New York, Chicago, and Cincinnati.[24] It was in Cincinnati where he introduced substantial elements of the modern musical festival to an American public, and it was in Cincinnati where the two strands most influencing American music festivals came together—English and German.[25] The major patrons of Cincinnati's first May Festival in 1873—Maria Longworth Nichols and her husband, George Ward Nichols—based their hopes on the success of the Birmingham Festival in England, and the widely separated Boston festivals of the Handel and Haydn Society.[26] These last Thomas himself had experienced as a musician. The Nicholses wished to see choral and orchestral masterworks performed as part of a larger program of cultural uplift in the city.

Thomas's ambitions were, if anything, even higher, and served to move the American festival into a new phase, one with didactic ambitions and increasingly rigorous expectations. In Thomas's case, cosmopolitan affiliations transcended ethnic origins. Earlier visits with a touring orchestra had solidified his local following in Cincinnati. In directing the city's first May Festival, he tested whether a four-day program of serious music, without the theatrics associated with the Gilmore Jubilees or the extensive socializing, beer drinking, and competitive performances of the German American meetings, could succeed. Despite their considerable contributions to the city's musical culture, German American elements in Cincinnati were largely shut out of the festival planning and management.[27] These German Americans raised questions, not only about their own exclusion but also about the Thomas festival's unremitting seriousness. Cincinnati was not alone, in the post–Civil War era, in experiencing tension between Anglo-American and ethnic groups over the control of public events. The histories of the Mardi Gras celebrations in both New Orleans and Mobile exhibited similar patterns.[28]

Thomas partly prepared for the great event by leading some major choral works at a somewhat hurriedly and haphazardly organized New York festival. In Cincinnati, with better planning and more elaborate forces, he conducted Handel's *Dettingen Te Deum* and Beethoven's *Ninth Symphony*, along with a series of excerpts from Handel, Haydn, and Gluck. Attendance was excellent, local critics were ecstatic, and backers promised more festivals to come. And they came quickly, with the rapid incorporation of the Festival Committee. During the 1870s, having learned both from Boston and Birmingham, Cincinnati emerged as America's musical festival capital—its residents claimed still broader cultural status—staging three festivals and using the third, held in 1878, as the basis for creating an enormous new auditorium, part of an exposition complex that was called the Cincinnati Music Hall. This was aided by the generosity of a single patron, a retired merchant, Reuben Springer, who had been impressed by the energy of the festivals and was determined to benefit his home town. A blend of grand philanthropy, local fund raising, and municipal ambitions, the Music Hall, inaugurated in May 1878, revealed the power of festivals to shape more permanent institutional structures. Festivals were rehearsals for local leadership networks as well as donor opportunities. Capital and enthusiasm were both necessary for the survival of ambitious organizations.

And Cincinnati was not alone in this linkage. It could be argued that the need to stimulate more permanent cultural structures and infrastructure helped nurture the festival mood of the late nineteenth century. Cities with important music festivals—Boston, Cincinnati, Worcester, New York, and Chicago—also became the sites of significant institutional accomplishments, again owing to the intervention of individual philanthropists. In the case of New York, the desideratum, according to Thomas and a number of others, was a permanent hall devoted to the presentation of large-scale musical performances. When, in 1882, New York hosted its first gargantuan music festival, it had to take place in the Seventh Regimental Armory. This was the city's first experience with a huge chorus and orchestra on the scale of the British celebrations. Thomas assembled a chorus of some 3,000 singers, taken not only from New York itself but from nearby eastern cities. The Handel and Haydn Society of Boston sent down more than 500 singers, who traveled in a boat, using it as their dormitory during the rehearsals and concert. The soloists included internationally established stars, one of whom had introduced the role of Brunhilde at Bayreuth, and the programs reflected the traditional obeisance accorded major works by Handel and Beethoven.

New York critics were ecstatic about finally bringing a great festival to their city, ending a vacuum they had long bemoaned. It seemed a signal of maturity, marking a triumphant phase in the evolution of local musical culture.[29]

Thomas, the festival conductor and longtime lion of the New York musical world, had been hoping for and occasionally planning a major concert hall for the city, one that would allow his orchestra to perform in an appropriate setting. As it turned out, the 1882 festival helped keep in motion events that would eventuate, a few years later, in just such a facility, Carnegie Hall, although by the time it would open Thomas himself had abandoned New York for Chicago, lured by the promise of generous private subsidies and a permanent orchestra.[30] Within a few years, Thomas would get a hall of his own, and at least partly, of his own design.

The Chicago Symphony Orchestra and the building of Orchestra Hall were certainly part of a broader pattern of cultural institutionalization in that city—a function of increasing wealth, social differentiation, ideology, and municipal ambition.[31] Lawrence Levine has placed its foundation within a broader process of sacralization applicable to other symphony orchestras, to art museums, and to a whole series of cultural practices formalized during the late nineteenth and early twentieth centuries in America.[32] But, within the area of music itself, the Chicago developments owed a good deal to the enormous success of the series of festivals that Thomas led there in the 1880s. These concerts were performed in an exposition building on Michigan Avenue, close to the business center of the Loop. Performing the same program he had organized in New York, now for audiences of 10,000, Thomas himself declared the Chicago festival superior in quality as well as scale. Local boosters, with characteristic restraint, crowed that the "railroad capital of the world" had suddenly become the "music capital of the world."[33] For high culture advocates, this ability to manage and publicize so complex an event, as well as attract large audiences and sustain a reasonable standard of musical competence, demonstrated the presence of appetite and resources. These could be translated into permanent institutions, which over time attracted a narrower wedge of the community than the festivals. Subscription audiences, for various reasons, had a more class-specific makeup than the larger crowds drawn to the spasmodic festival events. But the connection—and the tensions—between the more tolerant tradition of festivals and the greater rigor of the permanent orchestras flavored musical culture in cities like Chicago and shadowed the career of impresarios like Thomas.

Other, smaller cities also began to enjoy their festivals at just about this time. Hartford, for example, with a resident chorus, began its festival tradition in 1889, and over the next few years it presented—along with Bach, Handel, and Mendelssohn—Rossini, Saint-Saens, Berlioz, Sullivan, and some contemporary American composers. The music, according to the festival historian, was "bound to cover a good deal of ground, . . . arranged so as to attract all classes." Fundamental to each festival, the last of which took place in 1923, was a work "which could not be given without orchestra and chorus of the best training, as well as solo artists of some distinction."[34]

In some ways, festivals were the performance counterpart of the loan exhibitions that in many American cities, especially in the Midwest, typically preceded the establishment of art museums.[35] A group of art enthusiasts and "connoisseurs" would pool their resources and collections to produce a local art show. Exaggerated claims of authenticity and provenance aside, the shows drew large numbers of visitors; occasionally were repeated, like the festivals, on a biennial or triennial basis; and reassured backers about potential levels of support and existing art collections. The local loan exhibition, like the festival, was often a rehearsal for something else; like the festival, once it had served its immediate need, it would be subsumed within continuous cultural organizations and spaces. This may account for the fact that, unlike Europe, the American festival movement enjoyed a distinct peak in the late nineteenth century, standing in the vestibule of more permanent musical organizations and facilities. It was a demonstration, a pledge of fealty to a set of standards and kind of repertory that epitomized the highly ritualized world of American high culture.

For the American festivals, like their European counterparts, were extraordinarily repetitive. The programs have been analyzed in great detail, but the recurrence of particular pieces of music almost on an annual basis—Handel's *Messiah* and *Israel in Egypt*, Beethoven's *Ninth Symphony*, Mendelssohn's *Elijah* —reminds us of the difficulty of satisfying musical desire in a pre-phonographic age, particularly for large-scale musical compositions. The ecstatic mass responses to festival performances in Europe and America continued to stimulate religious analogies. In several ways, festivals can be likened to revival meetings, reassuring the congregants, after periodic lapses of time, that their faith still beat strong and they did not stand alone in their beliefs (or tastes).

Festivals were also like revivals in attracting the censure of those who thought they unfairly monopolized public attention. Their self-celebration and self-satisfaction in attendance levels disguised the humdrum, mundane duties necessary for the survival of musical institutions. Communities that boasted of the large crowds attracted to their festivals were not invariably hospitable to musicians. Sullivan, for one, likened Birmingham's musical activities and triennial festivity to a boa constrictor: gorging every three years but starving in between. Such views, both in Europe and America, qualified the ambitions of those who hoped to use festival enthusiasm as a basis for securing more permanent commitments to the arts. As with revivals, this debate over the respective value of sudden effusions or systematic worship would have no final resolution.

Experimentation for all the festivals was difficult because their box office results were so critical. The symphonic and oratorio works were lengthy and demanding, but they enjoyed a popular following. Festival directors tried from time to time to introduce contemporary compositions into their repertory, sometimes in surprising numbers. Most of these, both in Britain and America, were quite orthodox, modeled on the oratorios. But audience response to modernity proved to be tepid, and the traditional warhorses remained in their central positions.

Festival approaches were used in other American settings. Beginning with the Philadelphia Centennial of 1876 and continuing through the Panama-Pacific Exposition of 1915, the major world's fairs featured visiting bands, orchestras, and choirs, some of them gargantuan, from throughout the country and the world. These, along with famous soloists, performed a wide range of musical compositions, and even some pieces specially commissioned to mark the occasions. Few of these latter have survived, except as curiosities. Thomas, after some rueful experiences with world's fairs, advised managers to concentrate on entertainment; people did not come to expositions, he argued, to be improved or enlightened.[36] That function was better served by Chautauqua, both the assembly in upper New York State and the very popular, touring tent versions. Their combination of moral uplift, lectures, and musical entertainments constituted a species of intellectual vaudeville. Derided by later critics as a grotesquely flattened-out caricature of cultural ambitions, a monument to national philistinism, Chautauqua was a far more complicated movement than this, but its special complexities cannot be examined here.[37]

Except for the fact that they were nonrecurring events, at most expanded to a second season, the expositions did adapt many festival techniques, including the heavy advertising, emphasis upon scale and spectacle, and unique assemblies of performers and compositions. And like festivals and temporary exhibitions before them, the fairs stimulated the creation of permanent cultural institutions in their host cities. Museums, rather than symphonic ensembles or concerts halls, were the principal beneficiaries here.

One last American festival of this earlier period intimated changes ahead. This was the annual Bach Festival held in Bethlehem, Pennsylvania, which featured, at its opening session in March 1900, the first American performance of Bach's *B-Minor Mass*.[38] Situated in a city that had been founded by Moravian immigrants in 1741 but was now dominated by the Carnegie Steel works, Bethlehem became a place of pilgrimage, an American Bayreuth for Bach enthusiasts.

The Bethlehem audiences—specialized, even arcane in their tastes, and insistent upon high standards of musical performance—forecast a changing pattern for the American music festival, again imitative in everything but political itineraries of a transformed European model. It had been most decisively developed at Bayreuth in the 1870s and afterward, with the Wagner festivals. In the 1920s, the genre would be dominated by the overwhelming success of the newly created Salzburg Festival. Once contrasted with agenda-driven Bayreuth as an effusion of simple passion for Mozart and classical music, Salzburg's ideologically shaped bloodlines, as tortured in their ways as Bayreuth's own, have been uncovered by recent historians.[39] The festival gave an Austria that had been geographically and, some argued, spiritually emasculated by the post–World War I settlement the chance to turn back, for a time, to its folk roots and cultural past to nurture its national identity. Scholars have pointed to the conservative, Roman Catholic, and baroque flavor of the initial programs. Furious struggles erupted over the strategies, involving political, religious, and ethnic contests. But for an international assemblage of music lovers, Salzburg stood for the summertime consummation of musical habits and tastes nourished throughout the year, under conditions of great beauty and superb professionalism. The playing of the Vienna Philharmonic and the organization of extraordinary and innovative opera productions set a high international standard.

Modern American Festivals

A Salzburg ideal now descended upon American festival makers. America deserved a Salzburg, festival organizers cried; assuming that rank became the goal of both the Chautauqua Institute and the newly formed Berkshire Music Festival at Tanglewood, created in the mid-1930s and solidified just a couple of years after its establishment by a marriage between it and the Boston Symphony Orchestra.[40] Nazi domination of Salzburg created a vacuum that Americans might well fill. Rescue and asylum joined imitation as objectives, and these were applied more broadly to European high culture in the 1930s and 1940s.

The character of American interwar festivals had been, to be sure, irrevocably changed by the growth of film and radio, the proliferation of permanent cultural institutions like symphony orchestras and chamber music groups, and the construction of a more discriminating and cosmopolitan musical public. European conductors and performers now appeared regularly throughout the United States; and canonical works, even the most complex and demanding, were accessible to anyone with a radio or phonograph. It was no longer necessary to organize a festival to achieve the special musical effects brought by size. New performing festivals often reflected quite specialized interests. In the 1920s and 1930s, certain festivals stood out among the recent entries: contemporary chamber music, at Saratoga Springs, New York; dance, at Bennington, Vermont; and Bach, in Florida and California.[41]

There was also talk of using the American festivals as training grounds for a new cadre of American musicians and vocalists, as well as devices that might reduce the distance between high art and a mass audience. The fact that big music festivals, being summertime events, were held in the open air, serving ticket holders who picnicked before and during the actual concerts, offered some promise of accomplishing this last goal. At Tanglewood, Lucien Price wrote in 1940, with coatless artists sweating in the sun, "art begins to wear the look of honest toil." Music, originally an "out-of-door art, has been too much housed. . . . An art sinks its roots deeply into the soil of a nation only when it goes to and comes from the people—which is to say, when it can live in the open." The Boston Symphony, an "exotic hothouse plant, winter-grown under glass, is taken out into the Berkshire countryside to bloom by day under summer suns, to flower by night under summer stars, . . . to eat and sleep with the earth."[42] Such ambitions did not prevent critics from calling Tanglewood "swanky"; *Newsweek* complained about the ticket prices, bus fares, and hotel rates.[43]

In fact, Tanglewood was spectacularly successful, particularly in the years after World War II, drawing to its concerts, along with faithful devotees of the Boston Symphony Orchestra, large crowds of the unsophisticated, audiences whose dress and demeanor departed considerably from the formality of the early years. Not everyone was happy about the openness. Complaining about the crowd-pleasing antics of the visiting conductor Victor de Sabato, the *New Republic* critic Cecil Smith declared that appealing to the lowest common denominator would lead the festival down an unhappy path. "Tanglewood was not conceived as a forum for rabble-rousers. . . . Will it now become another Hollywood Bowl?"[44]

Smith's fears notwithstanding, a string of expanded facilities permitted this festival to serve a whole range of constituencies, whose diversity of interests— a tribute, some might argue, to democratic pluralism—would ultimately lead to tensions. This was especially true when it came to the vexing issue of contemporary music, which has had its own week-long festival (and festival director) at Tanglewood since the 1970s. Furious arguments about whether such arrangements marked a ghettoizing of nontraditional taste have threatened the longevity of managers and altered festival policies.[45]

By the 1950s and 1960s, of course, throughout Europe and America, a host of prospering summer festivals testified to increasing leisure, international mobility, and specialized, sometimes even arcane tastes. The Edinburgh, Holland, Aix-en-Provence, and Strasbourg festivals, along with a number of others, were all under way by 1950. Rather than stimulating permanent new ensembles, festivals now relied heavily on established and even venerable groups, from orchestras and choruses to quartets and trios. In or near Cleveland, Chicago, Philadelphia, and Washington, orchestral associations repeated the Boston pattern, extending their seasons by playing at specially created summer homes in festival formats. Occasionally, these orchestras would travel to one of the many European festivals flourishing at just the same time.[46] The performers at Edinburgh, Salzburg, Ravinia, or Aspen, as well as much of the repertory, were almost interchangeable. And so were the questions addressed to these festivals throughout the world: Had they grown too large? Had they become too commercial? Were they making too many concessions to popular audiences? Did they appeal primarily to older audiences, and what was the cause?[47] Were they insufficiently attentive to experimental or contemporary art practices?[48] Some festivals had become so enormous, Edinburgh being perhaps the major example, that they were accompanied by a range of unofficial events that dwarfed in number the actual festival performances.[49]

Conclusions

Today's festivals inhabit a performance culture quite different than that of a hundred years ago. Their credentialing and identifying functions contrast sharply with the needs met by festivals organized for nineteenth-century audiences. Festivals are now meeting places for practices of all kinds, competitions for distinction as well as simple vacation retreats. They are at one and the same time casual leisure pursuits and professional self-examinations, training schools for actors and musicians, opportunities for playwrights and composers, sites for scholarly symposia, and places to rehearse revolution. Woodstock, after all, was, officially, a festival. Some of them—film, jazz, and folk festivals in particular—have reversed historic flows from east to west, as American artists and performers have exported their talents and accomplishments, playing before appreciative European audiences and introducing them to entirely new repertories.

Festivals are also instruments of validation, legitimating areas of popular, ethnic, or commercial culture, sometimes by invading historic sites and storied landscapes, at other times merely demonstrating the presence of substantial enthusiasm. The extraordinary career of the Newport Jazz Festival and the folk festivals sponsored by the Smithsonian Institution on the Mall in Washington indicate the range. Mariachi lovers and Bach enthusiasts both have their respective venues. Straightforward linkages among traditional repertories, institutional structures, and festival forms are no longer standard. And today's festivals can easily become sites of contestation and challenge, shaking up accepted notions of artistic propriety and audience taste, shocking rather than confirming canonical faith in classics.

The Spoleto Festival in Charleston offers one of the most dramatic instances of this type of vibrant event. Created in 1977 as the sister to an already existing festival in Spoleto, Italy, the South Carolina version did more than simply feature operatic and theatrical performances, many of them by contemporary composers and playwrights. On a couple of occasions, it also hosted citywide, site-specific artworks, which characteristically and self-consciously challenged conventional images of the city and its history. Ann Hamilton's *Indigo Blue* of 1991, one of seventeen works commissioned by the festival, was dominated by 14,000 pounds of blue laundry, part of an "ode to the worker and to hand labor." At a corner of the garage she used for her site, a small, second-story room symbolized the management office and its surveillance function. A third section depicted the selective erasure of certain kinds of history from collective memory. The whole installation "encompassed the exploitation of the earth and humanity for the benefit of the few, now and in the past," concentrating "on those whom history has left unnamed, the individuals who make possible the success of the businessman, the victories of the general."[50] Other artists packed clay figures into cells, called into question historically defined female roles, and invoked—or targeted—the city's heritage of black slavery. The founder and spiritual leader of the Spoleto Festival in Charleston, Gian Carlo Menotti, angrily denounced the art and threatened for a time to abandon the undertaking entirely. But the festival managers sought deliberately, as they put it, to "reach audiences in ways that are more direct, unpredictable, and, often, confrontational, than can be achieved in gallery or museum."[51] Other festivals, not necessarily with the same intensity as in Charleston, also provided opportunities to question existing hierarchies—of power or values.

The late-nineteenth- and early-twentieth-century American festivals, conversely, had generally operated on a more basic level—as surrogates for an institutional life that was still undeveloped, as devices to concentrate and mobilize talents that were widely dispersed, and as validations for a European performance tradition that might otherwise have become too attenuated to thrive in new soil. But with their strong elements of showmanship and exaggeration, their huge audiences, their occasional informalities, their mingling of classes, and their sometimes startling match and mix of repertories, these earlier festivals also carved out a space resistant to the formalizing thrust of high culture. In their questioning of generic categories, their creative juxtapositions of normally separated groups, their irreverence, and their rediscoveries, these festivals may be said to have anticipated part of our current cultural situation. Thus they merit continuing attention, both as a genre in themselves and as a testimony to the ethnic, class, and regional affiliations that have, over time, shaped America's taste and performance rituals.

Notes

1. See, e.g., Tanya Gulevich, ed., *World Holiday, Festival, and Calendar Books* (Detroit: Omnigraphics, 1998); Carol Price Rabin, *Music Festivals in America* (Stockbridge, Mass.: Berkshire Traveller Press, 1979, 1983); and Helen R. Coates, *The American Festival Guide* (New York: Exposition Press, 1956, 1998).
2. "Festival Guides," *Yahoo! Internet Life*, July 1999, 128.
3. This is also true of European versions. Francis Shemanski, *A Guide to World Fairs and Festivals* (Westport, Conn.: Greenwood Press, 1985), organizes the festivals by forty-four different categories, although some of them are overlapping.
4. For scholarly commentary on contemporary festivals and celebrations see, among others, Ramon A. Gutierrez and Genevieve Fabre, eds., *Feasts and Celebrations in North American Ethnic Communities* (Albuquerque: University of New Mexico Press, 1995); and Theodore C. Humphrey and Lin T. Humphrey, eds., *"We Gather Together": Food and Festival in American Life* (Ann Arbor: University of Michigan Press, 1988).
5. Omission of the performance festival as an instrument of acculturation and transmission is pervasive, even in texts concerned with cultural transfer. To take two very different texts, in time frame and method, note its total absence in *Orpheus in the New World* by Philip Hart (New York: W. W. Norton, 1973), a work concerned with the development of the American symphony orchestra; and its prac-

tical invisibility in the invaluable survey *Not Like Us: How Europeans Have Loved, Hated, and Transformed American Culture since World War II* by Richard Pells (New York: Basic Books, 1997).

6. For a twentieth-century compilation of these religious and ethnic festivals, see Dorothy Gladys Spicer, *The Book of Festivals* (New York: Woman's Press, 1937). Musical and dramatic festivals are not represented here; the book's categories are by peoples and by calendar.

7. One useful, though possibly outdated, summary of this view can be found in Robert Briffault, "Festivals," *Encyclopaedia of the Social Sciences*, ed., Edwin R. A. Seligman (New York: Macmillan, 1934), vol. 6, 198–201.

8. See for example, within a considerable literature, Sydney Anglo, *Spectacle, Pageantry, and Early Tudor Policy* (Oxford: Clarendon Press, 1969); Anthony M. Cummings, *The Politicized Muse: Music for Medici Festivals, 1512–1537* (Princeton, N.J.: Princeton University Press, 1992); Gordon Kipling, *Enter the King: Theatre, Liturgy, and Ritual in the Medieval Civic Triumph* (Oxford: Clarendon Press, 1998); Bonner Mitchell, *Italian Civic Pageantry in the High Renaissance: A Descriptive Bibliography* (Firenze: Olschki, 1979); Barbara Wisch and Susan Scott Munshower, *"All the World's a Stage . . .": Art and Pageantry in the Renaissance and Baroque*, Part I, *Triumphal Celebrations and the Rituals of Statecraft, Papers in Art History from The Pennsylvania State University*, vol. 6; and Edmund A. Bowles, *Musical Ensembles In Festival Books, 1500–1800. An Iconographical & Documentary Survey* (Ann Arbor, Mich.: UMI Research Press, 1989).

9. For the English festival tradition, I have relied on Howard E. Smither, *A History of the Oratorio: The Oratorio in the Classical Era* (Oxford: Oxford University Press, 1987); and William Weber, *The Rise of Musical Classics in Eighteenth-Century England: A Study in Canon, Rituals, and Ideology* (Oxford: Oxford University Press, 1992).

10. *European Magazine*, supplement to June 1784, 1, quoted in Weber, *Rise of Musical Classics*, 225. Chapter 8 of the Weber book is devoted to this commemoration and analyzes its rich political implications. See also Smither, *Oratorio in the Classical Era*, 222–31.

11. Weber, *Rise of Musical Classics*, 222.

12. For the Birmingham festivals, see Chris Upton, *A History of Birmingham* (Chichester: Phillimore, 1993); and John Money, *Experience and Identity: Birmingham and the West Midlands, 1760–1800* (Montreal: McGill–Queen's University Press, 1977). There were also major festivals held in the cathedral cities of York and Norwich.

13. For details on these festivals, see Michael Musgrave, *The Musical Life of the Crystal Palace* (Cambridge: Cambridge University Press, 1995).

14. [Moncure D. Conway,] "The Handel Festival at the Crystal Palace, 1868," *Harper's Monthly* 37 (November 1868), 754.

15. For the history of this organization, see H. Earle Johnson, *Hallelujah, Amen! The Story of the Handel and Haydn Society of Boston* (Boston: Bruce Humphries, 1965).

16. According to Johnson, the new president of the organization, Charles Francis Chickering, conceived "a brilliant idea based on European custom: a Festival of several days duration at which favorite works would be presented in subscription performance aided by soloists of note." Johnson, *Hallelujah, Amen!* 81. The festival began May 21, 1857, with performances of Haydn's *Creation*, Mendelssohn's *Elijah*, and Handel's *Messiah*.

17. There were also frustrations to festival planning. Thus in 1847 Henry Meiggs, a New York music promoter, planned a festival to rival the Birmingham events for September, doing works by Handel, Haydn, and Mendelssohn. It came to nothing, although a series of oratorios were performed by both the American Musical Institute and the Sacred Music Society. See Vera Brodsky Lawrence, *Strong On Music: The New York Music Scene in the Days of George Templeton Strong, 1836–1875*, vol. 1 (New York: Oxford University Press, 1988), 477–79.

18. Gilmore's career is summarized in Marwood Darlington, *Irish Orpheus: The Life of Patrick S. Gilmore Bandmaster Extraordinary* (Philadelphia: Oliver-Maney-Klein, 1950); and H. W. Schwartz, *Bands of America: A Nostalgic, Illustrated History of the Golden Age of Band Music* (Garden City, N.Y.: Doubleday, 1957), chaps. 2–6.

19. [William Dean Howells,] "Jubilee Days," *Atlantic*, August 1869, 145–54. This essay would be reprinted in *Suburban Sketches*. Howells reported that he had no distinct impression of the orchestra "save of the three hundred and thirty violin-bows held erect like standing wheat at one motion of the director's wand, and then falling as if with the next he swept them down" (247).

20. Under P. T. Barnum's sponsorship, Jullien presented his *Quadrille* and other extravaganzas at New York's Crystal Palace in 1854, part of an unsuccessful effort to sustain the World's Fair building. A total of 1,500 performers entertained crowds in the tens of thousands, anticipating although not realizing the gargantuanism of Gilmore's day. See Vera Brodsky Lawrence, *Strong On Music: The New York Music Scene in the Days of George Templeton Strong*, vol. 2 (Chicago: University of Chicago Press, 1995), 459–68.

21. As quoted in Joseph A. Mussulman, *Music in the Cultured Generation: A Social History of Music in America, 1870–1930* (Evanston, Ill.: Northwestern University Press, 1971), 86.

22. [George William Curtis,] "Boston's Peace Jubilee of 1872," *Harper's Monthly* 45 (September 1982), 619. To assemble foreign bands and Strauss's orchestra, Curtis declared, "was no more a humbug than the pleasure which they gave."

23. For more on the Saengerfests, see [George William Curtis,] "Festivals," *Harper's Monthly* 63 (July 1881), 618–20; F. Karl Grossman, *A History of Music in Cleveland* (Cleveland: Case Western University, 1972); E. Irenaeus Stevenson, "The Saengerfest at Philadelphia," *Harper's Weekly* 41 (June 3, 1897), 667; J. Heywood Alexander, *It Must Be Heard: A Survey of the Musical Life of Cleveland, 1836–1918* (Cleveland: Western Reserve Historical Society, 1982); and Suzanne G. Snyder, "The Indianapolis Mannerchor: Contributions to a New Musicality in Midwestern Life," in *Music and Culture in America, 1861–1918*, ed. Michael Saffle (New York: Garland, 1998), 111–40.

24. The most recent study of Thomas is Ezra Schabas, *Theodore Thomas: America's Conductor and Builder of Orchestras, 1835–1905* (Urbana: University of Illinois Press, 1989). See also George P. Upton, ed., *Theodore Thomas: A Musical Autobiography*, 2 vols. (Chicago: McClurg, 1905); and Lawrence W. Levine, *Highbrow/Lowbrow: The Emergence of Cultural Hierarchy in America* (Cambridge, Mass.: Harvard University Press, 1988), chap. 2.

25. For the significance of Cincinnati as the home of American music festivals, see Henry Edward Krehbiel, "Cincinnati and Its Music Festivals," *Harper's Weekly* 38 (May 12, 1894), 440–41; and Robert C. Vitz, *The Queen & The Arts: Cultural Life in Nineteenth-Century Cincinnati* (Kent, Ohio: Kent State University Press, 1989),

chap. 4, "Of Musical Matters," 80–100, and chap. 6, "Advances and Retreats," 133–51.

26. For more on this festival and the Cincinnati festivals of the period, see Robert C. Vitz, "Starting a Tradition: The First Cincinnati May Musical Festival," *Cincinnati Historical Society Bulletin* 38 (Spring 1980): 33–50; and Zane Miller and George F. Roth, *Cincinnati's Music Hall* (Virginia Beach: Jordan & Co., 1978).

27. Vitz, "Starting a Tradition," passim.

28. See Samuel Kinser, *Carnival American Style: Mardi Gras at New Orleans and Mobile* (Chicago: University of Chicago Press, 1990), 90–97. For the ethnocentric orientation of most Mannerchore, as well as the attention given them outside the German community, see Mary Sue Morrow, "German Mannerchore in New York and New Orleans," in *Music and Culture in America*, ed. Saffle, 79–109.

29. For some of the excited comments, see [George William Curtis,] "Editor's Easy Chair," *Harper's Monthly* 65 (July 1882), 306–8; "The Programme of the Music Festival," *Harper's Weekly* 26 (April 15, 1882), 227; "The Musical Festival," *Harper's Weekly* 26 (May 6, 1882), 279; and "The Music Festival," *Harper's Weekly* 26 (May 13, 1882), 291.

30. See "New York's New Music Hall," *Harper's Weekly* 33 (November 9, 1889), 895. Carnegie Hall was opened by a special festival in May 1891. See "Tchaikovsky and the Music Festival," *Harper's Weekly* 35 (May 9, 1891), 347.

31. See especially Helen Lefkowitz Horowitz, *Culture and the City: Cultural Philanthropy in Chicago from the 1880s to 1917* (Lexington: University of Kentucky Press, 1976).

32. Levine, *Highbrow/Lowbrow*, 116–19.

33. Quoted in Schabas, *Theodore Thomas*, 119.

34. Frances Hall Johnson, *Musical Memories of Hartford: Drawn from Records Public and Private* (Hartford: AMS Press, 1970 [1931]), 80.

35. This happened, among other places, in Detroit, Cincinnati, and Indianapolis.

36. Thomas wrote that "people go to a World's Fair to see and not to hear, to be amused, and not to be educated." Upton, *Theodore Thomas*, vol. 1, 67.

37. For more on Chautauqua, see Theodore Morrison, *Chautauqua: A Center for Education, Religion and the Arts in America* (Chicago: University of Chicago Press, 1974). For the tent Chautauquas, see, among others, Gay MacLaren, *Morally We Roll Along* (Boston: Little, Brown, 1938); Victoria Case and Robert O. Case, *We Called It Culture: The Story of Chautauqua* (Garden City, N.Y.: Doubleday, 1948); and Harry P. Harrison, as told to Karl Detzer, *Culture Under Canvas: The Story of Tent Chautauquas* (New York: Hastings House, 1958). Chautauqua festivals, both the portable tent variety and the more ambitious Lake Chautauqua programs, deserve more attention than they have received in recent years.

38. This festival is summarized briefly by Harry Haskell, *The Early Music Revival: A History* (London: Thames & Hudson, 1988), in chap. 5, "Old Music in the New World," 94–111. See also J. Bunker Clark, "The Beginnings of Bach in America," in *American Musical Life in Context and Practice to 1865*, ed. James R. Heintze (New York: Garland, 1994), 337–50.

39. See, most notably, Michael Steinberg, *The Meaning of the Salzburg Festival: Austria as Theater and Ideology, 1890–1938* (Ithaca, N.Y.: Cornell University Press, 1993). See also Stephen Gallup, *A History of the Salzburg Festival* (Topsfield, Mass.: Salem House, 1987). For Bayreuth, an enormous literature exists, but see, among others,

Frederic Spotts, *Bayreuth: A History of the Wagner Festival* (New Haven, Conn.: Yale University Press, 1994); and Joseph Horowitz, *Wagner Nights: An American History* (Berkeley: University of California Press, 1994), passim.

40. "It is high time that America had its own Salzburg," the president of the Berkshire Symphonic Festival declared at the annual meeting that set up the first festival. The speech has been quoted in many places, but for an early version see "Berkshire's 'American Salzburg' Not for the Masses," *Newsweek*, August 22, 1936, 27. Two years later, Julius King, the publicity director for the Chautauqua Institution, wrote a letter published in the *New York Times*, May 29, 1938, which the paper published under the title "Is it in Keeping to Suggest That Chautauqua Is the American Salzburg?" and King titled his résumé of the coming season "Chautauqua: The American Salzburg." See Robert H. Cowden, *The Chautauqua Opera Association 1929–1958: An Interpretative History* (New York: National Opera Association, 1974), 30.

41. For press coverage, see Paul Rosenfeld, "The Second Yaddo Festival," *New Republic*, October 18, 1933, 280–82; "The Arts," *Newsweek*, August 22, 1926, 27; *Theatre Arts Monthly*, May 1938, 394; "The World and the Theatre," *Theatre Arts Monthly*, January 1931, 3–5. And see the references to pre–World War II music festivals in Rabin, *Music Festivals in America*. Folk and jazz festivals were also being created. See, e.g., Dorothy Thomas, "That Traipsin' Woman," *Independent Woman*, June 1934, 169, 188–89.

42. Lucien Price, "Music in Shirt Sleeves," *Atlantic*, July 1940, 108.

43. "Miracle in the Berkshires," *Time*, August 24, 1942, 38; "Berkshire's 'American Salzburg' Not for the Masses," *Newsweek*, August 22, 1936, 27.

44. Cecil Smith, "Musical Incidents & Altercations," *New Republic*, September 18, 1950, 23.

45. See Andrew L. Pincus, *Scenes from Tanglewood* (Boston: Northeastern University Press, 1989), 110. This book also contains a helpful summary of American musical festival traditions.

46. See Cecil Smith, "Music: The Americanization of Europe," *New Republic*, July 24, 1950, 21–22.

47. For Tanglewood and this issue, see Joseph Berger, "When the Face in the Crowd Is Grandmotherly," *New York Times*, August 24, 1999. Letters to the *Times* in subsequent days discussed the reasons for the aging of the audience.

48. See, e.g., the protests of Hugh MacDiarmid against the Edinburgh Festival, quoted in Eileen Miller, *The Edinburgh International Festival, 1947–1996* (Aldershot, U.K.: Scolar, 1996), 19; and the arguments advanced in Andrew L. Pincus, *Tanglewood: The Clash between Tradition and Change* (Boston: Northeastern University Press, 1998).

49. This has been studied, in some detail, by Wesley Monroe Shrum Jr., *Fringe and Fortune: The Role of Critics in High and Popular Art* (Princeton, N.J.: Princeton University Press, 1996), chap. 4, "Festivals and the Modern Fringe." The Edinburgh Fringe, as these nonofficial events are called, consists of some thousands of different shows.

50. *Places with a Past: New Site-Specific Art at Charleston's Spoleto Festival* (New York: Rizzoli, 1991), 75–76.

51. These words were taken from a festival press release as quoted by Arthur C. Danto, "Site-Specific Works at the Spoleto Festival," in *Embodied Meanings: Critical Essays & Aesthetic Meditations* (New York: Farrar, Straus & Giroux, 1994), 199.

CHAPTER 2

Norman Rockwell, Public Artist

MICHELE H. BOGART

In the United States, questions about culture and the public sphere often center on public art. Public art used to be a straightforward matter. From its "beginnings" in the mid–nineteenth century on into the 1930s, public art was generally defined in terms of four interlocking concerns and conditions: (1) enlightened state or "disinterested" corporate patronage; (2) a location in outdoor or communal spaces; (3) high-minded ideals of democratic citizenship, progress, and social harmony; and (4) a community with shared ideals.

This conception of public art went by the wayside in the course of the last half century. New styles, new constituencies, and increased social divisions

The author acknowledges the assistance of a National Endowment for the Humanities Fellowship for College Teachers and Independent Scholars, which enabled her to begin thinking about the issues that resulted in this chapter. She is also indebted to Maud Ayson, Maureen Hennessey, Maryann Joyner, and Linda Szekely of the Norman Rockwell Museum at Stockbridge, without whose generous assistance she could not have completed the research for this chapter. She thanks Casey Blake, Herman Lebovics, Susan Nugent, and Michael Lacey of the Woodrow Wilson International Center for Scholars for providing her with the opportunity to participate in the conference that resulted in this chapter. She is also grateful to Leo Bogart, Josh Brown, Peter Buckley, Sarah Burns, Ruth Schwartz Cowan, Ann Gibson, Krin Gabbard, Richard Hoggart, E. Ann Kaplan, Charles McGovern, Paul Mattick Jr., Nicholas Mirzoeff, Masako Notoji, James Rubin, Philip Pauly, David Schuyler, Atsushi Yoshida, and Rebecca Zurier; to members of the Imagining the Social Seminar at the New York University Institute for the Humanities; and to audiences at Franklin and Marshall College, Indiana University, Stony Brook University, the Japanese Association of American Studies Annual Conference in Tezukayama University, and the Woodrow Wilson International Center for Scholars for comments and suggestions on versions of this chapter.

fragmented the traditional vision of public art. The enterprise came under attack from both the left and the right. Scholars and arts advocates have attempted to respond to the challenges to public art. Some have gone on the counterattack. Some have undertaken historical studies to explore the roots of the political and aesthetic tensions.[1] But differences remain; the meaning and future of public art are unresolved.

One reason for this impasse, I suggest, is that conceptions of public art continue to be too straightforward. For all the debates, the concept has been framed too rigidly. This chapter reexamines the assumption that public art demands the existence of a public sphere defined as the union of state support, locale, civic values, and communal audience. It argues that historians should take a broader, more inclusive perspective. Public art is not limited to statuary in public squares or murals in post offices. Individuals, frequently working in a commercial context, have often functioned as public artists.

This phenomenon was particularly important in the years around midcentury. As Gary Larson and others have noted, the period from the late 1940s to the middle 1960s was marked by a reduction of federal sponsorship of the arts and by an political-cultural emphasis on the private realm and individual freedom of expression.[2] With the muting of two of the primary characteristics identified with public art, other forms of art production and producers (among them Leonard Bernstein; Frank Capra; Walt Disney; Theodore Geisel, known as Dr. Seuss; and Norman Rockwell), expressed high-minded ideals and engaged broad numbers of people. Thus, to consider empirically the historical trajectory of American public art during this era, we need to explore both its relationship with popular art and the importance of certain key artistic popularizers.[3]

This chapter examines the case of Norman Rockwell (1894–1978). Unlike Walt Disney or the composers of Broadway musicals, Rockwell painted on canvas. His work conformed to traditional notions of visual art, and thus it functioned within a frame of aesthetic reference closely comparable to that of state-supported fine arts projects.

The inquiry consists of three sections, which together explore the public roles played by Rockwell's commercial art in the postwar, Cold War period. First, a brief consideration of Rockwell's critical reputation between 1945 and 1965 will shed light on how the "popular" emerged in opposition to, and in an important sense superseded, "the public" in art during this period. The second section, an analysis of several Rockwell covers for the mass market magazine the *Saturday Evening Post*, shows how the artist himself worked through matters of artistic identity and attempted to bridge the widening divisions, generated through the critical discourse on art and experience, between "public" and "private," "public" and "popular," and "fine" and "commercial" domains. Finally, I focus on Rockwell's fan mail, pointing to both the range and depth of people's responses to Rockwell's work and the degree to which those responses constituted part of the public's sense of itself—as a public. I argue in addition that Rockwell's fans were not passive or unthinking, as some critics portrayed them. His admirers spanned a surprisingly broad social and intellectual spectrum, and they engaged with his work and art generally in reasoned fashion.

The chapter argues that press criticism, image content, and fan response, when taken together, offer an alternative way of envisioning artistic endeavor, reception, and meanings, both during the period in question and more broadly. During this era, a moment marked by the collapse of the traditional public art complex, Norman Rockwell's art served to a significant degree as a meaningful replacement. His images, though ridiculed by intellectuals, generated a metaphorical "web" of discourse on art, culture, and citizenship in a democracy. An examination of his activity and impact broadens understanding of the history of the public art experience.[4]

Rockwell and the Culture Wars

Norman Rockwell was one of the most famous American artists. For the last fifty years, his pictures have been acclaimed as symbols of "America." Even in the present, his work is championed by media personalities (like the late celebrity attorney Johnnie Cochran) and innumerable pundits as an expression of traditional ideals and the American experience.[5] Rockwell's was a public art, in the sense that it was widely visible, engaged large numbers of people, and communicated values that many regarded as typical, meaningful, national in spirit, and communally shared.

Rockwell's work had this decidedly public dimension, but his work was certainly "private" in other respects. For the most part, he worked for private-sector, commercial enterprises: advertisers and popular magazines like the *Saturday Evening Post* and *Look*. He was a producer of "privatized," commodified easel pictures, whose specific meanings were mediated by the institutional exigencies of businesses and the mass print media. Much of his work was disseminated through mass publishing, but it was experienced, in general, in the private sphere of the home or office.[6]

Rockwell's uncertain status as public artist was an outgrowth of his ambiguous artistic reputation. The popular appeal of his pictures made him decidedly unpopular among certain constituencies. Artists and intellectuals in particular tended to examine his images (and popular art more generally) from the perspective of their own (culturally influential) aesthetic preferences and hierarchies. Regarding "good" art history as being the history of "good" art—abstract, politically progressive, and vigorously noncommercial—art historians presented, until quite recently, a very limited picture. The popular, public aspects of Rockwell's work notwithstanding, he has been notably absent from art historiography. When not completely ignored, his pictures have been the subject of derision.[7]

The present-day censures of Rockwell's work largely follow the lead of influential intellectual critiques of the 1940s, 1950s, and 1960s—a period of cultural "cold wars," with battle lines drawn along several related cultural and political fronts.[8] Clashes erupted around three sets of divisions: between supporters of traditional versus modernist formal styles; between advocates of complex, conceptually, and pictorially nuanced "high" culture, and purveyors and consumers of commercial and popular texts; and between champions of government patronage of the arts and those who preferred a definite no-support policy.

During this historical interval, conservatives mounted virulent attacks on art revealing leftist sympathies or modernist formal abstractions. Emerging within and in response to this climate of heightened suspicion and intolerance, American avant-garde (and social progressive) artists and critics returned fire, launching a wide-ranging critique of mass culture. Rockwell became embroiled in the conflict. He was a target in part because he was a holdover from an earlier period, circa 1880 to 1935, in which the kinds of cultural tensions mentioned above (e.g., between fine and commercial art), though certainly present, were effectively negotiated.[9] He became caught in the transition between this older, more pliant cultural nexus and a newer postwar framework in which sociocultural polarities were more extreme and partisan, and cultural boundaries were more strictly delineated and patrolled.

Having been assigned into the traditionalist, popular camp of commercial private-sector interests, Rockwell was identified as an adversary by artists and intellectuals who believed it morally necessary to establish well-defined cultural divisions. These negative assessments represent a first important node in the public web of discourse circulating around Rockwell's art.

The basic contours of the aesthetic and mass culture critiques are by now quite familiar. Stated simply, Rockwell's work, in its use of a conventional, illusionistic style and legible, predictable, nostalgic narratives, was inauthentic, commercial kitsch. It represented the antithesis of "real" painting, which, according to critics like Clement Greenberg, should articulate literally, through expressive flat color on canvas, the essential properties of the medium. In true modern art, formal values had to bear meaning in their own right. By manipulating the formal components of line, form, and color merely for the spurious purpose of sentimental storytelling, the artist invoked a mythical, false representation of life. Rockwell's formulaic, mechanical images, argued detractors, blinded people to the nuances, complexities, and liberating effects of true art. Produced on contract to pander to a mass and ignorant audience, Rockwell's work epitomized commercial compromise, the antithesis of artistic authenticity and freedom.[10]

The concerns for freedom articulated in the aesthetic critiques were often motivated by political considerations, arising from the context of the Cold War, left liberal critiques of mass culture, and debates over national identity in the 1950s and 1960s. For novelist critics like Wright Morris and Benjamin De Mott, for example, Rockwell's idealizations and retrospections were profoundly disturbing. Because Rockwell's paintings appealed to the private interests of "middlebrow" individuals and articulated the logic of the marketplace, these works hindered opportunities to mold a thoughtful, civic-minded polity. Rather than exposing harsh realities like poverty, Rockwell simply fabricated nostalgic myths that absolved the populace of any responsibility for confronting hard and painful social questions. De Mott characterized him as a "prophet of mindlessness, a man who knows as a matter of instinct where and how the national brain will next shut off."[11] Rockwell's accessible, earnestly humorous, and seemingly apolitical art represented all that was wrong with the dominant political culture.

Finally, for advocates of federal arts funding like the Democratic representative Eugene McCarthy, Rockwell's art represented an additional negative factor: the specter of arts privatization and the undermining of state-supported public art. For McCarthy, striving to defend congressional arts funding, the options were clear. If arts supporters caved to conservatives (who insisted that state-supported arts programs were mere havens for communist subversives), then the work of Norman Rockwell and other popular illustrators might soon be the only mode of pictorial social criticism available to the American populace—not a happy prospect.[12]

Intellectuals believed it was imperative to banish an artist like Rockwell to reclaim "high art" and the public and civic art mantle. Thus critics were expansive and sweeping in their condemnations of popular culture, yet at the same time, more narrowly focused on aesthetics than reception. Spokesmen were concerned with how Rockwell's images measured up to their own progressive political and aesthetic standards and agendas rather than with how those images resonated with viewers who did not share their tastes or politics. From this perspective, Rockwell did not measure up.

These criticisms of Rockwell's art have had tremendous cultural weight. The problem with these arguments in their present incarnations is that they are too unidirectional, examining Rockwell's work solely in relation to a relatively narrow audience of intellectuals and chastising him for failing to live up to goals that he could never fulfill. It is necessary to balance the historical record, to reposition Rockwell and his publics as actors in the cultural domain. The historical importance of his work becomes more compelling if we incorporate a perspective that considers the broader public dialogue and also his communications with his audiences, his public statements, and how these statements resonated with average people. Such an inquiry is crucial for gaining better comprehension of the processes and meanings of public art in a democratic society.

Rockwell's Public Art

The critics say that any proper picture should not tell a story but should be primarily a series of technical problems of light, shadow, proportion, color and voids. I say that if you can tell a story in your picture, and if a reasonable number of people like your work, it is art. Maybe it isn't the highest form of art, but it's art nevertheless, and it's what I love to do. I feel that I am doing something when I paint a picture that appeals to most people. This is a democracy, isn't it?

—NORMAN ROCKWELL, 1945

Norman Rockwell's critics used his work as an occasion to carve out, in public spheres of the bar, the studio classroom, and the press, a space to reflect upon art, mass culture, and national identity. For the most serious of these commentators, nothing less than the future of the democracy was at stake. Rockwell did not engage with his critics in those same social and institutional spaces. The quotation above, from the *New Yorker*, was an exception, but it reveals that Rockwell was not aloof, as one might surmise from some of his critics' negative charges.[13] Although he left little correspondence on the subject, he responded to his critics in several interviews and in his popular autobiography. More significantly, Rockwell responded on his own terrain, through his art. The following analysis of select *Post* covers illustrates how Rockwell actively constructed his own "public sphere," a commercialized space in which to ponder art practice and purpose in modern democratic America.

Beginning as early as the mid-1920s, Rockwell's *Saturday Evening Post* covers on artistic subjects exemplified and articulated the permeability of cultural borders, the interconnecting threads of commercial and public art.[14] These covers, though often humorous, were serious stuff. They revealed that art produced within a commercial framework could be thoughtful, nuanced, and noncommercial in emphasis. They addressed significant concerns: questions of art and artistic identity, and the place of the artist in art history and in the age of mass media. Rockwell explored these matters in public, representing them for scrutiny by an audience of millions. In the 1950s and 1960s, when efforts to segregate cultural realms were rapidly gaining momentum, Rockwell attended to these issues of cultural spheres, boundaries, and hierarchies with greater urgency. Insofar as the postwar statements were consistent with the perspectives put forth earlier, it is worth taking a brief look further back.

The 1926 *Pipe and Bowl Sign Painter* (figure 2.1), one of Rockwell's first depictions of the artist at work, is, on the face of it, a humorous evocation of the past, harking back to simpler, more "honest" times to bridge the psychological gap between past and mechanized present. An expression of the Colonial Revival movement all the rage in the 1920s and 1930s, *Pipe and Bowl Sign Painter* was one of many images of this period in which Rockwell depicted

Figure 2.1. Norman Rockwell, *Pipe and Bowl Sign Painter*, originally appeared in the *Saturday Evening Post*, February 6, 1926. Courtesy of the Norman Rockwell Family Agency.

colonial types as being much like contemporary "average" white middle-class Americans.[15]

Yet the image is more than just that. For one thing, it is a parody of the long-standing tradition, in painting, of the artist at work with the tools of his trade: palette, oil paints, mahlstick, brushes. It deflates reigning high cultural hierarchies and pretensions while engaging with art history. In Old Master paintings like Johannes Vermeer's *Artist and His Muse* (1670–75, Kunsthistorisches Museum, Vienna), the artist would be depicted in his spacious studio. Rockwell, conversely, depicts the sign artist hunched over and all scrunched up, seated on a rough, makeshift stool fashioned from tree branches. Traditional representations usually highlighted the hallowed object (the model) and subject (the image rendered on canvas) of the artist's inspiration. Vermeer, for example, depicted the artist's muse; and Diego Velasquez, in *Las Meninas* (1656, Museo del Prado, Madrid), the king, queen, and infanta, to accentuate the ennobled stature of both the artist and his subject. Their importance *removed* them from the realm of ordinary mortals.

Rockwell's model is *not* visible, and the object of his painstaking labors is *not* a noble, "fine" art portrait but rather a Revolutionary-era version of the billboard—a shop sign—and one for a tavern at that—a not unnoteworthy sign of nostalgia at the height of Prohibition. In the mid-1920s, a moment when the artistic and social merits and effects of billboard and print advertising were being hotly debated among advertising professionals, artists, and civic reformers (and not the least of their concerns was the impact of local billboards for "sinful" products like tobacco!), Rockwell conjured up an image whose humor was rooted in its implicit contrast between the diligently handcrafted signage of the past—artful, local, and "sinful" in emphasis—and the slick, impersonally rendered images of present-day, alcohol-free national advertising. Yet Rockwell also presented an insider's rationalization and point of view. By rendering the sign painter as "artist," he suggested something of the rarified, aesthetic decisionmaking injected into the art-making process by the artist in advertising. Rockwell also intimated that although commercial art was intended to lure and sell, the best of its practitioners were nonetheless serious workers, dedicated to producing works of excellence.

Nine years later, in 1935, Rockwell presented an updated version of *Sign Painter, Billboard Painter* (figure 2.2). Here, the importance of the artist's work is highlighted by the fact that the man is at work on a *painted* sign. In contrast to the twenty-four-sheet lithographed billboard posters that pervaded American highways and urban streets during the Depression, painted showings (which were hand-painted, smaller-scale advertising displays) were more limited in numbers and were often placed with specific local markets and contexts in mind. Nonetheless, this image sets up a pointed contrast between the individual craftsman (who is working on a scale too large for "fine art" easel painting) and the stereotypical and dehumanizing forces of commercial culture—exemplified by the glamour girl billboard.

Figure 2.2. Norman Rockwell, *Sign Painter, Billboard Painter,* originally appeared in the *Saturday Evening Post,* February 9, 1935. Courtesy of the Norman Rockwell Family Agency.

Although most of the poster image is rendered only in outline form, enough is visible to discern the typical glamour girl image of feminine allure, which had been exploited since the turn of the century to sell entertainment and a multitude of other products. The image's wide-eyed gaze is one of feminine and corporate power, seducing the viewer to buy. That aura of power is reinforced by the glamour girl image's monumental scale and by the erotic innuendoes of the words "kiss" and the strategic placement of the woman's lips "against" the painter's body. Although rendered lightheartedly, in typically Rockwellian fashion, these features convey the potential attraction, influence, and potential threat to individual autonomy, exerted by mass media images. The 1934 cover *Boy Gazing at Glamour Stars* (figure 2.3) and *Double Take* (March 1, 1941), also underscored the fantasies and desires aroused by such imagery. In the case of these two pictures, however, Rockwell emphasized the impact of movie stars' images and of magazines like the *Post* upon American youth, spotlighting more generally the tensions among the unattainable ideals presented in the magazines, the awkward body image of adolescent "reality," and the travails of Depression reality.

If these covers offered observations on the impact of mass publishing and advertising on constructing the subject and subjectivity, especially among American teenagers, Rockwell's cover of October 8, 1938, *The Deadline* (figure 2.4), featured the impact of the *Saturday Evening Post* on the illustrator. Here, as with *Pipe and Bowl Sign Painter*, Rockwell established a humorous dialogue with art history. Famous masters like Velasquez and Vermeer knew exactly what inspired them, but the one artist who is working under a real deadline does not have a clue.

In his 1960 reminiscences, Rockwell dwelt at some length upon the challenges of coming up with his *Post* cover subjects. *The Deadline* is a visual rendition of this excruciating process.[16] Far from churning out homogeneous, thoughtless images, Rockwell intimated, the true illustrator, who took his tasks seriously, encountered significant creative obstacles. Inspiration had to come from within—this, despite the hundreds of "idea" suggestions Rockwell received from his fans. Yet Romantic ideals of inspiration notwithstanding, the artist in commerce could not afford the indulgence of time. Rockwell conveyed this aspect of the illustrator's practice, his desperation, not only by depicting the stopwatch but also by rendering the disarray of his work area—by contrasting the empty, white canvas with the cluttered reams of discarded sketches and the mass of crumpled books. The feeling of agitation, enhanced via Rockwell's wiry lines and his gawky physique, is rendered almost palpable.

Rockwell's 1938 cover depicted the challenges of working on deadline. His April 29, 1950, cover, *Shuffleton's Barber Shop* (figure 2.5), painted after he had left the pressures of New York City (in 1939) to reside in Vermont, displays the mastery he could achieve when that inspiration arrived. *Shuffleton's Barber Shop* represents the tension between modernity and tradition, regionalism and national culture, privatized space and public spheres, filtered

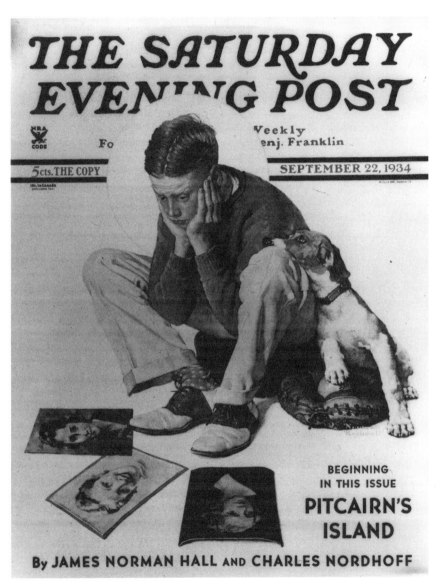

Figure 2.3. Norman Rockwell, *Boy Gazing at Glamour Stars,* originally appeared in the *Saturday Evening Post,* September 22, 1934. Courtesy of the Norman Rockwell Family Agency.

Figure 2.4. Norman Rockwell, *The Deadline*, originally appeared in the *Saturday Evening Post*, October 8, 1938. Courtesy of the Norman Rockwell Family Agency.

through the lens of art. The scene, a slice of "real life" through a transparent barbershop window, makes reference to the centuries-old conventions of naturalism, an artistic experience ordered through the system of Renaissance perspective. The scene is much more than just a transparent "window" onto the world of a small-town Vermont barbershop. The viewer's consciousness of artistic intervention is heightened by the artist's (and the beholder's) implied presence outside the frame of the window and canvas—whose literal planarity is emphasized through the flattening mullions and such modernist devices as the cropped lettering.[17] These devices in turn evoke the sense of immediacy of the moment glimpsed inside.

Rockwell depicts Shuffleton's barbershop as a place where the disruptive effects of modern culture have seemingly not taken hold. Shuffleton's is a place where profits, if any, are modest. It is a place of hard work, community, and camaraderie, where the spaces of work and leisure are still integrated. Shuffleton's is a place where essential services are provided, with no frills or excess. It is also a place of culture. The players are not provincial rubes. They play violin and cello; they use sheet music. Shuffleton's thus seems to exist outside the national consumer culture that was transforming postwar American cities and suburbs. Yet the magazine and comic book display to the left suggests that the lures and distractions of urban commercial culture were nonetheless a presence even in small town America.

In *Shuffleton's Barbershop*, the self-conscious commentaries on the relationships of art, life, and mass media were rendered quite subtly. During the next decade, a period of significant soul searching for Rockwell, his explorations of art and the public realm became more obvious and prominent in a number of his *Post* covers. Like the earlier covers discussed above, these images ruminated on what the commercial artist could and did do, but they dealt more explicitly with criticism, reception, and the increased authority of aesthetic standards and hierarchies that excluded popular images like his.

The Art Critic (1955; figure 2.6) is obvious, for a reason. An impoverished youthful copyist strains to examine through his looking glass a small detail of a seventeenth-century Dutch portrait. He employs the Morellian techniques of the connoisseur—close scrutiny of small details as a method of attribution and aesthetic evaluation.[18] For the critic, the subject matter is secondary to the formal characteristics he is assessing. Rockwell gently mocks the earnest artist's aesthetic blinders. The "critic" stares squarely into the collarbone of the buxom maiden but is totally oblivious to her charms. The moral in part is that those who claim to be experts, or those who parrot the received wisdom regarding art's meanings, may be blind to deeper meanings that are right there on the surface. Even artists and critics themselves may be missing something.

In 1960, a very painful moment in the immediate aftermath of the death of his wife, Rockwell returned to the subject of artistic identity. The *Triple Self-Portrait* (figure 2.7), painted for a *Post* cover of February 13, 1960, explored further just *what* kinds of meanings Rockwell felt his artistic and critical de-

Figure 2.5. Norman Rockwell, *Shuffleton's Barber Shop*, originally appeared in the *Saturday Evening Post*, April 29, 1950. Courtesy of the Norman Rockwell Family Agency.

tractors might be missing. In *Triple Self-Portrait*, Rockwell sought to show that there was much more to the man and his art than some might believe.

Triple Self-Portrait is about the multiple and conflicting influences and identities of the artist in commerce, the conflict between public image and private character, myth and reality, high and low pigeonholing. Through symbols like the old-fashioned ladderback chair and the mirror with its eagle and stars-and-stripes crest, Rockwell acknowledges the linkages between his own popular reputation and myths of national identity. That public image, undergirded by the impeccably rendered formal self-portrait on canvas, a sign of "high" artistic status, is called into question through contrast with the conflicting representations of the "private" individual: the bewildered-looking Rockwell, the precariously balanced cola, the smoking cigarette butt (an allusion to the kind of human foible that culminated in the 1943 fire that devastated Rockwell's studio), and the scumbled painterly treatment of the painting's white background, signifier of individuality (but invisible in the reproduction). The image of the blank-eyed Rockwell, together with the rear-view depiction, form public references to the private realm, its inaccessibility. Hence *Triple Self-Portrait* underscores the tension between public and private identities and character. The man hiding behind the confident self-portrait was a man of many doubts.

Figure 2.6. Norman Rockwell, *The Art Critic*, originally appeared in the *Saturday Evening Post*, April 16, 1955. Courtesy of the Norman Rockwell Family Agency.

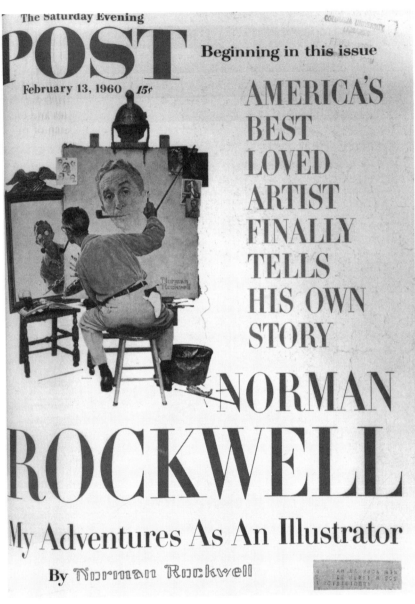

Figure 2.7. Norman Rockwell, *Triple Self-Portrait,* originally appeared in the *Saturday Evening Post,* February 13, 1960. Courtesy of the Norman Rockwell Family Agency.

Those doubts were triggered in part by the attacks on the worthiness of Rockwell's "transparent" narratives. Although Rockwell's reminiscences show that he was prone to self-deprecation, *Triple Self-Portrait* functioned as a retort to critics like Greenberg and Morris. The pictorial counterpart to his 1943 statement, it was an assertion that art had to go beyond the formal literalness of the avant-garde project in order to reach people. It showed, literally, through props like the medieval helmet and cola, that Rockwell's images were rooted in rigorous observation. Through the inclusion of multiple self-portraits and "great artist" images, it likewise asserted that his art was an act of imagination constructed by the artist, but rooted in tradition. The Van Gogh and Picasso self-portraits showed that Rockwell was open to diverse stylistic influences and that, indeed, his full-scale paintings were part of a larger Art enterprise, even as they constituted part of the modern commercial framework of mass reproductions and magazine publishing. Through such juxtapositions, Rockwell asserted that commercial and fine art were integrally connected in twentieth-century America. Through the mechanisms of mass media, old masters, and modern ones—illustrators—shared the spotlight as public artists.

In contrast to *Triple Self-Portrait*, which addressed artistic hierarchies and the significance of Rockwell's work in broadly probing fashion, *The Connoisseur* of 1962 (figure 2.8) pinpointed aesthetic issues specific to that particular cultural moment. Like *The Critic*, it highlighted problems of reception and expertise, and evoked similar tensions between formalist literalism and popular narratives. A lone viewer stands before a simulated Abstract Expressionist painting: painting of a style that represented the ultimate in Greenbergian literalism and self-expressivity in 1962. The single viewer in the empty gallery stood as a measure of Abstract Expressionism's still exclusive, elite status. Although the style was becoming more familiar to many Americans through articles in *Life* and *Vogue*, and through exhibits at international trade fairs, it still represented the antithesis of Rockwell's accessible, mass-reproduced art. To most people, Abstract Expressionism was "difficult" abstract art, whose appreciation hinged on a contemplative encounter between sensitive, educated viewers and a unique, authentic painting.[19]

The Connoisseur's meanings are both obvious and literal, and subtle and ironic. What was the significance of the painting in the painting? Intriguingly, as with so many of his "art" covers, Rockwell renders the subject with his back turned *away* from the viewer, shielded from and oblivious to the outside world. We do not learn his response. It would appear that on one level, such work represented the artistic challenge Rockwell sought to master and felt he could not. At the same time, the painting within the painting served as a response to those connoisseur/critics, like Greenberg (who championed Abstract Expressionists like Jackson Pollock). For on the surface, Rockwell's "Pollock" seemed indistinguishable from the real thing.[20] It invoked the common uninformed critique of Abstract Expressionist painting: "My child of ten could do it." Turning his back on critics like Greenberg, Rockwell showed that *he*

Figure 2.8. Norman Rockwell, *The Connoisseur*, originally appeared in the *Saturday Evening Post*, January 13, 1962. Courtesy of the Norman Rockwell Family Agency.

could do it, in miniature, no less (the entire cover painting is 31.75 by 31.5 inches).

Through such appropriations, *The Connoisseur* insinuated that, from a technical standpoint, the illustrator and advertising artist was just as accomplished as any "fine" artist. Boundaries asserted firmly by cosmopolitan critics were exposed as arbitrary, narrow-minded, and elitist. There was added significance in the fact that the whole "fine art" image was absorbed into the parameters of the mass market magazine letterhead. Rockwell was simply following the precedent set by *Vogue* and *Life* magazines (and countless other examples) in rendering fluid the boundaries between fine art and commercial art. The straightlaced connoisseur, with the Abstract Expressionist painting in a sanitized gallery, underscored the "reining in" of bohemianism by the institutional forces of the commercial gallery and the museum. Like *Triple Self-Portrait*, the image signified the interdependence of fine art and commerce within the institutional frameworks of both art and publishing.

Other factors shaped *The Connoisseur*'s meanings. By 1962, Abstract Expressionism—as both a style and a symbol of freedom and humanism—was a force to be reckoned with. Indeed, there is no indication that Rockwell was mocking Abstract Expressionist techniques. In a sense, the care with which he rendered the image was a form of tribute. At that moment, however, Abstract Expressionism was also being challenged even from within the New York art world by pop artists like Andy Warhol, who was inspired as much by advertising and mass media as by his predecessors in fine art. The dichotomy of abstract and realist styles pictured in Rockwell's image, an expression of the establishment art world's investment in a gap between abstract fine art and realist commercial art was, then, being contested by the fine artists themselves. Although *The Connoisseur* showed a tension regarding artistic borders that still existed for many, it was no longer the hot issue it had once been. Absorbing the literal (Abstract Expressionist) image into a narrative framework, *The Connoisseur* articulated the contradictions and failures of the modernist project even as it paid tribute to its aesthetic and cultural influence.

On yet another level, as well, *The Connoisseur* was a study of modern obsolescence. If on the one hand artists like Warhol were highlighting the blurring of borders, advertisers on the other hand considered the boundaries between commercial art and fine art to be quite clear. They increasingly shunned "art" in advertising. Moreover, with photography and television taking the lead in advertising representation, both "modernistic" representation and hand-crafted "realism" were becoming obsolete from a marketing standpoint.[21] Significantly, the dandified connoisseur is depicted in a state of absorption akin to the numerous contemporary photographs of people watching television, the new popular medium soon to put illustration and magazines like the *Post* out of business. Turning his viewer's back to the beholder, Rockwell evoked a realm of unique, private challenging Art experience that represented a notable "about-face" to the ubiquitous images of publicly grinning faces, both staring *at* the tube and gazing *out* from it—images that evoked the simpleminded pleasures of commercial media, pleasures of the sort that critics condemned in *Rockwell's* own work. Rockwell, the quintessential artist of the modern print media, here relayed, through paint and offset, the capacity of traditional media to resist the seductively mind-numbing effects of the new mass medium, television.

Was this cover meant to be humorous or serious? Was the connoisseur's response positive or negative? Rockwell never lets his viewers know. He did write to one fan, however, "Don't worry. I'm not going modern. But I did have fun painting the abstraction. It was my first and my last."[22]

Rockwell's Letter-Writing Publics

This fan letter and Rockwell's response were a reminder. Rockwell's work did not float into a void, unnoticed. It reached many people who responded actively and in diverse ways. Far from assuming that the meanings of Rockwell's work were obvious, many of the artist's admirers sought to communicate how his paintings were significant, to provide their own accounts in writing.[23] Their commentaries, some quite lengthy, were often reasoned and thoughtful.

Rockwell's publics have been stereotyped and caricatured, yet such voices are crucial to any consideration of cultural and public spheres. Rockwell's fan mail offers a concrete look at one aspect of the popular response to his pictures and, as such, represents a third stratum of critical discourse. This correspondence helps to reveal an additional realm of Rockwell's art, and people's engagement with images generally, that has not been adequately examined. Fans' actions and reactions resonated with Rockwell's characterization of art in a democracy. Collectively, they affirmed the centrality of visual narratives and the emotional needs such stories could fulfill, at a moment when such genres and responses were being forcefully challenged. Many letter writers expressed dissatisfaction with mechanisms of cultural distinction that they perceived to be operative in metropolitan art worlds and in the press. In several ways—by offering personal information, suggestions for cover subjects, and explicit critical commentary—fan letters constituted a cultural space in which "ordinary" citizens asserted their democratic right to experience art on their own terms. The correspondence shows how Rockwell's art operated in public to constitute that public's sense of self-identity at a point when more official, established public arts were in recession or struggling for an audience. Together with more high-minded, intellectual criticism and with Rockwell's pictorial responses, this fan mail is indicative of the complexity and expansiveness of the public fields generated by the forces of commerce.

Norman Rockwell was not a celebrity on the order of contemporaries like Charlie Chaplin, Franklin Roosevelt, Marilyn Monroe, Elvis Presley, or the Beatles, but it is nonetheless reasonable to apply the term to him. The Norman Rockwell Museum in Stockbridge, Massachusetts, houses at least thirty cartons packed with letters, most of which postdate the 1943 studio fire. (In all likelihood, Rockwell received additional correspondence that was lost or destroyed.)[24]

Letters to Rockwell came from all corners of the United States, and from abroad; most came from outside the largest American cities. Letter writers' self-descriptions, handwriting styles, commentaries, and stationery suggest that this writing public fit the typical profile of the *Saturday Evening Post* reader, of modest or comfortable income, blue- and white-collar workers, with a few people from the topmost and lowest financial strata.[25] Correspondents included college students, struggling and established writers and artists, a typewriter repair man, advertising and public relations professionals, doctors, bank workers, a drugstore owner, a boxmaker, a construction engineer, a wealthy heir, newspaper reporters and editors, judges, members of Congress, engineers, pilots, a bus driver, and hundreds of homemakers.

Authors ranged in age from seven to (approximately) eighty-seven years, with most being over thirty, married, and female.[26] The majority of letter writers' names were Anglo or Germanic. Although one person identified himself as Jewish, no one explicitly referred to himself or herself as Negro, Mexican, or Italian. In other words, Rockwell's work found its most vocal admirers among a large yet limited segment of the U.S. public that was constituted at the time as the white "cultural majority." Significantly, the profile of this public was more akin to the older, relatively more affluent people who wrote politicians than to the more youthful and penurious supporters of avant-garde artists, or fans who wrote stars like Sinatra, Elvis, or Lennon. Many wrote out of a sense of purpose rather than in response to the kinds of fantasies that often roused the youthful fans of commercial rock.[27]

The People as Public

Norman Rockwell's art was not made public through originals but rather through the mediation of mass reproductions. The Rockwell persona likewise was experienced through the mass media. Thus many were prompted to write after seeing one of his magazine covers or, by the early 1960s, after viewing him on television.[28] Quite a few expressed an awareness of Rockwell as a public, mass media figure, opening their letters, for example, with an acknowledgment of being part of a mass audience of admirers. ("You give pleasure to millions like myself who will probably never see a collection of portraits" was a standard remark.[29]) This confession made many people all the more determined to "break through" that "mass" media wall and to communicate with Rockwell personally.

Yet few seem to have considered the intervention of mass media as a significant factor or influence. The media representations were taken at face value, as transparent. Many admirers perceived Rockwell's public persona to be pleasantly consistent with their conception of his "private" character: decent, honest, down to earth.[30] To a good number of fans, Rockwell represented a kindly father figure. Consequently, many people poured out their hearts and recounted their backgrounds and life experiences.[31] Rockwell received hundreds of solicitations, for assistance, autographs, artwork, and his philosophy of life. The following request was typical:

> I would appreciate it greatly if you would answer the following question for me: *In general, what is your aim in life?* I want this answered on an unfolded sheet of paper (. . . because I want to frame it).[32]

Such solicitations indicated the extent to which Rockwell and his art were the focus of desire and dreams. In addition, thousands offered both suggestions of "stories" for Rockwell to picture and commentaries upon Rockwell's own work. Some letters were obviously self-serving. All types, however, reflected the desire to connect with something authentic and meaningful in an unstable world.[33]

For some Rockwell fans, that search entailed self-constitution as part of a national public of individual subjects. Numerous admirers expressed such convictions quite forthrightly, maintaining that Rockwell's art was inspired by real-life, "typically" American experiences. "I believe you can present Americans to the world as few men can," wrote one fan. "Keep up the great contributions to our Way of Life. I can't think of an artist whose works are so meaningful to common people," remarked another, sentimentally. "Your art work, I feel, is a part of Americana, times when people were neighborly, movies were purely entertainment, and the world was a nice and cozy place to live in."[34]

For numerous others, Rockwell's works evoked, both nostalgically and inspirationally, more "universal" emotions, ideals, and behaviors. The "suggestion" letters in particular articulated these concerns. In many ways, they confirmed Wright Morris's assertion that people viewed America through the eyes of Norman Rockwell. ("I'd like to describe a scene which to me was a Norman Rockwell painting come to life.")[35] For these letter writers, Rockwell's narratives served as models of the actual and the ideal (depicting actions or outlooks worthy of emulation); they articulated ways to make sense of experience. At the same time, they highlighted common and significant tensions between real and ideal existence, present and past, loss and memory.[36]

The structure, as well as the content of these suggestion narratives, was important. The letters intimated that Rockwell's visual rhetorical strategies were also consistent with the ways that fans constructed narratives of their own lives, and that they were suitable for structuring stories of their own experiences. Hence the stories fans recounted were similar to Rockwell's art.[37]

Most of the idea proposals were, like Rockwell's covers, subjects from white middle-class life. Rarely overtly unsettling, they tended to focus on the privatized realm of the home and family (hardly surprising in this period of heightened economic and political insecurity). Social protests, urban street life, the civic realm, and commercial culture were ignored (with the exception of a few ideas suggesting male amusement or disgust with female engagement with shopping). Dominant themes included the ages of humanity, generation gaps (the industriousness or mischievousness of children), the awkward transition between youth and adulthood (with an emphasis on teenagers), human foibles, American heroes, and mundane incongruities and confrontations with modern life (e.g., the tensions arising from gender constructions—particularly during and after the war—young mothers grappling with the demands of motherhood and housewifery; husbands coping with female empowerment in the home, the marketplace, and workplace). A few topics highlighted class differences.

The pattern of structural repetition, of providing the "same in the different" through *Post* cover suggestion letters, was a testament to the extent to which Rockwell's pictures inflected people's worldviews and their vision of their life experiences. Yet the penchant for Rockwell-like subjects in fact indicated that his work was not mindlessly fulfilling. The idea letters were, as well, an expression of the continual need to make sense of the world in *that* particular narrative fashion. In other words, Rockwell's familiar, banal narrative strategies, as well as his subject matter, resonated with broadly felt interests and responses to the world.

Yet although the proposed stories centered on the private sphere, letter writers sought to present such local, privatized encounters in public terms. People recounted these stories to Rockwell in the hopes of making them public, via the commercial print media. They assumed that others could relate to their Rockwell-like narratives.[38] Hence they also conveyed a belief that art produced for the millions should articulate [white] "Americans'" shared human experiences.

The story suggestion letters served the performative function of creating social and psychological order; as with other narratives, they offered ways of understanding life and rules for living. The desire for order was conveyed explicitly, for example, in one of the very few idea letters to propose an art-related subject. A cartoonist, possibly inspired by *Sign Painter, Billboard Painter* and *The Connoisseur,* suggested to Rockwell a cover in which two billboard painters, "one lean, one a little heavy, or any two good types for contrast," would be painting "the usual hard boiled commercial poster, y'know pretty girl head, smoke this, or drink that." The one commercial artist, tired of selling, would live out his fantasies of artistic freedom and personal autonomy. "To the surprise and perplexed expression of one, the other has had enough; he is painting an abstraction a la Jackson Pollock with lots of verve." The letter writer saw humor in the contrast of physical and stylistic "types." But this contrast was meant in turn to highlight the real point of the story: the incongruity and the implausibility of abandoning a stable and rational artistic enterprise.[39]

In correspondence, at least, fans sought to make sense of the world by not confronting the senseless. These letters did not offer critical, ironic, or satirical narratives of a sort that might find approval among art experts. Indeed, significantly, as mentioned, most suggestions for covers steered clear of art. The writers of this particular group, "cover suggestion" letter writers, evidently were not sufficiently familiar with art to feel inclined to tell stories about art encounters. Or, quite conceivably, they felt uncomfortable about broaching the subject as knowledgeable amateurs or authorities. The word from the critics, after all, was that the general public was ignorant; its tastes were a problem.

If letter-writing fans were hesitant to suggest their own art covers, many were not afraid to offer opinions on art subjects. For our purposes, one thematic strain in these letters is especially noteworthy: an insistence that art in a democracy allows for some measure of democratic participation. Few correspondents presented the issue as explicitly as had Rockwell in 1943. The more common preoccupations that masked these concerns were mistrust of cultural expertise and professional art power brokers. Letters often began with an explicit acknowledgment of the cultural force of expertise and the class dimensions of competence, an awareness of the need for certain kinds of schooling and the importance of social connections. ("I am not an artist, nor a critic . . ." was a typical introduction. "Do you mind if a horribly-low-brow comments on your pictures?" queried another letter writer.) But when it came down to assessing the merits of Rockwell's art versus others', particularly modernists', fans felt emboldened to challenge professional authority.[40]

Most writers provided opinions on art off-the-cuff, in response to a range of cover images. But in the 1950s and 1960s, the combination of critical media coverage, institutional activities, and Rockwell's own art covers and published reminiscences provoked more pointed responses concerning art meanings and boundaries.

The Connoisseur in particular elicited the majority of specifically art-related comments. Responding to uncertainties regarding Rockwell's artistic stature, raised in part by his own pictures and reminiscences and in part by magazine accounts of art debates, a few fans praised his "abstract" painting, tongue in cheek. Many more expressed their unease with the cultural tensions raised by the image. Disturbed by his confessions of a lack of confidence, many people wrote to reassure Rockwell that he was indeed an artist—that he should not belittle himself.[41]

Fans made their counterassertions through negative comparisons between Rockwell and stylistic "modernists" (the sort who made abstract paintings like the one in *The Connoisseur*). To this end, some fans parroted the sweeping antimodernist rhetoric that had been spewed by certain artistic and political conservatives over the previous fifty years (but had been especially pervasive since the ascendance of the American avant-garde and of television in the mid-1950s): Modern artists were mere "bad-boy paint daubers . . . bitter misanthropes," lacking "self-discipline," too lazy to paint in detail, realistically.[42]

Significantly, letter writers reserved their most negative remarks not for "modern" artists but for art critics. Rightly or wrongly, by the late 1950s and early 1960s, many of these fans associated modernism and art critics with snobbish, powerful, impersonal, and threatening special interests ("The damn critics and art curators are mainly responsible for this insane rage"), upscale publications, museums, art dealers, and art professionals, who belittled the unsophisticated tastes of the general public.[43] In light of these concerns, some reacted indignantly to the artistic insecurities expressed by Rockwell in his *Adventures* and in *The Connoisseur.* "It is with real consternation that I note you are experimenting with a new style," wrote one admirer, who continued:

> As a long-standing lover and patron of art, with a catholicity of taste extending to appreciation of the extreme modern as well as the more conventional styles, I think yours is one of the great arts of all time. . . . Hogarth is a Toonerville Trolley cartoonist alongside of you. Your work outclasses the best in the Dutch genre school. The failure of museums to hang your work reflects the narrowness of professional critics. . . . Undoubtedly slick sales promotion has entered into the acclaim for some of the latest fair-haired "boys." . . . There is room for all kind of painting. However, in my opinion, it is ridiculous to rate the opaque above the lucid, and to attribute profundity to the obscure. . . . For heaven's sake, don't change your style, and don't worry about a new style.[44]

Another letter writer exclaimed:

> If all the modernists' paint-pot accidents exemplify art, and if most of the "fine" artists' nightmare distortions are traded as art, then let me and the rest of unaesthetic America have—ad infinitum—Norman Rockwell with only the very artful ability to delight and please a multitude of people with fine portrayals of humor, wisdom and understanding. Whether the so-called critics call a rose by one name or another—Artist or Illustrator—it still adds up to the well-put caption on the *Post*'s February 13 cover: "America's best-loved artist."[45]

For these fans, Rockwell's expressions of doubt had disturbing implications; such admissions seemed to signal the dominance of elite cultural and economic fractions, who, fans believed, scorned their tastes and values and effectively excluded them from the public sphere of art.[46]

Letters to Norman Rockwell served in part to counter the rising cultural legitimacy of attacks upon Rockwell and "middlebrow" culture in general. Fan responses, sometimes quite vehement, were evidence not necessarily of the philistinism of educated (if not intellectual) middle-class people, but rather of a stance of defiance, in reaction to feeling ridiculed and locked out of important cultural matters.[47] On the defensive, admirers sought contact with the artist-celebrity in order to affirm the centrality of his "unoriginal" art, the purposefulness and commonality of values and ideals it evoked, and the legitimacy of the emotions and concerns it elicited—no matter what the contentions of art critics.

Although stated in private, the weight and numbers of these responses were such as to make a claim for attention, to constitute an alternative "space" in the broader spectrum of public debates over art and culture. Rockwell's fan letters confirmed that his popular art had a public magnitude and legitimacy, that his audience constituted a bona fide public. It enabled his admirers to participate in the web of public culture in ways that they felt not possible with other art forms. By highlighting an ideal order that helped people ruminate on the world and cope with their everyday lives, Rockwell's art served deep-seated and widely felt emotional needs that state-sponsored, nonprofit, and publicly located art did not necessarily fulfill. For those who engaged positively with Rockwell's art, the commercial sponsorship and purposes of his images were irrelevant.

As I have shown, however, the commercial aspects of Rockwell's art were *not* irrelevant. In contrast to publicly sponsored work, whose producers often operated on the premise that experts and artists should bring excellence to the masses, no matter what their tastes or opinions, purveyors of commercial culture literally could not afford to take such a stance. A mass magazine like the *Saturday Evening Post*, with its particular image and market, placed definite limitations on the themes and scope of Rockwell's work. The artist knew quite well that certain kinds of visual statements were simply unacceptable.[48] The publishers and editors of Rockwell's principal outlets, moreover, did little to provide a forum for thoughtful public exchanges on art and its publics within the framework of the magazine. Instead, commentaries on Rockwell's work were relegated to short (undoubtedly heavily edited) paeans or jabs in the "Letters to the Editor" sections. Such evasions thwarted opportunities for public dialogue and enlightenment. And to be sure, editorial policies on what constituted appropriate imaging often resulted in more aesthetically and politically conservative and less intellectually challenging work than that produced by artists in other venues (e.g., those sponsored by select New York galleries or later in the 1960s by the newly funded programs of the National Endowment for the Arts). There were clearly limits to Rockwell's public impact.

Nevertheless, Rockwell's attempts to make art that would resonate with his fans' concerns had positive effects. He let his publics know that their input in art discussions mattered. Mass dissemination of his work offered the possibility for multiple interpretations and meanings, even in circumstances in which the channels of communication were influenced by large-scale corporate interests. This chapter has attempted to move beyond the stance that commercial culture is meaningless or manipulative. By highlighting how the commercial art of Norman Rockwell functioned as a form of public art, it has sought to show cultural alternatives that coexisted with, and at times replaced, the older vision. It has also sought to point to the limitations of a constricted vision of public art twinned with an ideal disinterested public sphere. Such a model, often premised upon a commitment to cultural stratification, was—in its most compelling and pivotal expressions—a product of the 1950s and 1960s. In asking how culture might contribute to a more humane and democratic polity, we should broaden our scope of inquiry and explore further the public dimensions of popular art. Such an project requires taking Norman Rockwell and his admirers very seriously.

Notes

1. Important work on recent public art debates includes Casey Nelson Blake, "An Atmosphere of Effrontery: Richard Serra, *Tilted Arc,* and the Crisis of Public Art," in *The Power of Culture: Critical Essays in American History,* ed. Richard Wightman Fox and T. J. Jackson Lears (Chicago: University of Chicago Press, 1993), 270–71; Michael Kammen, "Culture and the State in America," *Journal of American History* 83 (December 1996): 791–814; Jane Kramer, *Whose Art Is It?* (Durham, N.C.: Duke University Press, 1994); W. J. T. Mitchell, ed., *Art and the Public Sphere* (Chicago: University of Chicago Press, 1992); Harriet F. Senie and Sally Webster, eds., *Critical Issues in Public Art: Content: Context, and Controversy* (New York: HarperCollins, 1992); Harriet F. Senie, *Contemporary Public Sculpture: Tradition, Transformation, Controversy* (New York: Oxford University Press, 1992); and David Abramson, "Maya Lin and the 1960s: Monuments, Time Lines and Minimalism," *Critical Inquiry* 22 (Summer 1998): 678–709. Also relevant is Wendy Steiner, *The Scandal of Pleasure: Art in an Age of Fundamentalism* (Chicago: University of Chicago Press, 1995).
2. Gary Larson, *The Reluctant Patron: The United States Government and the Arts, 1943–1965* (Philadelphia: University of Pennsylvania Press, 1983). See also Karal Ann Marling, *As Seen on TV: The Visual Culture of the 1950s* (Cambridge, Mass.: Harvard University Press, 1995). Michael Leja, *Reframing Abstract Expressionism: Subjectivity and Painting in the 1940s* (New Haven, Conn.: Yale University Press, 1993), offers important insights and background on these issues. Karal Ann Marling and John Wetenhall, *Iwo Jima: Monuments, Memories, and the American Hero* (Cambridge, Mass.: Harvard University Press, 1991), illuminates controversies that arose over one of the important public monuments that was erected in this period.
3. This line of thinking has been pursued in other ways by Casey Blake, Erika Doss, Neil Harris, Karal Ann Marling, W. J. T. Mitchell, as well as scholars of cultural studies and fandom, who have examined meanings of public art as they arise from the popular, commercial sector and from the segmented ranks of "ordinary," middle-class people. See Erika Doss, *Spirit Poles and Flying Pigs: Public Art and Cultural Democracy in American Communities* (Washington, D.C.: Smithsonian Institution Press, 1995); Mitchell, *Art and the Public Sphere.* On fandom, see Eric Smoodin, " 'This Business of America': Fan Mail, Film Reception, and 'Meet John Doe,' " *Screen* 37, no. 2 (Summer 1996): 111–28; Barbara Ehrenreich, Elizabeth Hess, and Gloria Jacobs, "Beatlemania: Girls Just Want to Have Fun," in *The Adoring Audience: Fan Culture and Popular Media,* ed. Lisa Lewis (London: Routledge, 1992), 84–106; Kathryn H. Fuller, *At the Picture Show: Small-Town Audiences and the Creation of Movie Fan Culture* (Washington, D.C.: Smithsonian Institution Press,

1996), 115–68; Miriam Hansen, *Babel and Babylon: Spectatorship in American Silent Film* (Cambridge, Mass.: Harvard University Press, 1991), 245–68; Karal Ann Marling, *Graceland: Going Home with Elvis* (Cambridge, Mass.: Harvard University Press, 1996); Karal Ann Marling, *The Colossus of Roads: Myth and Symbol along the American Highway* (Minneapolis: University of Minnesota Press, 1984); Erika Lee Doss, *Elvis Culture: Fans, Faith, and Image* (Lawrence: University Press of Kansas, 1999); and Gilbert B. Rodman, *Elvis after Elvis: The Posthumous Career of a Living Legend* (London: Routledge, 1996). See also Angela McRobbie, *Feminism and Youth Culture: From "Jackie" to "Just Seventeen"* (Houndmills, U.K.: Macmillan, 1991); and Angela McRobbie, *Postmodernism and Popular Culture* (London: Routledge, 1994).

4. On the public sphere, see Jürgen Habermas, *The Structural Transformation of the Public Sphere: An Inquiry into a Category of Bourgeois Society,* trans. Thomas Burger with Frederick Lawrence (Cambridge, Mass.: MIT Press, 1991 [1962]). Habermas envisioned the enlightened public sphere as emerging outside and in critical opposition to the power of the state. For responses to the Habermasian model, see Craig Calhoun, ed., *Habermas and the Public Sphere* (Cambridge, Mass.: MIT Press, 1962).

5. In preparation for a jurors' visit to the home of the football star O. J. Simpson, on trial for double murder, the Simpson defense attorney Cochran replaced the sexy pictures of Simpson's girlfriend, adorning the walls, with Rockwell's *The Problem We All Live With,* a powerful illustration of youthful determination triumphing over racial hatred. See "The Great O. J. Legacy," *Economist,* November 30, 1996, 23.

   Former speaker of the House (1995–99) Newt Gingrich implored Americans to cull through the *Saturday Evening Post*s of 1955 "for a sense of the personal values we should be communicating to our children." Rockwell's work figures large in the *Saturday Evening Post* of 1955. Newt Gingrich, *To Renew America* (New York: HarperCollins, 1995), 78. The businessman and presidential candidate (1996 and 1992) Ross Perot owns several Rockwells. The film director Stephen Spielberg, also a collector, borrowed from Rockwell for scenes of "typical Americana" in *Close Encounters of the Third Kind.* In 1995 the U.S. Postal Service reproduced Rockwell's *Triple Self-Portrait* on a 29¢ (standard) stamp.

6. His work was an early example of what W. J. T. Mitchell characterized, with respect to popular films like Spike Lee's *Do the Right Thing,* as the erosion of the public and private spheres. W. J. T. Mitchell, *Picture Theory: Essays on Verbal and Visual Representation* (Chicago: University of Chicago Press, 1994), 372–82.

7. In the early 1990s, American Studies scholars began to examine Rockwell's images, particularly with regard to themes of gender and sexuality, and national identity. On Rockwell and gender, see Melissa Dabakis, "Gendered Labor: Norman Rockwell's *Rosie the Riveter* and the Discourses of Wartime Womanhood," in *Gender and American History,* ed. Barbara Melosa (New York: Routledge, 1993), 182–204. On Rockwell, citizenship, and national identity, see Robert Westbrook, "Fighting for the American Family: Private Interests and Political Obligations in World War II," in *The Power of Culture,* ed. Fox and Lears, 194–221; Stuart Murray and James McCabe, *Norman Rockwell's Four Freedoms: Images That Inspire a Nation* (Stockbridge, Mass.: Berkshire House and the Norman Rockwell Museum, 1993); William Graebner, "Norman Rockwell and American Mass Culture: The

Crisis of Representation in the Great Depression," *Prospects* 22 (1997): 323–56; and Karal Ann Marling, "Norman Rockwell: Citizenship, Criticism, and Affirmation," paper delivered to the Organization of American Historians, San Francisco, April 19, 1997.

The publication of Eric Segal's "Norman Rockwell and the Fashioning of American Masculinity," *Art Bulletin* 78 (December 1996): 633–46, signaled that the tides were turning in art history as well; even the professional journal of record now acknowledged Rockwell as a worthy subject of scholarly investigation. See also Sarah Burns, *Inventing the Modern Artist: Art and Culture in the Gilded Age* (New Haven, Conn.: Yale University Press, 1996), 321–27.

A major traveling exhibition—initiated by the Norman Rockwell Museum in Stockbridge, Mass., and the High Museum of Art in Atlanta—has further affirmed Rockwell's significance as a cultural figure, and, in an odd twist, positioned him (for some, at least) within the fine arts canon. The following books were published after work for this chapter was completed: Karal Ann Marling, *Norman Rockwell* (New York: Harry N. Abrams, 1997); and Maureen Hart Hennessey and Anne Knutson, eds., *Norman Rockwell: Pictures for the American People* (New York: Harry N. Abrams, 1999); Laura Claridge, *Norman Rockwell: A Life* (New York: Random House, 2001); and Richard Halpern, *Norman Rockwell: The Underside of Innocence* (Chicago: University of Chicago Press, 2006). Their findings complement but do not supersede my own.

8. I am using the term "cultural cold wars" loosely, to allude to national cultural debates. The phrase, as employed by historian Christopher Lasch, referred more specifically to international affairs and to Central Intelligence Agency exploits in the cultural sector. See Christopher Lasch, "The Cultural Cold War: A Short History of the Congress for Cultural Freedom," in *Towards a New Past: Dissenting Essays in American History*, ed. Barton J. Bernstein (New York: Pantheon Books, 1968), 322–59.

9. For consideration of these earlier tensions and resolutions, see, e.g., Burns, *Inventing the Modern Artist;* Michele H. Bogart, *Public Sculpture and the Civic Ideal in New York City, 1890–1930* (Washington, D.C.: Smithsonian Institution Press, 1997 [1989]), chaps. 9–13; Michele H. Bogart, *Artists, Advertising, and the Borders of Art* (Chicago: University of Chicago Press, 1995), 290–300; and William Leach, *Land of Desire: Merchants, Power, and the Rise of a New American Culture* (New York: Pantheon, 1994).

10. The most preeminent source of this critique is Clement Greenberg, "Avant-Garde and Kitsch" (1939), in *Art and Culture* (Boston: Beacon Press, 1961), 14. See also Howard Warshaw, "Return of Naturalism as the 'Avant-Garde,' " *Nation*, April 22, 1960, 344–50.

11. See Benjamin DeMott, "When We Were Young and Poor," *Nation*, April 2, 1960, 299–300; and Wright Morris, "Norman Rockwell's America," *Atlantic*, December 1957, 133–38. See also Richard Reeves, "Norman Rockwell Is Exactly Like Norman Rockwell," *New York Times Magazine*, February 28, 1971, 14–15, 36–37, 39, 42.

On the American critiques of mass culture during this period, see Erika Doss, *Benton, Pollock, and the Politics of Modernism: From Regionalism to Abstract Expressionism* (Chicago: University of Chicago Press, 1991), 368–92; Herbert Gans, *Popular Culture and High Culture: An Analysis and Evaluation of Taste* (New York:

Basic Books, 1974), 19–64; Paul Gorman, *Left Intellectuals and Popular Culture in Twentieth-Century America* (Chapel Hill: University of North Carolina Press, 1996), 137–85; Robert H. Haddow, *Pavilions of Plenty: Exhibiting American Culture in the 1950s* (Washington, D.C.: Smithsonian Institution Press, 1997), 1–17, 122–23; Michael Kammen, *American Culture American Tastes: Social Change in the Twentieth Century* (New York: Basic Books, 1999), 3–27, 166–89; Jackson Lears, "A Matter of Taste: Corporate Cultural Hegemony in a Mass-Consumption Society," in *Recasting America: Culture and Politics in the Age of Cold War,* ed. Lary May (Chicago: University of Chicago Press, 1989), 38–57; Marling, *As Seen on TV,* 243–83; and Andrew Ross, *No Respect: Intellectuals and Popular Culture* (London: Routledge, 1989), 42–64.

For comparisons with Europe, see, e.g., Pierre Bourdieu, *Distinction: A Social Critique of the Judgment of Taste,* trans. Richard Nice (Cambridge, Mass.: Harvard University Press, 1984 [1979]); and Richard Hoggart, *The Uses of Literacy* (New Brunswick, N.J.: Transaction Books, 1992 [1957]).

12. Larson, *Reluctant Patron,* 36.
13. Rockwell was quoted by Rufus Jarman, "Profiles: U. S. Artists—II," *New Yorker,* March 24, 1945, 36.
14. Rockwell designed *Post* covers intermittently from 1916 to 1963. Rockwell's *Post* covers can be compared with those of other illustrators by consulting Jan Cohn, *Covers of the Saturday Evening Post: Seventy Years of Outstanding Illustration for America's Favorite Magazine* (New York: Viking, 1995). See also Marling, *Norman Rockwell,* 111–33.
15. Rockwell's advertisement for Interwoven Socks, appearing in the *Post* on June 15, 1935, is another example of how the distant past was brought down to earth.
16. Writing of the 1920s, Rockwell stated: "I'd stare at the wall and doodle. Then I'd begin to examine the wall more closely and wonder how they got the strips of wallpaper to match so perfectly. . . . And I'd notice a little cobweb in a corner and a black spider crawling toward it. Why don't spiders fall off the wall? I'd think. . . . Then I'd look for the spider again . . . and wonder about where he was going since he'd already passed the cobweb." He'd continue to struggle, then turn in. "The next morning I'd be desperate. . . . What was I going to do? No ideas. I'd kick my trash bucket and suddenly, as it rolled bumpety-bump across the floor, an idea would come to me, lighting up the inside of my brain like a flash of lightening in a dark sky." Norman Rockwell, as told to Thomas Rockwell, *My Adventures as an Illustrator* (New York: Harry N. Abrams, 1988 [1960]), 200–1.
17. The tension between modernist "literalism" and traditional illusionistic narratives are, for a brief instant, reconciled. On the "literalism" of modern painting, see Clement Greenberg, *Art and Culture* (New York: Beacon Press, 1961), 136–38, 168.
18. On Morellian connoisseurship, see Edgar Wind, *Art and Anarchy* (New York: Vintage, 1969 [1963]), 32–57.
19. On Abstract Expressionism, *Vogue,* and *Life* magazine, see Doss, *Benton, Pollock, and the Politics of Modernism,* 393–414; Bradford Collins, "*Life* Magazine and the Abstract Expressionists, 1948–1951: A Historiographic Study of a Late Bohemian Enterprise," *Art Bulletin* 73 (June 1991): 283–308; Timothy J. Clark, "Jackson Pollock's Abstraction," in *Reconstructing Modernism,* ed. Serge Guilbaut (Cambridge, Mass.:

MIT Press, 1990), 172–238. On the display of abstract expressionist art in exhibitions like the 1958 Brussels World Fair, see Haddow, *Pavilions of Plenty*, 107, 222.

20. Or almost. As the Abstract Expressionism scholar Ann Gibson has noted, Rockwell "got the form right, but not the colors." From the standpoint of the aesthetics of the 1950s, Rockwell's "ab-ex" colors, brashly bright and "feminine," would represent "Jackson Pollock's worst nightmare." Ann Gibson, in conversation with the author, December 6, 1996. For additional discussion of Rockwell's *Connoisseur*, see Wanda M. Corn, "Ways of Seeing," in *Norman Rockwell*, ed. Hennessey and Knutson, 81–93.

21. Bogart, *Artists, Advertising, and the Borders of Art*, 290–300.

22. Rockwell, note on letter from Raymond P. Fraser, January 30, 1962, box 27, Norman Rockwell Archive, Norman Rockwell Museum at Stockbridge, Stockbridge, Mass. All letters cited hereafter are from this collection.

23. By the 1950s, the *Saturday Evening Post* had begun to offer its own brief interpretations of the covers on the table of contents page. These were typically humorous, cast in questions, or left open-ended. The blurb for *The Critic*, for example: "This museum seems to be exhibiting a remarkable new art form; would you call it unstill life? Presumably when nobody is around, those Dutch gents are able to relax from their canvas-stiff poses and enjoy a round of flirtatious chitchat with Gretel Van der Redhead. If the art scholar could see Gretel now, he would get quite a belt, eh? Trouble is, he is so preoccupied with technique that actually he is the dead one and it's the gal in the painting who is alive—which profound critique on painting is tossed in here for free. Well, the student will evolve. Maybe he'll go through a phase of painting cuckoo clocks growing on hat trees, then pull himself together and do Post covers almost as well as the man whose magic brush created him." *Saturday Evening Post*, April 16, 1955, 3. Although summaries like this were undoubtedly sufficient for many people, they by no means exhausted the possibilities of meaning or interpretation, as the fan letters make clear.

24. The analysis in this chapter is based on correspondence dating from the years 1939 through about 1970, with greatest emphasis on years 1943 to 1965. My search was not exhaustive. It is thus impossible to gauge with any absolute certainty the degree to which my sample was typical of the full range of Rockwell correspondents. It is highly unlikely that the sample (or even the entire body of Rockwell's correspondence) was itself representative of Rockwell's audience as a whole. Public opinion specialists have shown that those who write letters are generally admirers, not detractors. Even when they voiced criticisms, fans were generally the ones willing to take the trouble to write, and the majority of letters to Rockwell were, by far, letters of praise. Rockwell undoubtedly had many other viewers who either admired or detested his work but did not bother to write.

The typologies and writer profiles that I did examine were sufficiently consistent (and remained so over time) to convince me that my sample was, at the very least, representative of the tenor of the correspondence as a whole. I scrutinized the letters for their individual contents, categorized them by type, and compared these types with those developed with regard to mail sent to political leaders, institutions, and other celebrities. Studies that offered instructive comparisons were Smoodin, " 'This Business of America,' " 111–28; Leo Bogart, "Fan Mail for the Philharmonic," *Public Opinion Quarterly* (Fall 1949): 423–34; Fuller, *At the Picture Show*, 115–68; Lewis, *Adoring Audience*; Constance Penley, "Feminism, Psychoanalysis, and the Study of Popular Culture," in *Cultural Studies*, ed. Lawrence

Grossberg, Cary Nelson, Paula Treichler (London: Routledge, 1992), 479–500; Leila Sussmann, *Dear FDR: A Study of Political Letter Writing* (Totowa, N.J.: Bedminster Press, 1963); and James Hay, Lawrence Grossberg, Ellen Wartela, eds., *The Audience and Its Landscape* (Boulder, Colo.: Westview Press, 1996).

The thirty boxes represent a fraction of the millions of letters received by Franklin Delano Roosevelt. In contrast to Roosevelt, however, Rockwell did not solicit correspondence; nor did he devote comparable resources to respond to it.

But respond to it he did. In contrast to some celebrities, Rockwell read all his fan mail and appears to have answered most all of it. He had a secretary and relied upon an array of stock responses, but additional notations indicated concerted efforts to personalize responses. Rockwell's receptiveness to communicate with his fans was consistent with his congenial personality; at the same time, his responses served as a calculated strategy to sustain the "nice guy" persona that enabled audiences to find a positive consistency between artist and work. By contrast, the sociologist Gib Fowles has shown that many celebrities, especially contemporary rock stars, do not respond to fan mail, in part because of the volume of mail, in part because of the sexual or threatening nature of many of the letters, and in part because a response (a kindly, personal gesture) would be insistent with the aloof, "macho," or "bad girl" persona that a rock star or superstar has taken such pains to project and that is part of the basis for his or her popularity. On celebrity, see Gib Fowles, *Starstruck: Celebrity Performers and the American Public* (Washington, D.C.: Smithsonian Institution Press, 1992), 131; and Joshua Gamson, *Claims to Fame: Celebrity in Contemporary America* (Berkeley: University of California Press, 1993). On artist-celebrities, see Burns, *Inventing the Modern Artist*, 221–46.

25. Roland Marchand, *Advertising the American Dream: Making Way for Modernity 1920–1940* (Berkeley: University of California Press, 1985), 64; Jan Cohn, *Creating America: George Horace Lorimer and the Saturday Evening Post* (Pittsburgh: University of Pittsburgh Press, 1989).

26. One might interpret the fact that women wrote more often as proof that they responded more, or at least differently, than men to Rockwell's work. A more likely factor was that more women worked at home, on their own time, and thus had more flexibility or leisure to put their responses on paper. Within my sample, there were few discernable differences of interest, focus, or tone that could be readily ascribed to gender difference. One exception was the tendency, on the part of a few female writers, to praise Rockwell's images for counteracting the typical, yet false portrayals of glamorous, attractive men and women in magazine illustrations and advertisements. "I look about at my neighbors and see how plain looking they are (and as I am, too)," wrote one woman. "Then I thank God for giving America an artist like Norman Rockwell, who paints people as they are and is not afraid to face reality." Frankie B. Krzympiec, n.d. (ca. 1963), box 12.

27. On socioeconomic differences among those who wrote politicians vs. celebrities, see Sussmann, *Dear FDR*, 133–39; on youthful fans and celebrities, see Ehrenreich, Hess, and Jacobs, "Beatlemania." By the 1970s, the profile of Rockwell's increasingly elderly and small-town audiences, unappealing to advertisers, would kill off the *Saturday Evening Post*.

28. Mrs. Guert Leih, March 15, 1959, box ST3 FM (DBP) #24, Mostly About, fifties and fifties envelope; Mike Leahy, August 4, 1960, box ST6 FM (GS) #1; Janice Edmonson, September 18, 1962, box 27.

29. Lela Kaufman, September 3, 1939, box ST3 FM (DBP) #24, Replies and Information envelope. ". . . I'm sure you can't really know, how much pleasure your illustrations . . . and pictures . . . give to thousands of people." Susan A. Tice, September 18, 1942, box ST3 FM (DBP) #24, 40s and 50s Detailed Appreciation envelope. "I am one of those uncounted hordes of people. . . ." Ruth Berkshire, March 15, 1960. See also Jay Darling, February 13; Lewis J. Clark, March 29, 1960; James W. Burbank, March 30, 1960, all in box ST6 FM (GS) #1; Betty Wilson, March 30, 1960, box 33; Mary L. King, July 2, 1964, box 1, Fan Mail 1960–64, Mrs. Barnett answered envelope.

30. Mary Jo Schwin, March 12, 1960, box 33; Robert Finney, October 19, 1960, box ST6 FM (GS) #38; Mrs. A. Grant, October 8, 1962, Box 1, Fan Mail 1960–64, Mrs. Barrett answered envelope.

31. This was also a common tendency in fan mail to other celebrities. Just a few of the many examples include William L. McGhee, February 10, 1960, box 33; James W. Burbank, March 30, 1960; Mike Leahy, August 4, 1960, both in box ST6 FM (GS) #1.

32. Harold Leonard Krevolin, July 6, 1955, ST3 FM (DBP) #24, Replies and information envelope. The sociologist Leila Sussmann characterized such letters as "personal service" letters; *Dear FDR*, 123. Other examples include February 7, 1959, box ST3 FM (DBP) #45, 60s request envelope; William L. McGhee, February 10, 1960, box 33.

   Many fans invited Rockwell to be a speaker, or a juror for art shows or beauty pageants. Quite a few sought career advice. Such entreaties indicated that many people associated Rockwell with artistic expertise, and not only acknowledged but also actively pursued such connotations. See, e.g., Leona Carrick, February 10, 1943, box ST3 FM (DBP) #24, Mostly About, Fan, himself, 40s and 50s envelope; Mary Jo Schwin, March 12, 1960, box 33. Rockwell responded honestly when people asked his advice on their talents, e.g., telling Vickie Colestock that she had "no great talent" and "little likelihood of becoming a commercial illustrator." Rockwell notes on letter from Vickie Colestock, February 26, 1960, box ST6 FM (GS) #1.

   Much like the narratives in Rockwell's own paintings, the desired "collectibles" people requested, represented what the anthropologist Grant McCracken characterized as a symbolic "bridge"—a psychological mechanism that made life more bearable, by negotiating the gap between the disappointments of "real" life and the "ideal" world, where hopes and dreams still reigned. These requests for objects also exemplified what the media scholar John Fiske termed "semiotic productivity," a process whereby fans actively construct their own internal identities and meanings from the "the semiotic resources of the cultural commodity." See Grant McCracken, *Culture and Consumption: New Approaches to the Symbolic Character of Consumer Goods and Activities* (Bloomington: Indiana University Press, 1988), 104–17; John Fiske, "The Cultural Economy of Fandom," in *Adoring Audience*, ed. Lewis, 37. For examples of such hundreds of requests, see J. Roy Ildstad, February 23, 1960, ST3 FM (DBP) #24, Mostly About, Fan, himself, 40s and 50s envelope; Clayton H. Collins, February 10, 1963, box 27, Letters February 1963 folder.

33. Such "idea" letters exemplified fandom's "textual productivity," representing texts and meanings that were inspired by positive and active readings of Rockwell's art but that differed from any actual Rockwell image. See Fiske, "The Cultural Economy of Fandom," in *Adoring Audience*, ed. Lewis, 37; Penley, "Feminism, Psycho-

analysis, and the Study of Popular Culture," 479–500; Smoodin, " 'This Business of America,' " 111–28; and McRobbie, *Feminism and Youth Culture*, 81–188.

The psychological mechanisms at work among these fans was analogous to those described by the critic J. Hillis Miller as undergirding the production of narratives; they simultaneously reinforce the dominant culture (through their search for and reinforcement of an ideal of stability and order) and put it into question (through the insistence of that search and, as we shall see, through the continual construction of new narratives). J. Hillis Miller, "Narrative," in *Critical Terms for Literary Study*, ed. Frank Lentricchia and Thomas McLaughlin (Chicago: University of Chicago Press, 1990), 70. See also Jean-François Lyotard, *The Postmodern Condition: A Report on Knowledge*, trans. Geoff Bennington and Brian Massumi (Minneapolis: University of Minnesota Press, 1984 [1979]); Jerome Bruner, "The Narrative Construction of Reality," *Critical Inquiry* 18 (Autumn 1991): 1–21.

34. Lew Waterman, April 11, 1959, ST3 FM (DBP) #24, box 27, April 1959 folder; Irene Domzalsh, September 30, 1975, box 27. See also Frankie B. Krzympiec, n.d. [ca. 1963], box 12. Typical comments about Rockwell's "real life" detail went as follows: "Every time I stop and enjoy your Jury Room Post cover of February 14, I am struck with its reality in every detail—the pinned up pony tail and flat scuffs of the determined young matron and everything and every person in the picture including your good self." Annabel Joy, May 6, 1959, box 27.

35. Cornelia I. Wenzel, April 15, 1959, box 27, Letters, April 1959 folder. Although a few people suggested biblical subjects, and a few devised their own subjects, the majority suggested ideas based upon their own life experiences.

"Hope you'll pardon the familiarity but we just saw a 'picture' that only you can paint," wrote Mary and Harry Young. "We were shopping, papa and I, we have a typical California shopping area, bottle shop at one end, ending with a Laundromat. . . . Well, along comes this lovely girl, she was 15–16, so naturally she was lovely, wouldn't you say? Looking back when you are in your late 50s anybody young is lovely. So anyway, she has on tight riding pants, regular riding boots and a western hat, flannel shirt and over her shoulder she has this fuller than full half slip that the youngsters wear under a full dress? and she is headed for the cleaners and it just made us think Norman could do something with this. . . . Simple but it's your simple ones that keep us looking for more signed by yourself. . . . PS This girl had a long bob, hair no special color but she was nice and thin, long legs, lucky lucky girl." Mary and Harry Young, April 3, 1959, box 27, Letters, April 1959 folder.

"The other day I saw my employer sitting at the drug store counter where he invariably lunches. This, on the face of it, does not sound unusual but, if you were to see the boss in these surroundings, you, too, would gasp in astonishment. . . . For the boss makes an appearance of dignified splendor. On this particular day he wore a handsome dark blue overcoat, a matching Homburg hat—and shirt, tie and highly polished shoes of the very highest quality. Visible under the bottom of his overcoat were two carefully pressed, expensive looking trouser legs. The boss's face is dignified, too, almost to the point of austerity. . . . Why does he eat at this lunch counter? Because he is pressed for time and can eat a hasty lunch without the absorption of too many calories. . . . On the day I write of, there were some rough-looking laborers at the counter and the usual assortment of indifferently dressed office workers. The boss stood out startlingly. . . . Couldn't you draw a picture of just this sort of counter and this sort of boss, and depict another of life's incongruities?" Edith Hammond, March 5, 1948, box 12.

36. Miller, "Narrative," 70. Memory and loss are evoked in Mrs. Claude Haskell, June 29, 1958, box ST3 FM (DBP) #24, Mostly From, Fan, himself folder; Pauline Roesch, April 9, 1960; Jessie MacMellen, April 15, 1960, both in box ST6 FM (GS) #1.

37. "Since your pictures are so marvelously human, I thought I would suggest another to you that is also very 'human,' " wrote one Seattle woman. "I was suddenly seeing my teen-age son (he will be 15 this month) as he really looked. He is lean as a string-bean and a little under 6 ft. . . . He was seated at the kitchen table, his long, lean legs partly folded and partly sprawling, and he was seriously going about the business of eating a breakfast-lunch combination he had prepared for himself. . . . If you are ever in Seattle and want to do this picture I will gladly lend you my son and my kitchen and table." Mrs. Robert H. Grace, October 8, 1955, ST3 FM (DBP) #24, Suggestions for subject envelope.

38. Herminie Cooke, ca. 1960, box 27; J. Roy Ildstad, February 23, 1960, ST3 FM (DBP) #24, Mostly About, Fan, himself, 40s and 50s envelope; name unintelligible, ca. 1960, box 33.

39. Emidio Angelo, February 12, 1960, box ST 6 FM (GS) #1.

40. The letters quoted are March 2, 1943, box ST3 FM (DBP) #24, and Rose Green Bishop, May 1, 1940, box 32, Suggestion for pictures, 40s envelope. See also February 20, 1943, March 2, 1943, Heinz Frost, May 17, 1955, both in box ST3 FM (DBP) #24; Joseph Hunter, April 21, 1959, box 27.

41. Sue Turner, March 24, 1960, box 33; Lewis J. Clark, March 29, 1960, Jessie MacMellen, April 15, 1960, both in box ST6 FM (GS) #1; Regina Shannon, n.d. [1962?], Raymond P. Fraser, January 30, 1962, R. W. MacGibbon, February 10, 1963, all in box 27; Mrs. A. Grant, October 8, 1962, box 1, Fan Mail 1960–64, Mrs. Barrett answered envelope.

42. "Bad-boy" in J. Roy Ildstad, February 23, 1960, ST3 FM (DBP) #24, Mostly About, Fan, himself, 40s and 50s envelope; lack of "self-discipline" in Delia Jelenko, March 28, 1960, box ST6 FM (GS) #1; W. Merritt Gaunt, Thanksgiving 1959, ST3 FM (DBP) #24, Mostly About, Fan, himself, 40s and 50s envelope; Roberta Swift, October 7, 1964, box 24; Ruth Radford, July 4, 1963, box 27.

Just as prevalent were more moderate comments such as "Modern art may be all right, but those of us who are not educated to it, like to know what we are looking at." Edith E. Clark, April 4, 1960, box 33; Pauline Roesch, April 9, 1960, box ST6 FM (GS) #1; Robert Finney, October 19, 1960, box ST6 FM (GS) #38; Regina Shannon, n.d. [1962?], box 27; Theodora Ostroff, ca. May 17, 1964, ST6 FM, box 14; Walter A. Johnson, April 10, 1964, box 32, 40s envelope.

43. J. Roy Ildstad, February 23, 1960, ST3 FM (DBP) #24.

44. Edward B. Benjamin, November 15, 1958, ST6 FM, box 33, Letters, September 1957 folder. See also Joseph Hunter, April 21, 1959, box 27.

45. Mrs. Otto Rehak, February 9, 1960, box ST6 FM (GS) #1.

46. Jay Darling, February 13, 1960, Delia Jelenko, March 28, 1960, Jessie MacMellen, April 15, 1960, Hazel and Ed Barr, n.d., all in box ST6 FM (GS) #1; Raymond P. Fraser, January 30, 1962, box 27.

"I don't like too much sentiment personally, but we don't need to sneer at people because they are decent and honest and have other so called old fashioned ideas."

Mrs. A. Grant, October 8, 1962, box 1, Fan Mail 1960–64, Mrs. Barrett answered envelope. See also Walter A. Johnson, April 10, 1964, box 32, 40s envelope.

47. Casey Blake and Erika Doss's studies of public art of the 1980s offer important comparisons and parallels. See Blake, "An Atmosphere of Effrontry," 282–87; and Doss, *Spirit Poles and Flying Pigs*, 35–69.

48. Even when conditions were right for making controversial and explicitly political statements, as in the powerful civil rights illustrations commissioned for *Look* magazine (*The Problem We All Live With*, January 14, 1964, and *Southern Justice*, June 29, 1965, accompanying attorney Charles Morgan Jr.'s article on the murder of the three civil rights workers in Mississippi.), Rockwell appears to have received few written responses. The latter were mixed in opinion and provide little sense of the images' impact. *Look* editors then had second thoughts about making public a gruesome antiwar illustration they had commissioned from Rockwell. *Blood Brothers* (c. 1968)—depicting black and white soldiers lying side by side, dead in a pool of blood, and with eyes wide open—was never published.

These three paintings, ruminations on fortitude, citizenship, the state, and the nation, spotlighted the horrors of the civil rights struggles and the Vietnam War. They also represented an ideological shift on Rockwell's part, from the post–New Deal liberal outlook of paintings like the *Four Freedoms*, with their emphasis on the state's role as protector of families and individual liberties, to more of a "Kennedy" liberalism, supporting deployment of federal power to protect the rights of the poor and racial minorities. In *The Problem We All Live With*, the contrasts among the clenched fists of the federal marshals, the calm, yet resolute posture of the little Ruby Bridges, and the despicable, abstract splat of the thrown tomato (the literal traces of hate) also offer a grimly ironic spin on the abstract canvas of the earlier *Connoisseur*.

Rockwell's activist stance in the middle to late 1960s seems to have been prompted by a combination of factors, including the death of his second wife and his remarriage to the staunchly liberal Molly Punderson. Rockwell and the *Post* editors (who would not have condoned such overtly political subjects) were also becoming increasingly disenchanted with each other and parted ways in 1963. Rockwell commenced work for *Look* in 1964. Rockwell, *My Adventures as an Illustrator*, 411–24.

PART TWO

Cultural Policy
and the State

CHAPTER 3

Culture and the State in America

MICHAEL KAMMEN

During the period 1989–90, the National Endowment for the Arts (NEA) underwent a fierce attack because it indirectly funded allegedly anti-Christian work by Andres Serrano and an exhibition of photographs by Robert Mapplethorpe considered pornographic by some. In 1991 a revisionist, didactic display of Western art at the National Museum of American Art (part of the Smithsonian Institution) aroused congressional ire. Yet that fracas now seems, in retrospect, fairly calm compared with the controversy generated in 1994–95 by The Last Act, a long-planned exhibition concerning the end of World War II in the Pacific slated to appear in the National Air and Space Museum (also part of the Smithsonian). This exhibit was cancelled by the secretary of the Smithsonian because of immense political pressure and adverse publicity emanating from veterans' organizations and from Capitol Hill.

Throughout 1995, those who hoped to eliminate entirely the National Endowment for the Humanities (NEH), the NEA, the Institute of Museum Services, and the Corporation for Public Broadcasting and to reduce support

This chapter was previously published in a slightly different form as "Culture and the State in America," *Journal of American History* 83, no. 3 (December 1996): 791–814. Copyright December 1996, Organization of American Historians. Reprinted by permission. The author thanks the following for their critical yet constructive readings of this chapter in draft form, even though they still may not share some of his views: Susan Armeny, Thomas Bender, Paul J. DiMaggio, Douglas S. Greenberg, Neil Harris, John Higham, James A. Hijiya, Arnita A. Jones, Stanley N. Katz, Walter LaFeber, Sheldon Meyer, Mary Beth Norton, Dwight T. Pitcaithley, Richard Polenberg, Joel H. Silbey, and David Thelen. He is also very grateful to Steven L. Kaplan and Jamil Zainaldin for information and insights.

for the National Trust for Historic Preservation did not succeed, but they did achieve devastating budgetary cuts. Moreover, Speaker of the House Newt Gingrich insisted in a two-page essay in *Time* magazine that "removing cultural funding from the federal budget ultimately will improve the arts and the country."[1]

These controversies and attacks, taken together, have had me wondering why it is that most nations in the world have a ministry of culture in some form, whereas the United States does not. Indeed, the very notion seems politically inconceivable in this country. It has been proposed from time to time, most notably in 1936–38 (offered in Congress during Franklin D. Roosevelt's second term as the Coffee-Pepper Bill), but each time abortively.[2] It has been considered and rejected by several presidential administrations. Comparative investigation of state support for cultural projects, examined in historical perspective, provides grist for the mill of anyone inclined toward a belief in American exceptionalism, by which I mean difference, not superiority.[3]

The purpose of this chapter, therefore, is to examine the development of a historical context that has shaped contemporary relationships between government and culture in the United States along with contested attitudes concerning those relationships. I am persuaded that our controversies (as well as our current options) cannot be understood without historical perspective.

As a historian who entered the profession in the mid-1960s, my own views on this subject have been formed by essential legislation and events that occurred in 1965, a year that seems to me the pivotal (and positive) turning point in the relationship between government and culture in the United States. I do not believe that the federal government should have or seek a national cultural policy in the French sense, meaning a specific agenda for a ministry of culture and related agencies determined in a highly centralized fashion.[4] I do, however, believe in government funding at all levels, sometimes on a collaborative basis, for cultural programs and institutions of many different sorts. Although I certainly cherish and applaud support from foundations, corporations, and private individuals, there are cultural imperatives, ranging from preservation to scholarly innovation, that will only be achieved with encouragement and help from the state. Although he carries the idea to an extremist conclusion that I do not share, I am intrigued by an assertion once made by the philosopher Horace Kallen: "There are human capacities which it is the function of the state to liberate and to protect in growth; and the failure of the state as a government to accomplish this automatically makes for its abolition."[5]

Complexities, Ironies, and Anomalies

Numerous complexities, ironies, and historical anomalies are evident in the relationship between government and culture in the United States. Three of them seem especially noteworthy. First, it has not simply been persons uninterested in cultural programs and those with a reflexive distrust of federal expansion who have opposed government support for culture in the United States. To be sure, such conservative politicians as Representatives George A. Dondero of Michigan, H. R. Gross of Iowa, and Howard W. Smith of Virginia were frequent and formidable opponents. When legislation creating the two endowments neared passage in 1965, it was the irrepressible Representative Gross who offered an amendment that would have expanded the definition of arts activity to include belly dancing, baseball, football, golf, tennis, squash, pinochle, and poker. A year later, when the Historic Preservation Act moved haltingly toward approval, Representative Craig Hosmer of California presented a comic version of a time-honored argument in opposition, using Al Capp's America as his point of reference. "Let us keep the hands of Washington, its resources, and its politics out of the arena of local historical interest," he declared. "In short, if Jubilation T. Cornpone's birthplace is to be preserved, Dogpatch should do it."[6]

Gross and Hosmer provide familiar voices of protest. Much less expected, however, is the opposition, mainly before 1965 to be sure, of such creative figures in American culture as the painters Edward Hopper and Thomas Hart Benton, the musician Duke Ellington, and the writers George Jean Nathan, Gilbert Seldes, and John Cheever. The painter John Sloan said that he would welcome a ministry of culture because then he would know where the enemy was. And in 1962 Russell Lynes, a widely read cultural observer, warned that

> those who administer the subsidies first must decide what is art and what is not art, and they will have to draw the line between the "popular" arts and the "serious" arts, a distinction that is increasingly difficult to define. . . . Having decided what is serious, it will follow that those who dispense the funds will also decide what is safe . . . able to be defended with reasonable equanimity before a Congressional committee.[7]

From a historian's perspective, then, there really has been an astonishing reversal. We tend to forget that in 1964–65, when the NEA was being hesitantly created, some of the most prestigious artists, art critics, and arts institutions felt suspicious of politicians and believed that they had more to lose than to gain from any involvement in the political process. Three decades later, that pattern of mistrust has been turned inside out. Now it is numerous politicians who regard artists and arts organizations as tainted and unreliable. Consequently, the former feel that they have much to lose if they endorse government backing of cultural programs.

A second anomaly worthy of attention arises from the fact that the United States does not lag behind all other industrial countries in every approach to preserving the national heritage and environmental culture. The United States was the very first nation to set aside large and spectacular natural areas as national parks, a precedent followed by Canada and eventually by other countries. Moreover, the United States created a precedent in 1917–18, when it became the first nation to allow tax deductions for cultural gifts to museums and nonprofit cultural organizations. The pertinent legislation has been altered several times since, sometimes in ways that seem inconsistent to the point of being bizarre, but the operative principle has been an immense boon to cultural institutions. Moreover, the principle has become increasingly attractive to European countries during the past decade or so.[8]

A third complexity verges upon anomaly in the eyes of some, but it is not widely or well understood. In accord with the American commitment to a federal system of government, the United States has had state agencies for the arts since the early 1960s and a network of state humanities councils since the mid-1970s. Their existence is reasonably well known to scholars, to nonprofit organizations such as local historical societies, and to civic leaders. Less familiar, however, are the separate state offices of "cultural affairs" (in some but not all states), which frequently have as their primary mission the promotion of tourism and related commercial activities within the state.

Quite a few of these agencies have been created in recent decades to do at the state level, and with little or no controversy, what many Americans apparently mistrust at the national level. In North Carolina, what is now called the Department of Cultural Resources was the first such cabinet-level entity to be established in any state. It emerged from the State Government Reorganization Act of 1971 as the Department of Art, Culture, and History. The legislature of West Virginia created a Division of Culture and History in 1977 that includes archives and history, historic preservation, arts and humanities, museums, and administrative sections. The state museums of New Mexico are run by the Office of Cultural Affairs. In Iowa, the Cultural Affairs Advisory Council's mission is to advise the director of the Department of Cultural Affairs on "how best to increase the incorporation of cultural activities as valued and integral components of everyday living in Iowa." Wyoming now has a Division of Cultural Resources. In Hawaii, the State Foundation on Culture and the Arts prepares programs designed to promote and stimulate participation in the arts, culture, and humanities.[9]

As more American states create such government departments and programs, the process suggests a gradual, almost evolutionary (rather than revolutionary) departure from the long-standing preference for leaving to private and local groups decisions affecting the creation and conduct of cultural institutions. In some states, these bureaus cooperate harmoniously with the state arts and humanities councils, while in others rivalry exists; in a few, the bureaus keep one eye nervously on the state legislature and the other one warily on the arts and humanities councils that really ought to be their natural allies.

Thoughts on Not Having a National Cultural Policy

At the end of the 1960s, the United Nations Educational, Scientific, and Cultural Organization (UNESCO) mobilized in Monaco a Round-Table Meeting on Cultural Policies and commissioned booklets about state cultural programs in diverse nations of the world. The paper prepared for presentation in Monaco by representatives of the United States opened with this categorical yet enigmatic statement: "The United States has no official cultural position, either public or private." The author of the booklet that resulted, Charles C. Mark, called his opening chapter "Cultural Policy within the Federal Framework" and offered this explanatory definition: "The United States cultural policy at this time is the deliberate encouragement of multiple cultural forces in keeping with the pluralistic traditions of the nation, restricting the federal contribution to that of a minor financial role, and a major role as imaginative leader and partner, and the central focus of national cultural needs."[10]

Roger Stevens, the first chairman of the NEA (1965–69), declared that his agency did not have a cultural policy as such; his successor, Nancy Hanks, reiterated that position. By the autumn of 1977, however, spokespeople for the Jimmy Carter administration asserted that by means of special task forces in tandem with state and national conferences, a cultural policy for the United States would be forthcoming. The following year, Joan Mondale, the wife of Vice President Walter Mondale, led a concerted effort to activate the Federal Council on the Arts and the Humanities, which had been inert since its legislative creation in 1965. One of the council's first responsibilities would be to review "the arts and cultural policy of the United States."[11]

Ambivalence and uncertainties ensued. In 1980 Representative Sidney R. Yates of Chicago, chairman of the House Appropriations Subcommittee on Interior and Related Agencies, requested a full-scale review of both NEH and NEA operations. The report that emerged more than eight months later concluded that the NEA had failed to "develop and promote a national policy for the arts." When Yates called for clarification of the NEA's objectives, its chairman, Livingston Biddle, was distressed on the grounds that compliance would require him to become a "cultural czar" and exercise control, a role highly inappropriate in a democratic society. After two intense days of hearings, Yates shelved the committee report and did not subsequently mention the need for a national cultural policy. Former representative Thomas J. Downey puts it this way, semifacetiously: "We have a cultural policy by the seat of our pants. We do it ad hoc."[12]

I am persuaded that what emerged during the Carter years—namely, the desire by a few people to articulate a national cultural policy—represented an aberration, albeit a recurrent one in the American past. For the most part, the United States has not had such a policy because it has seemed inappropriate in such a heterogeneous society as well as a potential flash point in the view of many political leaders. (The 1965 legislation creating the two endowments explicitly advocated "a broadly conceived national policy of support for the humanities and the arts.") Ever since the administration of John F. Kennedy, despite very significant changes in the visibility of cultural activities in public life, it has remained inexpedient or imprudent to advocate a full-blown national cultural policy.[13]

A notable exception to that generalization, however, involves Nelson A. Rockefeller, a man who once remarked that "it takes courage to vote for culture when you're in public life." Rockefeller remained a staunch advocate of government support for culture. New York created the first state council on the arts in 1960, a major precedent, during Rockefeller's first term as governor, and not by happenstance. Nancy Hanks served her apprenticeship as an arts administrator when Rockefeller hired her as a member of his advisory staff. It has not been adequately recognized that Kennedy, Lyndon B. Johnson, and Richard M. Nixon all, despite personal reluctance, accepted the idea of federal support for culture because Rockefeller loomed as a potential threat for the presidency. Political consultants warned them that the active government role envisioned by Rockefeller appealed to an increasing number of major campaign contributors and influential local elites as well as voters. That was the advice given to Nixon, for example, by Leonard Garment, his closest adviser on cultural matters. It is revealing that directly following his reelection in 1972, Nixon no longer felt any need to keep pace with Rockefeller's freewheeling agenda for cultural programs. "The arts are not our people," Nixon told his aide H. R. Haldeman. "We should dump the whole culture business."[14]

Nixon unleashed his cynicism once he knew that he would never again have to compete with Rockefeller for the White House. When Kennedy campaigned in 1960, he refused to commit himself to federal support for cultural programs. During his presidency, according to August Heckscher, Kennedy always used the word "marginal" when questions of federal funding arose. And considering Johnson's rage at writers and artists as a result of their critical reaction to his foreign policy and, more particularly, their negative response to the White House Festival of the Arts in June 1965, it seems almost a miracle that only a few months later, he signed the legislation that created the NEH and NEA.[15]

So the U.S. government has never had a national cultural policy—unless the decision not to have one can, in some perverse way, be considered a policy of sorts. (Unquestionably, the creation of the national endowments in 1965 marked a notable break with tradition and legitimized the concept of federal support for culture.) Two partial exceptions to my assertion ought to be acknowledged, however.

It became apparent during the first half of the nineteenth century that public architecture would follow the classical revival model, a policy strengthened and extended between 1836 and 1851, when Robert Mills served as architect of public buildings in Washington. Having been a student of Thomas Jefferson, James Hoban, and Benjamin H. Latrobe, Mills mingled Palladian, Roman, and Greek motifs. By the end of his tenure, a pattern had been firmly established that would endure. Although Mills certainly did not create the classical revival, he made it ubiquitous in prominent public structures. In this particular instance, the government's architectural policy turned out to be the lengthened shadow of one man's drafting board and engineering skills.[16]

The second partial exception, in my view, occurred during the Cold War decades, most notably 1946 to 1974, when a pervasive concern to combat and contain communism prompted an unprecedented yet uncoordinated array of initiatives by the federal government to export American culture as exemplary illustrations of what the free world had to offer Europe as well as developing nations. A new position was created, undersecretary of state for cultural affairs, with Archibald MacLeish as the first incumbent—the closest American counterpart, perhaps, to André Malraux of France. The State Department actually purchased and sent seventy-nine works by contemporary artists abroad for exhibitions. The Fulbright Scholarship Program emerged. The United States Information Agency came into being in 1953, and soon it had jazz bands such as Dizzy Gillespie's making international tours. Such exports achieved undeniable popularity wherever they went, and they were perceived as the music of individualism, freedom, pluralism, and dissent—fundamental qualities obliterated by communism.[17]

From 1950 until 1967, the Central Intelligence Agency (CIA) covertly funded the Congress for Cultural Freedom, whose publications ranged from the widely admired monthly magazine *Encounter* to a slew of foreign-language journals. What their editors and authors held in common was a liberal or even a radical hostility to communism. Although Allen W. Dulles and other leaders of the CIA did not exactly share the values of such men as Dwight Macdonald and Melvin Lasky, they assumed that anticommunist statements coming from the Left would carry special credibility.[18]

After 1963, when rumors of CIA support for the Congress for Cultural Freedom began to spread, the organization became discredited, especially following the escalation of U.S. bombing of North Vietnam in the spring of 1965. Stalwarts such as George Kennan, however, defended the millions of dollars used by the CIA to disseminate Western values, and he based his support on curious yet symptomatic grounds. "The flap about CIA money was quite unwarranted," Kennan wrote. "This country has no ministry of culture, and the CIA was obliged to do what it could to try to fill the gap. It should be praised for having done so, and not criticized."[19] I find it intriguing that an American ministry of culture, rarely considered politically viable by anyone, might be envisioned by Kennan as an appropriate vehicle for anticommunist and ideologically related literature.

Culture and the State before 1965

Taking the long view, some unsuccessful efforts at government support, highly expedient initiatives, and embryonic moves provide historical context for the major breakthrough that occurred in 1965. Yet these developments also help to explain why many participants in the polity still have ambivalent or even negative feelings about the existence of the NEH and NEA.

Let us begin late in 1825, when President John Quincy Adams sent Congress his recommendations for a national university, astronomical observatories, and related programs. Congress scornfully rejected his initiatives, and they never even reached the stage of serious consideration. Martin Van Buren and John C. Calhoun led the opposition with contemptuous charges of "centralization," a catchphrase that would become a standard rallying cry for more than a century among opponents of federal support for cultural projects.[20]

The federal government funded exploring expeditions at intervals throughout the nineteenth century, the best known being the ones led by Meriwether Lewis and William Clark, Charles Wilkes, Ferdinand V. Hayden, and John Wesley Powell. Although each of their ventures had scientific objectives, sometimes including ethnography, they received validation primarily because they served the national interest, and in the trans-Mississippi West especially, they also opened entrepreneurial vistas, ranging from railroad routes to water use for agriculture and ranching.[21]

The early history of the Smithsonian Institution provides us with a symptomatic object lesson for the subsequent story of government and culture in the United States: uncertain, politically troubled, and contentious. In the very year of the institution's inception, 1846, a Princeton University scholar offered these rhetorical warnings to Joseph Henry, the first secretary (i.e., director):

Is there any adequate security for the success or right conduct of an Institution under the control of Congress, in which that body have a right and will feel it to be a duty to interfere? Will it not be subject to party influences, and to the harassing questionings of coarse and incompetent men? Are you the man to have your motives and actions canvassed by such men as are to be found on the floor of our Congress?

As for inconsistency and uncertainty, Henry spent much of his tenure as secretary, 1846 to 1878, trying to prevent any merger between a proposed national museum and the Smithsonian. His successor, Spencer Baird, however, promptly reversed that policy.[22]

There would be many other vacillations and reversals in years to come. Cultural institutions, like any other kind, are bound to redirect their course; but the Smithsonian's prominence and its peculiar circumstances as a privately endowed public institution meant that its policies would be closely scrutinized. Unpredictability in those policies, especially under Baird's successor, Samuel P. Langley, made it all the more likely that the Smithsonian would come to be regarded as the "nation's attic," an institution of memory rather than its guiding gyroscope or compass for cultural affairs.

In 1904, two years before his death, Secretary Langley included at the outset of his annual report an upbeat assessment of the Smithsonian's political autonomy. He even specified the principal sources of that sheltered status: Congress and the institution's Board of Regents:

> The appreciation of the work of the Institution by the American people is best testified by their representatives in Congress. This has been clearly demonstrated through many successive terms regardless of political change; by the judgment with which their representatives upon the Board of Regents are selected; by the care by which they protect the Institution in its freedom from political entanglements.[23]

During the 1920s, a decade before the one we customarily emphasize in regard to federal support for cultural activities, the American film industry received major federal support. It should be acknowledged, however, that the film industry's "angel" was the Commerce Department, which assumed that it was helping to sustain a fledgling but potentially important international industry, rather than "culture" as such. When World War II cut off the extremely lucrative European market that provided half the income for Walt Disney's corporate enterprises, the U.S. government helped Disney develop audiences in Latin America. In 1941, moreover, when Disney was on the verge of bankruptcy, the federal government began to commission propaganda films that became Disney's mainstay for the duration of World War II.[24]

The proliferation of cultural programs during the New Deal—almost entirely for reasons of economic relief rather than as a result of any sudden epiphany about the importance of art for its own sake—has been so well documented that it requires no more than a mention here. Writers and painters, sculptors and photographers, folklorists and dramatists were able to feed their families and to sustain or even launch careers, and they made some innovative as well as enduring contributions to the arts in the United States.[25]

We cannot ignore, however, the lingering hostility that led Congress to end these programs in the years 1939 to 1941. It was not simply that the programs had already served their purpose or that funds and human resources had to be redirected to a global military struggle. A great many politicians did not believe the products had justified the expense. Member of Congress had not been converted to the notion that government had a permanent role to play as a cultural entrepreneur or advocate. And theatrical productions, in particular, came to be regarded as leftist critiques of traditional American values. Representative Clifton Woodrum of Virginia, chairman of the House Appropriations Committee, expressed his determination to "get the government out of the theater business," and he succeeded.[26]

Nevertheless, the middle and later 1940s, not customarily regarded as a propitious decade for government support of culture, produced promises of changes to come. Discussions of a national portrait gallery occurred even as World War II drew to a close. (The initiative for such a gallery dated back to the efforts of the painter Charles Willson Peale in the early national period;

was raised again when the British Portrait Gallery was created in 1856; resurfaced once more after World War I when paintings of the Versailles peace treaty negotiators and war heroes like General John J. Pershing were commissioned; and was envisioned by Andrew Mellon during the 1930s when he purchased works specifically for a portrait gallery that would be a separate entity from the projected National Gallery of Art.) As an illustration of how indirect support for the arts could occur, in 1949 Alan Lomax got Woody Guthrie a job writing and singing songs about venereal disease for a radio program on personal hygiene sponsored by the U.S. government. (Guthrie produced at least nine songs, a few of them clever and moving but most considered raunchy or outrageous.)[27]

During the 1950s, the long-standing pattern of hesitancy and inconsistency persisted. In 1954, a special subcommittee of the House Committee on Education and Labor considered bills to establish arts foundations and commissions, including a proposed national memorial theater. A majority recommended against the bill, explaining that it would be an inappropriate expenditure of federal funds. "It is a matter better suited to state, local, and private initiative," they said. A forceful minority report, however, called attention to the propaganda value to the Soviet government if the United States stopped participating in international festivals of art, music, and drama. A New Jersey Democrat warned that the Soviet Union and its satellite states "picture our citizens as gum-chewing, insensitive, materialistic barbarians." Albert H. Bosch, a Republican from New York City, responded and probably spoke for many Americans at that time: "We are dubious, to say the least, of the contention that people abroad are drawn more easily to Communism because we have failed to subsidize, or nationalize, the cultural arts in the United States." No one involved in that dialogue, however, had said anything about nationalizing the arts.[28]

Change was clearly in the air by the later 1950s—notably an awakening sense of popular pride in American cultural activities, broadly defined, and the proliferation of cultural centers all across the country that could house those programs. The renaissance in American cultural awareness customarily identified with the Kennedy years actually had its genesis several years before Kennedy took office. In 1960, for example, *Life* magazine devoted a laudatory two-page editorial in its twenty-fifth anniversary issue to "The New Role for Culture."[29] Simultaneously, the American Assembly, based at Columbia University (created in 1950 by Dwight D. Eisenhower while he served as president of Columbia and later acquiring quasi-official status), invited August Heckscher, a patrician long prominent in New York's cultural life, to contribute an essay titled "The Quality of American Culture" to a volume published in 1960 under the title *Goals for Americans: Programs for Action in the Sixties, Comprising the Report of the President's Commission on National Goals*.

The penultimate section of Heckscher's essay, called "Government and the Arts," acknowledged that "where government has entered directly into the field of art, the experience has too often been disheartening. Political influences have exerted themselves. . . . The art which has been encouraged under official auspices has almost always favored the less adventurous and the more classically hide-bound schools." Heckscher then proceeded to turn the discussion in a new direction, one that would be followed during the Kennedy and Johnson administrations and beyond. "From this experience," Heckscher observed,

> leading figures in the art world have drawn the conclusion that anything is better than the intrusion of government. It may be questioned, however, whether such men are not thinking too narrowly as professionals, without adequate understanding of the governmental methods and institutions which in other fields, no less delicate than art, have permitted the political system to act with detachment and a regard for the highest and most sophisticated standards.

(Heckscher clearly had the National Science Foundation in mind.) During 1961 and 1962, when Kennedy and his advisers briefly considered the creation of a cabinet-level department of fine arts or cultural affairs, Heckscher was envisioned as the secretary of such a department. He served JFK as special consultant on the arts in 1962–63.[30]

Meanwhile, in the spring of 1960, eight months before moving from Harvard University to Washington as special assistant to the president, Arthur M. Schlesinger Jr. published a short piece titled "Notes on a National Cultural Policy." Much of it addressed what he called "the problem of television" and revealed a perspective very different from the hands-off stance of cultural critics from Gilbert Seldes's generation. Schlesinger insisted that "government has not only the power but the obligation to help establish standards in media, like television and radio, which exist by public sufferance." There seemed to be no other way, he continued, "to rescue television from the downward spiral of competitive debasement." Much in this vigorous piece anticipated the famous address given by the head of the Federal Communications Commission, Newton N. Minow, in May 1961 to the National Association of Broadcasters, the well-remembered "Vast Wasteland" speech in which Minow threatened government regulation in order to improve the quality of television. (Late in 1960, Walter Lippmann called for the creation of a federal television network because he felt that program quality on the commercial networks was so low.)[31]

In his final two pages, Schlesinger moved more expansively to the difficult issue of broad responsibility for cultural policy in general. He acknowledged that compared with regulation of the media, "the case for government concern over other arts rests on a less clear-cut juridical basis." He reminded readers that John Quincy Adams had "clearly stated that a government's right and duty to improve the condition of the citizens applied no less to 'moral, political, [and] intellectual improvement.'" He did not mention that most Americans had ignored President Adams. He did concede, however, that "the problem of government encouragement of the arts is not a simple one; and it has never been satisfactorily solved." His closing remarks anticipated the new endowment initiatives implemented in 1965, whose emergence has been fully described in several histories and memoirs.

> Government is finding itself more and more involved in matters of cultural standards and endeavor. The Commission of Fine Arts, the Committee on Government and Art, the National Cultural Center, the Mellon Gallery, the poet at the Library of Congress, the art exhibits under State Department sponsorship, the cultural exchange programs—these represent only a sampling of federal activity in the arts. If we are going to have so much activity anyway, . . . there are strong arguments for an affirmative governmental policy to help raise standards. . . . Whereas many civilized countries subsidize the arts, we tend to tax them. [Note: A series of recommendations followed.] . . . As the problems of our affluent society become more qualitative and less quantitative, we must expect culture to emerge as a matter of national concern and to respond to a national purpose.[32]

The extent to which Schlesinger's recommendations (along with those of Robert Lumiansky of the American Council of Learned Societies and others a few years later) were implemented during the mid-1960s and afterward surely must have exceeded even the wildest dreams of any wistful or visionary academic historian.

Some Problematic Developments since 1965

The history of government support for cultural programs and related activities during the past three decades is familiar in certain respects yet obscure and sorely misunderstood in many others.[33] Although space does not permit even a cursory survey, I want to call attention to four problematic issues.

First, because the perception of a tension between "quality and equality" has been troublesome, most of the conferences and blue-ribbon reports that have appeared since 1965 emphasize, pari passu, the goals of "supporting excellence" and "reaching all Americans. One rubric that has resulted from these dual goals is "excellence and equity." Many of the key figures in the post-1965 period have believed that they could square the circle and achieve both. Hence Ronald Berman at the NEH and Nancy Hanks at the NEA both loved the so-called blockbuster museum exhibits during the 1970s because they brought first-rate materials to audiences of unprecedented size. When Joan Mondale led the Federal Council on the Arts and the Humanities late in the 1970s, she declared: "If being an elitist means being for quality, then yes, I am for quality. If being a populist means accessibility, then yes, I am a populist. I want the arts to be accessible."[34]

Key participants have insisted during the past twenty-five years that "excellence versus equity" is a false dichotomy, a nonissue, a diversion that obscures more important matters. As I read through pertinent texts and historical records, however, it is clear that keen observers have regarded the tension as real and problematic. Many crucial policymakers, moreover, are divided, explicitly advocating more emphasis either on excellence or on the democratization of resources and opportunities.[35]

I find it curious that in so much of the discourse (including speeches, testimony, and commission reports), "excellence" is casually used with positive implications while "elitism" has pejorative connotations. Yet many of the advocates of excellence are elitists in wanting quality control, and many of the so-called elitists are guilty of nothing more than insisting upon rigorous peer review procedures because they believe that taxpayers' money should be used accountably to support those projects most likely to have enduring value. Livingston Biddle, who drafted much of the 1965 legislation that created the endowments, recently clarified for me his vision at that time: Excellence would be made available to the largest number of people, which is not the same thing as "trying to make everyone excellent," an unrealistic goal.[36]

My second observation is that the art forms that are most distinctively American—musical theater, modern dance, jazz, folk art, and film—had to struggle very hard indeed to achieve recognition as genuine cultural treasures. For many years, for example, the NEA was not notably supportive of jazz, a pattern that changed in 1977–78 because Billy Taylor, the jazz pianist, played a persuasive role on the National Council for the Arts, the governing council of the NEA.[37]

The third problematic issue is that the two endowments have sparred with each other on occasion, competing in ways that were not constructive for the politics of culture in the United States. During the 1970s, Nancy Hanks and Ronald Berman, respectively the heads of the NEA and NEH, had different agendas and developed a cordial disdain for one another, although each endowment, at other times, has done much to sustain its sibling politically. Moreover, relations have not always been optimal between the NEA and the National Assembly of State Arts Agencies. Ever since the mid-1970s, many of the state arts agencies have wanted something closer to partnership with their federal parent, not just patronage. They have sought, and even demanded, a larger role in policy formation.[38]

My fourth observation concerns a phenomenon that may, in the long run, be just as significant as the much-noticed politicization of the endowments: the proliferation of state humanities councils and state and local arts agencies. State arts agencies first appeared early in the 1960s, were mandated by the federal legislation of 1965, and became a complex, architectonic reality by the mid-1970s and a major source of cultural funding by the 1980s.

The structural and funding differences between the state agencies and councils are significant but not widely or well understood. All arts agencies are funded by their states as well as by the NEA (at a higher percentage of its annual budget than what the NEH is required to provide for its dependents). They are much broader in their operations than the state humanities councils, and collectively they now receive four times as much annual funding as the NEA itself. State arts agencies fund institutions, organizations, and individuals. They are the single most important source of support for the arts, and their work is supplemented by local arts agencies, which are funded by the states, mayors' offices, small foundations, businesses, and county boards.[39]

State humanities councils, conversely, are not state agencies. They are comparatively small nonprofit organizations that fund projects, usually ones involving support for scholars along with other expenses associated with a program. Because they do not fund institutions, they tend to be mission- and theme-driven. More often than not, their objective is to shape a civic culture in their respective states by providing support for humanities programs that engage public (i.e., nonacademic) audiences. A fundamental distinction also remains as true today as it was thirty years ago: Most people who are at all interested in culture understand what the arts are and mean far better than they understand what the humanities are all about. According to a catchphrase that some administrators use, "If they do it, it's art. If they talk about it, it's humanities."[40]

The unwanted aspect of this bilevel, federal, yet asymmetrical structure is that rivalries and tensions occasionally occur between the state and national bodies. (For those with historical knowledge reaching back to New Deal cultural programs, this offers a vivid sense of déjà vu. The state-based writers' projects during the 1930s chafed at the degree of control exercised by officials in Washington.) The competitiveness and occasional resentments are more serious on the arts side than on the humanities side. There has also been cooperation, and during 1985 the state bodies did a great deal that was politically efficacious in helping, quite literally, to save the national endowments.[41]

The endowments and their state programs have gone far beyond the New Deal arts projects in intellectual coherence and enduring value. New Deal relief programs improved people's cultural lives in ways that were positive yet utilitarian and largely passive in terms of public engagement. There were guidebooks, murals, and plays for viewers to enjoy. But the cultural heritage of the United States was more often romanticized than preserved; and the New Deal programs provided scant basis for the public to become culturally interactive, except perhaps to protest some murals that they did not want in their local post offices and courthouses.[42]

In contrast, engagement has been a major success of government support at several levels during the past thirty years: preservation, creation, dissemination, and interaction. Museum attendance and activities have reached unprecedented and unanticipated levels during the past quarter century. Diverse stimuli are responsible, but major ones, surely, have been initiatives of both endowments.[43]

Essential though they were at the time, New Deal projects did not sustain exhibits of history and art (accompanied by conferences and symposia) that enlarged understanding of American culture in multifaceted ways. They did not support seminars for the enrichment of teachers and the overall improvement of education. They did not sustain humanistic research, especially long-term projects that require collaborative efforts, such as bibliographies, encyclopedias, dictionaries, and critical translations. They did not launch interactive public programs by promoting partnerships among libraries, historical societies, universities, and schools. They did not engage the public culture through innovative films with compelling humanistic content, up-to-date interpretation of historic sites, and stimulating occasions that bring scholars together with lay audiences.

Despite some slips of judgment, inevitable elements of trial and error, and unhelpful competitiveness and bureaucratization, the two endowments, the Smithsonian Institution, the Institute of Museum Services, the National Park Service, the National Trust for Historic Preservation, and the array of state cultural agencies that have emerged or been transformed during the past generation have all redefined their mandates and modes of operation as circumstances dictated. In doing so, they have altered not merely the nature but the very meaning of public culture in the United States.

If we believe that culture is a necessity rather than a luxury, if we feel that public dialogue and comprehension of a heterogeneous social heritage are essential, if we are committed to a more inclusive audience for scholarship, then there simply has to be sufficient government support for such an agenda. What our historical experience has shown, beyond any doubt, is that public money spent on cultural programs has a multiplier effect—not only economically but in participation by people. What the critics of state support for culture dismally fail to understand is that a diminution or elimination of public support will not prompt an increase in private support. Quite the contrary, it leads to a loss of private support. That, in turn, impoverishes the nation, with implications and outcomes that are truly lamentable.[44]

Comparisons and Explanations

Most industrial nations and many of the so-called developing ones have cabinet-level ministries of culture. Poland, Denmark, Argentina, Haiti, and France are among the highly diverse examples. André Malraux wrote the script for such a department in France, and the actress Melina Mercouri made its Greek analogue quite visible. In Spain the minister of culture played an important role in 1992–93, when his country arranged a genuine coup: the acquisition for $350 million of a phenomenal art collection belonging to the Swiss industrialist Baron Hans Heinrich Thyssen-Bornemisza.[45]

Because a full-scale comparative study of these ministries has not yet been made, however, those of us in the United States who think about them at all tend to assume that they must do about the same things because they have fundamentally similar titles and mandates. In reality, there is significant variation. (The European Economic Community even has a commissioner of cultural affairs; and the European ministers of culture meet regularly on a monthly or sometimes a bimonthly basis to discuss their differences and possible modes of cooperation.)

The French Ministry of Culture, created in 1959 under Malraux, who earnestly wished to democratize culture, is probably the best known and surely the most publicized. A four-page explanation of the government's cultural policy, prepared in 1983, begins:

> France has long had a tradition of supporting the arts. French monarchs considered themselves protectors of the arts, and since the republic was founded the public sector has viewed "culture" (the arts and the humanities) as its responsibility to encourage. And though private support for the arts and the humanities has existed, the major thrust most often has come from the central government if only to preserve the heritage of the country.

Although particular projects or initiatives of the minister may turn out to be controversial, the ministry itself normally is not.[46]

In Germany, by way of contrast, because of the federal form of the republic but also because of pressure from the Western Allies following World War II, the establishment and maintenance of most cultural facilities are the responsibility of provincial governments (Laender). The Allies wanted an end to state-controlled culture as propaganda. All legislation pertaining to cultural matters, therefore, with a few exceptions, is the prerogative of the separate federal states. There is no federal ministry of culture.[47]

In Great Britain, where the Department of National Heritage enjoys cabinet-level status, the most significant connections between culture and the state for more than four decades have been found in national museums and archaeological sites, in broadcasting, in arts councils, and in historic preservation activities. Under prime ministers Margaret Thatcher and John Major, however, the Department of National Heritage has been quite candid about its entrepreneurial aspirations. It also runs the National Lottery (a modest portion of the take goes to support cultural programs), it advocates "sport and recreation," and it lists as its sixth objective on page 1 of its informational brochure that it seeks to "encourage inward [from abroad] and domestic tourism so that the industry can both make its full contribution to the economy and increase opportunities for access to our culture and heritage."[48]

In Botswana, the Ministry of Culture deals primarily with the preservation of aboriginal culture because the Bushmen of the Kalahari are a diminishing presence. In some other so-called developing nations, the ministry of culture enjoys an autonomous existence; in some, it is combined with the ministry of education; and often it is mainly concerned with tourism. In Brazil, individual states have secretaries for cultural affairs. In Bahia during the early 1990s, for example, that position was held by Gilberto Gil, an immensely popular musician and advocate of Afro-Brazilian culture.

To the best of my knowledge, virtually no historian has systematically examined two closely related questions: Why is the United States so distinctive in not having a ministry of culture? And why is that office comparatively noncontroversial in some nations yet politically or ideologically problematic in others—above all, in our own? Although I cannot answer these questions exhaustively, I would at least like to propose a plausible hypothesis.

Suppose we consider those countries of continental Europe where the ministry of culture not only is ordinarily noncontroversial, but where the cultural authority of the state is highly centralized—a concentration of control long feared and resented by so many in the United States. We can illuminate the contrast if we look back more than three centuries to a period when the consolidation of royal power occurred in such sovereign entities as France and what became the Austro-Hungarian Empire.[49]

Because the appearance of royal strength and attendant splendor mattered a great deal, patronage of the arts developed in an uncontested manner. The Hapsburgs seem to have sponsored music because the Roman Catholic Church had done so. The Bourbons were more attracted to theater, and the French were especially partial toward regally supported architecture and music. The Louvre, which became the model for all state art museums, had its origins in the French royal picture collections. It opened as a public museum in 1793, at the height of the French Revolution.

Whatever their pet projects may have been, and they changed from one ruler to the next, all these regimes established and sustained cultural institutions on a grand scale: opera houses, theaters, museums, and so forth. Equally important, perhaps, they created an enduring environment in which support of the arts came to be widely accepted, both among those at the very apex of the social pyramid and among those who aspired to be. Even municipalities felt a sense of civic responsibility for culture. In 1767, for example, the city of Paris decided that it would make an annual subvention to the Opera.[50]

What seems notable and significant is that such supportive attitudes survived the overthrow or decline of absolute monarchy, enlightened or otherwise. Moreover, the diverse regimes that succeeded those absolute rulers continued to support the cultural institutions that had been lavishly established by the dynasties they replaced. (In nineteenth-century France, a struggle took place between church and state for control of cultural patronage.) The blurred lines of distinction that dated back to the later Renaissance—did cultural patronage truly come from the state, or from the private purse of a monarch or some noble grandee?—remained ambiguous, albeit less so, even in the nineteenth and early twentieth centuries.

By contrast, in countries whose destinies were determined by the Protestant Reformation and by the evolution of constitutional monarchies, such as Great Britain and the Netherlands—the nations that founded the colonies that became the original United States—kings and queens did not find themselves in such an absolute position to spend quite so lavishly on cultural projects as a means of glorifying their reigns. Consequently, they relied more heavily on what we would consider the private sector, as a matter both of policy and of necessity. Moreover, the appearance (if not always the reality) of austerity required by Calvinism, even in historically modified forms, would not allow for the kinds of cultural luxury and artistic life that continued to flourish in Roman Catholic countries such as France and Austria-Hungary.

The constitutional monarchies were not exactly abstemious, to be sure; they also provided varying amounts of cultural patronage. But compared with the courts of central and southern Europe, conspicuous consumption in the realm of culture was not commonplace. The historian Janet Minihan demonstrated how stingily Parliament supported the British Museum during the nineteenth century, and as a consequence that national treasure grew haphazardly. Although the government eventually purchased those notorious Greek marble reliefs from Lord Elgin, it did so reluctantly and ungraciously.[51]

In sum, state support for cultural endeavors has obviously been much weaker in the United States than in Europe. We can locate the antecedents of our own reluctance to spend public money on artistic and humanistic programs in the eighteenth- and especially the nineteenth-century cultural costiveness of the very countries that colonized what became British North America. We also know that Congress looked carefully at the Arts Council of Great Britain as a model when launching the two endowments in 1964–65, especially in seeking to maximize protection for the endowments from political interference. In 1946, Britain became the first country to create a quasi-autonomous nongovernmental organization ("quango") to be the primary conduit for government support of the arts.[52]

In closing this section devoted to comparisons, it is essential to acknowledge a major irony.[53] For more than a decade now, there have been clear signs that European countries are increasingly interested in and attracted to the American model. Without exception, they all insist that they would like a policy of decentralizing support for art and culture. More particularly, as government budgets grow leaner, political leaders abroad express envy for the American tradition of private support. They are especially fascinated by the use of matching grants, even though there have been only modest attempts to implement that mechanism in Europe. Matching grants have worked successfully at the provincial level in Canada.[54]

Owing to economic contraction, moreover, Europeans are becoming more inclined to emphasize excellence above equity and to insist that cultural creativity can be encouraged but not purchased. We now hear echoes of a letter written by Gustave Flaubert back in 1853:

Have you ever remarked how all authority is stupid concerning Art? Our wonderful governments (kings or republics) imagine that they have only to order work to be done, and it will be forthcoming. They set up prizes, encouragements, academies, and they forget only one thing, one little thing without which nothing can live: the atmosphere.[55]

When budgets shrink in our own time, encouraging an optimal "atmosphere" looks like a prudent yet easy alternative. Mere encouragement is not sufficient, however.

Conclusions

Anxiety at the prospect of a leviathan state—ranging from social services to cultural programs—has been a long-standing and persistent legacy in American political culture. Fears about centralization prompted the opposition of Van Buren, Calhoun, and many others to the cultural and scientific agendas of John Quincy Adams. Those concerns resurfaced prominently during the later years of Franklin D. Roosevelt's second term, once again during the early years of Ronald Reagan's presidency, and in 1995 when Republicans sought to fulfill their Contract with America.[56]

I believe that such nagging concerns can be turned to the advantage of those who value cultural growth, achievement, and institutions—in particular, those of us who are persuaded that the NEH has been the single most important source of support for humanistic endeavors in the United States during the past generation. Major cultural organizations and significant, broad-gauge scholarship must be sustained at the national level. Federal dollars are absolutely indispensable to leverage local and private funds. The federal imprimatur has meant legitimacy for cultural programs at all levels.

An important rationale for fostering closer collaboration between federal and state entities (meaning consultation and the sharing of resources) is that it might help depoliticize culture. Support at the state and local levels is less likely to provoke controversy. Cultural localism and regionalism may not make a big splash, but neither do they ordinarily alienate citizens and suffer from distortion or sensationalism in the national media. Increased cooperation among levels and sources of government support simply makes sense in a country that everyone acknowledges is diverse in taste levels, opinions, and what is perceived as the public interest. It is worth bearing in mind that Nancy Hanks's phenomenal success as the chair of the NEA owed a great deal to her carefully organized network of support at the grass roots. Former representative Thomas J. Downey, who chaired the Congressional Arts Caucus from 1982 until 1987, regarded the state arts agencies as "invaluable" because they constantly pressured members of Congress and made them aware that support for cultural programs was both essential and politically viable. As Downey put it, they provided validation from the districts on economic as well as cultural grounds. They also undercut those who contended that federal support for the arts was elitist.[57]

It is particularly noteworthy, I believe, that during the 1995 campaign to save the NEH and NEA, advocates scored effective points by constantly calling attention to positive achievements made at the state and local levels. Those are the levels most appealing to members of Congress, and we cannot escape the reality that we are discussing a highly political process. Congressional supporters of cultural programs are partial to the phrase "building from the bottom up." That is a crucial reason why the state councils and agencies are so essential.

From the perspective of historians, state programs have had, and will continue to have, the salutary effect of broadening the audience for history. They transmit far beyond academe new historical interpretations and an understanding of what American history is all about—something that many scholars have long been saying needs to be done. State councils transmit money to local historical societies and discussion groups that meet at public libraries; and professional historians play a prominent role on state humanities councils. They can have a profoundly influential impact by determining what kinds of history will be disseminated and discussed at the grassroots level.

I do not for a moment mean to suggest that the state agencies and councils are prepared or able to resolve all the vexed issues involving culture and government in the United States. Historical experience has demonstrated their limitations. Generalizations about fifty-six different entities are dangerous, but overall they are more oriented to the contemporary than to the historical. They do not directly support scholarship. Their assistance to museums goes for public and educational programs rather than for basic curatorial, cataloging, or even exhibition needs. Some members of the state councils have even been disdainful of scholarship.[58]

State and local cultural organizations do things that complement what only the national entities are able to do. We need all of them, working in concert, if we genuinely hope to achieve excellence and equity. It is imperative that we strengthen the connective links of cultural federalism, because that is often the way American governmental politics works most successfully.

Above, when I supplied cursory descriptions of the state humanities councils and arts agencies, I emphasized contrasts between the two because their histories are so asymmetrical and not clearly understood. There is, however, a key area in which they have been moving in sync. In more than thirty states (by the mid-1990s), the state agencies and councils do some cooperative or shared programming. Several states now have a joint standing committee on the arts and the humanities, a collaborative arrangement in which Ohio has been the leader.[59]

For about two decades, the humanities councils have emphasized what they call the public humanities, the dissemination of fresh perspectives to a broad, nonacademic audience. As the philosopher Charles Frankel phrased it: "Nothing has happened of greater importance in the history of American humanistic scholarship than the invitation of the government to scholars to think in a more public fashion, and to think and teach with the presence of their fellow citizens in mind."[60]

Similarly, both the NEA and the state arts agencies have promoted what is called "the new public art," meaning art put in public places for its own sake rather than the commemoration of some politician or military hero. Doing so entails a vision of art that can humanize and enliven public places—art to be enjoyed. Needless to say, the sculpture *Tilted Arc* by Richard Serra did not achieve such an outcome in lower Manhattan, but responsibility for that debacle rests with misunderstanding on all sides. Alexander Calder's *La Grand Vitesse*, a comparable commission for Grand Rapids, provides an illustration of communication and explanation eventually leading not merely to acceptance but also to pride.[61]

It may help clarify our thinking if we reflect comparatively on the historically determined nature of the U.S. situation. During the eighteenth century, what later became Germany was a fragmented set of societies partially bonded by a common culture. A Kulturvolk existed rather than a cohesive polity. In the nineteenth century, after the fall of Napoleon, when Germans wanted a political structure worthy of that rich culture and commensurate with it, they regarded the nation that emerged as a Kulturstaat: a state defined by the vigorous presence of a common culture.[62]

In striking contrast, when the United States emerged as a nation in 1789, it came to be defined by its distinctive political structure and by the Founders' desire and rationale for that republican structure. Unlike Germany, the country did not yet possess a defined common culture; and it might well be argued that the task of defining a common culture in the United States has become more difficult, rather than less, in the intervening two centuries.

Henry Adams perceived that problematic reality more than a century ago when he wrote an open letter to the American Historical Association, which he served as president in 1894. He fully anticipated the flowering of intellectual and cultural diversity in the United States. An effort to "hold together the persons interested in history is worth making," he wrote. Yet his candid realism followed directly. "That we should ever act on public opinion with the weigh of one compact and one energetic conviction is hardly to be expected, but that one day or another we shall be compelled to act individually or in groups I cannot doubt."[63]

I feel certain that solutions to the complex interaction between culture and the state in the United States can be found in improved institutional and organizational relationships—connections that belong under a rubric that might be called cultural federalism. The state now has a strong tradition of encouraging and supporting cultural activities when doing so seems to be in the interest of the state. That is exactly why federal support for culture accelerated during the Cold War decades.

It is no coincidence that a broadly based acceptance of government support for culture waned precipitously once the Cold War ended in 1989. Many of those who had long feared alien ideologies have subsequently projected their anxieties onto domestic "enemies," such as artists, intellectuals, and institutions that communicated unfamiliar views or unconventional positions critical of orthodox pieties. The historic hostility toward unusual, dissident, or revisionist views described so forcefully by Richard Hofstadter in his 1963 book *Anti-Intellectualism in American Life* resurfaced with renewed political potency after 1989, resulting in mistrust of artists, intellectuals, and many cultural programs because they appeared elitist, "revisionist," or unpatriotic.[64]

Cultural federalism—government support for cultural needs along with collaboration at all levels—could go a long way toward minimizing anti-intellectualism, fear of innovation, and mistrust of constructive cultural criticism. That is why the notion of public humanities really matters. It is an idea whose time has come, because it is sorely needed at this juncture.

Notes

1. Newt Gingrich, "Cutting Cultural Funding: A Reply," *Time*, August 21, 1995, 70–71.
2. A. Hunter Dupree, *Science in the Federal Government: A History of Policies and Activities* (Baltimore: Johns Hopkins University Press, 1986), 215–20, 293; Richard McKinzie, *The New Deal for Artists* (Princeton, N.J.: Princeton University Press, 1973), 151–54, 185; Gary O. Larson, *The Reluctant Patron: The United States Government and the Arts, 1943–1965* (Philadelphia: University of Pennsylvania Press, 1983), 42, 221.
3. J. Mark Davidson Schuster, *Supporting the Arts: An International Comparative Study* (Washington, D.C. : National Endowment for the Arts, 1985); Richard M. Merelman, *Partial Visions: Culture and Politics in Britain, Canada, and the United States* (Madison: University of Wisconsin Press, 1991).
4. On the French approach, see *New York Times*, February 25, 1996.
5. Horace Kallen, *Culture and Democracy in the United States: Studies in the Group Psychology of the American Peoples* (New York: Boni & Liveright, 1924), 123.
6. Stephen Miller, *Excellence & Equity: The National Endowment for the Humanities* (Lexington: University Press of Kentucky, 1984), 21–22; *Congressional Record*, 89 Cong., 2nd sess., September 19, 1966, 22957.
7. See Gail Levin, *Edward Hopper: An Intimate Biography* (New York: Alfred A. Knopf, 1998), 277; McKinzie, *New Deal for Artists*, 58; Jerre Mangione, *The Dream and the Deal: The Federal Writers' Project, 1935–1943* (Boston: Little, Brown, 1972), 102–3; Michael Kammen, *The Lively Arts: Gilbert Seldes and the Transformation of Cultural Criticism in the United States* (New York: Oxford University Press, 1996), 11–12, 200, 319, 371. For John Sloan's remark, see Alice Goldfarb Marquis, *Art Lessons: Learning from the Rise and Fall of Public Arts Fun*ding (New York: Basic Books, 1995), 242–43; and Russell Lynes, *Confessions of a Dilettante* (New York: Harper & Row, 1966), 22–23. As late as 1953, symphony orchestra di-

rectors were almost unanimously opposed to any government subvention for orchestras, preferring to rely on socially elite patrons and foundations. See Marquis, *Art Lessons*, 30.

8. Alfred Runte, *National Parks: The American Experience* (Lincoln: University of Nebraska Press, 1979), esp. chaps. 2, 3; Hal Rothman, *Preserving Different Pasts: The American National Monuments* (Urbana: University of Illinois Press, 1989); Marquis, *Art Lessons*, 170–71; Schuster, *Supporting the Arts*. In 1991, private individuals contributed $8.8 billion to the arts and humanities in tax-deductible donations, a figure widely noticed and deeply envied abroad. See Marquis, Art Lessons, 170.

9. See Lisa A. Marcus, ed., *North Carolina Manual, 1993–1994* (Raleigh, N.C.: Rufus Edmisten, 1994), 268–75; and Sharon J. Marcus, ed., *The National Directory of State Agencies* (Gaithersburg. Md.: Cambridge Information Group, 1989).

10. Charles C. Mark, *A Study of Cultural Policy in the United States* (Paris: UNESCO, 1969), 11. For an astute account of the historical background, see Stanley N. Katz, "Influences on Public Policies in the United States," in *The Arts and Public Policy in the United States*, ed. W. McNeil Lowry (Englewood Cliffs, N.J.: Prentice Hall, 1984), 23–37. Cf. Margaret Jane Wyszomirski, "The Politics of Art: Nancy Hanks and the National Endowment for the Arts," in *Leadership and Innovation: A Biographical Perspective on Entrepreneurs in Government*, ed. Jameson W. Doig and Erwin C. Hargrove (Baltimore: Johns Hopkins University Press, 1987), 207–45, esp. 219–20.

11. See Marquis, *Art Lessons*, 88; Michael Straight, *Twigs for an Eagle's Nest: Government and the Arts, 1965–1978* (New York: Devon Press, 1979), 96; and Michael Macdonald Mooney, *The Ministry of Culture: Connections among Art, Money, and Politics* (New York: Wyndham Books, 1980), 49, 250–51. More than one scholar considers it a functional "myth" that the United States has no national arts policy. See Margaret Jane Wyszomirski, "Federal Cultural Support: Toward a New Paradigm?" *Journal of Arts Management, Law, and Society* 25 (Spring 1995): 76–77.

12. Marquis, *Art Lessons*, 157; Livingston Biddle, *Our Government and the Arts: A Perspective from the Inside* (New York: American Council for the Arts, 1988), chap. 5, esp. 398–99; Thomas J. Downey interview by Michael Kammen, January 11, 1996, notes (in Michael Kammen's possession). Cf. Samuel Lipman, "The State of National Cultural Policy," in *Culture and Democracy: Social and Ethical Issues in Public Support for the Arts and Humanities*, ed. Andrew Buchwalter (Boulder, Colo.: Westview Press, 1992), 47–57.

13. Miller, *Excellence & Equity*, 54 (emphasis added); Terri Lynn Cornwell, "Party Platforms and the Arts," in *Art, Ideology, and Politics*, ed. Judith H. Balfe and Margaret Jane Wyszomirski (New York: Praeger, 1985), 252–53.

14. Marquis, *Art Lessons*, 42, 96–97, 93; H. R. Haldeman, *The Haldeman Diaries: Inside the Nixon White House* (CD-ROM)(Santa Monica, Calif.: Sony ImageSoft, 1994), entries for November 11 and 20, 1972.

15. August Heckscher interview by Kammen, December 19, 1995, notes (in Kammen's possession). For John F. Kennedy's vagueness on what the government actually do in support of culture, see *Public Papers of the Presidents of the United States: John F. Kennedy, Containing the Public Messages, Speeches, and Statements of the President, Jan. 1 to Nov. 22, 1963*, 3 vols. (Washington, D.C.: U.S. Government Printing Office, 1962–64), vol. 3, chap. 16, esp. 427, 448, 450.

16. Rhodri Windsor Liscombe, *Altogether American: Robert Mills, Architect and Engineer, 1781–1855* (New York: Oxford University Press, 1994).

17. For raised eyebrows by art critics in response to this innovation, especially its emphasis on modern art, see *New York Times*, October 6, 1946. For congressional resistance and actual curtailment in 1947, see *New York Times*, May 6, 1947; Gilbert Seldes, "MacLeish: Minister of Culture," *Esquire*, June 1945, 103; Taylor D. Littleton and Maltby Sykes, *Advancing American Art: Painting, Politics, and Cultural Confrontation at Mid-Century* (Tuscaloosa: University of Alabama Press, 1989); Jane De Hart Mathews, "Art and Politics in Cold War America," *American Historical Review* 81 (October 1976): 762–87; and *New York Times*, May 19, 1996.

18. Peter Coleman, *The Liberal Conspiracy: The Congress for Cultural Freedom and the Struggle for the Mind of Postwar Europe* (New York: Free Press, 1989); Christopher Lasch, "The Cultural Cold War: A Short History of the Congress for Cultural Freedom," in *Towards a New Past: Dissenting Essays in American History*, ed. Barton J. Bernstein (New York: Pantheon, 1968), 348–49.

19. For George Kennan's statement, see Coleman, *Liberal Conspiracy*, 234. For the Central Intelligence Agency's (CIA) public defense of its policy, see Thomas W. Braden, "I'm Glad the CIA Is 'Immoral,' " *Saturday Evening Post*, May 20, 1967, 12, 14.

20. Mary W. M. Hargreaves, *The Presidency of John Quincy Adams* (Lawrence: University Press of Kansas, 1985), 165–72; James D. Richardson, comp., *Messages and Papers of the Presidents, 1789–1897*, 10 vols. (Washington, D.C.: U.S. Government Printing Office, 1899), vol. 2, 311–17.

21. See William Stanton, *The Great United States Exploring Expedition of 1838–1842* (Berkeley: University of California Press, 1975); William H. Goetzmann, *Exploration and Empire: The Explorer and the Scientist in the Winning of the American West* (New York: Alfred A. Knopf, 1966); and Wallace Stegner, *Beyond the Hundredth Meridian: John Wesley Powell and the Second Opening of the West* (Boston: Houghton Mifflin, 1954).

22. Wilcomb E. Washburn, "Joseph Henry's Conception of the Purpose of the Smithsonian Institution," in *A Cabinet of Curiosities: Five Episodes in the Evolution of American Museums*, ed. Walter Muir Whitehill (Charlottesville: University of Virginia Press, 1967), 113, 145–46.

23. *Annual Report of the Board of Regents of the Smithsonian Institution . . . for the Year Ending June 30, 1904* (Washington, D.C.: U.S. Government Printing Office, 1905), 5–6.

24. Victoria de Grazia, "Mass Culture and Sovereignty: The American Challenge to European Cinemas, 1920–1960," *Journal of Modern History* 61 (March 1989): 53–87 (the citation here is on 59); Ariel Dorfman and Armand Mattelart, *How to Read Donald Duck: Imperialist Ideology in the Disney Comic* (New York: International General, 1975), 18–19.

25. See, among others, Mangione, *Dream and the Deal*; Karal Ann Marling, *Wall-to-Wall America: A Cultural History of Post-Office Murals in the Great Depression* (Minneapolis: University of Minnesota Press, 1982); Barbara Melosh, *Engendering Culture: Manhood and Womanhood in New Deal Public Art and Theater* (Washington, D.C.: Smithsonian Institution Press, 1991); and Michael Kammen, *Mystic Chords of Memory: The Transformation of Tradition in American Culture* (New York: Alfred A. Knopf, 1991), chap. 14.

26. Mangione, *Dream and the Deal*, 321–22. See also Melosh, *Engendering Culture*; Jane De Hart Mathews, *The Federal Theatre, 1935–1939: Plays, Relief, and Politics*

(Princeton, N.J.: Princeton University Press, 1967); and Carol Brightman, *Writing Dangerously: Mary McCarthy and Her World* (New York: Clarkson N. Potter, 1992), 258.

27. Marcia Pointon, "Imaging Nationalism in the Cold War: The Foundation of the American National Portrait Gallery," *Journal of American Studies* 26 (December 1992): 791–814; Joe Klein, *Woody Guthrie: A Life* (New York: Random House, 1980), 363.

28. On the House committee discussion, see *New York Times*, September 29, 1954. See also Karal Ann Marling, *As Seen on TV: The Visual Culture of Everyday Life in the 1950s* (Cambridge, Mass.: Harvard University Press, 1994), 270.

29. "The New Role for Culture," *Life*, December 26, 1960, 44–45. See also William Attwood, "A New Look at America," *Look*, July 12, 1955, 48–54.

30. August Heckscher, "The Quality of American Culture," in *Goals for Americans: Programs for Action in the Sixties, Comprising the Report of the President's Commission on National Goals and Chapters Submitted for the Consideration of the Commission*, ed. President's Commission on National Goals (Englewood Cliffs, N.J.: Prentice Hall, 1960), 141. See also August Heckscher, *The Public Happiness* (New York: Atheneum, 1962); and August Heckscher, *The Arts and the National Government: A Report to the President* (Washington, D.C.: U.S. Government Printing Office, 1963). In November 1963, the *New York Times* announced that Richard N. Goodwin would succeed Heckscher, who had left the position in June. The article noted that many in Washington were puzzled by the delay in naming a successor. One observer said: "You hear a lot of talk about culture in this town, but there's not much action." *New York Times*, Nov. 22, 1963. See Richard N. Goodwin, *Remembering America: A Voice from the Sixties* (Boston: Little, Brown, 1988), 222–25.

31. Arthur M. Schlesinger Jr., *The Politics of Hope* (Boston: Houghton Mifflin, 1962), 254–61, esp. 255; James L. Baughman, *The Republic of Mass Culture: Journalism, Filmmaking, and Broadcasting in America since 1941* (Baltimore: Johns Hopkins University Press, 1992), 95.

32. Schlesinger, *Politics of Hope*, 259–60.

33. See Milton C. Cummings, "To Change a Nation's Cultural Policy: The Kennedy Administration and the Arts in the United States, 1961–1963," in *Public Policy and the Arts*, ed. K. V. Mulcahy and C. R. Swaim (Boulder, Colo.: Westview Press, 1982), 141–68; Milton C. Cummings, "Government and the Arts: An Overview," in *Public Money and the Muse*, ed. Stephen Benedict (New York: W. W. Norton, 1991), 31–79.

34. Ronald Berman, *Culture and Politics* (Lanham, Md.: University Press of America, 1984), chap. 8. For Joan Mondale's statement, see Mooney, *Ministry of Culture*, 21. Whether the humanities can "provide a level of excellence toward which all should strive and through which all can derive pleasure" was the focus of a major conference, "Government and the Humanities," held in 1978 at the Lyndon B. Johnson School of Public Affairs, University of Texas, Austin. See Kenneth W. Tolo, ed., *Government and the Humanities: Toward a National Cultural Policy* (Austin: University of Texas Press, 1979), 1–2, 7–8, 28, 33–34, 38, 70–71, 74, 131. For a comment by Mondale similar to the one quoted above, see ibid., 7–8.

35. See Tolo, *Government and the Humanities*, 134 and passim; Judith Huggins Balfe to editor, *New York Times*, March 22, 1995; and Joseph Duffey to Michael Kammen, January 18, 1996 (in Kammen's possession).

36. Straight, *Twigs for an Eagle's Nest*, 175; Marquis, *Art Lessons*, 165; Livingston Biddle interview by Kammen, January 11, 1996, notes (in Kammen's possession).
37. See Marquis, *Art Lessons*, 180; Biddle interview.
38. Biddle, *Our Government and the Arts*, 319–20, 330–31; Berman, *Culture and Politics*, 47, 148, 151–58; Marquis, *Art Lessons*, 106–8, 110, 112, 139, 229; Margaret Jane Wyszomirski, "The Politics of Arts Policy: Subgovernment to Issue Network," in *America's Commitment to Culture: Government and the Arts*, ed. Kevin J. Mulcahy and Margaret Jane Wyszomirski (Boulder, Colo.: Westview Press, 1995), 58.
39. Jeffrey Love, "Sorting Out Our Roles: The State Arts Agencies and the NEA," *Journal of Arts Management and the Law* 21 (Fall 1991): 215–26; Jonathan Katz interview by Kammen, January 10, 1996, notes (in Kammen's possession). (Katz is director of the National Assembly of State Arts Agencies.) I have learned from pamphlets received from Katz and from the seminar led by Robert L. Lynch, president of the National Assembly of Local Arts Agencies, February 13, 1996, at the American Council of Learned Societies offices in New York City.
40. For Charles Frankel's version of this phrasing in 1978, see Tolo, *Government and the Humanities*, 124. Jamil Zainaldin, president of the Federation of State Humanities Councils, to Kammen, December 4, 12, 1995, enclosing brochures and pamphlets (in Kammen's possession).
41. Monty Naom Penkower, *The Federal Writers' Project: A Study in Government Patronage of the Arts* (Urbana; University of Illinois Press, 1977), 26–27, 29, 31–33, 39, 48, 50, 98. For illustrations of grassroots support for retaining the national endowments and the state-based councils, see *New Orleans Times-Picayune*, January 15, 1995; *Maine Sunday Telegram*, January 22, 1995; *Wichita Eagle*, January 30, 1995; *Hartford Courant*, February 8, 1995; *Boston Sunday Globe*, April 23, 1995; *Albuquerque Journal*, June 19, 1995; and *Box Elder* [Brigham City, Utah] *News Journal*, August 9, 1995. 2. On August 21, 1995, radio station KPBS in northern California did a program on the impact of humanities funding in northern California. Similar programs aired in other states. On April 7, 1995, the CBS Evening News "Eye on America" did a close-up of "The Piney Woods Opry" in Abita Springs, Louisiana. Similar close-ups appeared on the other major television networks.
42. See McKinzie, *New Deal for Artists*; Marling, *Wall-to-Wall America*; and Melosh, *Engendering Culture*.
43. See Fannie Taylor and Anthony L. Barresi, *The Arts at a New Frontier: The National Endowment for the Arts* (New York: Plenum Press, 1984); Mulcahy and Wyszomirski, eds., *America's Commitment to Culture*.
44. There were 160 local arts agencies in 1965; there are 3,800 in 1996. In 1983 state support for the NEH state humanities councils was $150,000. By 1995 it was close to $3 million. See Nina Kressner Cobb, *Looking Ahead: Private Sector Giving to the Arts and the Humanities* (Washington, D.C.: President's Committee on the Arts and Humanities, 1995); Commission on the Humanities, *The Humanities in American Life* (Berkeley: University of California Press, 1980); and Merrill D. Peterson, *The Humanities and the American Promise: Report of the Colloquium on the Humanities and the American People* (Charlottesville: Colloquium on the Humanities and the American People, 1987).
45. "Paying for Culture," Thematic Issue, *Annals of the American Academy of Political and Social Science* 471 (January 1984): esp. 117–31. On Spain, see *New York Times Magazine*, October 4, 1992, 27; and *New York Times*, June 19, 1993.

46. Robert Wangermee, *Cultural Policy in France* (Strasbourg: Council of Europe, 1991); Antoine Bernard, *Le Ministère des Affaires Culturelles et la Mission Culturelle de la Collectivité* (Paris: Ministry of Cultural Affairs and Cultural Mission of the Collectivity, 1968). See *New York Times*, March 24, 1993; and *Ministère de la Culture, de la Communication et des Grands Travaux* (Ministry of Culture, Communication, and Public Monuments) (Paris: Ministère de la Culture, de la Communication et des Grands Travaux, 1990), an elegant promotional booklet.

47. Schuster, *Supporting the Arts*, 18.

48. Janet Minihan, *The Nationalization of Culture: The Development of State Subsidies to the Arts in Great Britain* (New York: New York University Press, 1977); Raymond Williams, "The Arts Council," in *Resources of Hope: Culture, Democracy, Socialism*, by Raymond Williams (London: Verso, 1989), 41–55; the essay dates from 1979.

49. For helpful information and insights supporting the four paragraphs that follow, see Frederick Dorian, *Commitment to Culture: Art Patronage in Europe, Its Significance for America* (Pittsburgh: University of Pittsburgh Press, 1964); Milton C. Cummings Jr. and Richard S. Katz, "Government and the Arts: An Overview," in *The Patron State*, ed. Milton C. Cummings Jr. and Richard S. Katz (New York: Oxford University Press, 1987), 5–7; and John Pick, *The Arts in a State: A Study of Government Arts Policies from Ancient Greece to the Present* (Bristol: Bristol Classical Press, 1988).

50. See Martin Warnke, *The Court Artist: On the Ancestry of the Modern Artist* (Cambridge: Cambridge University Press, 1993 [1985]); Andrew McClellan, *Inventing the Louvre: Art, Politics, and the Origins of the Modern Museum in Eighteenth-Century Paris* (Cambridge: Cambridge University Press, 1994); and Cecil Gould, *Trophy of Conquest: The Musée Napoleon and the Creation of the Louvre* (London: Faber and Faber, 1965).

51. Minihan, *Nationalization of Culture*, esp. 9, 12, 18; Shannon Hunter Hurtado, "The Promotion of the Visual Arts in Britain, 1835–1860," *Canadian Journal of History*, 28 (April 1993): 59–80.

52. John S. Harris, *Government Patronage of the Arts in Great Britain* (Chicago: University of Chicago Press, 1970).

53. There is an unnoticed lesser irony. In 1989, the very year of the Robert Mapplethorpe exhibition brouhaha, Beijing's Museum of Fine Arts in the puritanical People's Republic of China mounted an exhibition of nude paintings to stimulate ticket sales. The show set a new attendance record for the museum! See also Jianying Zha, *China Pop* (New York: New Press, 1995), 105.

54. See Schuster, *Supporting the Arts*, 1, 41, 48; Dorian, *Commitment to Culture*, 446–47; Christopher Price, "Culture in a Cold Climate," *Annals of the American Academy of Political and Social Science* 471 (January 1984): 122; Hans F. Dahl, "In the Market's Place: Cultural Policy in Norway," ibid., 123, 127; *Toronto Globe and Mail*, May 10, 1995; and *New York Times*, November 14, 1995.

55. Gustave Flaubert to Louise Colet, [Dec. 28, 1853], in *The Letters of Gustave Flaubert, 1830–1857*, 2 vols., ed. and trans. Francis Steegmuller (Cambridge: Cambridge University Press, 1980), vol. 1, 206.

56. See Albert Jay Nock, *Our Enemy, the State* (New York: William Morrow, 1935); and Wilfred M. McClay, *The Masterless: Self and Society in Modern America* (Chapel Hill: University of North Carolina Press, 1994), 222–23.

57. William J. Keens, "The Arts Caucus: Coming of Age in Washington," *American Arts* 14 (March 1983): 16–21; Downey interview.
58. For the view that absolute partnership between state and national entities is unattainable because achieving a consensus among the diverse sectors and policymakers, public and private, is impossible, see Paul J. DiMaggio, "Can Culture Survive the Marketplace?" in *Nonprofit Enterprise in the Arts: Studies in Mission and Constraint*, ed. Paul J. DiMaggio (New York: Oxford University Press, 1986), 73.
59. Jamil Zainaldin interview by Kammen, January 11, 1996, notes (in Kammen's possession).
60. Merrill D. Peterson, "The Case for the Public Humanities," in *The Humanities and the American Promise* [Report of the Colloquium on the Humanities and the American People] (Austin University of Texas Press, 1987), 5–19; National Task Force on Scholarship and the Public Humanities, *American Council of Learned Societies Occasional Paper 11* (New York: American Council of Learned Societies, 1990). For Charles Frankel's statement, see Miller, *Excellence & Equity*, 130.
61. Special issue, "Critical Issues in Public Art," *Art Journal* 48 (Winter 1989); Margaret Jane Wyszomirski, "Public Art Issues," in *Arts and the States: Current Legislation*, ed. Catherine Underhill (Denver: National Conference of State Legislatures, 1988), 3; Casey Nelson Blake, "An Atmosphere of Effrontery: Richard Serra, Tilted Arc, and the Crisis of Public Art," in *The Power of Culture: Critical Essays in American History*, ed. Richard Wightman Fox and T. J. Jackson Lears (Chicago: University Of Chicago Press, 1993), 270–71.
62. See James J. Sheehan, *German History, 1770–1866* (New York: Oxford University Press, 1989), chaps. 3, 6, 9, 13.
63. Henry Adams, *The Degradation of the Democratic Dogma* (New York: Macmillan, 1969 [1919]), 125.
64. See Richard Hofstadter, *Anti-Intellectualism in American Life* (New York: Alfred A. Knopf, 1963).

CHAPTER 4

The Happy Few—en Masse:
Franco-American Comparisons in Cultural Democratization

VERA L. ZOLBERG

Beaubourg meant the end of the era of the temples of culture. It marks the onset of vast supermarket-like spaces open to the public, without ever giving up concern with quality.

—Claude Mollard[1]

When I was ten, my father used to take me to the Louvre on Sunday mornings. It was a tranquil place. That's where I learned that to look at a painting you need time, calm, silence. And I cannot believe that the crowds parading through the Louvre today can undergo anything resembling what we used to think of as an aesthetic experience. They go to carry out a ritual, a duty that they've been taught they ought to accomplish.

—Claude Lévi-Strauss[2]

The American Museum is . . . neither an abandoned European palace nor a solution for storing . . . national wealth. . . . It is an American phenomenon developed by the people, for the people, and of the people.

—Francis H. Taylor[3]

One cannot help feeling that for the educator, social justice has a higher museum priority than historical truth or aesthetic quality. One cannot turn this position around and state that the museum should support social injustice, but one might wonder whether it would not be better for it to leave the solution

*of socio-political problems to those who know more about them.
Having said this much, one is accused of considering the
museum as an ivory tower. What is wrong with an ivory tower?*

—GEORGE HEARD HAMILTON[4]

How can the "Happy Few," the sensitive elite that Stendhal saw
as his fellow aesthetes, and for whom he considered himself the spokesman,
have anything in common with the mass audience targeted by contemporary
cultural policy? The Happy Few rejected insensitive philistines, the newly
wealthy for whom art was validated by monetary value rather than some
higher, disinterested motive. Their stance was akin to the overthrown nobil-
ity's, to whose condition writers and artists, dependent upon the literary and
artistic marketplace, aspired.[5] For the nineteenth-century emerging high culture, the rising middle classes[6] and certainly peasants and unschooled workers
did not come into serious consideration as a public.

Since Stendhal's time, these lower strata no longer constitute an unedu-
cated mass; bankers and businessmen are increasingly well schooled, and the
success or failure of artworks is not determined by elite patronage or market
value alone. As indicated by the quotations above from Claude Mollard, at
the time secretary general of the Centre Georges Pompidou, and Francis
Henry Taylor, then director of the Metropolitan Museum of Art, democratizing ideas are neither exclusively French or American. But, conversely, as
the assertions by the anthropologist Claude Lévi-Strauss and the art historian
George Heard Hamilton quoted above show, neither is wishing that cultural
institutions were less open. Modern liberal democratic states, and even more
authoritarian ones, proclaim that certain forms of aesthetic culture that were
previously associated with elites should be available to those wishing access
to them. They want their nationals to be educated and prepared to associate
with that culture. From being treated as a private good, based on personal
taste, the arts and accessibility to them have come to be considered a right of
citizenship and a badge of national prestige. Yet while the large number of
visitors and audiences for museums, operas, concerts, and theaters suggests
that democratization has been attained—even to the point of alarming those
such as Lévi-Strauss, who long for the serenity of old-time high cultural institutions—a closer look suggests that despite crowding, the social attributes
of most members of these throngs testify that in many countries democratization remains elusive.[7]

This chapter explores how the democratization of culture has been thought
of, acted upon, and instituted in France and the United States. I look at long-
term changes in public policies with respect to expanding access to culture for
previously excluded or neglected groups. I also consider recent artistic transformations and ideas about aesthetic quality in light of the increasingly mul-

ticultural makeup of the two nations' populations. The two countries constitute a revealing pair because they share certain attributes as the original democratic republics but differ sharply with regard to political traditions, structures of governance at the national and local levels, and population composition. Though the hallmark of the United States has long been a population of extreme diversity—racially, ethnically, regionally, and linguistically, which is crosscut by a huge variety of religions—France has emphasized its relative homogeneity, in reality achieved by being largely imposed on those defined as different. Both in the metropole, with a relatively generous naturalization policy, and in its colonies, France adopted a policy of assimilation to a single model of Frenchness, whose centerpiece is its language. French remains the official language, and notwithstanding recent concessions to certain previously suppressed regional languages, such as Occitan or Breton, it retains pride of place in the nation's cultural policies. From the standpoint of religion, the vast majority of French men and women identify themselves as Catholic, even though their religious practice is minimal at most. Other religions have been tolerated, as have racial differences, though in practice this has varied according to circumstances and the particular race in question. The criterion of assimilation to Frenchness remains paramount.

Despite this striving for homogeneity, diversity is becoming a fact in many countries, including France. Whereas in the past the condition of monoculturalism was probably more *uncommon* in most nation states than imagined or desired by their leaders, today, as human migrations attain unprecedented levels, monoculturalism is becoming even rarer throughout the world. This is relevant to our present understanding of democratization. Until recently, the process of democratization largely entailed incorporating members of lower status and class categories by giving them access to positions from which they had previously been excluded. In European countries, this meant that democratization was directed primarily at working-class citizens, while in the United States socioeconomic status was added to race. In France the situation of foreign immigrants had tended to be omitted from the purview of most analyses of trends in social class and citizenship.[8] Despite the increase in the movement of people into countries such as France, the gap shows little sign of being filled by more recent work.[9]

The importance of official French policy toward culture cannot be overstated. A strong state has been an outstanding attribute of France for centuries, almost regardless of regime, although only a relatively recent characteristic associated with the United States. The legendary prominence and power of the French state continue to provide it with enormous means to enhance the symbolic standing of those it honors or, conversely, to diminish those it condemns to marginality. Even with a relatively weaker state, however, the importance of the state on the western side of the Atlantic should not to be underestimated.

A focus on official policy directed to the support and dissemination of high culture, however, is too narrow a perspective because it neglects the profound changes that have taken place in the arts over the past century, the most striking of which involve the crossing of genre boundaries in almost all art forms. The seemingly impermeable barrier between high art and popular art has been breached countless times. In the past few decades, the massive wall between commercial art forms and the "serious" or "disinterested" arts has been shaken to the point of crumbling. By now Latin American, Asian, and African visual and musical forms have increasingly gained legitimacy and, to some extent, admission into the Western-dominated canon. Moreover, any kind of art, whether popular, commercial, or serious, is disseminated through the same channels of distribution, commercial or noncommercial. Thus, the interplay of official policy, often originating in France, with market forces of high culture and with the culture industry, predominantly in the United States, is the key to the process of understanding the process of democratization at the start of the twenty-first century.

Contrasts in the Culture of Cultural Democratization

"Democratization" tends to be used loosely by social scientists, social critics, and policymakers alike. It risks remaining an empty and overly abstract concept unless contextualized within its societal environment in a historically informed manner. Conventionally, it has signified making available what has come to be viewed as traditional elite culture to broader publics, and inducing these publics to use or appreciate it. More recently, however, it has also come to encompass the enlargement of the content of aesthetic culture itself, by including cultural forms and genres hitherto unrecognized or previously excluded from this hierarchically defined construct.

In its first connotation, if high culture represents valued symbolic capital, then its possession, as Pierre Bourdieu insists, is as necessary an element of upward social mobility as is one's educational attainment. Bourdieu argues convincingly that elite-connected culture is a component of the means whereby dominant groups exercise and maintain control over members of subordinate strata. He treats this relationship as a zero-sum game: To the extent that the dominant succeed in defining the culture of the dominated as unworthy, their judgment buttresses the rationale for excluding them from valued social standing. The dominated come to see themselves in terms of elite values and evaluations, as praiseworthy or blameworthy. Repeated assaults on the dominated shake them to the point of embedding in their habitus the visible marks of failure.[10]

Parallel to this process, cultural forms that are excluded from recognition by high-level official bodies or prestigious institutions may wither or remain marginalized. If, however, previously excluded forms should be drawn into the institutions of the society's cultural core, those individuals associated with the cultural forms may correspondingly gain in stature. That process is represented in the transformation of previously repugnant forms, such as jazz and folk culture into acceptable—even revered—genres.[11]

Both forms of democratization are occurring simultaneously, though not at equal rates in France and the United States. These disparities in timing and rates of change arise as a result both of mediation by the two countries' respective political structures and of economic developments. French political culture is associated with a strong and extremely centralized state, usually seen as the heritage of its absolutizing monarchs; American political culture is based on its organization in a federation that until relatively recently kept the national state at bay.[12] Equally important, and interacting with the political realm, is the early market development and commercial dominance over cultural creation and distribution in the United States.

In the United States, in line with the country's heritage of decentralization and relative freedom from state interference in business, the democratization of access to culture has produced characteristic unevenness, of advances and retreats. Until the twentieth century, the federal government tended to be excluded from playing a major role in culture, as well as from many other domains. To the extent that government played a part at all, it was at the local or state levels. This was in sharp contrast to France, which adopted the goal of cultural democratization more recently, but in a more centralized, state-impelled, top-down manner. These dissimilarities will become evident below as I consider how each nation tried to attain its democratic ideal.

Toward Democratization in American High Culture

For the better part of American history, the preference of the federal government, to be kept and keep itself at arms' length from the arts, would not have been surprising to Alexis de Tocqueville. Among many astute observations, he remarked on the strikingly pervasive uncertainty in the American attitude toward the arts.[13] At one extreme, the fine arts embodied an elitism at odds with the nation's democratic project; at the other, the fine arts were vulnerable to the contamination of tasteless commercialism.

Beyond nuanced considerations such as these, at a mundane level, most politicians strongly resisted attempts to expend tax monies for cultural purposes, sharing a view common among certain opinion leaders in the "mother country," which provided a "model" for a patronage characterized by "noblesse oblige." As in England, where aesthetic culture was considered to be a private pleasure, not to be paid for by ordinary rate-payers, in the United States, particularly with the rise of Jacksonian democracy, the fine arts seemed to bear the taint of aristocratic decadence.[14] A similar populist logic persists to the present day, though additional reasons are adduced to buttress it. Certain politicians and their constituents assert their revulsion from what they see as obscenity (e.g., photographs by Robert Mapplethorpe) or treasonous (works that involve "desecration" of the American flag). It is on grounds such as these that many reject state support for culture altogether.[15] Gingerly straddling commercialism and disinterest, autonomy and decency, the arts have never become securely entrenched as a national government obligation. Still, despite these seemingly insuperable barriers, a realm of culture to which is imputed special value, and whose appreciation was considered to distinguish elites from others, has come to be constructed in the United States. It is one in which tax policies encourage the establishment of cultural institutions such as museums in cities and states by municipal and state agencies, in response to initiatives by local elites rather than from central planning.

Because a single official national cultural policy has been nonexistent or, at most, barely discernible except in very rare circumstances, mapping American culture policy and its democratizing project is no simple matter. Simply focusing on the national government level of enacted legislation does not permit us to grasp the whole picture, and it would give a distorted impression. Instead, what exists by way of American cultural policy is a patchwork of disparate elements located at various levels of government. It encompasses the private as well as the public sectors, functioning as a hybrid of the two, which together compose the functional equivalent of what elsewhere, especially in France, might be a neater, more coherent cultural policy.

As in other domains, a plethora of laws and regulations, emanating from every level of government—national, state or municipal—enacted for other more general purposes, has impinged upon the arts and their publics.[16] Directly and, to a great extent, indirectly, they affect the creation, distribution, and reception of the arts. Not only may the nation, the states, and many municipalities provide or withhold subsidies to artists or institutions, but at the national level, tariff regulations also affect the art market; citizenship laws or passport and visa regulations and statutes foster or trammel travel by American artists and writers abroad, and the entry into the United States of foreign artists. The national government thereby sets the broad parameters within which creative artists function.

Although the national government holds jurisdiction over certain overarching areas that may affect artistic work—civil rights, sex discrimination, job or product safety—and the physical or "moral" safety of audiences, the arts and their publics are at least as much affected by rules at local and state levels. State government agencies and municipal bodies play a considerable part in defining the environment within which creative artists work and attempt to distribute their works. State and local laws still largely determine the nature of pornography (though within a framework of national standards of freedom of speech, established or interpreted by the Supreme Court); regulate zoning uses; set fire safety standards; grant or withhold liquor licenses for nightclubs where bands may perform; tax theater tickets; and accredit educational programs in the arts, among other fields of study. The local level of government was, if anything, even more prominent in the formative decades of the nineteenth century, when the uniquely American structures of support were created. Nor has it entirely lost its force since then. As consideration of important cultural institutions such as museums and symphony orchestras indicates, paradoxically, their legitimation came to depend upon their supposed importance for a democratic polity. But they owed their very existence to the local level.

The center of national government, Washington, was for much of the nineteenth century a cultural backwater, based on a temporary community capital when Congress was in session. It is important to bear in mind that there was no major publicly owned art museum or major performing organization in the nation's capital until the twentieth century. In the country as a whole, high culture was unevenly distributed, with most of it concentrated in the northeastern region. In the deliberate absence of a strong national state, the early part of the nineteenth century was characterized by a largely market driven, varied, localized, mostly ephemeral series of cultural activities. With the exceptions of a few, primarily East Coast cities where high cultural activities had become regularized or frequent,[17] cultural life was a mixture of elements, with little distinction between high arts and entertainment.

Symphonic music tended to be performed at first by British musicians, often itinerant players; museums were largely cabinets of curiosities, adjuncts of local philosophical societies, of varying quality; opera companies were, for the most part, itinerant troupes of Italian or pseudo-Italian performers. Following the changing trends in immigration patterns, with the midcentury influx of German immigrants, symphony orchestras came increasingly to be led and staffed by German players and conductors, playing their preferred repertoires. Museums or protomuseums began to diverge between the serious-respectable and the demotic-vulgar; the popular and (for a considerable time) commercially successful American Museum of P. T. Barnum, with its "Freaks" and curiosities of nature, came to rest in the sphere of popular entertainment; its serious side became oriented to historicizing, evolution-based, professionalized, academic disciplines. Thus, a Barnum descendant was involved in the founding of the noncommercial, academically aspiring American Museum of Natural History.

This divergence of popular from serious was enhanced in the latter half of the century, by the rise of a status-seeking, newly moneyed elite, wishing access to an appropriately distinguishing culture. Their patronage permitted cultural entrepreneurs from local cultural institutions (impresarios, conductors, artists) to accelerate the process of improving their quality. Local elites and arts managers followed the model of Boston, whose art museum and symphony orchestra were transformed into high-quality institutions by, among other things, eliminating accessibly pleasing elements that did not sufficiently discriminate among their audiences. This was the case, in particular, for the newer cities of the "middle border," such as Chicago, which were competing with other rising cities. Eventually art museums—such as Boston's Museum of Fine Arts, the Metropolitan Museum of Art, and the Art Institute of Chicago

—relegated their plaster cast copies of classical art to their cellars and accepted into their collections only (what were thought to be) authentic artworks by esteemed masters.[18]

The idea of what constituted a "public" was far more limited than is commonly implied by the term today. Where and if cultural institutions existed, the public that elites sought was mostly among those who were already drawn to it, preferably from their own social sets. Beyond that, these civic boosters targeted their cities' middle classes and, to some extent, skilled workers and tradespeople. But they either excluded or discouraged as much as possible African Americans or Indians, and they only grudgingly if at all made way for newly arrived immigrants or rural folk.

The unique American pattern of local support for high cultural institutions can be seen in New York City, which under state laws regulating nonprofit charitable institutions pioneered in bringing together elite patrons with subsidies, direct or indirect, from the municipality. These structures of support remain in place for a number of New York institutions, among them the American Museum of Natural History and the Metropolitan Museum of Art, both built on city-owned land and both receiving an important part of their operating budgetary expenses from the city, under the authority of the State of New York. But the taxpayer received something in return. The quid pro quo is that the institutions are expected to provide access for a broader population than elite patrons. Thus, even when devout Presbyterian trustees on the board of the Metropolitan Museum of Art wished to keep the museum closed on Sundays by threatening to withdraw their funding, the municipal council forced it to remain open, enabling working people to attend on the one day when they were not likely to be on the job. Several other institutions are also supported in this way, most of them built in the last part of the nineteenth century; but new ones have also gradually been added. In New York City the expenditures for a number of these cultural institutions are built into the city's Charter, and they compose about 90 percent of all city expenditures on culture. Thus, although there is little funding available for grants to individual creative artists or, now, to emergent artistic groups, certain established museums can rely on a specified subsidy.

It is difficult to know what proportion of museum visitors came out of the more modest strata of the population, because attendance data in the nineteenth century (and a good part of the twentieth) are extremely scattered and unsystematic. Moreover, to the extent that figures are available, they were obtained for the most part by museum management for purposes that were far from disinterested. To support their claim for municipal subsidies, they had to show that large numbers of visitors were drawn to them. Nevertheless, using the available data with extreme caution, it seems that by the last decade of the nineteenth century, the Metropolitan Museum of Art in New York, which already came closest to being the nation's art center in size if not in stature (Boston still outclassed New York), had proportionally fewer visitors than art museums in some other cities. For instance, in 1900 the Metropolitan claimed 703,000 visitors, while the Art Institute of Chicago reached 851,000 for a population half the size! How can we account for this difference?

Part of the answer may lie in the extraordinary efforts that the Art Institute's leaders had to make to increase its public in order to justify their funding from the local government unit known (later) as the Chicago Park District: They provided popular shows, such as on home decorating, as well as exhibitions devoted to what had come to be considered high culture.[19] Chicago's museum welcomed about a half million visitors each year, far more than the most prestigious art museum at the time, Boston's Museum of Fine Arts. Although the Museum of Fine Arts was a decade older than the Art Institute, it opened itself to only 224,000 visitors. Granted that Boston was a smaller city (though surrounded by many small towns); but as DiMaggio has pointed out, few of Boston's trustees were interested in expanding the size and breadth of its public.[20] The fact that its leaders tended to equate what appear to have been striving middle-class visitors with lowly slum dwellers may help to account for their reluctance. Thus, whereas the board of the Metropolitan Museum of Art had agreed to an arrangement with the political machine of New York City to move into the building erected for the Met in Central Park at city expense, the Museum of Fine Arts raised funds privately to build its own quarters.

Orchestras share some of the same attributes as museums, as may be seen when we consider the differences between the democratic policies of Chicago's orchestra and those of the more patrician Bostonians. Whereas the Boston Symphony Orchestra adopted a fairly austere repertoire, the Chicago Symphony Orchestra, also known for performing some of the most advanced and "difficult" works at the time (Wagner and Debussy), nevertheless persisted in playing popular music as well.[21] To fill its too-large hall (the over-3,000-seat Auditorium Theatre), its board members encouraged local businessmen to purchase blocs of cheaper tickets to resell at subsidized prices to their employees. This promotion, which was intended to appeal particularly to German or Austro-Hungarian, Czech, and other immigrants, had the consequence, whether intended or not, of ringing the death knell for the several local German-run orchestras that had provided a steady diet of symphonic and related music for this immigrant population. Instead—although, like most nineteenth-century American symphony orchestras, the Chicago Symphony was led by a German conductor, with mainly German players—its administration was dominated by members of much the same Anglo-American elite that had taken over or launched the city's burgeoning museums, opera companies, and libraries.

To a limited and indirect degree, these cozy arrangements at the local level sometimes helped civic boosters and art lovers gain legal advantages for their city even at the national level. Thus, local elites were able to lobby their members of Congress to pass legislation that eliminated tariffs on the importation of artworks. This had the immediate effect of permitting J. P. Morgan to repatriate with no duty the immense art collection he had acquired and kept in England. Eventually, he willed a substantial part of it to the Metropolitan Museum of Art, which had made him its president. Though this legislation came at a loss to the national revenue because of forgone taxes, and had the most immediate advantage for elite art collectors, in the long run it benefited cultural institutions that were open to anyone. Later, in the twentieth century, laws providing tax incentives for charitable donations would indirectly foster donations to high cultural institutions. But without support from the partnership of elites and elected officials, it is difficult to envisage how the dense cultural matrix that came to characterize the United States could have grown. As has been put succinctly and accurately, the American nation-state has been and continues to be "a reluctant patron."[22]

Many argue that the arts should not be confined only to elites, because they were supposed to elevate the spirit of ordinary people. In that light, it is necessary to imbue the public with proper respect for the arts, a rationale that their predecessors had used to loosen municipal, state, and, eventually, national purse strings. It was largely on that basis that individual patrons, clergymen, civic boosters, businessmen, and professionals gained support from local or state governments. They were obliged to inject a dose of didactic purpose for civic betterment, patriotism, and democracy to justify whatever tax support, direct or indirect, their institutions received. The large numbers of visitors to many American museums and opera and symphony societies of the late nineteenth century seemed to provide evidence for their trustees' claims to have accomplished democratization. Yet despite these concessions, these art forms were not immediately opened to all on an equal basis.

Although it is difficult to generalize, in light of the decentralized character of cultural institutions and various local practices, even when admission was free, structural barriers intervened for the less educated in facing an unfamiliar setting: the intimidating atmosphere characteristic of many museums. Access to orchestral, theatrical, and operatic performances was even more difficult because of the relatively high admission costs, and the lack of preparation of the least educated for the increasingly esoteric repertoire.

Obtaining national support for the arts might have been more feasible if there had been a large, unified, and powerful lobby of art world people, both patrons and artists, to demand it. But members of the American arts community were not unequivocally in favor of urging the national government to support the arts. Just as many Americans feared what they saw as the potentially overwhelming power of the central government in relation to the autonomy of the states, many in the arts worried that central government support of any kind was a danger to the autonomy of their art form. Wanting to have their cake and eat it too produced concerns that they might lose *their* artistic freedom, control over *their* public, and freedom to manage *their* institutions.

Although it is true that without substantial government support, many cultural institutions suffered materially, the absence of centralization also offered them certain opportunities. Without an official academy, the founders of music and art institutions were relatively free to adopt models congenial to themselves and their clientele, the audiences they were trying to build. In the absence of an official academic system, they were relatively free to permit experiments with repertoires and collections, seek advice from sources they trusted, accept the tastes of their local elite collectors and patrons, and modify their institutions in a flexible manner. Perhaps unintentionally, patrons, politicians, and arts entrepreneurs together produced a complex system of organized patronage that relied on donations from individuals or foundations and intersected with local, state, and federal government programs. In the process, they created a *culture of donation* to cultural creators and institutions, in which traditional arts as well as new artworks were encouraged, or at least not forbidden.

Once the culture of donation had become established and structurally embedded, another important legacy of its proponents' arguments for arts patronage became the insistence by funding agencies—whether government, foundation, or corporate—that whatever else they do, cultural institutions need to provide opportunities for non-elite publics to benefit from them as well. A turning point in this process was the innovation of federal funding under the New Deal. Among many other programs, national agencies paid unemployed artists to instruct teachers and schoolchildren in the arts. Well over two decades after the demise of the first New Deal, its legacy was renewed under the Great Society programs of President Lyndon Johnson, when policies of this kind were relaunched. This time, partly because of federal government requirements for "outreach" and to take into account local conditions,[23] and the Texan origins of the president, the Great Society went beyond bringing fine art to economically deprived people in general. Instead of assuming a monocultural ideal, the Great Society expanded its outreach to a bilingual, especially Spanish-speaking, public.

Among the strategies used to gain support for the enactment of new laws in a particular domain is to show that their own country compared unfavorably with others of significance. This argument, implicit and explicit during the United States' Cold War rivalry with the Soviet Union, was the basis of the rhetoric used by American proponents of national government support for the arts. Indeed, the role of foreign policy "intruding" to promote a certain "Display Democracy" seems an anomaly in the long-standing tradition of keeping the federal government at arms length."[24] In this period, it was commonly employed to highlight the disadvantages suffered by the arts in America, in contrast to cultural subsidies by European states. For example, conveniently leaving aside local and state patronage, in a 1978 study, the economist Dick Netzer argued that the United States lagged far behind the generous aid provided by many countries, with France a leading case. Despite its wealth and power, in the United States the national government's role as cultural patron, as emphasized above, had always been deeply troubled and largely rejected.[25] From the perspective of supporters of state support of the arts, why could the United States not be more like France?

Cultural Democratization à la Française

France, a country with a democratic tradition as old as America's, had a history of promoting high culture, especially in the arts and sciences, that was based, almost regardless of regime, on the belief that the arts represented the soul of the nation, a patrimony in which contemporary generations were rooted, the marker of *civilisation*. Although this idea has persisted for centuries, it was, however, not applied in the same way, to the same degree, or with the same outcomes under different regimes. Long before the Great Revolution, the absolutizing monarchy's policy was to use culture to glorify the Court, the State, the Nation, or all three combined. This symbolic project, pursued through conspicuous consumption in cultural activities, predates by far its democratizing policies. It pervades the activities of its monarchs, nobles, academic officials, government ministers, and magnates.[26]

In his account of the development of French cultural policy, André-Hubert Mesnard states that throughout the ancien régime, as in most absolutist states, cultural policy meant cultural control and glorifying the principal patron, the king. Mesnard perceives a linear pattern in which the only constant has been expansion and retention: New bureaus, institutions, and regulations are added and, once instituted, rarely eliminated.[27] Its primary purpose, he argues, was far removed from democratization. During the eighteenth century, when the Louvre and the Royal Library were opened, they were not intended for the general public but rather for scholars, to foster higher learning to the glory of France. The Revolution provided only a temporary hiatus in this long-term policy, and even during the nineteenth century, French cultural institutions were not oriented toward attracting non-elite publics except on such special occasions as international expositions.[28]

Even under the Third Republic, when the state undertook to create a new, democratically based culture, government patronage continued to be directed at enhancing the reputation of art patrons or the prestige of the state rather than to expand the public. Though its principal activity lay in preserving the artworks and buildings of the past, it purchased (or acquired as booty from French colonies) works of art; distributed more or less working administrative positions, as well as pensions to certain artists; and supported institutions such as the Opéra and Opéra Comique.[29] Paris was its headquarters, with the provinces treated either as sources of major works, usually from churches and official city buildings, or if there were political reasons to do so, as recipients of favors for local officials, who received loans or gifts of artworks from national collections or salons.

As far as its democratizing project is concerned, the Third Republic's greatest cultural achievement was not directly in the arts and sciences but in the crucial domain of primary education.[30] Underlying this expansive policy was the political goal of propagating, in the face of reactionary Catholicism, a unified national secular culture. The Third Republic's leaders entertained other new ideas, such as recognizing the leisure needs of adolescents; but only from 1935, with the advent of the Popular Front, did ways to democratize by enlarging the public culture really take off. As did other countries during this period of world economic crisis (including, as shown above, even the typically reluctant United States), the French government undertook to expand the audience for the arts. This moment of high unemployment served as a turning point: acknowledging that workers had a right to a week's paid vacation during the work year. The state's approval provided an important source of legitimation for leisure, the arts, recreational activities, and spectator events. Even though it took decades before this policy was implemented for the majority of workers, the idea retained its symbolic importance through decades of war, enemy occupation, and periods of economic uncertainty.[31]

This policy had counterparts, mutandis mutandi, in authoritarian and totalitarian countries during the 1930s, which reduced culture largely to ideology in service to the party in power. In France, because the arts made up only a very small part of regular education's curriculum, relatively few students were prepared for or inclined to profit from their availability. Not being a high curricular priority, music and art tended to be taught either privately (for those who could afford it) or in public conservatories or academies, largely for professional training for evidently gifted students, and with extremely limited availability. Budgetary allocations were so sparse that except for Paris, few conservatories actually came into being. In the 1930s the few that were established received, at most, 2 percent of their budget from the national state. In reality, the "sociocultural" aspects of cultural policy, which implies an educational policy committed to the student's social mobility, existed more on paper than in fact.

The gap between goals and their implementation was even more evident when it came to various programs of adult education and programs related to social services. These programs generally involve cultural dissemination that is incidental to other social service–oriented projects, such as popular or continuing education for older adults and after-school programs outside the regular educational system. These "sociocultural" activities were often located outside official cultural agencies or ministries and usually had been left to various political, syndical, lay, confessional movements.[32] But neither the Popular Front nor, after the Liberation, the Fourth Republic cared to spend enough to implement as policy these sociocultural domains. By default, therefore, with a minimum of rather desultory oversight by government bureaus or ministries, the preexisting organizations, usually representing particular ideological or religious positions, remained in effective control of popular education, and of the many cultural associations associated with it.[33]

As with many prewar socialist ideals, it was not until several years after France was recovering from the effects of World War II that sustained efforts were made to implement expanding secondary and higher educational opportunity and democratizing the culture more generally. The greatly enlarged postwar cohort of adolescents met a world in which schooling was called upon urgently to prepare them for an economy requiring more highly educated workers. The government's response was to extend and diversify education, a move that had the advantage as well of delaying entry into a labor force that was, in any case, not ready to receive them. Thus, although the term "sociocultural," with its connotations of cultural expansion and democratization, was occasionally voiced under the Fourth Republic, it was largely under the Fifth Republic that it came to prominence.[34]

Herman Lebovics has pointed out that effectuating a program of democratization of the arts dates from the late 1950s, when Charles de Gaulle created a niche for his preferred cultural entrepreneur, André Malraux, whom he made the first minister of cultural affairs.[35] The Fifth Republic reinforced cultural institutions created by the Third and Fourth republics, especially with respect to private activities and social movements, encouraging them with the promise of subsidies to clarify, codify, and organize themselves more rationally. Given the Fifth Republic's reputation for conservatism, it may seem uncharacteristic that the decree establishing the Ministry of Cultural Affairs specifically makes it a primary goal to bring the greatest possible number of French men and women into contact with the chief works of humanity, to create the broadest audience for the French cultural patrimony, and to foster the creation of artworks. The emphasis, to be sure, was less on the creation of new works than creating an audience for existing and already consecrated works of French culture. This was to be done to a large extent, at Malraux's initiative, through one of the institutions, the Maisons de Jeunes et de la Culture. These maisons, which were established on a fragile footing mostly from the Liberation on, saw their numbers multiplied by Malraux, eventually amounting at their height to roughly one thousand throughout France.

Cultural programs came to be a regular part of central economic planning, launched regularly as initiatives in the public sector and goading the private sector. Though French plans did not have the authority and force of the central planning associated with the illiberal states of the Soviet bloc, they were intended to suggest broad, more or less urgent, directions and goals for the economy. Along these lines, the Third Plan stated that "culture . . . [is to be considered] not as a luxury but as the expression of an essential need, to improve people's spirit, life, relations to the environment." It further pointed out that "[because] education does not seem to create equality, . . . culture must be taught as well, including music, architecture, plastic arts, theater, and other domains." The approach was broadly holistic, addressing itself to culture as what are now referred to as quality-of-life issues.

Included under the rubric of culture in France were domains that are left to commerce in the United States: book publishing and distribution, radio and television. As in many European nations, electronic media were largely paid for by fees levied on set owners, and a part of those revenues was allocated to subsidizing movie making. The ambition of this overarching cultural policy was to replace ideologies (including religious and political totalitarianism) in the modern world by making its aims compatible with the supposedly neutral requirements of economic development. In its breadth, it even laid down guidelines to discourage massive building programs, which might create too much impersonality in the life of its citizens.

Centralized plans and eloquent policy addresses of Minister Malraux notwithstanding, however, many of the cultural programs were not realized or fell short of their goals. On the one hand, the pattern in France of policymaking and, especially, of policy *changing* involves foot dragging by entrenched bureaucracies, made up of civil servants who remain in office while ministers and regimes change. The frustration that this structural inertia causes was expressed by the critic Pierre Cabanne in a diatribe directed against Malraux. In Cabanne's terms, Malraux emerges a tragic figure, more capable of histrionics than of implementing a worthwhile policy.[36] At the time Cabanne was writing, less than 0.75 percent of the national budget had been assigned to cultural affairs. Whereas this was generous compared with the American government's, Cabanne believed that it was inadequate, resulting in many missed opportunities. The ambitious statement of principles continued to produce little by way of implementation.[37] Regardless of regime, the situation by the end of the 1980s had changed little from the days of the Popular Front, which had wished to fund such initiatives as music conservatories.[38]

If the assertion by Claude Mollard is taken literally, then this pattern appeared to be broken when, under the presidency of George Pompidou, the Centre Beaubourg was created.[39] One of the first postwar presidential "monuments" (to which François Mitterand's Bibliothèque Nationale was a worthy addition), this was to be the first French cultural center combining art museum, public library, media center, creative centers for experimentation in music (appended somewhat later), and art. As a teaching, multimedia, and multipurpose institution, the Centre Pompidou, as it was later renamed, was intended to preserve aesthetic culture (by including the National Museum of Modern Art) and to promote creativity (Institute for Music and Acoustic Research and Coordination—IRCAM—and for children's art), but most important, to disseminate culture as widely as possible. Its programs include changing displays of popular cultural forms from all regions of France and the world, lectures, panel discussions, movies, and cutting-edge exhibitions.[40]

However, in light of opposition by established museum and music officials, who saw the Centre Beaubourg as a threat to their cultural institutions, in order to bring it into existence, the ambitious cultural complex had to be created as an entity outside existing government institutions and bureaus. The reasons for these agencies' reluctance stemmed in part from the fact that certain major institutions require so much money for their maintenance that, as is the case of the Paris Opera, they gobbled up much of the French music budget. This combination of motives has had a long tradition in French centralized institutions and persists today. Moreover, as in the nineteenth century, when the Academic system was at its height, driving artists to seek other outlets than official ones, the Beaubourg represented an aesthetic that was completely at odds with the conception of fine art defended by the officials and staffs of the established institutions.

Achievements and Shortfalls

It is easy to exaggerate the differences between the United States—a country lacking a feudal or courtly tradition, where the arts are more dependent on the private sector, either of the commercial realm or the world of benevolence—and Europe, with its tradition of royalty and, at times, absolutism, and government culture subsidy. Despite the long history of state patronage, in one respect the trajectory of European countries has recently come to parallel that of the United States: Many of them are being called upon to take on the relatively recent concern that state support be contingent on reaching out to underserved populations. When Joshua Taylor, the director of the National Collection of the Fine Arts at the Smithsonian Institution, wished that cultural institutions would provide "an elite experience for everyone," he may have been voicing an oxymoron, but this goal is in keeping with American ideals.[41] In France, similar goals have been announced, but even as Malraux's Maisons de Jeunes et de la Culture are being eliminated, even at their height they paid more attention to artists and performers than to reaching out to new publics. Instead of workers, small business owners, and farmers, they drew largely students, teachers, clerks, middle managers, professionals, and executives.

Both American and French surveys over many decades indicate that participants in high cultural activities belong to the highly educated.[42] The Fifth Republic under Charles de Gaulle and Georges Pompidou did enlarge audiences for culture, but it is difficult to sustain the argument that they actually expanded access so as to democratize the audience. Even at the Centre Pompidou, with its democratic surface offering its varied fare, like the user-friendly supermarket that Mollard envisaged (see the epigraph at the start of the chapter), Nathalie Heinich found that offerings are received according to the usual social categories, or as Bourdieu would have it, according to the cultural capital that individuals bear with them. Within this mall-like institution, visitors carve a minimuseum appropriate to their educational level.[43]

This does not mean that the state has simply permitted the public to be thrown into the intimidating world of high culture to sink or swim. Rather, the pedagogic mission that the planners of the Centre Beaubourg foresaw led only slowly and halfheartedly to the creation of new intermediaries, charged with orienting visitors to the arts. This was to be done by the *animateurs*, officially designated organizers of cultural activities, who were to work with various age groups. But having started as a semiprofession, the position of *animateur* seems to have taken hold. At the outset, and for a long period thereafter, *animateurs* in museums were left largely to fend for themselves, receiving little by way of information and training.[44] Through their efforts, they soon sought to upgrade their position, demanding and eventually receiving official status based on a diploma and official certification. Museums were to be redirected from object preservation to public *animation*, or education for the general public. But the problem of reaching traditionally underserved segments of society is not easier to resolve in France than in the United States.

In a study of fifteen countries, the economist Mark Schuster found that as income rises, participation rates rise as well.[45] In fact, virtually all participation studies indicate that as education increases, so does participation in cultural activities—thus from 4 percent for those with only a grade school education to 55 percent with some graduate school education. It is painful for democratizing reformers to learn that (with few exceptions) in the fifteen countries, fewer than 25 percent of the population had actually visited an art museum, yet museums are among the cultural institution with the broadest appeal. As Schuster puts it, "Overall participation rates are surprisingly similar to one another."[46] The relatively small variations among countries occur *despite* differences in government policies; the mix of private, quasi-public, and public institutions; levels of public subsidy; and admission charges. Interestingly, despite the sharp divergences between them, the United States and France show nearly the same levels of museum attendance.

But what of the quality of participation? To what degree do visitors appreciate and understand what they see and hear? Is their visit merely a quick look at high culture, with little real impact on their senses and life, a ritualized activity engaged in from a sense of obligation, as Lévi-Strauss asserts (see the epigraph at the start of the chapter), or do these accidental visitors become discerning habitués? American and French museum people often bewail what they consider a lack of discernment among visitors, but little direct empirical research has been done to verify their impression. Schuster has noted that in Nordic countries, individuals seem to have more contact with art museums and galleries than elsewhere, but both France and the United States are more successful than other countries in attracting *repeat* visits. From the standpoint of art museums, this is a happy finding, indicating that, contrary to Lévi-Strauss's forebodings, their future may be in the good hands of a dedicated audience. Conversely, from the perspective of expanding the reach of high cultural institutions to a more diverse population, the results are actually disquieting. In a study of Dutch museums, researchers found that museums and exhibitions for which intensive efforts had been used to promote and attract visitors ended up drawing a better-educated population than usual, but not a more diverse one.[47]

What this suggests is that as Bourdieu and Darbel found in their now-classic study of museum visitors in five European countries that had a declared policy commitment to democratization, the range of habitus of actual visitors continues to be nearly as narrow today as it was a generation ago.[48] Those in the same strata who did not participate in cultural activities earlier continue not to participate—rural dwellers, the aged, those with little education. Because the level of education in France has increased and is considerably higher, why does only a continuing narrow range of individuals participate in cultural institutions? The growing numbers of secondary school or higher education graduates have become more active than in the past. To be sure, the range and frequency of their activity are likely to be enhanced if they live in Paris rather than elsewhere.[49] But as regional cities develop further, a more varied cultural menu would be likely to mitigate this pattern. Moreover, under the presidency of Mitterand, the long and popular tenure of the minister of culture, Jack Lang, did a great deal to legitimate the active participation in culture of the citizenry (summer music nights, festivals, etc.) and its expansion to new fields of creation.

The Elitism-versus-Populism Controversy Revised?

The question of how institutions founded by and for social elites could possibly serve the population at large has been a central issue for many scholars and policymakers. Until relatively recently, debate has revolved around the familiar incompatibility of populism versus elitism. Populists are usually accused by their opponents of being too willing to sacrifice aesthetic standards merely to appeal to a middle-level or, some suggest, even lower-level public, with damaging results for what they consider *true* art lovers and for *great* art. On the other side, elitists are denounced for forgetting that if the culture to which they are devoted is so worthwhile, it should not be withheld from the majority of the population to whose tax payments, in any case, high cultural institutions owe their existence.

The arts of high cultural institutions are faced with challenges to their underlying conceptual foundations. For example, over two centuries, museums have striven to bring the arrangement of their collections into line with Enlightenment thought, the Gutenberg pattern of the illustrated book, as Marshall McLuhan suggested. Art museums came to pride themselves on their orderliness based on chronology along national lines, in which the objects of art themselves reigned supreme. But now museums face the challenge of intellectual outlooks whose categories are less apparent and unified. History museums, once unselfconsciously in service to the "prince" or to the nation-state, were intended to help legitimize national policies and regimes.

If increasing the numbers of visitors is a perennial concern, the new demands for access now include not merely visitors from modest economic backgrounds—a goal that, as we have seen, is far from being attained—but also the crosscutting aspects of gender, ethnicity, and racial or religious distinctions. Each of these may have aesthetic implications that the conflict, as usually expressed—quantity versus quality—does not encompass. Now, in more inclusive democratic societies, cultural institutions and implementers of state policies more generally are called upon to reconstruct that history in a more equitable manner, so that the "losers" of the past may regain their place as worthwhile *people*, rather than as inferior or peripheral beings. In the United States, for example, American Indians, African Americans, Japanese Americans, and other groups marginalized by powerful social forces and the politics of dominant groups are struggling for and, in some cases, winning a more accurate depiction. In France, particularly during the mid-1970s, and under the pressure of considerable political activism, the national state has made some concessions to the recognition of Occitan and Breton regional cultures. Whereas in the United States, there is increasing recognition of the disparities in access to culture by ethnically diverse groups, in France, where for several decades studies of cultural practice by the population have been carried out, little attention has been given to ethnics or immigrants.[50]

This relegation of cultural practices of diverse groups has its counterpart in the content of the culture that is deemed worthy of official recognition and dissemination. With the opening up of the arts and letters to varied new forms, and the blurring of artistic genres, cultural institutions face knotty problems of aesthetic judgment. As boundaries among art forms and genres become blurred, those art museums that wish to incorporate the new art genres are challenged not only by the unwieldiness or space-greediness of some aesthetic forms and by those who speak for them, a problem of long standing, but also by new demands. These demands are voiced not merely for space to display what has become canonic avant-garde work but also for previously unrecognized genres, some imbued with political resonance. Attacks on politically and sexually controversial art forms have been followed by a serious diminution of national (and local) government support for the arts in the United States. Yet dealing with this crisis may be less problematic in the United States than in France. To a great extent, the de-centered fragmentation of the American art world is an asset when it comes to incorporating innovation. In France, conversely, creators continue to have to seek the support of the state for material and symbolic acknowledgment.

How should art museums deal with art that arises from the increasingly migratory character of the world's peoples? How can works be aesthetically evaluated in light of political and social critique, or should such criticism be disregarded as irrelevant to aesthetics? There are few clear answers to these questions, although many art museums are trying new modes of presentation to draw their potential publics into the conversation with the arts. Museum people cannot assume that these publics will be attracted by displays that do not speak to them directly. Their most serious challenge is the demand by previously excluded social categories or groups to be welcomed into the institutional world of high culture, a world of whose existence many in those groups have had little awareness. Official national recognition of artists, both in the fine arts and the popular arts, has added glamour to already highly esteemed art forms, as well as raising the standing of popular commercial arts, such as jazz, to the position of a disinterested art form. In fact, the line between the fine arts and the popular arts has faded so much that the term "crossover" has gone from being an industry term to becoming a legitimating category. But because, in the process of acquiring stature, these forms are transformed by learned or sophisticated discourses, they are usually assumed to be beyond the comprehension of the very social groups whence they emerged. Instead, they are appropriated by dominant cultural agents and assume a level of esotericism vis-à-vis their originators' heirs.

Interestingly, as Peterson and Simkus suggest in recent studies, the relationship of social status to artistic preferences may need to be reformulated. In their research on musical preferences, instead of finding the expected relationship between high occupational standing and high art music, their data suggest that those in prestigious (i.e., those based on high educational levels) occupations have a broader range of likes than do those in less prestigious occupations (i.e., those associated with lower educational standing). Instead of an orthogonal relationship between hierarchically ranked tastes and occupational statuses, the highly educated turn out to be "omnivores," in that they choose to listen to a broad range of music, including, but not confined to, classical or serious music, while those in low-status occupations behave as "univores," whose musical preferences are narrow and are largely devoted to one kind of music.[51]

This finding indicates that to think productively about cultural democratization, we need to take into consideration popular and commercial cultural forms as well as traditional high culture. It may be that in conceptualizing democratization, too much emphasis has been placed on a formulation closely tied to a nineteenth-century idea in which the fine arts are unquestionably superior to all other forms of creation, entertainment, and leisure activities. At a time when other activities compete for audiences—sports events, rock concerts, and movies, to name only a few—for defenders of artistic autonomy, the arts play a unique role as media of human interaction. As such, they function far beyond mere entertainment; and as sources for the creation of cultural meanings, they need to be given serious attention.

Indeed, they are already given serious attention, both in the United States and in France, though for different reasons. Europe has for over a century been a *market* for American popular culture, from Buffalo Bill's Wild West performances to Hollywood movies and jazz. The liking for these cultural exports has not faded, but the conditions under which the French state receives the vibrant popular culture forms of the United States (and of Britain) have changed. Whereas, previously, American popular culture was treated as a pleasant curiosity, with the development of the mass media—motion pictures, recordings, and television—certain European states, including France, introduced regulations to subsidize and protect their own blossoming culture industries. For example, television channels that air films are required to fulfill a quota of 60 percent made in Europe, and 40 percent of them must be French.[52] What many French intellectuals fear is that their nation's identity is threatened.

It is unclear to what extent such policies can actually succeed in protecting national identity today. The conditions under which states maintain their sovereignty have become transformed in the post–World War II, postcolonial era. Economically, multinational corporations that produce and disseminate a vast array of commercial culture are difficult to control. Politically, the success of the European community implicitly diminishes barriers against former rivals. With the gradual expansion of international agreements to decrease tariffs and eliminate the protection of national products and services, it may be that requirements of quotas for media and other cultural production will become untenable. Finally, the trend to privatize culture, as well as other former state functions, which began in the United States and Britain, is likely to have an impact on democratization and also on national identity. This has been of particular concern to France, and indeed it was the dismay expressed by French intellectuals that has gained the most prominence. Other Europeans have also expressed apprehension as to whether their nations' identity will be recognizable as the new millennium proceeds. Are all European national languages fated to become no more than "dialects" in relation to the lingua franca of rock and rap? Will the opportunities that are opened by the great "information highway" lead to the museumification of cherished cultures of earlier generations—as has already happened in folk life museums?[53]

Although the shift away from virtually complete national government support has not yet occurred in France (nor in the other countries that are trying to adopt it), the privatization process will set the parameters within which changes of the form and substance of the arts, and their publics, are likely to develop. The dissemination of a global culture has had both positive and negative consequences; positively, for instance, it has led to the creation of transnational networks of people united through a common love of music, both popular and classical.[54] Cultural institutions that wish to incorporate the new art genres of their time or of the immediate past are challenged both by their aesthetic forms and by those who speak for them. Even when they emphasize works of the past, art museums implicitly take a stance toward works created by individuals and groups previously excluded from established aesthetic canons because of the condition of their makers, as female or black. Are art museums obligated to maintain silence about the exclusion of these groups from access to the legitimate institutions that trained and certified artists? How should cultural institutions respond to the challenge by women and minorities for employment at higher levels? How can they balance aesthetics with political or social critiques?

These questions have few easy answers, although some museums, orchestras, opera companies, and theaters are trying to develop new and different modes of presentation to draw their potential publics into the ongoing conversation that the arts have come to represent. Many American institutions react with fear of being overwhelmed by a parochialism that threatens their universalizing orientation. Yet by responding to the challenges of these demands, both artistic and social, and by taking them seriously enough to argue with those making them, these institutions have an opportunity to broaden access to a new public, to reexamine their aesthetic conceptions, and to underwrite their survival.[55]

Notes

1. "Avec Beaubourg l'ère des temples culturels prend fin. Arrivent les grandes surfaces largement ouvertes au public sans que jamais le souci de la qualité soit abandonné." Claude Mollard, *L'Enjeu du Centre Georges Pompidou*, Collection 10/18 (Paris: Union Générale d'Éditions,1976), 26; this excerpt translated by the author.
2. "Quand j'avais dix ans, mon père m'emmenait le dimanche matin au Louvre. C'était un lieu paisible. J'ai appris là que pour regarder un tableau, il faut du temps, du calme, du silence. Et je ne peux pas croire que les foules qui défilent au Louvre actuellement éprouvent quoi que ce soit qui ressemble à ce qu'on entendait jadis par émotion esthétique. Elles vont accomplir un rite, quelque chose d'obligatoire, qu'on leur a appris qu'il fallait faire." Claude Lévi-Strauss with Isac Chiva, "Qu'est-ce qu'un musée des arts et traditions populaires?" *Le Débat* 70 (1992): 171; translated by the author.
3. Francis Henry Taylor, *Babel's Tower: The Dilemma of the Modern Museum* (New York: Columbia University Press 1945), 21.
4. George Heard Hamilton, "Education and Scholarship in the American Museum," in *On Understanding Art Museums*, American Assembly Report, ed. Sherman E. Lee (Englewood Cliffs, N.J.: Prentice-Hall, 1975), 126.
5. Pierre Bourdieu, *Distinction: A Social Critique of the Judgment of Taste* (Cambridge, Mass.: Harvard University Press, 1984 [1979]); César Graña, "The King's Shadow: The Aesthetic Legacy of the Aristocracy" in *Meaning and Authenticity: Further Essays on the Sociology of Art* (New Brunswick, N.J.: Transaction Publishers, 1989), 158.
6. Paul J. DiMaggio, "Cultural Entrepreneurship in Nineteenth-Century Boston: The Creation of an Organizational Base for High Culture in America," in *Media, Culture and Society: A Critical Reader*, ed. Richard Collins et al. (London: Sage Publications, 1986), 194–211.
7. J. Mark Davidson Schuster, "The Public Interest in the Art Museum's Public," in *Art Museums and the Price of Success: An International Perspective*, ed. Truus Gubbels and Annemoon Van Hemel (Amsterdam: Boekman Foundation, 1993).

8. Henri Mendras with Alistair Cole, *Social Change in Modern France: Towards a Cultural Anthropology of the Fifth Republic* (Cambridge: Cambridge University Press, 1991 [1989]).

9. Ministère de la Culture, *Les pratiques culturelles des Français 1973–89* (Paris: La Découverte / La Documentation Française, 1990), 8; Loïc Wacquant, "Review of Henri Mendras, *Social Change in Modern France* (1991) in *Contemporary Sociology* 22 (January 1993): 84–86.

10. Bourdieu, *Distinction*.

11. The inclusion either in toto or as "influences" on "serious" (or "academic") art encompass Pop Art, Readymades, or their equivalents in music, dance, and dramatic performance. This is also the case of the "primitive" in art, which has come to rest in the world's most esteemed art museums. See, e.g., Vera L. Zolberg, "African Legacies, American Realities: Art and Artists on the Edge" in *Outsider Art: Contesting Boundaries in Contemporary Culture*, ed. Vera L. Zolberg and Joni M. Cherbo (New York: Cambridge University Press, 1997). Of course, there is no guarantee that the creators of these forms benefit from such reverence. It may be that acceptance is no more than the appropriation of their creations by others who themselves gain.

12. Only during periods of emergency was the American national state permitted to expand, e.g., during the Civil War, itself primarily based on the attempt of southern states to secede from the Union. It was during the Civil War that a federal income tax was enacted, only to be successfully contested at its end and eliminated for several decades, until 1913. The contrast with France's centralization is startling. But France and the United States share a long history as democratic republics based on universal suffrage for males, albeit in effect excluding African Americans in the American South. In the twentieth century, suffrage was extended to women, in the 1920s in the United States, and only after World War II in France.

13. Alexis de Tocqueville, *Democracy in America*, vol. 1 (New York: Vintage, 1955 [1835]).

14. Karl E. Meyer, *The Art Museum: Power, Money, Ethics*, Twentieth-Century Fund Report (New York: William Morrow, 1979), 269; Janet Minihan, *The Nationalization of Culture: The Development of State Subsidies to the Arts in Great Britain* (New York: New York University Press, 1977), 9.

15. Vera L. Zolberg, "Censorship in the United States: Politics, Morality, and the Arts," in *Social Problems*, ed. Craig Calhoun and George Ritzer (New York: McGraw-Hill, 1992).

16. Kevin Mulcahy has clearly delineated this multilevel pattern of American cultural support in comparison with a number of other countries in "Public Support for the Arts in the United States, Western Europe and Canada: Polities, Policies, Politics," paper presented at "The Arts and the Public Purpose," American Assembly conference, Columbia University, New York, May 29–June 1, 1997.

17. The most prominent during the early and middle nineteenth century was Boston, with competing centers such as Philadelphia and New York. A few outliers with a long cultural tradition included Charleston and New Orleans, where the earliest opera performances had taken place and companies were established.

18. This process, taking Boston as a model, is carefully analyzed by DiMaggio, "Cultural Entrepreneurship in Nineteenth-Century Boston."

19. If, as seems likely, the Art Institute was striving to impress local officials with their popularity among ordinary Chicagoans, it succeeded.

20. DiMaggio, "Cultural Entrepreneurship in Nineteenth-Century Boston."

21. Vera L. Zolberg, "Displayed Art and Performed Music: Selective Innovation and the Structure of Artistic Media," in *Art and Society: Readings in the Sociology of the Arts*, ed. Arnold W. Foster and Judith R. Blau (Albany: State University of New York Press, 1989), 325–41.

22. Gary O. Larson, *The Reluctant Patron: The United States Government and the Arts, 1943–1965* (Philadelphia: University of Pennsylvania Press, 1983).

23. E.g., The Museum of Contemporary Art in Los Angeles has made available informative pamphlets in English, Spanish, Japanese, and Korean so that parents can introduce their children to modern art. This technique is becoming increasingly widespread in American museums.

24. I owe this concept to my husband, Aristide Zolberg.

25. Dick Netzer, *The Subsidized Muse: Public Support for the Arts in the United States* (New York: Cambridge University Press, 1978).

26. Pascal Ory, "Politiques culturelles avant la lettre: Trois lignes françaises, de la Révolution au Front populaire," in *Sociologie de l'Art*, ed. Raymonde Moulin (Paris: La Documentation Française, 1986), 23–30; Meyer, *Art Museum*.

27. André-Hubert Mesnard, *La Politique culturelle de l'État* (Paris: Presses Universitaires de France, 1974), 23–32

28. Elizabeth Gilmore Holt, ed., *The Art of All Nations: 1850–1873* (Garden City, N.Y.: Anchor Press/Doubleday, 1981).

29. On the whole, despite the long-standing belief that all things are centralized in France, it should be noted that the state was often rather timid about its role as art patron, preferring to establish councils that decided on the commissioning of artworks, discernment of scholarships, and architectural design. One result was that, willy-nilly, almost all such decisions ended up being under the control of the most conservative, academically oriented figures.

30. Even though there had been quite a high proportion of school-age children in school already, this was a truly spectacular achievement. Primary schooling was made universal and compulsory, and a popular form of secondary schooling was expanded, extended, and regularized. Antoine Prost, *Histoire de l'enseignement en France, 1800–1967* (Paris: Armand Colin, 1968), 101.

31. Since then, the week has expanded to a month or more for the regularly employed. There is clearly a parallel in demands for a more educated workforce, and the desire by an enlarged adolescent cohort after the World War II for more education.

32. Mesnard, *La Politique culturelle.*

33. In 1936, an Undersecretariat for Sports and Leisure was established, followed in 1947 by a Ministry of Youth, Arts, and Letters and, in 1951, under the Ministry of Education, a section on Youth and Sports, separate from a Secretariat of Fine Arts. In 1956, a Secretariat of Arts and Letters was established. An important idea of the Front Populaire was that of *comités d'entreprises*, to provide opportunities for cultural life within the workplace. This was generalized after the Liberation, according to Mesnard, *La Politique culturelle*, 30.

34. Prost, *Histoire de l'enseignement*, 422–26.

35. Lebovics notes that by being placed at the helm of the new Ministry of Cultural Affairs, Malraux was able to have the idea of French *civilisation* reformulated into a Gallic *Kultur.* See Herman Lebovics, "Malraux's Mission," paper presented at New York Area French History Seminar, New York, 1997, 17–18.

36. Pierre Cabanne, *Le pouvoir culturel sous la Vème République* (Paris: Olivier Orban, 1981).

37. E.g., during the events of May 1968, the government tried to take control of the *maisons de la culture*, which, they believed had come to be dominated by leftist art leaders. This persisted throughout the Fifth Republic, under Malraux's successors. Moreover, at the same time that under De Gaulle regional cultures were promoted by extending recognition for higher education chairs in certain previously suppressed language groups (Breton and Occitan), the Ministry of the Interior also tried to control private associations in those regions.

38. Antoine Hennion, *Comment la musique vient aux enfants: Une anthropoloogie de l'enseignement musical* (Paris: Anthropos, 1988).

39. Mollard, *L'Enjeu du Centre Georges Pompidou*, 20.

40. A consequence of the architectural plan was that the plaza in front of the building became an informal setting where street performers (jugglers, fire eaters, living statues, and assorted others) ply their skills for passersby, many of whom may not enter the center itself.

41. Zolberg, "Displayed Art and Performed Music."

42. Paul J. DiMaggio, Michael Useem, and Paula Brown, *Audience Studies in the Performing Arts and Museums: A Critical Review* (Washington, D.C.: National Endowment for the Arts, 1978).

43. Institut National de la Statistique et des Études Économiques, *Données Sociales,* 3rd ed. (Paris: Imprimerie Nationale, 1978); Nathalie Heinich, "The Pompidou Centre and Its Public: The Limits of a Utopian Site," in *The Museum Time Machine: Putting Cultures on Display,* ed. R. Lumley (New York: Routledge & Kegan Paul, 1989), 199–212; Gérard Mermet, *Francoscopie: Les Français: Qui sont-ils? Où font-ils?* (Paris: Larousse, 1985); Ministère de la Culture, *Pratiques culturelles des Français: Description socio-démographique, évolution 1973–1981* (Paris: Dalloz, 1982); Bourdieu, *Distinction.*

44. *Animateurs* are expected to hold a diploma in education or obtain training while studying art or general educational subjects.

45. The major exception that Schuster notes is American students, whose current income is relatively low but whose cultural choices are oriented toward the taste associated with their expected future economic standing. Schuster, "Public Interest."

46. Schuster shows that other demographic variables—e.g., occupation, age, gender, race, and the metropolitan area in which one resides—vary in expected fashion, but their effects are confounded with those of education and income. Ibid., 44–45, 47.

47. Ibid., 50–51; H. Ganzeboom and F. Haanstra, *Museum and Public: The Public and the Approach to the Public in Dutch Museums* (Rijswijk: Ministry of Welfare, Health, and Culture, 1989).

48. Pierre Bourdieu, Alain Darbel, et al., *The Love of Art: European Art Museums and their Public,* trans. C. Beattie and N. Merriman (Stanford, Calif.: Stanford University Press, 1990 [1969]).

49. Ministère de la Culture, *Pratiques culturelles* (1982).
50. Ministère de la Culture, *Pratiques culturelles* (1990), 8.
51. Richard A. Peterson and Albert Simkus, "How Musical Tastes Mark Occupational Status Groups," in *Cultivating Differences: Symbolic Boundaries and the Making of Inequality*, ed. M. Lamont and M. Fournier (Chicago: University of Chicago Press, 1992), 152–86.
52. Marlise Simons, "France to Form New Body to Further Protect Culture," *New York Times*, February 25, 1996.
53. These concerns gave rise to an international conference in the Netherlands, in which French, Dutch, British, and American scholars participated. They explored the facts and implications of international free trade agreements on national identity. The papers have been published in *Trading Culture: GATT, European Cultural Policies, and the Transatlantic Market*, ed. Annemoon Van Hemel, Hans Mommaas, and Cas Smithuijsen (Amsterdam: Boekman Foundation, 1996).
54. E.g., adolescents and young adults have been brought together through music to raise substantial sums of money for people in distress as a result of warfare or natural disasters ("Live-Aid" concerts); classical music students from all over the world are peopling the new campuses of the European Mozart Foundation in several countries—the Czech Republic, Hungary, and Poland—to bridge the cultural gap between Eastern and Western Europe. Negatively, the impact of popular commercial culture is seen as a threat—the decoloration of "local color" through "Coca-colonization" or the more recent "McDonaldization." Even more threatening, however, are the attempts to spread censorship through force or duress, beyond the national boundaries of particular states. See Zolberg, "Censorship in the United States."
55. In France, the debate concerning the founding a new museum that would recognize "*les arts premiers*" (a term including "primitive" or developing-world art) is exemplary of one aspect of multiculturalism, and the resistance to it by established arts administrators.

CHAPTER 5

Exporting America: The U.S. Propaganda Offensive, 1945–1959

LAURA A. BELMONTE

In the wake of the September 11, 2001, terrorist attacks, the catchphrase "Why do they hate us?" entered the American lexicon with light-ning-like speed. Popular demand for a more concerted effort to explain the United States abroad grows. Politicians turn to Hollywood for guidance on how best to package the American way of life for international audiences. Diplomats call for greater expenditures on public diplomacy. Journalists and public relations experts advise the U.S. government on crafting effective prop-aganda. At the same time, the American defense budget and military presence on the global stage increase exponentially.

To those of us who specialize in Cold War studies, this scenario sounds eerily familiar. Throughout America's decades-long battle with communism, the U.S. government mounted elaborate media campaigns designed to explain, to use the current phraseology, why they should *hate* the communists and why they should *like* democratic capitalism. Propagandists played a crucial role in advancing this foreign policy agenda.[1] Facing threats of communism, anti-Americanism, and totalitarianism, U.S. information officials at the State De-partment and the United States Information Agency (USIA) began America's first peacetime propaganda offensive.[2] Though the information programs were an integral element of early Cold War diplomacy, they also represented a concerted effort to define American national identity. Through radio shows, art, sports, architecture, material culture, films, and publications, U.S. policy-makers propagated a carefully constructed narrative of progress, freedom, and happiness. They not only "imagined" an American "community" but also pre-sented their vision to the world in hopes of persuading foreign peoples to re-ject communism and adopt democratic capitalism.[3]

Returning to the early Cold War, this chapter examines the U.S. propaganda offensive and its efforts to export American political culture and the foreign policy of the United States. The decade following the collapse of the Berlin Wall witnessed a wide array of assessments of the causes, interpretations, and implications of the end of the Cold War.[4] Some authorities extolled the "triumph" of American culture and institutions over communism.[5] Alarmed by this chorus of praise, other scholars stressed the social, financial, and political costs of America's Cold War victory.[6] The dissolution of the Soviet Union did not enable the American people to reach a consensus on the proper role of the state or the defining characteristics of U.S. political culture. But the wave of patriotism immediately following the tragedies of 9/11 demonstrates that shared ideals of democratic freedom and individual rights remain powerful. As the nation defines its global war against terrorism, it is highly instructive to examine the initial American response to the Cold War.

The American Response to the Cold War

In the immediate aftermath of World War II, U.S. policymakers faced circumstances strikingly similar to those currently confronting the United States. Facing a changed world marked by terrifying weapons, economic uncertainty, and shifting political allegiances, public officials and private citizens struggled to reconcile "the American way of life" with America's role as a global superpower. During World War II, the collective imperative of defeating fascism subsumed various manifestations of domestic discord.[7] Following V-J Day, the national sense of mission quickly gave way to a series of bitter conflicts over which beliefs, aspirations, values, and symbols exemplified the United States. Americans experienced great dislocations in politics, family life, race relations, the economy, culture, and society.[8]

Although they were dismayed by this instability, members of the U.S. foreign policy establishment knew it paled in comparison to the devastation, starvation, and chaos engulfing much of the world.[9] Such conditions, they feared, could jeopardize their hopes for a postwar world dominated by the United States. Elites in government, business, and the media—determined to safeguard American economic, political, and military interests—embraced new strategies and tactics for defending national security.[10] But protecting America meant far more than guarding tangible assets. It also signified a commitment to preserve the ideals and institutions embodying the exceptionalism of the United States.[11]

The intersections of culture and foreign relations are yielding a number of important academic studies. Inspired by the work of postmodern and poststructuralist theorists, scholars are examining the multivariate discourses and spectacles of international relations.[12] Other researchers are examining the impact of American products, values, and culture upon a variety of foreign audiences. Though some critics denounce American "cultural imperialism" as hegemonic and unstoppable, others stress the complicated processes by which nations selectively adopt or reject Americanization.[13] Throughout this literature, we are learning a great deal about the wide-ranging number of individuals who engage in a variety of transnational exchanges—including tourists, international businesspeople, soldiers, journalists, missionaries, and public health workers.[14]

Following a similar line of inquiry, this chapter examines the state's attempts to define itself, its people, and its culture for foreign audiences. Exploring the totality of the images of America offered by U.S. propagandists provides a means of assessing the state's construction of national identity as a means of protecting national security.[15] The promotion of democracy formed a critical component of the U.S. information campaigns. Yet, despite a massive amount of scholarship on the relationship between political ideology and U.S. foreign policy, we know surprisingly little about how U.S. officials defined democracy in order to appeal to the widest possible global audience.[16] How did they compare democratic governments to communist systems? How did they convey the advantages democracy accorded individual citizens? How did they articulate the freedom and equality imbued in the American political ethos?

Contrary to interpretations commonly found in foreign policy historiography, U.S. policymakers did not define the national interest exclusively in concrete political, economic, and military terms. Nor were they blind to the ways in which America's pluralistic society could complicate—or facilitate—the pursuit of global power. Instead, American officials fused the material and immaterial into a narrative justifying American predominance in international affairs. Whenever possible, they provided foreigners with visual demonstrations of the political freedoms, economic opportunities, technological innovation, and cultural vibrancy found in the United States.

Working closely with leaders from the private sector, government officials constructed portraits of U.S. race relations, family life, politics, culture, labor relations, consumerism, and religious communities. But the task of defining the American people for foreign audiences was never easy. Most propagandists were former journalists and advertisers with liberal anticommunist sympathies. Their emphasis on mass communication clashed with older notions of cultural diplomacy. Their attempts to explain unsavory aspects of American life such as segregation and McCarthyism drew the ire of conservatives who associated propaganda with political radicalism. Although congressional investigations of the USIA and Voice of America (VOA) yielded little evidence of communist subversion, propagandists wrestled with fluctuating budgets and loyalty investigations for years. Because of the difficulties in defining what "an American" was, U.S. policymakers focused instead on what "an American" was not. Information experts, unified in their belief in the superiority of democratic capitalism, depicted communists as dishonest, atheistic, militaristic, antifamily, violent, unfree, undemocratic, uncultured, and—definitively—un-American.[17]

In contrast to communist deception, U.S. propagandists extolled the "truth" of the American way of life.[18] Tailoring their methods and tactics to appeal to different countries, U.S. officials defined America as a nation in which families, workers, and freedom flourished. Suburbs, unions, churches, voting booths, and many other "uniquely American" items filled U.S. propaganda materials. Men and women raised happy families and lived comfortably. Employers and employees enjoyed the benefits of capitalism. Artists, architects, writers, and musicians produced original, exciting works. Life under democratic capitalism meant far more than escaping communist oppression. It signified a world of spiritual, material, social, political, and cultural benefits of which communists could only dream. The following brief snapshot of the U.S. propaganda offensive explores some of the visions of America exported by policymakers.[19]

A Snapshot of U.S. Cold War Propaganda

During the Great Depression and World War II, fascist propaganda had fostered negative stereotypes of politics in the United States. Charged with articulating an appealing and nonthreatening image of the United States, U.S. information experts expressed dismay at international distortions of American democracy. On February 26, 1946, William B. Benton, the assistant secretary of state for public affairs, told the House Appropriations Committee:

> The nature of the American democratic system, with its disagreements and its individual liberty, is bewildering to a world emerging from the throes of authoritarianism. It is easy for foreigners, without knowing the real situation, to get the impression that this is a land of strife and discord, with race set against race, class set against class, religion set against religion, the rich oppressing the poor, the poor revolting against the rich, gangsters roaming the streets of our cities, cowboys shooting up Wild West saloons, and Congress weltering in a whirl of filibusters and cocktail parties.[20]

Disturbed by these stereotypes and confronting communist expansionism, U.S. propagandists recognized the need to impart the advantages of the American democratic system.[21]

U.S. officials considered freedom the most appealing element of democracy. They distinguished the national and individual liberties of the Free World from the "slavery" of communist countries. On March 12, 1947, President Harry S Truman enunciated this contrast between democracy and communism. "Nearly every nation," he proclaimed, "must choose between alternative ways of life." "One way of life," he continued, is based upon the will of the majority, and is distinguished by free institutions, representative government, free elections, guarantees of individual liberty, freedom of speech and religion, and freedom from political oppression. The second way of life is based upon the minority forcibly imposed upon the majority. It relies upon terror and oppression, a controlled press and radio, fixed elections, and the suppression of personal freedoms.[22]

Although Truman did not mention the Soviet Union, he eloquently enunciated the emerging struggle between democratic liberty and communist subjugation.[23]

When attacking communism, U.S. officials broadly defined democratic freedom.[24] They simultaneously advocated national self-determination and individual liberty. They stressed the freedom of worship, freedom of assembly, freedom of expression, and freedom of speech nurtured by democratic government. They emphasized that democracies protected civil rights, personal property, and individual dignity. They presented the United States as a pluralistic society characterized by widely dispersed power and the reconciliation of conflicting interests. By extolling these liberties, U.S. policymakers hoped to gain adherents to the democratic way of life and to discredit communism.

To counteract communist depictions of the United States as an oligarchic, racist, imperialist, and immoral nation, U.S. information strategists employed a variety of propaganda tactics. Their arsenal included radio broadcasts, trade fairs, photography exhibits, musical and dance performances, athletic events, and films. To reach the widest audience possible, most campaigns used simple language and images. Whenever possible, foreigners were encouraged to touch displays and props, such as furniture, voting machines, telephone books, stereos, televisions, and computers. At international exhibitions, U.S. pavilions featured modernist architecture, cutting-edge industrial designs, and innovative films projected inside geodesic domes. With the aid of American corporations such as IBM and General Electric, the USIA produced spectacular displays of consumer products and heavy machinery. Buckminster Fuller, Charles Eames, Ray Eames, Russel Wright, Edward Steichen, and Peter Blake are only a few of the artists and architects who helped convey the wonders of democratic capitalism to foreign audiences (figures 5.1 and 5.2).[25]

An avalanche of publications and cartoons satirized the communist system. U.S. embassies, United States Information Service (USIS) reading rooms, and bookmobiles distributed millions of these pamphlets. Some emulated the glossy photography of *Life* and *Look* magazines. Others were crudely drawn caricatures printed on inexpensive paper. In 1951–52, for example, the USIS released 500,000 copies of *Glossary of Soviet Terms*, a booklet of sardonic cartoons illustrating the terms. For the term "classless society," there was a picture of the "people's commissariat" riding in a limousine past two Soviet beggars. For "people's democracy," there was a cartoon of two Soviet policemen forcing a couple to enter a detention camp. And the picture for "democratic elec-

Figure 5.1. U.S. information officials highlighted the loving nature of American family relations as part of their efforts to demonstrate communism's deleterious effects on marriage, childhood, and intimate life. Courtesy of the National Archives.

tions" featured an armed soldier guarding a single ballot box labeled "yes." All the cartoons in the *Glossary* attacked communist attempts to usurp democratic rhetoric.[26]

Other publications celebrated U.S. democracy. *A Picture Story of the United States* quoted famous American historical figures describing freedom in the United States. Roger Williams declares, "I'll start a settlement where all can worship as they please, government must never interfere with a man's belief!" John Peter Zenger asserts: "The press must be free to print the truth, no matter whom it offends!" Other cartoons portray abolitionism, women's rights, and the rise of organized labor. After illustrating the growth of U.S. industrial and economic power, the booklet defends the capitalist system, stating, "But with all this material progress and prosperity, Americans did not lose sight of the foundations on which their blessings rested; free education for all, the free spread of knowledge and ideas, the right to worship as they chose." Overall, the pamphlet presents the United States as a nation of diversity, equality, and morality.[27]

In addition to championing individual liberties, U.S. policymakers advocated independence for all nations. Determined to counter Soviet accusations

Figure 5.2. In this U.S. Information Service photograph, a woman visiting the National Gallery of Art scrutinizes Benvenuto Cellini's *Salt Cellar*. Such images formed an integral element of U.S. efforts to promote American cultural vibrancy and to stress opportunities for personal enrichment in the United States. Courtesy of the National Archives.

of U.S. imperialism, U.S. propagandists denied that Wall Street financiers dominated American politics.[28] They defined the United States as an anticolonial power with genuine interest in the principle of national liberation. U.S. information strategists assailed the Soviet Union for exploiting weaker nations. In late 1949, the State Department released *Russia the Reactionary*, a booklet denouncing Soviet attacks on national and individual liberties. A chapter titled "Russia Destroys National Independence" condemned the Soviets' seizure of land and personal property for collective farms. After recounting the communist annexation of Eastern Europe, the text asserted:

> Throughout the USSR and the satellite countries the entire educational, informational, and legal structure has been used to wipe out every culture, every belief, every person that stood in the way of complete conformity to the Moscow party line. Experiences of all nations under the domination of the Kremlin prove that only one way of life is tolerated among those nations—the Soviet way of life. National independence and love of country must be subordinated to allegiance to the Communist Party. There can only be one kind of patriotism—Soviet patriotism.[29]

The Soviets, U.S. officials argued, completely disregarded legitimate aspirations for national independence among Eastern Europeans. Instead, communist authorities created police states that consigned satellite peoples to lives of poverty, desperation, and subjugation.[30]

When presenting images of the American government, U.S. information officials offered a meticulous depiction of the benefits fostered by democracy. They extolled America's participatory democracy, laws, welfare programs, and commitment to peace and freedom.[31] In contrast to the ruthless destruction of personal liberties by Soviet authorities, American propagandists emphatically stressed the dignity of individuals living in the United States.

U.S. policymakers assailed communist restrictions on freedom of thought and expression. They emphasized that democracies permitted ideas to flourish unfettered. In 1952, the USIS released *Soviet Communism Threatens Education*, a pamphlet urging foreign educators to resist communism. The booklet warned:

> One of the targets of a Communist regime would be the school system. The Communists realize that to survive they must destroy free thought. While democracy works through a free people, Communism must have blind, unthinking obedience. Communists secure that obedience through controlled, regimented instruction and the brutal suppression of free thought.[32]

Other USIS publications ridiculed Soviet attempts to censor scholars, artists, and writers. In *It's a Great Life, Comrades*, U.S. information strategists used satirical photographs with captions such as "I will not compose bourgeois music" and "Who cares about facts? I'm an historian."[33]

U.S. propagandists glorified the political freedoms characterizing democratic societies. They praised the multiparty elections and diverse political opinions in the United States. During the 1948 presidential campaign, VOA broadcasters portrayed the Dixiecrat rebellion and growth of the Progressive Party as evidence of the vitality of U.S. democracy.[34] Showing participatory democracy in action, they profiled American political organizations such as the League of Women Voters.[35] They attacked the staged elections, one-party ballot system, and persecution of political dissenters behind the Iron Curtain. In publications like the *Facts about Communism* series, U.S. information experts juxtaposed the democratic traditions of free citizenship with the political abuses rampant behind the Iron Curtain. They derided the Soviet justice system for enforcing draconian laws antithetical to communist rhetoric that espoused the primacy of individual rights.[36]

Religious Freedom Moves to Center Stage

U.S. officials, being cognizant of the tremendous importance of religion in the lives of individuals everywhere, privately criticized the official atheism of the Soviet state.[37] They castigated the antireligious statements in communist youth newspapers and the exclusion of Jews from top-ranked posts in the Soviet government.[38] Nonetheless, religious themes did not initially play a prominent role in U.S. propaganda.

As the Cold War intensified, however, American policymakers began placing religious freedom at the core of their defense of democracy. Communist persecution of European clerics compelled State Department leaders to escalate public attacks on Soviet repression of religion. When the Hungarian government arrested Joszef Cardinal Mindszenty on December 27, 1948, U.S. officials quickly grasped the political implications of the case. Seldon Chapin, the U.S. minister in Hungary, warned acting secretary of state Robert Lovett that if the United States failed to condemn the worst human rights violations since the Holocaust, Eastern Europeans "will regard [the] West as morally bankrupt." Agreeing with Chapin, Lovett ordered State Department aides to issue press statements linking the Mindszenty arrest to the systematic destruction of human rights and liberties behind the Iron Curtain.[39]

But using religion as a means of discrediting communism proved challenging. U.S. propagandists searched for ways to emphasize religious themes without offending different foreign audiences. Internal State Department memoranda from the spring of 1949 demonstrate these difficulties. When John C. Wiley, an American Foreign Service officer in Tehran, suggested that all religions shared common beliefs in "peace," Charles Thayer, the chief of the VOA Russian Desk, disagreed. "It would be difficult," Thayer asserted, "to divorce the concept of peace as taught by Christ from some of the war-like measures that have been introduced to spread Christianity. The same would be true, of course, with the Moslem faith." Unable to resolve such conflicts, U.S. information officials adopted a general, though unwritten, policy of advocating no particular denomination while stressing freedom of religion as a political civil right.[40]

With the assistance of American and foreign clergy, the State Department and USIA acknowledged important religious holidays. On April 9, 1950, VOA broadcasts to Czechoslovakia featured Francis Cardinal Spellman, the archbishop of New York, offering a special Easter message for people living behind the Iron Curtain. Spellman assured the Czechs that Americans "are mourning over your enslavement and your misery, praying for your delivery from persecution and suppression, beseeching God that you also may enjoy the blessings with which we are blessed in America."[41] Other VOA programs commemorated Christmas, Good Friday, and the holy days of non-Christian religions such as Yom Kippur. VOA disc jockeys included religious music on their playlists.[42]

Printed propaganda materials included "spiritual content." *Wireless Bulletin*, a weekday digest of news events, printed speeches of "a religious nature" by President Harry S Truman or other noted Americans. Special articles described the Quakers, the chaplains in the United States Congress, and Catholic adult educators. *Air Bulletin* reports on American life and culture contained stories such as "Books of the Spirit," "Church Women's Aid," "Bible Reading Program," and "Salvation Army, Flying Missionaries." The USIS photography exhibits "Small Town USA" and "Meet the Temples—An American Family" included churchgoing scenes in their depictions of American family life.[43]

Propaganda films also accentuated the role of religion in U.S. communities. Filmmakers strove "to reflect the religious freedom and tolerance that prevails throughout the United States." Stressing the general message "I am my brother's keeper," one film showed a farmer doing chores for his sick neighbor. Pictures of "unguarded milk bottles on the doorstep" represented "the fact that Americans are generally trustworthy, honest, and forthright." At the same time, State Department film crews paid close attention to the religious mores of other nations. Films shown in Hindu nations minimized "any reference to raising, slaughtering, marketing, and eating of cattle." In the Near East and Far East, filmmakers avoided images of pork, liquor, and "feminine undress."[44]

Such tepid religious programming made little impact upon foreign audiences. In March 1951, State Department administrators discussed new guidelines on moral and spiritual factors in U.S. propaganda. They expressed dismay that American foreign policy was "being handicapped abroad by suspicion of U.S. motives, questioning of our moral and spiritual stamina, and a general cynicism toward what are construed to be the American standard of values." U.S. propaganda strategists attributed this distrust to a variety of factors. Foreigners envied America's prosperity, but they also believed that Americans "are concerned only about economic and material matters with little or no thought for moral and spiritual values." Countries with national religions misunderstood the U.S. separation of church and state. American notions of religion as "strictly a personal matter in which each individual is entitled to his own private convictions" also confused foreign audiences.[45]

Information officials assiduously considered their response to this delicate situation. Afraid that the U.S. propaganda program's primary emphases on "military strength, material wealth, and economic power" were contributing to international perceptions that Americans lacked religious and ethical convictions, they offered suggestions for forging "a community of interest between ourselves and other peoples who possess like moral and spiritual values." They proposed more coverage of U.S. foreign aid programs, relief efforts, and private humanitarian endeavors. They identified possible linkages among the Christian, Hebrew, Moslem, Buddhist, Hindu, Confucian, and Shinto communities, including "freedom of conscience (at least as long as it does not lead to heresy), respect for human life and the human spirit, love of one's neighbor, truthfulness, honesty, loyalty to one's convictions." Yet, however intent they were on improving the international image of American moral and religious values, the propagandists also stressed the importance of convincing more noncommunists of "the deadly threat to freedom of spirit and religion, to freedom for all religions and even the right to adhere to no formal religion or ideology" posed by communism.[46]

Finding Universal Themes, Embracing Capitalism

Throughout the 1950s, propaganda materials reflected the twin goals of embracing ecumenical themes and promoting capitalism while attacking communism.[47] VOA broadcasts and USIS publications denounced "the Stalinist attack on God, on His brotherhood of Man, and His Peace" and publicized communist assaults on religious worship in Asia and Eastern Europe.[48] The pamphlet *Red Star over Islam* detailed Soviet persecution of Moslems. Declaring that "the Communists will never succeed in destroying Islam," the pamphlet urged Moslems to "join with all other free and God-fearing peoples of the world in the struggle to stop communism."[49] More than 150,000 copies of the special Christmas pamphlet *Peace under God* were disseminated in German, Persian, Spanish, Sinhalese, Tamil, and Vietnamese. The pamphlet featured quotes from Jesus Christ, Buddha, Confucius, the Bhagavad Gita, and the Koran. Extolling "the peace of human brotherhood, dignity, and freedom," it then attacked "the tyranny of Soviet imperialism," which sought "to kill the divine and good in men to impose the equality of death and the peace of the graveyard."[50]

U.S. information officials found the tangible benefits of capitalism much easier to promote than the spiritual values of religion. Avoiding abstract economic concepts, American propagandists articulated the material attractions of capitalism in individualistic terms designed to reach the average foreigner.[51] Visions of the typical American worker figured prominently in U.S. attempts to make capitalism appealing internationally.

Following World War II, U.S. leaders worried that less fortunate countries would resent—and perhaps sabotage—America's economic and political success. To avert such suspicion and resistance, U.S. policymakers dedicated themselves to explaining the U.S. economic system to foreign audiences. From the inception of the postwar information program, American propagandists linked the defense of liberal capitalism to the preservation of world peace and freedom. But not all of America's motives were altruistic. U.S. officials also believed that nations familiar with American technology and production methods were more likely to purchase U.S. goods and services. American propaganda on economic issues, therefore, protected commerce as well as national security.[52]

As the ideological battle between capitalism and communism intensified, U.S. information leaders escalated their efforts to promote the American economic system abroad. They insisted, however, that the United States did not view itself as a model for all nations. A 1959 USIA policy paper read, "The Agency does not attempt to 'sell' the American economic system as a blueprint for other countries to follow."[53] Despite this disclaimer, U.S. information officials were quite willing to advocate American economic ideals and to extol the virtues of life in a capitalist democracy. The State Department employed labor advisers charged with "winning the support of the working people of foreign countries for free institutions and against totalitarianism."[54]

U.S. information authorities hoped to capitalize on the high level of international curiosity about living conditions in the United States. Consequently, they shaped programs designed to stress three basic elements of the American economy: free competitive enterprise, free trade unionism, and limited government intervention. In creating this picture of capitalism, USIA administrators emphasized that the American economic system, unlike socialism or communism, did not leave laborers beholden to an uncaring bureaucracy. "We *do* insist," information leaders asserted, "that the economy should exist for the benefit of the citizen, not for the state." Therefore, their portrayal of the American economy highlighted "related themes," such as the quest for social justice, the equitable distribution of income, "the growing classlessness of our society," the potential growth of the U.S. economy, and the thriving culture of the United States.[55]

U.S. information strategists meticulously interwove the economic and social benefits capitalism could produce.[56] Information packets prepared for distribution in all American embassies featured stories like "Labor's Drive for Guaranteed Annual Wages," "Union Plan Opens New Careers for Disabled Miners," "Wider Employment Opportunities for Women," and "Profit-Sharing Plans in U.S. Industry." Overall, U.S. propagandists accented harmonious labor and management relations, movement toward racial and gender equality in the workplace, and the material benefits capitalism afforded the typical worker, especially when juxtaposed with his or her Soviet counterpart.[57]

In advocating the American economic system, U.S. policymakers had to overcome negative international perceptions of capitalism. Soviet propagandists bombarded foreign audiences with reports of widespread labor unrest, insoluble social problems, economic instability, and high unemployment in the

United States.[58] These accounts resonated abroad. U.S. information leaders anticipated these criticisms. The USIA distinguished American capitalism from the "cartel-like or feudalistic" European variety. Officials praised the U.S. "mixed economy" characterized by federal regulations, individual freedom, collective bargaining, and economic competition. They accented the stability and productivity of the U.S. economy.[59]

U.S. propagandists stressed the impact of communism on laborers. Some USIS publications, such as *The Truth Crushes Commie Lies*, bluntly attacked communist labor laws. "Communism means no freedom for workers," the pamphlet declared. The text pointed out that Soviet workers could not bargain collectively, choose or quit their jobs, strike, or form their own unions.[60] U.S. information officials frequently criticized slave labor in the USSR. Through stories like "Slave Labor Follows the Russian Flag" and "The New Slavery," they contrasted oppressive working conditions in communist nations with the freedom and prosperity found among American laborers.[61] Communism, U.S. information officials maintained, devalued workers.

In contrast, capitalism enabled individuals to fulfill their career ambitions and to live in comfort. In the early 1950s, the USIS distributed more than 1 million copies of *Meet Some Americans at Work*, a lengthy pictorial essay portraying a variety of U.S. workers. All appeared content. Not a word about racial and gender discrimination, wage inequities, or labor unrest accompanied the photographs.[62] In October 1955, USIA guidelines on the American economy stressed the salary increases, investment opportunities, and fringe benefits available to productive U.S. workers.[63] The 1957 USIA pamphlet *Thomas Brackett* emphasized the lifestyle of the average American. Brackett, a Ford Motor Company employee, owned a house stocked with appliances and a car. He planned to send his four children to college. His high wages enabled his wife to remain at home. "There are millions of American capitalists like the Bracketts," the booklet concluded.[64]

International trade fairs became another forum for highlighting the U.S. economy. American displays often featured a fully furnished house, manufactured goods, appliances, mail-order catalogues, television shows, and motion pictures. Representatives of the Department of Commerce and private U.S. firms explained living conditions in the United States to thousands of visitors.[65] The exhibits usually accented U.S. consumer goods. At the Barcelona International Samples Fair in June 1956, workers at the American Pavilion distributed doughnuts, ice cream cones, cups of milk, samples of cheese, baked goods made from prepared mixes, and cigarettes. Other aides staged a continuous fashion show featuring nine models wearing the latest American designs. Such displays illustrated the purchasing power of the American consumer and his or her ability to choose among competing goods and services.[66] Enthusiastic visitors appropriated the props used in these exhibitions. At the American National Exhibition in Moscow in 1959, hundreds of books, dozens of *Monopoly* games, and even frozen food items vanished.[67]

Nonetheless, U.S. policymakers recognized that American material wealth was not necessarily a propaganda asset. Communist propagandists seized on international promotions of U.S. consumer goods as evidence of materialism and immorality in the United States. To prevent such distortions, U.S. propagandists linked the success of the American economy to its democratic system. Communism, they insisted, destroyed individual initiative.[68] On April 23, 1953, William L. Grenoble, an administrator of the International Motion Picture Service, explained:

> One of our biggest jobs—this is of course directly related in antipathy to the Communist line—is to demonstrate that although the average American has a good deal more of the material things of life than many people throughout the world, he has attained those by the application of hard work and ingenuity, and other people can do the same.[69]

Americans, in short, were not lazy. They had earned their possessions by performing well in an economy that valued productivity and creativity.

But even accurate portrayals of the lifestyle of a typical U.S. worker could produce undesirable results. Although broadcasts extolling capitalism generated fan mail, some of the letters contained comments such as "I listen to the Voice of America everyday. Please send me a Buick automobile. Yours sincerely."[70] Accounts of American economic performance intimidated some audience members. In December 1954, Clifton B. Forster, the public affairs officer of the USIA post in Fukora, Japan, recounted his difficulties in reaching Japanese laborers. When presented with factual representations of "the daily activity of an American laborer which show him driving to work in his own car, eating a steak by a Westinghouse Refrigerator, etc.," Foster explained, the Japanese expressed strong resentment and feelings of inferiority. "You are much too advanced over there," one labor leader in Onga commented.[71]

Yet foreigners were fascinated by U.S. consumer goods. Mail-order catalogues from U.S. stores ranked among the most popular materials at USIS libraries. In Finland, U.S. embassy officials claimed back issues of the Sears, Roebuck & Company catalogue "have been worn out through use, rebound with stronger covers and put back into circulation." In West Berlin, USIS authorities chained the catalogues to the tables as Germans crowded four deep to glimpse the illustrations. An airport bookstore in Jakarta reported selling the catalogues for $20 each despite currency restrictions that prevented Indonesians from ordering the items featured.[72]

Such popularity encouraged U.S. propagandists to respond assertively to Soviet distortions of the American economy. Because they were certain that the Soviet Union could not match U.S. levels of productivity, State Department analysts expressed little concern over improvements in the Soviet standard of living.[73] Accordingly, USIS materials emphasized the comparative work time required to buy certain items in the United States and the Soviet

Figure 5.3. This 1951 U.S. Information Agency photograph painted a bleak portrait of Soviet daily life. Its caption read: "Soviet farm women in the Ukraine look at a consignment of over-shoes just received at the village store. Such shipments are scarce and are eagerly awaited. Notice the empty bins and shelves in the foreground." U.S. Information Agency Photo 51-18041, kit no. 14, Words and Deeds, Library of Congress Prints and Photographs Division, Washington.

Union. For example, an April 1953 pamphlet featured a chart showing the buying power of an average Moscow worker as far lower than that of a laborer in New York. "For a pound of bread, he has to work twice as long as the American worker; for potatoes, he has to work about three times as long; for beef, 5 times; for eggs, about 7 times; and for sugar, 25 times."[74] USIA researchers noted clothing, housing, and food shortages in the USSR (figure 5.3).[75]

Not surprisingly, U.S. information strategists were less willing to acknowledge economic problems in the United States. In March 1957, USIA director Arthur Larson ordered his staff to prepare materials on unemployment, installment buying, and Wall Street capitalists. To correct Soviet distortions of the U.S. unemployment situation, Larson urged USIA officials to emphasize the number of vacant jobs, the seasonal nature of some jobs, and the existence of unemployment compensation. Because of the social welfare programs in America, Larson reminded his colleagues, unemployment "quite definitely should not and does not necessarily mean breadlines, soup kitchens, squalor, starvation." To deflect communist accusations that financiers controlled the United States, USIA officials explained the benefits and liabilities of the use of credit, the structure of American corporations, and buying power of American consumers.[76]

Juxtaposing the gains in wages and benefits won by American unions with the existence of forced labor camps behind the Iron Curtain, USIA administrators sought to define unions as the force protecting the typical American worker and his place under "People's Capitalism."[77] The USIS booklet *American Labor Unions: Their Role in the Free World* exemplifies these efforts, asserting that

> American workers know how difficult is the struggle for security and justice. Through their unions, they triumphed after many failures. . . . Capitalism in a democracy uses its forces not in a negative way, to depress and exploit the masses, but to expand production, to create new ideas and new wealth.[78]

USIA authorities frequently cited American labor leaders to demonstrate widespread domestic support for the objectives espoused by the U.S. information establishment.[79] They pointed to union programs for women and African Americans as examples of progressive, democratic attitudes.[80]

The role of organized labor, however, formed only a portion of the larger image of the American worker disseminated by the USIA. Rarely focusing on white-collar workers, the USIA usually highlighted factory workers in materials directed at foreign laborers. For example, a December 1955 article titled "An American Worker's Family" featured Ray Bellingham, a mill operator at General Electric's locomotive and car equipment department in Erie, Pennsylvania. The Bellinghams discussed Ray's wages, mortgage payments, workday, and taxes. His wife, Helen, described her attempts to maintain a budget while feeding and clothing their family of six.[81]

The Bellinghams exemplified how the "classlessness" of U.S. society enabled individuals to reap the benefits of capitalism. These gains, the USIA showed, extended beyond corporate executives and reached even manual laborers. Profit sharing, paid vacations, company-sponsored scholarships, and health insurance provided additional examples. Job security, worker's compensation, and unemployment stipends demonstrated the existence of an American social welfare system.[82] The success of "People's Capitalism" hinged upon making individuals like Ray and Helen Bellingham readily identified with the

American economic system. In this way, individuals as much as material items became props in the USIA narrative of democracy.

In contrast to the dignity and decent standard of living accorded American workers, USIA materials showed "Soviet drones" locked in a despotic system plagued by sinecures, forced labor camps, and oppressive working conditions.[83] Communist unions, American information officials alleged, existed only to ensure worker discipline and production quotas set so high that no worker could ever meet them.[84] Simple factual accounts of Communist slave labor camps provided USIA policymakers with propaganda more effective than anything they could create.[85]

Images of American gender roles and families also proved valuable tools in distinguishing democratic capitalism from communism.[86] U.S. information strategists quickly recognized that notions of gender could be used to discredit the communist economic and political system. They ridiculed Soviet claims of gender equity.[87] They claimed communism devalued workers and families.

On May 13, 1953, John Albert, the chief of the USIA's German service, articulated these sentiments:

> In the Soviet Zone in Germany, as in all the satellite countries, the women have equality. They have the equality to work in coal mines, work night shifts in heavy work. They can do everything which nobody in a free country would ask a woman to do. There is only one thing they can't do. They can't have time to raise their children, to provide for their home and take part in community life, because they are much too tired for it.

Albert, like most of his agency colleagues, believed that American consumer goods enabled U.S. women "to have a decent life, to have a job, to bring up children and still take time out for cultural and economic life." Convincing people behind the Iron Curtain of the possibility of a better family life, Albert concluded, inspired them to continue resisting the Soviets.[88]

Rather than deny inequities among American workers, U.S. information officers exposed degrading working conditions in the Soviet Union. "Emancipated" Russian women performed heavy labor in mines, construction sites, and shipyards. In the USSR, equality of opportunity "allowed" women to work as stevedores, street cleaners, and forge operators.[89] State Department analysts considered the exploitation of women one of the principal psychological vulnerabilities of the USSR. In 1950, they described the low wages and high prices that forced the majority of Soviet women to work. They wanted their superiors to publicize the plight of Soviet women—but without suggesting women belonged at home.[90]

Within two years, American information experts implemented this strategy. They emphasized U.S. labor laws safeguarding women from dangerous occupations. For example, a 1952 edition of *Labor Air Bulletin* declared:

In contrast with conditions in communist countries, where the much advertised equality and rights of women means the right to work in coal mines, the United States has shown a growing concern for the health and welfare of working women because of their role as home makers and future bearers of children.

Labor laws regulating hours, wages, and working conditions indicated a higher regard for women and children. The United States, the article implied, cared too much about its women and children to permit equality in the workplace.[91] The presentation of the American family abroad involved more than a defense of capitalism. U.S. information experts also sought to convey the quality of life in the United States. USIS libraries distributed material on American health, nutrition, and education.[92] They extolled the political and social freedom fostered by democracy. The USIA denigrated the ethical standards behind the Iron Curtain. Agency materials implied that communist parents failed their children. In February 1955, the USIA published "Russian Children to Throw Hand Grenades"—a description of newly established "physical culture tests" in the USSR.[93] An August 1953 USIA women's packet asserted, "Many Soviet women leave their children in State-run nurseries, and many mothers don't see their children from Monday morning until Saturday night."[94] In 1958, the American Pavilion at the Brussels World's Fair included a kindergarten to highlight innovative child-rearing and educational techniques.[95]

U.S. information experts claimed that communism impeded emotional intimacy, commitment, and family fealty. Communists considered love and marriage "capitalist stupidities." USIS pamphlets derided the absence of honeymoon trips in the USSR. Furthermore, American propagandists contended that communism destroyed families. In June 1951, the caption for a USIS cartoon titled "Communism and the Family" read "Communists take your young, but they cast aside the aged. Communism turns sons against fathers . . . and takes daughters for slave labor. Under Communism she [a mother] loses her loved ones . . . and gains a 'family' of strangers!" The USIS center in Manila distributed 10,000 posters proclaiming, "The Red target is *your* home." The placards featured Communist soldiers separating two women and a young boy. The text read, "Happy family life cannot exist in the communist scheme of things."[96]

According to the USIA, families thrived in democratic capitalist societies. The agency presented a carefully fashioned image of American families emphasizing community involvement, rewarding employment, and material comfort. To support these claims, the agency released stories about individual U.S. families. In April 1953, the USIA women's packet featured Gail Forster, a Philadelphia housewife and mother of three. The Forsters lived well, but not lavishly, on the wages of husband William, a radio engineer. In response to communist criticisms of American wealth and materialism, the USIA emphasized the Forsters' middle-class status. "Like most American families, they have no servants." Mrs. Forster, the text stated, "cooks the meals, cleans the house, washes, irons, and mends the clothes, cares for the children, and works in her flower garden." Despite her heavy workload, Mrs. Forster remained active in her neighborhood. She taught one day a week in her children's cooperative nursery school and volunteered for a housing committee in Philadelphia. Every Sunday, the Forsters attended a church. "Mrs. Forster," the publication concluded, "would never consider herself or her life unusual." According to the USIA, the Forsters exemplified the American family.[97]

Conclusions

By placing the advantages of democratic capitalism within the context of the lives of individual Americans, U.S. information experts articulated, in human and emotional terms, the reasons for combating communism. Though the Soviets denigrated American morality and culture, U.S. propagandists emphasized the freedom and comfort among citizens of the United States. In contrast to communist exploitation and misery, American information experts offered the physical and emotional fulfillment available in the United States. Fighting communism, they implied, involved much more than guarding U.S. material interests and power. It meant protecting average Americans and their way of life.

U.S. policymakers drew stark distinctions between democratic and communist nations. Where democracies permitted patriotism and individuality to flourish, communist states compelled nations and peoples to abandon their identities. Where democratic countries allowed multiparty elections, representative government, and open political debate, communist societies deprived their citizens of genuine political participation. Where democratic legal systems protected civil liberties and personal property, communist laws authorized widespread police surveillance, detention camps, and dramatic restrictions of individual liberties.

In contrast to the communists' prosecution of the faithful, democracies embraced religion as a vital part of family and community life. Where "free" nations enjoyed the fellowship fostered by religion, communist states used terror to enforce atheism. Where religious peoples embraced principles of love and peace that transcended nationality, "godless" communists spread dissent and hatred to divide the world's peoples. Where communist countries persecuted religious minorities, the United States cherished its tradition of religious tolerance.

Although the U.S. information campaigns evince arrogance and naiveté, they also demonstrate patriotism and conviction. Although their methods and messages were occasionally awkward and manipulative, American propagandists truly believed in the superiority of democratic capitalism over communism. The American economy *did* allow many individuals to flourish as citizens and consumers. Capitalism *did* accord the average worker dignity as embodied in personal buying power and fringe benefit programs. Accordingly, American information officials had little difficulty making the image of a typical U.S. housewife more attractive than that of a Soviet woman working on the railroad or the Communist man suffering in a labor camp.

When assessing the U.S. "victory" over communism, we must evaluate the totality of images of the United States that endure. For however alluring American consumerism, democracy, and popular culture are, anti-Americanism also erupts on a regular basis—a fact made horrifyingly clear on 9/11. In a world saturated not only with propaganda but also with mass media, tourists, businesspeople, soldiers, and consumer goods, we have no way of isolating the sources of foreign opinions of the United States. But by analyzing America's propaganda offensive, we get a powerful glimpse of how U.S. policymakers understood their country and their fellow citizens in ways reflecting all the contradictions and complexity of America itself.

Notes

1. Throughout this chapter, I refer to "propaganda" and "information." I use these terms interchangeably and not usually in a pejorative way. Like Clayton Laurie, I define propaganda as "any organized attempt by an individual, group, or government verbally, visually, or symbolically to persuade a population to adopt its views and repudiate the views of an opposing group." See Clayton D. Laurie, *The Propaganda Warriors: America's Crusade against Nazi Germany* (Lawrence: University of Kansas Press, 1996), 6. For a helpful historical overview, see Richard Alan Nelson, "Propaganda," in *Handbook of Popular Culture*, 2nd edition, ed. M. Thomas Inge (New York: Greenwood Press, 1989), 1011–123.

2. On the genesis of the postwar information program, see Frank Ninkovich, *The Diplomacy of Ideas: U.S. Foreign Policy and Cultural Relations, 1938–1950* (New York: Cambridge University Press, 1981); and Walter F. Hixson, *Parting the Curtain: Propaganda, Culture, and the Cold War, 1945–1961* (New York: St. Martin's Press, 1997).

3. On the challenges posed by defining "nation," see Homi K. Bhabha, "Introduction: Narrating the Nation," in *Nation and Narration*, ed. Homi K. Bhabha (New York: Routledge, 1990), 1–7. For an eloquent discussion of America's political discourse during the Cold War, see Nikhil Pal Singh, "Culture/Wars: Recording Empire in an Age of Democracy," *American Quarterly* 50 (September 1998): 471–522. On nations as "imagined communities," see Benedict Anderson, *Imagined Communities: Reflections on the Spread of Nationalism*, rev. ed. (New York: Verso, 1991).

4. Some important examples include Matthew Evangelista, *Unarmed Forces: The Transnational Movement to End the Cold War* (Ithaca, N.Y.: Cornell University Press, 1999); Raymond L. Garthoff, ed. *The Great Transition: American-Soviet Relations and the End of the Cold War* (Washington, D.C.: Brookings Institution Press,

1994); and Michael J. Hogan, ed. *The End of the Cold War: Its Meanings and Implications* (Cambridge: Cambridge University Press, 1992).

5. "American," "liberal," and "Western" values are usually used interchangeably in these accounts. See, e.g., John Lewis Gaddis, *We Now Know: Rethinking Cold War History* (New York: Clarendon Press, 1997); Arthur Schlesinger Jr., "Some Lessons from the Cold War," *Diplomatic History* 16, no. 1 (Winter 1992): 47–53; and Robert Heilbroner, "The Triumph of Capitalism," *New Yorker*, January 23, 1989, 98–109. The CNN television series on the Cold War sparked some particularly vociferous denunciations of communism; see Ronald Radosh, "Finding a Moral Difference between the U.S. and the Soviets," *New York Times*, January 9, 1999; Charles Krauthammer, "CNN's Cold War: Twenty-Four Hours of Moral Equivalence," *Washington Post*, October 30, 1998.

6. Robert Buzzanco, "What Happened to the New Left? Toward a Radical Reading of American Foreign Relations," *Diplomatic History* 23 (Fall 1999): 575–607; Cynthia Enloe, *The Morning After: Sexual Politics at the End of the Cold War* (Berkeley: University of California Press, 1993); Richard Ned Lebow and Janice Gross Stein, *We All Lost the Cold War* (Princeton, N.J.: Princeton University Press, 1994); Tom Englehardt, *The End of Victory Culture: Cold War America and the Disillusioning of a Generation* (New York: Basic Books, 1995); Thomas J. McCormick, "Troubled Triumphalism: Cold War Veterans Confront a Post–Cold War World," *Diplomatic History* 21 (Summer 1997): 481–92; Walter LeFeber, "The Tension between Democracy and Capitalism during the American Century," *Diplomatic History* 23, no. 2 (Spring 1999): 263–84.

7. See, e.g., John Morton Blum, *V Was For Victory: Politics and American Culture During World War II* (New York: Harcourt Brace Jovanovich, 1976); George H. Roeder, *The Censored War: American Visual Experience during World War Two* (New Haven, Conn.: Yale University Press, 1993); and Michael C. C. Adams, *The Best War Ever: America and World War II* (Baltimore: Johns Hopkins University Press, 1994).

8. On domestic life, see, e.g., Michael J. Hogan, *A Cross of Iron: Harry S. Truman and the Origins of the National Security State, 1945–1954* (Cambridge: Cambridge University Press, 1998); Joanne Meyerowitz, ed., *Not June Cleaver: Women and Gender in Postwar America, 1945–1960* (Philadelphia: Temple University Press, 1994); Ellen Schrecker, *Many Are the Crimes: McCarthyism in America* (Boston: Little, Brown, 1998); George Lipsitz, *Rainbow at Midnight: Labor and Culture in the 1940s*, rev. ed. (Urbana: University of Illinois Press, 1994); and James T. Patterson, *Grand Expectations: The United States, 1945–1974* (New York: Oxford University Press, 1997).

9. For powerful descriptions of the war's devastation and American reactions to the desolation, see Melvyn P. Leffler, "The Cold War: What Do 'We Now Know'?" *American Historical Review* 104 (April 1999): 513–17; and Thomas G. Paterson, *On Every Front: The Making and Unmaking of the Cold War*, rev. ed. (New York: W. W. Norton, 1992), 3–15.

10. Hogan, *Cross of Iron*; Melvyn P. Leffler, *A Preponderance of Power: National Security, the Truman Administration, and the Cold War* (Stanford, Calif.: Stanford University Press, 1992). On the elite backgrounds of U.S. policymakers and leading journalists, see Walter Issacson and Evan Thomas, *The Wise Men: Six Friends and the World They Made: Acheson, Bohlen, Harriman, Kennan, Lovett, McCloy* (New

York: Simon & Schuster, 1986); John Lamberton Harper, *American Visions of Europe: Franklin D. Roosevelt, George F. Kennan, and Dean G. Acheson* (New York: Cambridge University Press, 1994); H. W. Brands, *Cold Warriors: Eisenhower's Generation and American Foreign Policy* (New York: Columbia University Press, 1988); Edwin M. Yoder Jr., *Joe Alsop's Cold War: A Study of Journalistic Influence and Intrigue* (Chapel Hill: University of North Carolina Press, 1995); and Ronald Steele, *Walter Lippmann and the American Century* (New York: Vintage Books, 1981).

11. On exceptionalism as a guiding principle in American foreign policy, see, e.g., Michael H. Hunt, *Ideology and U.S. Foreign Policy* (New Haven, Conn.: Yale University Press, 1987), 19–45; Anders Stephanson, *Manifest Destiny: American Expansionism and the Empire of Right* (New York: Hill & Wang, 1996); and Emily S. Rosenberg, *Spreading the American Dream: American Economic and Cultural Expansion, 1890–1945* (New York: Hill & Wang, 1982).

12. Examples include David Campbell, *Writing Security: United States Foreign Policy and the Politics of Identity*, rev. ed. (Minneapolis: University of Minnesota Press, 1998); Amy Kaplan and Donald M. Pease, eds., *Cultures of United States Imperialism* (Durham, N.C.: Duke University Press, 1993); Anne McClintock, *Imperial Leather: Race, Gender, and Sexuality in the Colonial Contest* (New York: Routledge, 1995); Roxanne Lynn Doty, *Imperial Encounters: The Politics of Representation in North-South Relations* (Minneapolis: University of Minnesota Press, 1996); and Robert Rydell, *All the World's A Fair: Visions of Empire at American International Expositions, 1876–1916* (Chicago: University of Chicago Press, 1984).

13. Seminal critiques of cultural imperialism include Ariel Dorfman and Armand Mattelart, *How to Read Donald Duck: Imperialist Ideology in the Disney Comic*, trans. David Kunzle (New York: International General, 1975); Herbert Schiller, *Communication and Cultural Domination* (White Plains, N.Y.: International Arts and Sciences Press, 1976); and Edward Said, *Orientalism* (New York: Pantheon Books, 1978). Important studies that emphasize multinational processes of cultural dissemination and appropriation include Richard Pells, *Not Like U.S.: How Europeans Have Loved, Hated, and Transformed American Culture since World War II* (New York: Basic Books, 1997); Rob Kroes, Robert Rydell, and Doeko F. J. Bosscher, eds., *Cultural Transmissions and Receptions: American Mass Culture in Europe* (Amsterdam: VU University Press, 1993); John Tomlinson, *Cultural Imperialism: A Critical Introduction* (Baltimore: Johns Hopkins University Press, 1991); Ralph Willet, *The Americanization of Germany, 1945–1949* (London: Routledge, 1989); and Richard F. Kuisel, *Seducing the French: The Dilemma of Americanization* (Berkeley: University of California Press, 1993).

14. Frank Costigliola, *Awkward Dominion: American Political, Economic, and Cultural Relations with Europe, 1919–1933* (Ithaca, N.Y.: Cornell University Press, 1984); Rosenberg, *Spreading the American Dream*; Jessica Gienow-Hecht, *Transmission Impossible: American Journalism as Cultural Diplomacy in Postwar Germany, 1945–1955* (Baton Rouge: Louisiana State University Press, 1999); Gilbert M. Joseph, Catherine C. Legrand, and Ricardo D. Salvatore, eds., *Close Encounters of Empire: Writing the Cultural History of U.S.–Latin American Relations* (Durham, N.C.: Duke University Press, 1998).

15. On the tactics, strategy, and reception of U.S. propaganda, see Hixson, *Parting the Curtain*; Reinhold Wagnleitner, *The Coca-Colonization of the Cold War: The Cultural Mission of the United States in Austria After the Second World War*, trans. Di-

ane M. Wolf (Chapel Hill: University of North Carolina Press, 1994); Gerald K. Haines, *The Americanization of Brazil: A Study of U.S. Cold War Diplomacy in the Third World, 1945–1954* (Wilmington, Del.: Scholarly Resources, 1989), 159–84; Pells, *Not Like U.S.*, 37–93; and Seth Fein, "Everyday Forms of Transnational Collaboration: U.S. Film Propaganda in Cold War Mexico" in *Close Encounters of Empire*, 400–50.

16. Important recent examples include Abraham Lowenthal, *Exporting Democracy: The United States and Latin America* (Baltimore: Johns Hopkins University Press, 1991); Joshua Muravchik, *Exporting Democracy: Fulfilling America's Destiny* (Washington, D.C.: AEI Press, 1991); Robert A. Pastor, "A Discordant Consensus on Democracy," *Diplomatic History* 17 (Winter 1993): 117–28; and Tony Smith, *America's Mission: The United States and the Worldwide Struggle for Democracy in the Twentieth Century* (Princeton, N.J.: Princeton University Press, 1994).

17. This strategy was quite similar to that employed against the Japanese in World War II. See Robert B. Westbrook, "In the Mirror of the Enemy: Japanese Political Culture and the Peculiarities of American Patriotism in World War II," in *Bonds of Affection: Americans Define Their Patriotism*, ed. John Bodnar (Princeton, N.J.: Princeton University Press, 1996), 211–30.

18. U.S. propagandists frequently referred to their activities as "a campaign of truth" designed to expose the evils of communism. They also argued that the "truth" about the United States, whatever its failings, was better than the Soviet alternative. See, e.g., Allan A. Needell, " 'Truth Is Our Weapon': Project TROY, Political Warfare, and Government-Academic Relations in the National Security State," *Diplomatic History* 17 (Summer 1993): 399–420; Edward W. Barrett, *Truth Is Our Weapon* (New York: Funk & Wagnall's, 1953); Wilson P. Dizard, *The Strategy of Truth: The Story of the U.S. Information Service* (Washington, D.C.: Public Affairs Press, 1961).

19. Presentations of American race relations are a notable omission from this chapter. On this theme, see chapter 6 in this volume by Penny Von Eschen.

20. William B. Benton, testifying before House Appropriations Committee, 26 February 1946, RG 59, Lots 587 and 52–48, Records of the Assistant Secretary of Public Affairs, Memoranda, 1945–1947, box 14, National Archives II, College Park, Md. (hereafter NAII).

21. Ibid.

22. For the text of Truman's speech, see *New York Times*, March 13, 1947.

23. For more on the Truman Doctrine speech and its background, see Richard Freeland, *The Truman Doctrine and the Origins of McCarthyism* (New York: Alfred A. Knopf, 1975); *New York Times*, March 13, 1947, and May 9, 1947. In April 1950, Paul H. Nitze, the head of the State Department's Policy Planning Staff, defined the Cold War in similar terms. In National Security Council document NSC-68, Nitze described "a basic conflict between the idea of freedom under a government of laws, and the idea of slavery under the grim oligarchy of the Kremlin." In an impassioned defense of democracy, he praised "the marvelous diversity, the deep tolerance, [and] the lawfulness of the free society." Unless the United States protected these values, Nitze warned, communists would destroy freedom throughout the world. Truman approved NSC-68 on September 30, 1950, in response to the Korean War; see *Foreign Relations of the United States, 1950*, 1: 234–92 (hereafter *FRUS*, year, volume). NSC-68 is quoted in Ernest R. May, ed. *American Cold War Strategy: Interpreting NSC-68* (New York: Bedford Books, 1993), 27–9.

24. On the broad definition of freedom, see, e.g., Acting Secretary Robert Lovett to Certain American Diplomatic Officers, December 8, 1947, *FRUS, 1947*, 4: 630–32; Report Prepared by the National Security Council, March 2, 1955, *FRUS, 1955–57*, 9: 504–7; U.S. Information Policy with Regard to Anti-American Propaganda, December 1, 1947, RG 59, Lot 53D47, Records Relating to International Information Activities, 1938–53, box 3, NAII; "Soviet-Communism," December 29, 1948, RG 59, Lot 87D236, Historical Studies Division, Research Project, 1945–54, box 7, NAII; "USIA Basic Guidance Paper," October 22, 1957, File on Agency History, U.S. Information Agency Archives, Washington (hereafter USIAA). On the presentation of America as a pluralistic nation, see "USIA Planning Paper: Themes on American Life and Culture," July 14, 1959, USIA Subject Files, USIAA.
25. Robert Haddow, *Pavilions of Plenty: Exhibiting American Culture Abroad in the 1950s* (Washington, D.C.: Smithsonian Institution Press, 1997); and Eric Sandeen, *Picturing an Exhibition: The Family of Man and 1950s America* (Albuquerque: University of New Mexico Press, 1995).
26. Originally established by the Office of War Information, the U.S. Information Service remains the overseas apparatus of the U.S. Information Agency. *Glossary of Soviet Terms*, 1951–52, USIA Pamphlet Files, USIAA.
27. *A Picture Story of the United States*, rev. ed., 1961, USIA Pamphlet Files, USIAA.
28. See, e.g., "Voice of America Is Not the Voice of the American People," August 2, 1949, Iron Curtain Radio Comment on VOA, RG 306, Reports and Related Studies, 1948–53, box 8, NAII.
29. *Russia the Reactionary*, 1949, RG 59, Lot 53D47, Records Relating to International Information Activities, 1938–53, William T. Stone Files, box 1, NAII.
30. *The Free World Speaks*, USIA Pamphlet Files, USIAA.
31. Annual USIS Assessment Report, November 5, 1957, RG 306, Office of Research, Country Project Correspondence, 1952–63, box 10, NAII.
32. *Soviet Communism Threatens Education*, May 22, 1952, USIA Pamphlets, USIAA.
33. *It's a Great Life, Comrades*, 1956, USIA Pamphlets, USIAA. See also *The Glorious What?* 1953, ibid.
34. *New York Times*, October 11, 1948.
35. Transcript for October 14, 1952, German, RG 306, VOA Daily Broadcast Content Reports and Script Translations, 1950–55, box 53, NAII.
36. Transcript for October 29, 1952, Estonia, RG 306, VOA Daily Broadcast Content Reports and Script Translations, 1950–55, box 55, NAII; *Facts about Communism-Justice*, 1956, USIA Pamphlet Files, USIAA.
37. On religion and U.S. foreign relations, see J. Bruce Nichols, *The Uneasy Alliance: Religion, Refugee Work, and U.S. Foreign Policy* (New York: Oxford University Press, 1988); and Alfred O. Hero Jr., *American Religious Groups View Foreign Policy: Trends in Rank-and-File Opinion, 1937–1969* (Durham, N.C.: Duke University Press, 1973). On the domestic religious response to anti-communism, see Stephen J. Whitfield, *The Culture of the Cold War* (Baltimore: Johns Hopkins University Press, 1991), 77–100.
38. See, e.g., Dubrow to Secretary of State, October 28, 1946, *FRUS, 1946*, 4: 791–93; Dubrow to Secretary of State, December 2, 1947, *FRUS, 1947*, 4: 628–30.
39. Chapin to Secretary of State, December 29, 1948, *FRUS, 1948*, 4: 393–95; Lovett to the Legation in Hungary, December 31, 1948, ibid., 4: 395.

40. Wiley to Allen, April 15, 1949, RG 59, Lot 52-202, Records of Assistant Secretary of State for Public Affairs, 1947–50, General Correspondence, 1948–49, box 1, NAII; Thayer to Allen, May 25, 1949, ibid.; Free to Sargeant, April 27, 1949; ibid.
41. VOA Transcript, April 9, 1950, Czechoslovakia, RG 306, Voice of America Daily Broadcast Content Reports and Script Translations, 1950–55, box 1, NAII.
42. VOA Policy on Religion, April 12, 1951, RG 59, Records Relating to International Information Activities, 1938–53, Lot 53D48, box 110, NAII.
43. Pincus to Hulten, April 17, 1950, ibid.
44. Guarco to Grondahl, February 23, 1951, ibid.
45. Draft Special Guidance on Utilization of Moral and Religious Factors in USIE Program, March 8, 1951, RG 59, Records Relating to International Information Activities, 1938–53, Lot 52D365, box 63, NAII.
46. Ibid.
47. Basic Guidance and Planning Paper on Religious Information Policy, May 1, 1959, USIA Subject Files, USIAA.
48. VOA Transcript, January 29, 1952, Brazilian, RG 306, Voice of America Daily Content Reports and Script Translations, 1950–55, box 35, NAII; VOA Transcript, March 23, 1952, Armenian, ibid.; VOA Transcript, March 29, 1952, Latvian, ibid.; *Buddhism under the Soviet Yoke*, USIA Pamphlet Files, USIAA.
49. *Red Star over Islam*, USIA Pamphlet Files, USIAA.
50. *Peace under God*, USIA Pamphlet Files, USIAA.
51. Other scholars have noted the connections between U.S. foreign relations and the promotion of American consumerism and free enterprise abroad. See, e.g., Rosenberg, *Spreading the American Dream;* Wagnleitner, *Coca-Colonization and the Cold War;* Willet, *Americanization of Germany;* Kuisel, *Seducing the French;* and Hixson, *Parting the Curtain.*
52. Statement of William B. Benton, October 16, 1945, Interchange of Knowledge and Skills between the People of the United States and Peoples of Other Countries, Hearings before the Committee on Foreign Affairs House of Representatives, 79th Cong., 1st and 2nd sess., on October 16, 17, 18, 19, 23, and 24, 1945, and May 14, 1946, 7.
53. U.S. Information Agency Basic Guidance and Planning Paper 11, "The American Economy," July 16, 1959, Subject Files on Policy, USIAA.
54. See undated job description for the labor adviser position found in RG 59, Lot 52D365, Records Relating to International Information Activities, 1938–53, box 61, NAII. For more on the Labor Information Program, see file on Labor, ibid.
55. U.S. Information Agency Basic Guidance and Planning Paper 11, "The American Economy," July 16, 1959, Subject Files on Policy, USIAA.
56. On attempts to influence international labor, see Ray Godson, *American Labor and European Politics: The AFL as a Transnational Force* (New York: Crane, Russak & Company, 1976); Charles S. Maier, "The Politics of Productivity: Foundations of American International Economic Policy after World War II," in *Between Power and Plenty: Foreign Economic Policies of Advanced Industrial States,* ed. Peter J. Katzenstein (Madison: University of Wisconsin Press, 1978); Anthony Carew, *Labour under the Marshall Plan: The Politics of Productivity and the Marketing of Management Science* (Manchester: Manchester University Press, 1987); Michael J. Hogan, *The Marshall Plan: America, Britain, and the Reconstruction of Western Europe, 1947–1952* (New York: Cambridge University Press, 1987); and Mary Nolan, *Visions of*

Modernity: American Business and the Modernization of Germany (New York: Cambridge University Press, 1994).

57. See Feature Packets on Labor, RG 306, Feature Packets, Recurring Themes, boxes 7–14, NAII.

58. See, e.g., Harriman to Byrnes, November 19, 1945, *FRUS, 1945*, 5: 919–20; The U.S. Labor and Social Scene as Viewed by the Labor Press in the USSR, RG 59, Records Relating to International Information Activities, 1938–53, Lot 52D389, box 42, NAII. See also Draft Statement for Secretary of State George Marshall on the United States International Information and Cultural Relations Program for his Budget Presentation before the House Appropriations Subcommittee, January 27, 1947, RG 59, Lots 587 and 52-48, Records of the Assistant Secretary of State, 1945–50, Office Symbol Files, 1945–50, box 4, NAII.

59. *A Primer on the American Economy*, USIA Pamphlet Files, USIAA.

60. *The Truth Crushes Commie Lies*, RG 59, Lot 52D365, Records Relating to International Information Activities, 1938–53, box 61, NAII.

61. See, e.g., Labor Packet, June 1953, RG 306, Feature Packets, Recurring Themes, box 7, NAII; *The New Slavery*, USIA Pamphlets, USIAA.

62. *Meet Some Americans at Work*, USIA Pamphlets, USIAA.

63. Information Policy on the American Economy, October 3, 1955, USIA Subject Files on Exhibits and Fairs: People's Capitalism, USIAA.

64. *Thomas Brackett*, USIA Pamphlet Files, USIAA.

65. For an explanation of the objectives of U.S. trade exhibits, see House Committee on Foreign Affairs, Strengthening International Relations through Cultural and Athletic Exchanges and Participation in International Fairs and Festivals, 84th Cong., 2d sess., June 22, 1956, Committee Print.

66. Information Policy on the American Economy, October 3, 1955, Subject Files on Exhibits and Fairs: People's Capitalism, USIAA; "Western European Attitudes Related to the People's Capitalism Campaign," December 31, 1956, ibid.; and "Japanese Attitudes Related to the People's Capitalism Campaign," October 7, 1957, ibid. See also Themes on American Life and Culture, Basic Guidance and Planning Paper 10, July 14, 1959, Subject Files on Policy, USIAA.

67. Belmonte, "Defending the American Way," 311–22.

68. The USIS pamphlet *Sinews of America* provides a cogent example. See USIA Pamphlet Files, USIAA.

69. Testimony from April 23, 1953, *Overseas Information Programs of the United States*, Hearings before a Subcommittee of the Committee on Foreign Relations United States Senate, 83rd Cong., 1st sess., pt. 2, 986–87.

70. See the testimony of John A. Nalley, May 12, 1953, *Overseas Information Programs of the United States*, Hearings before a Subcommittee of the Committee on Foreign Relations United States Senate, 83rd Cong., 1st sess., pt. 2, 1298–99.

71. Bunce USIS Tokyo to USIA Washington, December 14, 1954, RG 306, Office of Research, Country Project Correspondence, 1952–63, box 13, NAII.

72. "Mail Order Catalogues a Hit Around the World," *New York Times*, October 5, 1955; *Christian Science Monitor*, April 13, 1956; Frank Sullivan, "Our Best Seller Abroad," *New York Times Magazine*, November 13, 1955.

73. See, e.g., Memorandum by W. K. Schwinn and A. A. Micocci, April 7, 1950, RG 59, Lot 53D48, International Information Director's Office, Subject Files, 1949–51, box 115, NAII. See also Emergency Plan for Psychological Offensive (USSR),

April 11, 1952, RG 59, Lot 52D432, Bureau of Public Affairs, Office Files of Edward W. Barrett, 1950–51, box 5, NAII.

74. Labor Packets, August 1953 and March-April 1954, RG 306, Feature Packets, Recurring Themes, boxes 7 and 10, NAII.

75. See, e.g., "Notes from the Soviet Provincial Press," May and June 1956, RG 306, Production Division Research Reports, 1956–59, box 1, NAII.

76. Larson to USIS Posts, March 1, 1957, Subject Files on "Disinformation," USIAA.

77. "Workers Win 10-Year Fight against Forced Labor," Labor Packet, Jul 1957, RG 306, Feature Packets-Recurring Themes, box 14, NAII; *The All Union Family*, an AFL-CIO publication included in Labor Packet, February 1957, RG 306, Feature Packets-Recurring Themes, box 11, NAII; *If You Were a Soviet Worker*, USIA Pamphlet Files, USIAA.

78. *American Labor Unions: Their Role in the Free World*, USIA Pamphlets, USIAA, 15–16. The USIS comic book, *Labor: United for Freedom* provides another example. See ibid.

79. See, e.g., George Brown, "Why Should We Be Interested in International Affairs?" Labor Packet, May 1957, RG 306, Feature Packets-Recurring Themes, box 14, NAII. Labor leaders also provided congressional testimony on behalf of the USIA. See the comments of Boris Shishkin, director of research, American Federation of Labor, Hearings before a Subcommittee of the Committee on Foreign Relations United States Senate, 83rd Cong., 1st sess., *Overseas Information Programs of the United States*, 1953, 731–43. The State Department also consulted union leaders. See Briefing for Labor Advisory Committee, December 19, 1950, RG 59, Lot 52D365, Records Relating to International Information Activities, 1938–53, box 61, NAII.

80. "U.S. Labor Unions Promote Political Education for Women," Women's Packet, October 1954, RG 306, Feature Packets-Recurring Themes, box 19, NAII; "Visitor Finds Negroes Active in U.S. Labor Movement," January 2, 1952, *Air Bulletin*, RG 306, Air Bulletin, box 2, NAII; William Green, "Organized Labor and the Negro," January 16, 1952, *Air Bulletin*, ibid.

81. "An American Worker's Family," Labor Packet, December 1955, RG 306, Feature Packets-Recurring Themes, box 12, NAII; "Living and Working in a Free Enterprise System," Labor Packet, July 1957, ibid., box 14, NAII. For an additional example, see the story of James Edward Barnes in the "People's Capitalism" exhibit, see Copy Text for People's Capitalism Exhibit, January 11, 1957, Subject Files on Exhibits and Fairs, USIAA.

82. "Manual Workers Gaining Over White Collar Groups," Labor Packet, October 1956; "Revolution in Income Distribution in the United States," Labor Packet, November 1956; "The Growth of Profit Sharing in the United States," Labor Packet, January 1957; "Low Cost Vacations for American Wage Earners," Labor Packet, July 1956; "American Industry Supports Higher Education," Labor Packet, August 1956; "Fringe Benefits Increase Among American Workers," Labor Packet, December 1956; all found in RG 306, Feature Packets, Recurring Themes, box 14, NAII.

83. Albert Parry, "Soviet Drones," *Wall Street Journal*, July 29, 1954, included in Labor Packet, September 1954, RG 306, Feature Packets, Recurring Themes, box 9, NAII.

84. "Hardships of Workers Behind the Iron Curtain Disclosed," *Air Bulletin*, January 23, 1952, RG 306, *Air Bulletin*, box 2, NAII.

85. "Refugee Returns from Grave of Communist Labor Camps," Women's Packet, November 1954, RG 306, Feature Packets, Recurring Themes, box 19, NAII; Matthew Woll, "Slave Labor Behind the Iron Curtain," *Air Bulletin*, March 7, 1951, RG 306, *Air Bulletin* files, box 2, NAII.

86. For analyses of gendered language in foreign policy, see Frank Costigliola, " 'Unceasing Pressure for Penetration': Gender, Pathology, and Emotion in George Kennan's Formulation of the Cold War," *Journal of American History* 83 (March 1997): 1309–39; Kristin L. Hoganson, *Fighting for American Manhood: How Gender Politics Provoked the Spanish-American and Philippine-American Wars* (New Haven, Conn.: Yale University Press, 1998); Robert D. Dean, "Masculinity as Ideology: John F. Kennedy and the Domestic Politics of Foreign Policy," *Diplomatic History* 22 (Winter 1998): 29–62; Carol Cohn, "Sex and Death in the Rational World of Defense Intellectuals," *Signs: Journal of Women in Culture and Society* 12 (Summer 1987): 687–718; Andrew J. Rotter, "Gender Relations, Foreign Relations, The United States and South Asia, 1947–1964," *Journal of American History* 81 (September 1994): 518–42; Emily S. Rosenberg, " 'Foreign Affairs' after World War II," *Diplomatic History* 18 (Winter 1994): 59–70; and Michelle Mart, "Tough Guys and American Cold War Policy: Images of Israel, 1948–1960," *Diplomatic History* 20 (Summer 1996): 357–80.

87. "Soviet Practices Refute Propaganda on Equality of the Sexes," October 1953, Women's Packet 7, *Air Bulletin*, RG 306, Feature Packets, Recurring Themes, box 17, NAII.

88. See *Overseas Information Programs of the United States*, Hearings before a Subcommittee of the Committee on Foreign Relations United States Senate, 83rd Cong., 1st sess., 1486.

89. *Labor Air Bulletin*, March 21, 1951, RG 306, Air Bulletin, box 2, NAII; October 1953, Women's Packet 7, RG 306, Feature Packets, Recurring Themes, box 17, ibid.

90. An Analysis of the Principal Psychological Vulnerabilities in the USSR and of the Principal Assets Available to the U.S. for Their Exploitation, 1950, RG 59, Lot 52 D 432, Bureau of Public Affairs, Office Files of Edward W. Barrett, 1950–51, box 5, NAII.

91. "Women Workers in U.S. Protected by Many Safeguards," January 23, 1952, *Labor Air Bulletin*, RG 306, Air Bulletin, box 2, NAII.

92. Hulten to Gould, March 20, 1951, RG 59, Lot 52D432, Bureau of Public Affairs, Office Files of Edward Barrett, 1950–51, box 2, NAII.

93. Women's Packet 23, February 1955, RG 306, Feature Packets, Recurring Themes, box 19, NAII.

94. "Rare Visitor to USSR Reports on Soviet Woman's Status," August 1953, Women's Packet 6, RG 306, Feature Packets, Recurring Themes, box 17, NAII.

95. Haddow, *Pavilions of Plenty*, 112–34.

96. *Communism and the Family* and poster for USIS film *This Is My Home*, USIA Pamphlet Files, USIAA.

97. "A Visit with Mrs. Forster," April 1953, Women's Packet 1, RG 306, Feature Packets, Recurring Themes, box 16, NAII.

CHAPTER 6

The Goodwill Ambassador:
Duke Ellington and
Black Worldliness

PENNY M. VON ESCHEN

In late August 1971, while preparing to tour the Soviet Union for the U.S. Department of State, the celebrated American composer and bandleader Duke Ellington told reporters for the Washington *Evening Star:* "After the Russian tour, we have our regular European concert tour, and then after that we go to South America and then we come back to the Rainbow Grill in New York, then to Japan and the Orient, then to Australia, New Zealand, and then we'll come back and probably catch another blizzard in Buffalo." As he went on in the interview to reject, for the umpteenth time, the category of jazz, he concluded, "I live in this music and this is the world."

Ellington was certainly a traveler and an international figure long before his first State Department–sponsored tour; but in this chapter I suggest that Ellington's extraordinarily expansive sense of "the world" was in no small way shaped by his experiences as a goodwill ambassador. His tours expanded the boundaries of Ellington's world in a remarkable and perhaps unparalleled way. Not only did he tour for the State Department more than any other musician, but the tours took him to places that would simply not have been possible—

Parts of this chapter have appeared in other forms in *Satchmo Blows Up the World: Jazz Ambassadors Play the Cold War,* by Penny Von Eschen (Cambridge, Mass.: Harvard University Press, 2004). Used by permission. The author is deeply grateful to the late Mark Tucker for generous advice and encouragement on this project and for giving her the opportunity to participate in the North Carolina Jazz festivals from 1997 to 1999. She thanks Ingrid Monson for her inspiration and for sharing her knowledge and research. The author also is grateful to Robert O'Meally for the opportunity to present an early version of the chapter at the Columbia University Jazz Institute. She is indebted to Brent Edwards, Kevin Gaines, and Travis Jackson for critiques and suggestions.

not commercially viable, nor politically or logistically negotiable—without government sponsorship. Moreover, as seen in his rejection of the term "jazz," Ellington had long resisted attempts on the part of white critics to define what was good or authentic black music. Insisting that "the music of my race is something more than the American idiom," he resisted the mainstream appropriation of what he thought of as "the music of my people."[1]

Ironically, the State Department tours gave Ellington an unprecedented opportunity and authority to carry out, on a world stage, his fight against the critics' attempt to define and appropriate black culture, even as he relished his role as goodwill ambassador. And the constant scrutiny of the category of jazz by one of the undisputedly greatest "jazz" ambassadors would shape his sensibilities as an ambassador. In coupling his insistence that "the whole scene outgrew the jazz category many years ago" with his statement that "I live in this music and this is the world," he insisted on the expansiveness of the music. And the music was more than baggage or something he carried along for a State Department show-and-tell.

The Cultural Cold War

Before turning to the Ellington State Department tours, it is necessary to briefly note the international context for the tours. Why was the State Department sending Ellington abroad? These tours represented the international arm of what Casey Blake has described as a distinctly modern moment in American art that was self-consciously tied to definitions of Cold War freedom.[2] For those who selected artists for the tours, the embrace of modernism was a way of distinguishing American art from classical Soviet and European forms.

The State Department began to send sent jazz musicians abroad in 1956, starting with Dizzy Gillespie. The department initially took up jazz with considerable reluctance. But with remarkable rapidity and in response to the glowing successes of the early tours, jazz became its pet project. Unlike classical music, theater, or ballet, U.S. officials could claim jazz as a uniquely American art form. And critically, jazz was an African American art form.[3] Jazz was embraced as a crucial part of a self-conscious campaign against worldwide criticism of U.S. racism; as an attempt to build cordial relations with formerly colonized peoples in Africa, Asia, and the Middle East; and as a way to woo the populations of the Soviet Union and Eastern Europe. From the time of Gillespie's tour in the months leading up to the 1956 Suez War, musicians were deliberately sent into tense situations in hopes of gaining political leverage via a build-up of cultural capital: Dave Brubeck ended up in Iraq in the Middle East crisis of July 1958; Louis Armstrong, in a 1960–61 twenty-seven-city tour of the African continent, played in several cities in the Congo in the weeks preceding the Central Intelligence Agency–backed assassination of Patrice Lumumba in January 1961; and as we shall see below, Ellington himself played next door to the Iraqi presidential palace in 1963 the day it was attacked in an attempted coup d'état.[4]

Edward Kennedy "Duke" Ellington was perhaps the ideal ambassador for one of the first tests of cultural exchange under the heightened international scrutiny of American race relations and the new official endorsement of civil rights. Having been born on April 29, 1899, in Washington and sixty-four years of age when he took his first tour in 1963, Ellington's international stature as a composer, pianist, and unparalleled bandleader matched that of Armstrong. Ellington's brilliance as an orchestra leader was legendary. He was renowned for getting the most out of musicians by featuring their talents in extended solos; his instrument of choice, it was said, was his orchestra. And in an era dominated by rock and roll, when most big bands had broken up long ago, he had managed against all odds to keep his orchestra together.

Not only did Ellington need a band to test out his newest compositions, but his orchestra also exemplified the success of big bands in providing gainful employment for African American men facing otherwise meager opportunities. Ellington's band on the State Department tour included such veteran members as Billy Strayhorn, Johnny Hodges, Paul Gonsalves, Cootie Williams, Sam Woodyard, Harry Carney, Ray Nance, Cat Anderson, and Russell Procope.[5] From the time the tour began, the State Department escort immediately discerned that "Ellington writes for his soloists" and "the members of the band are strongly individualistic not only as musicians but as personalities."[6] For the State Department, an orchestra filled with "stars" who were "all in a position to consider themselves exceptional artists," made for spectacular performances. It also led to conflict, difficulties in scheduling, and sometimes distinctly different views of the politics of the tours on the part of musicians and the State Department.

Ellington's cosmopolitanism—his worldliness as an international celebrity and his experience in leading a black big band in Jim Crow America—meant that he was uniquely situated to contend with the enormous tensions in the Cold War project represented by these government-sponsored tours. Between his first government-sponsored tour through the Middle East in 1963 and his death in 1974, Ellington toured the Soviet Union, made two trips to the continent of Africa, appeared in Eastern Europe, and toured South America and South Asia, all under the auspices of the State Department.

Indeed, this senior statesman of jazz brought a singularly complicated perspective to the tours. Over the course of his tours, Ellington appears to have been not only a patriot but also a sincere believer in the American Cold War mission of promoting the superiority of American democracy (a perspective not necessarily shared by members of his orchestra). Along with Lionel Hampton, Ellington was one of the very few Republican jazz musicians involved in the tours. Ellington's Republicanism best might be understood as a generational phenomenon, a residual effect of early-twentieth-century Washington, where he was born and raised in a relatively privileged middle-class black world. In his youth, the Republican Party was still the party of Abraham Lincoln. The Democratic Party was not only the party of the solid South but also the party of Woodrow Wilson, the president who brought legal segregation to the nation's capital and to the black Republic of Haiti after the U.S. invasion in 1915, when Ellington was an adolescent.[7] Thus, however anomalous in the jazz world, Ellington's "Republicanism" was consistent with his lifelong commitment to civil rights and the struggle over the control and representation of black cultural production.

Although Ellington relished his role as goodwill ambassador, as late as 1957, he had expressed profound reservations about the possibilities for America. In his essay "The Race for Space," he dispassionately observed that "America's inability to go far ahead or at least keep abreast of Russia in the race for space can be traced directly to this racial problem."[8] Noting that science and the arts were both fundamentally creative endeavors, he compared the satellite *Sputnik* with "a work of art in the sense that I view a great painting, read a great poem, or listen to a great work of music." Although he condemned the "regimentation of thought and the brutal subjugation of the individual to the state" in the USSR, for him, the achievement of *Sputnik* was possible because the USSR "doesn't permit race prejudice . . . to interfere with scientific progress." The United States, in contrast, was held back by racism, lacking the "harmony of thought [that] must have prevailed in order for the scientists to make a moon [satellite] that would work."[9] In other words, the United States could not be modern because of racism.[10]

For Ellington, Americans needed a "new sound. A new sound of harmony, brotherly love, common respect and consideration for the dignity and freedom of men."[11] When only six years later, President John F. Kennedy endorsed the civil rights movement, it meant that in his own lifetime, Ellington had witnessed both the imposition of Jim Crow laws in Washington and the unprecedented challenge of the movement in the late 1950s leading to Kennedy's condemnation of segregation in 1963. It was this dramatic shift that made him optimistic about the prospects for American liberalism. Thus, as Ellington embarked on his first ambassadorial trip in 1963, it was the civil rights movement that had created the conditions under which he could endorse the potential of the United States to enter the modern world.

Given Ellington's characterization of repression within the Soviet Union, it is understandable that he could endorse Cold War liberalism once the country had made an overt commitment to racial equality. But far more important than any direct consideration of U.S. Cold War foreign policy, for Ellington, being asked to serve as a cultural ambassador represented a belated, long-overdue recognition of his artistry. Though many considered Ellington the quintessential American composer, critical acclaim from the nation's cultural establishment continued to elude him. But if he did not share the critical perspectives on U.S. foreign policy of many in the jazz world, this did not, as many of his peers have suggested, make him "apolitical."

A master at the politics of representation, Ellington had long resisted the restrictive categorization of black music by white critics, maintaining that "the music of my race is something more than the American idiom."[12] His resistance to being defined contributed to the irony of this highly successful jazz ambassador's repeated rejection of the term "jazz."[13] As he consistently told audiences listening to his State Department lecture demonstrations that "jazz" was a misnomer, American officials cringed at the denial of the very existence of their prized cultural export. Yet if his explanations of why he did not use the term jazz could be frustrating to the State Department, it is critical for understanding his rejection of an exclusionary modernist canon that admitted no place for his hybrid musical sensibility encompassing African American and Western classical music, and running the gamut from popular dance numbers to ruminative extended form compositions.[14] Over time, as the tours enabled him to make further connections to African and African diasporic forms, his own struggles against appropriation would influence the way he approached new experiences and new musical influences.

Moreover, amid an ongoing battle over the politics of representation of black people, Ellington, like other black musicians and their allies, perceived the State Department jazz tours as a global platform from which to promote the dignity of black people and their culture in the United States and abroad in the era of Jim Crow. Indeed, on the 1963 tour, the moral authority that accompanied the high tide of the civil rights movement allowed musicians to assert egalitarian principles that challenged the State Department's priorities in cultural exchange. And for some musicians, these even reverberated into questions about foreign policy.

In exploring some of the tensions that arose between the State Department and the musicians during the tour, we might see the Ellington organization as a political entity unto itself, engaged in diplomatic relations and often advancing an interpretation of events that ran counter to those of the State Department. In those tensions we glimpse—to borrow a phrase from Paul Gilroy —a black counterculture of modernity, in, but not necessarily of, the bold, original, and violent U.S. project of hegemony through modernization and development that drove U.S. foreign policy in the post-1945 years.[15]

I invoke the notion of a black counterculture of modernity as a reminder that in the era of modernism in art and culture and the multifaceted American state-sponsored projects of global modernization, many black artists had their own deep investment in the notion and terms of modernity.[16] For those whose lives and professional careers had been molded amid the quotidian terror and petty restrictions of segregation—and this is true of virtually all the black artists because the tours began a full nine years before even the formal dismantling of Jim Crow—the "modern" connoted mobility and freedom, a cosmopolitan future where the tremendous constrictions of race in America would be transcended. Yet if black artists and writers embraced modernity, it was indeed a counterculture of modernity, both in the sense that they continued to confront such products of modernity as a racial, social, economic, and political order crafted from the vestiges of slavery. Ellington, like other jazz musicians, did not simply accept the way they were deployed by the State Department. Whether fostering informal musical connections after hours or backstage, pursuing romantic liaisons, or espousing political opinions in interviews and on stage, musicians slipped into the breaks and looked around, intervening in official narratives and playing their own changes on Cold War perspectives.[17]

Swinging into Action: State Department Agendas versus Artistic Adventures

The Duke Ellington Orchestra traveled to the Middle East for the first of its numerous State Department tours in 1963, visiting Syria, Lebanon, Afghanistan, Turkey, India, Pakistan, Ceylon, Iran, and Iraq.[18] The tour came just two months after the March on Washington and followed Ellington's production of *My People*, "a music and dance revue written to commemorate the hundredth anniversary of the Emancipation Proclamation."[19] A collaboration with choreographers Alvin Ailey and Tally Beatty, *My People* opened a week and a half before the March on Washington and ran daily at the Arie Crown theater in Chicago until September 2. As discussed by Ingrid Monson in "Duke Ellington and Civil Rights," her brilliant and path-breaking work on jazz and the civil rights movement, the production included a segment that "refashioned the spiritual 'Joshua Fit the Battle of Jericho' into 'King Fit the Battle of Alabam'" and "described some of the most dramatic moments of the spring 1963 [Southern Christian Leadership Conference] campaign."[20]

Ellington did not hesitate to carry this civil rights agenda abroad. The *New York Times* reported from Tehran on November 6, 1963, that "Ellington . . . tonight condemned racial segregation in the United States. He said he hoped the race problem in the United States would soon be resolved in favor of the Negro."[21] Reflecting on the significance of the tour, the *New York Herald Tribune* reported later that month on November 29 that Ellington emphasized that "aside from jazz, the people he met were most interested in talking about the United States' civil rights struggle."[22]

In his 1973 memoir *Music Is My Mistress*, Ellington placed his frank discussion of the civil rights struggle in the context of his explicit defense of American freedom. Remembering the 1963 tour, he was impressed that as the "various dos and don'ts which we are expected to observe are enumerated" during the briefings, "we are not required to restrain ourselves in the expression of our personal, political, social, or religious views. As citizens of a free country, there are not restrictions on our tongues. We are to speak as free men. They are very explicit in advising us that we should always say what we think in or out of favor of the U.S."[23] While in Delhi, Ellington took the offense when confronted by a critic of U.S. racial and economic policy:

> "The United States has an extremely accurate news service and the press enjoys almost complete freedom," I claim. "Did you incidentally, hear about the five little girls who were burned up in that church down in Alabama the other day?"
> "Yes," he says with great triumph.
> "Well, that was only a couple of days ago, and I'm not sure anybody else would have let such news out that quickly if it had happened in their backyard."

On the one hand, with the tense diplomatic situation raging at home—in the immediate aftermath of the assassination of Medgar Evers, the Birmingham campaign, and the Kennedy administration's belated embrace of civil rights—the State Department gave Ellington unprecedented latitude for the expression of political views. But in fact, Ellington was considerably more sanguine about American freedom while writing *Music Is My Mistress*—after the formal dismantlement of Jim Crow and in the afterglow of his own Soviet tour and having received honors from the Lyndon Johnson and Richard Nixon administrations—than he had been at the time of the 1963 tour. Along with his forthright comments to the press, he recounted in a 1963 interview having been deeply upset when asked "Why hasn't the Negro artist done more for the cause?" Along with his defense of artists, Ellington affirmed his personal investment in the civil rights struggle, arguing that "we had been working on the Negro situation in the South since the '30s, that we had done shows, musical works, benefits, etc., and that the American Negro artist had been among the first to make contributions."[24] In a struggle far from won, Ellington declined to discuss strategy, arguing that publicizing strategy "would help our opponents to build up an even more formidable resistance than they have now."[25]

Yet if Ellington was not as optimistic about American freedom in 1963 as he was a decade later, defending the black freedom struggle and American freedom were never incompatible. Indeed, his tours exemplify the coincidence of interests between black artists and civil rights activists on the one hand, and State Department personnel, who in the context of worldwide criticism of American racism became pro–civil rights liberals, on the other.

If the State Department agenda of emphasizing progress in civil rights and black freedom could at times allow the space for artists to promote civil rights, the agendas of the State Department and Ellington and his band did not always coincide. Band members felt that their own desires to play music and meet local musicians, as well as their genuine desire to bring jazz to new audiences, conflicted with the State Department's focus on neocolonial elites as target audiences. Members of the band overtly challenged the State Department's views of cultural exchange. Thomas W. Simons, the escort officer for the 1963 tour, was deeply sympathetic to the musicians. Ellington had taken him under his wing, recalling that "I am soon talking to him as is he were a relative, warning him against making the kind of mistakes that are all too easy, especially since the whole trip is east of Greece. If one is not socially aware, it is very easy to be caught in a position where one's chauvinistic shirttail is showing."[26]

Taking Ellington's advice to heart, Simons positioned himself as an advocate and interpreter for the musicians. Adopting the musicians' language, he discussed scheduling problems by explaining that the orchestra never "hit"— that is—began their performances on time. When the musicians protested that they were only playing for elites already familiar with jazz when they had expected to play for "the people," Simons struggled to reconcile his role in the State Department with the musicians' view of "the people." The orchestra members, Simons explained, had a "different conception of what they were to do" than the State Department. Simons reported: "The orchestra members had misunderstood the word 'people,' and were disagreeably surprised."[27] Positioning himself as a mediator between the musicians and the State Department, and not attempting to mask his sympathy for the musicians' perspective, Simons adopted the third person in his report:

> He could point out that societies in that part of the world are less fluid and more highly stratified than American society, . . . that the "people," the lower classes do not in fact "count" as much as they do with us, and that we are trying to reach out to those who did count. . . . Few of these arguments made any real impression. Band members continued to feel that they would rather play for the "people," for the men in the streets who clustered around tea-shop radios. More rationally, they believed that the lower classes, even if unimportant politically, were more worthy of exposure to good Western music than the prestige audiences for whom they played.[28]

Playing for the People

The theme of "playing for the man in the street" was raised repeatedly by members of the orchestra. Mercer Ellington explained that during the mixed State Department/commercial tour of Latin America in 1971, the performance in Uruguay had been especially rewarding because they had reached "the man in the street." Similarly, playing at the Sports Palace in Moscow was singled out for the same reason—they had been able to "reach the man in the streets."

Duke Ellington's sense of his audience also clashed with the State Department's when he learned while in Bombay of the black market for tickets and received numerous telephone calls and letters from musicians complaining of the impossibility of getting tickets. For Ellington, "All musicians are brothers in arms and it distresses me terribly that they could not get in to our concert, so we go about the business of readjusting the conditions. I insist that from now on, no matter how limited the space, all musicians are to be admitted."[29]

Robert O'Meally has discussed the complexity of Ellington's sense of who he was playing for, calling Ellington the "master of the fulfillment of wishes."[30] Under the spell of that mastery, the State Department perceived Ellington as the model gentleman and statesman. Other orchestra members, notably Paul Gonsalves and Mercer Ellington, similarly embraced the role of diplomat. Mercer explained that while on a commercial Latin American tour, "in a sense it was a good will tour. . . . Even when we were not appearing under the auspices of the State Department, it was good to go to the embassies."[31] State Department officials were greatly impressed with the charm and diplomatic acumen of Ellington and many members of the band. For Simons, despite illness and a taxing schedule, "in his off-stage appearances [Ellington] was without fail gracious, articulate, charming and absolutely winning, even when feeling poorly."[32]

Gonsalves demonstrated his diplomatic skills from the time of the first briefing in Damascus. After the ambassador finished briefing the band on its duties and local customs, Gonsalves, whom, Ellington recalls, had been sipping a few drinks, went over and put his arm around the ambassador. " 'Mr. Ambassador,' Paul says, 'you are absolutely right!' He then proceeds to make his own speech. His Excellency is astonished but feels it is wonderful and compliments Paul, telling him that he is a very good ambassador himself."[33] Gonsalves, Ellington concluded, "is a great diplomat, and sometimes, from the way he goes on, you think it is he who is really representing the government."[34]

Indeed, the State Department judged the diplomatic achievements of the whole band to be considerable. As Simons reported, "the group as a whole worked very hard to make offstage functions a success. Its members were almost without exception excellent ambassadors and representatives of America. . . . They were vivacious, direct, informal and intelligent. They were enormously friendly. They were excellent conversationalists."[35]

Yet the differences between musicians and government personnel in their sense of ideal audiences in the 1963 tour points to a number of tensions among these groups. Throughout, State Department officials' not so subtly coded discussions of "behavior" revealed prevailing anxieties about race, sexuality, and drug use. These anxieties erupted early on the tour, in Amman, when Ray Nance suffered an emotional breakdown, apparently brought on by drinking, stress, and fatigue. Nance's erratic behavior culminated in his refusal to stand for the national anthem while playing a concert at the Roman Theater in Amman.[36] Though officials were angered by conduct they attributed to drug abuse, Ellington and other band members spent hours with State Department officials, insisting that Nance was not using drugs. The stakes were very high because Nance had served time on a narcotics charge in 1955. To the contrary, the band members argued, Nance was drinking and depressed because he was *not* using drugs. Simons, clearly moved by the musicians "sorrow" over the problems of Nance, explained in his letter to Washington that "they had been with him for years and valued his true worth as a person and as a performer." Positioning himself as an advocate for the musicians and a buffer against official reprimand, Simons argued to Washington that "the embarrassment and harm which America has suffered as a result of Nance's conduct pales beside the tragedy of a fine American and a fine man."[37] All parties agreed that Nance should be sent back to the States.[38]

Underscored by Nance's departure, the 1963 tour turned out to be a strange, troubling, and ultimately tragic experience. Not only were the musicians often stunned and depressed by the widespread poverty they witnessed, but the band was playing in Baghdad next door to the presidential palace when it was attacked by Iraqi air force jets in an attempted coup d'état on November 12. (Ellington had been warned by the State Department of an impending coup and had agreed to continue the tour.) Then, the tour was cut short by the Kennedy assassination when the band was in Ankara. As David Hadju has told the story in *Lush Life*, Ellington, a close friend recalled, "was beside being beside himself. The whole tour was already strange, and now the president went and died on him."[39]

Devastated by the news of the assassination, Ellington nevertheless wanted to continue the tour, arguing that his music expressed the spectrum of human emotions and the orchestra's performances "would signify tribute rather than disrespect."[40] Indeed, his response to Kennedy's death was to stay up all night composing memorial music.[41] Though Ellington was persuaded that the remaining countries on the tour "might have thought that a continuation of the tour was in poor taste," he continued to defend his desire to complete the tour with memorial concerts.[42] In an interview with Sally Hammond of the *Washington Post*, he explained that "it would have meant a 'complete turnabout'" but that he had been "ready to sit up all night writing special memorial music." Outlining his vision of the music, he continued: "Of course I'd have cut out all the theatrical stuff and there wouldn't have been any swinging. But it would have had a beat. Religious music, you know, does have a beat."[43] The problem, he argued, came down to the word "jazz": "This word [jazz] has absolutely no meaning today. . . . If it hadn't been overplayed in the publicity, there would have been no reason to cancel the tour."

For Ellington, "jazz" should simply mean "freedom of expression through music," but because of the "shady associations" people have given it, concerts were canceled as country after country went into mourning. "They thought jazz might be considered in bad taste."[44] As evidenced in his desire to compose memorials for Kennedy, Ellington remained an active composer who was constantly writing through the most grueling itineraries. Throughout the tour and afterward, he responded to sorrows and triumphs by composing music.

Improvising Détente: From Africa to the Soviet Union

Ellington's next government-sponsored trip abroad and his first trip to the continent of Africa was for the First International Festival of Negro Arts in Dakar in April 1966. By the time of the festival, Congress had formally dismantled Jim Crow with the passage of the Civil Rights and Voting Rights acts. For the State Department, Ellington's presence at the festival—along with that of Alvin Ailey, Marion Williams, and Langston Hughes as the senior emissaries of black America—represented the triumph of American liberalism. State Department personnel were intensely proud of the art of Ailey and Ellington and of the Johnson administration's recent legislative achievements in civil rights, and with wide recognition of black American culture, it was a moment of great triumph for African American artists. With Ellington carrying away the greatest critical acclaim, many African American artists won awards. Best film went to *Nothing But a Man*, Michael Romer's realistic portrayal of black gender relations in the Jim Crow South with effective performances by Ivan Dixon and Abby Lincoln in roles of unprecedented depth. Mahalia Jackson won best female vocalist for the greatest hits of gospel; Louis Armstrong won best male vocalist for *Hello Dolly*. Ellington began work on the *Senegalese Suite* on his way to Dakar—although the composition ultimately became *La Plus Belle Africaine*. If the State Department perceived the festival as a triumph of American culture, Ellington experienced it as an affirmation of African diasporic ties. He wrote in his Dakar Journal: "After writing African music for thirty-five years, here I am at last in Africa. I can only hope and wish that our performance of *La Plus Belle Africaine*, which I have written in anticipation of the occasion, will mean something to the people gathered here."[45]

Ellington celebrated the Afro-diasporic spirit of the festival in the 1966 album *Soul Call*, which included the title track from the Louis and Henry Bellson composition, as well as Ellington's *La Plus Belle Africaine*, *West Indian Pancake*, and the Othello-inspired Ellington–Billy Strayhorn composition *Such Sweet Thunder*.[46] Continuing to pursue Afro-diasporic connections with a 1969 trip to Jamaica, where he recalled, "the band was uniformly dressed in dashikis," Ellington would return to the African continent for the State Department in 1973 to perform in Ethiopia and Zambia.[47]

Of all the State Department tours—by all artists—the department and observers alike considered Ellington's 1971 trip to the Soviet Union to be the greatest diplomatic triumph. The political context was critical: Ellington's trip followed the announcement of Nixon's impending visit to the Soviet Union. In *Music Is My Mistress*, Ellington wrote: "The anticipation of our tour of Russia is so great that there is a risk of being consumed by it."[48] And indeed, promotions and publicity for the tour presented him as the front man for the president! Before the tour, from September 13 to October 13, 1971, jazz had been incredibly embattled in the Soviet Union. Benny Goodman (1962) and Earl Hines (1966) had been the only jazz artists to represent the United

States in the Soviet Union. The Ellington orchestra played twenty-two concerts in five cities, reaching an audience of 126,000.[49] As one U.S. official reported: "Ellington was a mythical figure for the hardcore thousands of truly dedicated Soviet aficionados that waited for his arrival in the USSR with something akin to the anticipation of a Second Coming."[50] For some Soviet fans, it was if modernity itself had walked through the door with Ellington. The secretary of state, William P. Rogers, reported to President Nixon that one young fan yelled: "We've been waiting for you for centuries," a welcome Nixon would have envied.[51]

The American Embassy reported that "during the Band's appearance in Moscow, hundreds of travelers from distant places such as Odessa, Riga, and Yakutsk arrived in Moscow for the concerts. . . . Tickets in Moscow were being scalped for $50.00 each.[52] Describing Ellington as "ecstatic," the State Department and the Soviet public as "overjoyed," and noting that "even Pravda waxes rapturous with a long glowing review, . . . [the] first such acknowledgement . . . of the artistry of a visiting American musician," Leonard Feather called the tour "the greatest coup in the history of musical diplomacy."[53] Joseph A. Presel, the escort officer for the tour, called it an "immense success" for all parties and described Ellington as "a personage of immense historical importance to the Soviets. . . . He is, for them, composer of 'Take the A Train' [actually composed by Strayhorn], Willis Conover's theme song, he is one of the last survivors of the heroic age of jazz, and he is one of the seminal figures of jazz for the Soviet jazz buffs."[54]

No less than their counterparts in smaller posts around the world, for whom the visiting artist was welcomed as a Victrola in the wilderness, U.S. officials in Moscow relished the opportunity to be in the company of the charming Ellington. B. H. Klosson, the apparently star-struck American Ambassador in Moscow, spent no less than one single-spaced page explaining the "famous Ellington steaks."[55] For the U.S. officials, it was highly significant that the Soviets were acknowledging the accomplishments of an American artist."[56]

Subsequent to the Soviet tour and in the last three years of his life, Ellington's activities for the State Department actually accelerated. He was seventy-two years of age at the time of the Soviet tours, and he immediately followed up with performances in Western and Eastern Europe and a mixed commercial/State Department tour of Latin America, Brazil, and Mexico in November and December 1971. Ellington and his orchestra followed this up with a 1972 tour through East and Southeast Asia and 1973 visits to Ethiopia and Lusaka, Zambia, in the last year of his life.[57]

Ellington's final State Department tour began with a Newport Jazz Festival concert in Belgrade and continued in "pickup" appearances in Ethiopia and Zambia. In an otherwise celebratory piece titled "The Unique Duke Ellington," *Dnevnil* acknowledged that "the living legend of jazz" had "disappointed a part of the audience in Trivoi Hall," as "no more the musician they know from the numerous records so well." Though the critic cited the considerable changes in Ellington's orchestra, he surely did not know that Ellington had been diagnosed in January of that year with lung cancer, which already was rapidly spreading throughout his body.[58]

Although he was terminally ill, Ellington nonetheless welcomed the opportunity, following the Belgrade Newport appearance, for a pickup tour to Ethiopia and Zambia, arranged through Festival Productions. George Wein at Festival Productions did not know how sick Ellington was but sensed his vulnerability as he wrote to the Cultural Presentations Office that he was "very concerned" about the Ellington itinerary planned for Ethiopia. The band was scheduled to be up at 6:00 am two days in a row after flying all night from Europe. "That band will be whipped if we are not careful," Wein objected. "Let's not forget that Duke Ellington is 74 years old, although don't tell him I said so."[59]

The twenty-two-person Ellington Orchestra arrived in Addis Ababa on November 23. For the State Department, the tour was magical, with an "unforgettable" impact on U.S. Information Service (USIS) staff, Ethiopian youth, developing-world nationals, and the performing arts world alike. Publicity and media coverage had been superb, drawing on two U.S. Information Agency films about Ellington on the road and at the White House. U.S. officials ran newspaper advertisements and produced television and radio commercials, which the Ethiopian television service and Radio Ethiopia ran before and after the visit. At a critical moment in United States–Ethiopia relations, the State Department considered it not only an artistic success but also a great cooperative venture between U.S. officials and Ethiopians "from all professions and all walks of life."[60]

Emperor Haile Selassie I attended Ellington's opening "command performance," and at a special palace reception, he conferred the rank of commander in the Imperial Order of Ethiopia upon Ellington. The State Department explained that "we reaped an unexpected dividend in the unexpected calling of the eighth extraordinary session of the Organization of Africa Unity's Council of Ministers." The visiting dignitaries were invited to the opening concert and VIP reception that followed with the Ethiopian prime minister. American officials were impressed and grateful that Ellington insisted on being present to meet the prime minister and visiting officials at the event, though it was clear that he was suffering excruciating pain from arthritis following the concert.[61]

If Ellington worked his diplomatic charms in the world of dignitaries, USIS officials thought it "remarkable" that his music was received with such enthusiasm by the youth. This had been unexpected, because "our air waves here are almost dominated with recent contemporary American music." Yet, a student afternoon concert at reduced prices had the "most excitedly responsive audience" of all and, as a result, Ellington "played his best music. In effect, they metaphorically tore the theater apart with their enthusiasm and cheers."[62]

Ellington became "fast friends" with Mulatu Astatqé, Ethiopia's leading contemporary composer, arranger, conductor, and musician, "who was the Duke's constant companion and friend from the moment of arrival to departure."[63] Astatqé, a pioneer of Ethio-jazz, fused traditional Ethiopian music with a wide range of musical influences he had encountered while studying abroad in England from the age of seventeen. In England, he "was immediately taken with the Caribbean and Latin music present on the London scene, just before the onset of Beatlemania." He played with Frank Holder, a calypso musician from the Caribbean, and in Edmundo Ross's Latino band. He then studied in New York, where he founded the Ethiopian Quintet and went on to release two "Afro-Latin soul" albums with them in 1966, the same year that Ellington released *Soul Call*.[64]

It is no wonder that the two modern innovators got on famously. The State Department hosted Astatqé by putting him up in a room next door to Ellington at the Addis Ababa Hilton, where the band stayed. Astatqé brought "every available musician of note" to meet Ellington and brought a band together to play special arrangements of Ethiopian music that had been put together for Ellington's visit.[65] Six Ellington musicians joined artists from the famous traditional Orchestra Ethiopia and "modern musicians gathered by Ethiopian composer-musician Mulatu Astatqé in a jam session that the Ellingtonians will long remember." Within a few minutes, reported the delighted USIS, the American jazz stars were playing along—as one Ellington band member put it—"as if they were born here." A USIS press release reported that "the saxophone, trumpet and trombone met the traditional Ethiopian *masinko* and *washint* musical instruments and according to one Ellington bandsmen, 'music may never be the same again.' "[66] When Ellington had first visited Africa for the Dakar Festival in 1966, he had commented that after writing African music for thirty-five years, he was at last in Africa. Indeed, it seems fitting that even in the last months of his life and on his final State Department tour, he should contribute to yet another fusion in the seemingly infinite routes of Afro-diasporic innovation.

The Ellington Orchestra's next and final stop on the African tour was Lusaka. In a sobering reminder of the mining interests that had driven the U.S. interest in the region during the Congo crisis, the State Department's public affairs officer, Arthur Lewis, had apprised the Cultural Presentations Office that "the copper companies and the Zambian government are terribly interested" in a visit by Ellington, as part of independence celebrations.[67] The orchestra gave three concerts in two and a half days. In an "arrival day performance in Lusaka's famed Mulungushi Hall, well over 2,000 cheering, stomping fans welcomed the Duke and his Orchestra." "The crowds," reported the American Embassy, "were absolutely in love with the ageless Duke, who performed many of his old, familiar tunes to thunderous applause and whistles."[68] Early the next morning, they flew to the copper belt city of Ndola for a luncheon and afternoon performance in the Broadway Cinema. Returning to Lusaka for an evening reception sponsored by the American ambassador and the Zambian minister of education and culture, the orchestra then played a late Sunday afternoon concert at the State House.[69] A staff member of the American Embassy judged the value of the visit "immeasurable" and was "extraordinarily satisfied," calling Ellington "an unparalleled representative of the U.S., both personally and professionally."

The U.S. Embassy was clearly pleased with the visit for the "untold opportunities" it afforded for personal contacts with government officials. Embassy staff were also thrilled that Ellington's reception belied the notion that, as one put it, "American music, particularly jazz, is unknown to Zambians."[70] But many Zambians and the performing arts community might have taken issue with this emphasis on "American music." Ellington's music, reported the *Zambian Daily Mail* in a caption for a picture of the composer at the piano, "spans almost every style and mood of the world-wide music that has its roots in Africa."[71] Even more pointedly, the critic Valerie Wilmer argued in the *Zambia Daily Mail*, "the Western world deceives itself when they talk of Jazz—the only original American art form. What they should be saying and saying loud— is that Black Music is the beat to which the whole world is dancing."[72] And Ellington, who insisted that "the music of my race is more than the American idiom," would surely have agreed.

Against Appropriation

Ellington's death less than six months after his final State Department tour seemed to underscore the close relationship between the tours and his later career. It seems fitting then, in conclusion, to return to a consideration of the tours' impact on Ellington's music and composition. The musicologist Travis Jackson argues that "Ellington was not engaged in an attempt to *imitate* the different musics he heard during the tours. Rather, his primary aim was to allow all the experiences he had—musical and nonmusical—to *influence* his way of composing."[73]

In the liner notes to *The Far East Suite*, Ellington explained:

I don't want to copy this rhythm or that scale. It's more valuable to have absorbed while there. You let it roll around, undergo a chemical change, and then let it seep out on a paper in the form that suits the musicians who are going play it. But this takes quite a bit of doing, you don't want to underestimate or *understate the world out there*. (author's emphasis)

Ellington's emphasis on the diplomat-artist's delicate relationship with "the world out there" offers a clue to his sensibilities as a cultural ambassador. Recalling his warnings to Simons about the pitfalls of America chauvinism, Ellington's desire to let himself be influenced but not to imitate suggests his wariness of appropriation. This suspicion of appropriation, one might argue, was grounded in the resistance to being defined and categorized by critics that had long animated Ellington's life and work. Writing about the tours, he made no pretense of authority or even comprehension. He embraced the stance of misrecognition, calling attention to his frequent lapses in understanding, as when in Bombay, he misunderstood the gesture for "yes" and proceeded to eat the worst item off the menu for seven days in a row.

Further clues to Ellington's concern not to "understate the world out there" are found in his insistence that "the music of my race is something more than the American idiom." The passage continues: "It is the result of our transplantation to American soil, and was our reaction in the plantation days to the tyranny we endured. What we could not say openly we expressed in music. . . . It expresses our personality."[74] His insistence on music as expression, and specifically historical expression that marks a reaction to slavery and oppression, is critical. For him, "*stating* the world out there . . . takes quite a bit of doing," in part because music takes on the responsibility of representation. Indeed, Ellington's sense of music as historical expression mitigated against modernist forms of appropriation that posited art as pure expression abstracted from both history and its production through labor.[75] Not only was he wary of misrepresenting "the world out there," but his music had to *state* the world, to capture a changing cultural scene that was new to him and went beyond the questions of power and representation that he grappled with in a primarily American context.[76]

Yet as Ellington's work expanded further beyond the nation-state, to be involved in the tours at all was to be steeped in a national project of power and appropriation. Travis Jackson helps to illuminate Ellington's complex position vis-à-vis influence and appropriation. In letting himself be "influenced" by other music, Ellington was not engaging in a form of colonial appropriation. He was not trying to invigorate a seemingly dead or lackluster form of expression with more "primitive" or "emotionally engaged" music from places seen as "outside the West." Nor was he trying to give a flagging career a shot in the arm by coloring his work with exotica.[77] Rather than engaging in a colonialist form of appropriation, he was mining what he heard and saw to give him a way to think somewhat differently about composition. In doing so, however, he did sometimes resort to clichés that reduced the complexity of other people's music to a few musical signifiers. For example, he used phrasings to suggest snake charmers and "drones" in the *Far East Suite*.[78]

The metaphor of mining helps to remind us that while Ellington's State Department tours were not part of a colonial project, they were part of the U.S. pursuit of hegemony through policies of modernization and development. Indeed, it was no accident that jazz tours circled the quintessential Cold War commodities, oil and uranium, along with hitting the Cold War hotspots.[79] It would be wrong however, to comprehend the tours and their significance solely within the context of the vast and multifaceted American efforts to secure global resources.

To export American culture was to inevitably export its hybridity, its complexities, its tensions and contradictions. To export jazz was to export, in the words of Ellington, "an American idiom with African roots."[80] In 1963, that meant exporting the civil rights movement, and over the next and final decade of Ellington's life, that meant further exploring the transnational and improvisational foundations of jazz, from albums such as *Soul Call* to collaborations such as those with Astatqé.

During Ellington's tours, if the curious convergence of interests between State Department personnel defending American "race relations" and black artists fighting for civil rights could at times benefit the State Department, it also allowed for the projection of the optimism and vitality of black American culture abroad and the continuing transformation of that culture in transnational collaborations. The conflicts within the tours—over the meaning of "the people," the audiences; over the musicians' preference for interacting with other musicians and learning new music rather than attending official functions; indeed, over the musicians' insistence on putting their stamp on diplomacy—all speak to the impulse to refuse appropriation and the desire to project a cultural statement and musical expression that constituted "something more than the American idiom." In Ellington's long-standing fight against appropriation, in his attempt to be influenced but not imitate, there was an uneven match between what he intended and what he achieved in "the world out there," just as there was for the State Department.

Notes

1. Duke Ellington, "The Duke Steps Out" (1931), in *The Duke Ellington Reader*, ed. Mark Tucker (New York: Oxford University Press, 1993), 49.
2. See Chapter 8 in this volume.
3. For an elaboration of this strategy, see Penny Von Eschen, *Satchmo Blows Up the World: Jazz Ambassadors Play the Cold War* (Cambridge, Mass.: Harvard University Press, 2004).
4. Von Eschen, *Satchmo Blows Up the World*, 132–33.
5. For a discussion of idea that Ellington's orchestra was his instrument and the dynamics within the band, see Wynton Marsalis and Robert O'Meally, "Duke Ellington's Music Like a Big Hot Pot of Good Gumbo," in *The Jazz Cadence of American Culture*, ed. Robert G. O'Meally (New York: Columbia University Press, 1998), 147–50.
6. "The Duke Ellington Orchestra, September 6–November 28, 1963," Sixteen Weeks, Synopsis, series 2, box 9, Bureau of Educational and Cultural Affairs Historical Collection, J. William Fulbright Papers, University of Arkansas at Fayetteville (hereafter Bureau Historical Collection), General Report, Introduction, 1.
7. On the U.S. invasion and occupation of Haiti, see Mary Renda, *Taking Haiti: Military Occupation and the Culture of U.S. Imperialism, 1915–1940* (Chapel Hill: University of North Carolina Press, 2001).

8. Duke Ellington, "The Race for Space," in *Duke Ellington Reader*, ed. Tucker, 295.
9. Ellington, "Race for Space," 294.
10. The author is indebted to Paul Gilroy for a discussion about Ellington and modernity.
11. Ellington, "Race for Space," 296.
12. Ellington, "The Duke Steps Out," 46–50; Janet Mabie, "Ellington's 'Mood Indigo': Harlem's Duke Seeks to Express His Race," in *Duke Ellington Reader*, ed. Tucker, 41–43; Graham Locke, *Bluetopia: Visions of the Future and Revisions of the Past in the Work of Sun Ra, Duke Ellington, and Anthony Braxton* (Durham, N.C.: Duke University Press, 2000), 77–88.
13. "Duke To Play in Russia," *Evening Star*, August 30, 1971.
14. The quotation is from "Duke to Play." On this last point, see Kevin Gaines, "Duke Ellington: Black, Brown and Beige and Cultural Politics During the 1940s," in *Music and the Racial Imagination*, ed. Ronald Radano (Chicago: University of Chicago Press, 2001). See also Eric Porter, *What Is This Thing Called Jazz: African American Musicians as Artists, Critics, and Activists* (Berkeley: University of California Press, 2002), 37–39.
15. Paul Gilroy, *The Black Atlantic: Modernity and Double Consciousness* (Cambridge, Mass.: Harvard University Press, 1993). The term "counterculture of modernity" was originally used by Zygmut Bauman, who talked about the Left as a counterculture of modernity.
16. Certainly, all these variations of the term "modern" mean very different things and refer to radically different processes. Yet I would suggest that one might see modernity as the ideology of the United States' post-1945 hegemonic project and argue that the project worked precisely through the slippages in the meanings and uses of these terms.
17. For an elaboration of this point, see Von Eschen, *Satchmo Blows Up the World*, chap. 1.
18. This is found in series 2, box 9, Bureau Historical Collection.
19. Ingrid Monson, "Duke Ellington and Civil Rights," paper presented at Duke Ellington Centenary Conference, University of North Carolina Jazz Symposium, Chapel Hill, February 25–27, 1999.
20. Duke Ellington, *Music Is My Mistress* (New York: Da Capo Press, 1973), 197–99. Monson, "Duke Ellington and Civil Rights."
21. *New York Times*, November 6, 1963.
22. *New York Herald Tribune*, November 29, 1963.
23. Ellington, *Music Is My Mistress*, 302.
24. Stanley Dance, *The World of Duke Ellington*, (New York: DaCapo, 1970), 21.
25. Ibid.
26. Ellington, *Music Is My Mistress*, 302. Here, Ellington becomes the escort officers mentor, turning the tables on the escort officers usual function as supervisor, interpreter, and guide.
27. Thomas W. Simons Jr., Effectiveness Report, Ellington Tour 1963, series 2, box 9, Bureau Historical Collection, 15–17.
28. Ibid.
29. Ellington, *Music Is My Mistress*, 318. In Delhi, the band members were invited to the university, where they were given demonstrations of indigenous Indian instruments, and introduced to several forms of dance (p. 312).

30. Robert O'Meally, "Duke Ellington Plays the Audience," talk presented at the 1999 North Carolina Jazz Festival.

31. "The Long Road Home: Mercer Ellington Talks to Stanley Dance," *Downbeat*, April 13, 1972.

32. General Report, Bureau Historical Collection, 39–40.

33. Ellington, *Music Is My Mistress*, 302.

34. Ellington, *Music Is My Mistress*, 312.

35. General Report, 18.

36. From: Thomas W. Simons Jr., American Embassy, Amman Jordan, to Mr. Glenn Wolfe, Office of Cultural Presentations, Department of State, Washington, September 17, 1963.

37. Ibid.

38. Ibid.

39. David Hajdu, *Lush Life: A Biography of Billy Strayhorn* (New York: Farrar Straus Giroux, 1996), 230–31. On the tour's early ending see "Tour Curtailed," *Washington Daily News*, November 29, 1963; and "Jazz Seemed a Discord, Ellington Tour Ended," *New York Herald Tribune*, November 29, 1963, series 5, box 11, Educational and Cultural Exchange.

40. "Ellington Reaction of Cancellation of the Tour," Complete Itinerary of Ellington's 1963 Mideast Tour, Bureau Historical Collection, 16–17.

41. Interview, Von Eschen with Simons, June 17, 2003.

42. "Ellington Reaction to Cancellation of the Tour," 16–17.

43. Duke Ellington with Sally Hammond, *Washington Post*, December 6, 1963.

44. Ibid.

45. "Dakar Journal," in *Music Is My Mistress*, 337.

46. Duke Ellington, *Soul Call*, liner notes, Verve CD, 1999.

47. Ellington, *Music Is My Mistress*, 199.

48. Ellington, *Music Is My Mistress*, 364; for Ellington's recollections on the tour, see the chapter "Russian Journal, 1971," 364–80.

49. Recapitulation Report, Bureau Historical Collection.

50. To Department of State from American Embassy, Moscow, December 10, 1971, 2.

51. From Memorandum to the President, October 20, 1971, written by William P. Rogers, 2.

52. Memorandum to Department of State, Washington, from B. H. Klosson, U.S. Embassy, Moscow, on Duke Ellington in the USSR, December 10, 1971, Bureau Historical Collection, 9.

53. Leonard Feather, "Ellington Concert a Diplomatic Coup," October 24, 1971, series 2, box 9, Bureau Historical Collection; Ellington notes the acknowledgment of *Pravda* in Ellington, *Music Is My Mistress*, 374.

54. Joseph A. Presel (escort officer), "Duke Ellington in the USSR, September–October 1971" (trip report), series 5, box 9, Bureau Historical Collection, 2.

55. Klosson, Embassy Report, 9.

56. Presel, Escort Report, 5.

57. In another astounding chapter in the story of the ingratitude which the United States has shown its great artists, as Ellington carried out his "diplomatic coup" in the Soviet Union, a September 21, 1971, Internal Revenue Service memorandum to the State Department asked to put a levy on monies earned by Ellington, who had fallen behind on tax payments to the Internal Revenue Service. It is unclear

to me as to whether there was a connection between these developments and the acceleration of the Ellington tours.

58. Enclosure 1, 11; "Is Duke Tired of Everything?" *Delo*, November 9, 1973, enclosure 1, 14; John Edward Hasse, *Beyond Category: The Life and Genius of Duke Ellington* (New York: Simon & Schuster, 1993), 384.

59. George Wein to Mr. L. Dayton Coe II, Office of Cultural Presentations, August 6, 1973, Bureau Historical Collection.

60. Ibid., 3.

61. Ibid., 4.

62. Ibid., 3.

63. American Embassy, Addis Ababa, to Department of State, 5.

64. The biographical information on Astatqé is from the liner notes of *Ethiopiques: Golden Years of Ethiopian Music*, Amha Eshete/Amha Records.

65. American Embassy, Addis Ababa, to Department of State, 5.

66. News Release: Addis Ababa–USIS–Asmara, November 21, 1973, PR 74.

67. Arthur W. Lewis, Public Affairs Officer, Foreign Service of the United States of America, Lusaka; to Mark Lewis, Director of Cultural Presentations, August 23, 1973, Bureau Historical Collection.

68. American Embassy, Lusaka, to Department of State, December 18, 1973, 1–2.

69. Ibid., 1–5.

70. Ibid., 2–3.

71. *Zambian Daily Mail*, Lusaka, November 24, 1973; enclosure 1, p. 5 of 10, Bureau Historical Collection.

72. Valerie Wilmer, "Jazz: Africa Makes the People Dance," *Zambian Daily Mail*, November 24, 1973.

73. Travis A. Jackson, "Tourist Point of View: Ellington's Musical Souvenirs," paper presented at presented at Columbia University, Jazz Studies Group, November 30, 1999.

74. Ellington, "The Duke Steps Out."

75. The critic Randy Martin has astutely argued that the modernist appropriation of the art of "the other" rested on a denial of labor, positing art as pure expression (of the nation) rather than something technical and produced through labor. Randy Martin, "Modern Dance and the American Century," in *A Modern Mosaic: Art and Modernism in the United States*, ed. Townsend Luddington (Chapel Hill: University of North Carolina Press, 2000), 203–26.

76. The author is indebted to a conversation with Brent Edwards in elaborating this point. For a brilliant reading of Ellington's writing and use of language, see Brent Edwards, "The Literary Ellington," *Representations* 77, no. 1 (Winter 2002): 1–29.

77. Jackson, "Tourist Point of View." Practices of appropriation of such pop musicians as Paul Simon and David Byrne have been trenchantly critiqued by George Lipsitz, *Dangerous Crossroads: Popular Music, Postmodernism, and the Poetics of Place* (London: Verso, 1994), 56–63.

78. Jackson, "Tourist Point of View."

79. Von Eschen, *Satchmo Blows Up the World*.

80. Ellington, *Music Is My Mistress*, 436.

CHAPTER 7

A Modernist Vision:
The Origins and Early Years of the National Endowment for the Arts' Visual Arts Program

DONNA M. BINKIEWICZ

During the 1990s, the National Endowment for the Arts (NEA) became embroiled in controversy. Much criticism of the agency revolved around grants made to museums that had exhibited the works of such artists as Robert Mapplethorpe and Andres Serano during the late 1980s. The unsettling nature of their art (which included homoerotic images and a crucifix immersed in urine) brought widespread admonition not only to the artists but also to the agency that dared to fund such "gross, vulgar, offensive" pieces with hard earned taxpayers' money, in the words of Senator Jesse Helms.[1] Indeed, the NEA was besieged by conservatives who quite successfully branded it a harbinger of immorality and liberal excess unworthy of federal support.

These charges would have shocked the agency's founders and bipartisan backers who sought to build a showcase institution drawing national and international attention to American cultural excellence and the cherished American ideal of free expression. The NEA was a product of Cold War presidents John F. Kennedy's and Lyndon Johnson's liberalism, yet it never embodied the radical avant-garde facade that conservatives like Jesse Helms plastered upon it during the 1990s. Rather, in its efforts to cultivate an American "civilization" to rival that of Western Europe, the NEA promoted a well-established repertoire of classical music, opera, theater, and dance. Its Visual Arts Program funded a host of modernist abstract painters and sculptors who no longer pro-

This chapter is excerpted by permission from the author's larger work, *Federalizing the Muse: United States Arts Policy and the National Endowment for the Arts, 1965–1980* (Chapel Hill: University of North Carolina Press, 2004).

duced cutting-edge aesthetics but suited the agency's vision of high art symbolizing American freedom without messy political undertones.

This chapter focuses on the National Council on the Arts and the Visual Arts Program in their formative states between 1965 and 1975—an important component of NEA history. This was the crucial period in which the council formed the basic structures and goals for the NEA, which in many ways continue to guide the agency to this day. Placing the council historically within the intellectual and political milieu of the 1960s and carefully examining the first council members' decisions proves quite revealing. This chapter explores what these arts administrators considered to be "aesthetic excellence" in American painting and sculpture and how they organized the NEA to promote both artistic excellence and democracy through art funding. It also assesses their success at reconciling their ideal of high culture with democracy during a period of great stylistic and political change.

The Visual Arts Program developed two major components—the funding for works of art in public places and individual fellowships for visual artists. By analyzing the NEA's grant awards to painters and sculptors in these two areas, I demonstrate that federal support for the visual arts was less radical than many now believe. Rather, the Visual Arts Program in the 1960s and early 1970s funded modern abstract art of a nature that was politically acceptable and by then already long revered in the art world. While American visual art in the 1960s embraced pop, minimalism, performance, feminist, black, and Chicano arts that were more critical of American society, federal art support continued to favor older modernist forms. NEA grants tilted especially toward abstract expressionist and color field artists, who had risen to dominate the art world in the 1950s and whose works were seen as the best representation of American freedom during the Cold War.

The Origins of the NEA

Essentially, the National Council on the Arts was a product of Cold War–era liberalism and the ideology stressing excellence and problem solving that underlined the Kennedy and Johnson administrations. Establishing a federal arts policy was a measure designed to combat what many 1950s critics had labeled as the debased and increasingly materialistic nature of American culture in an age of abundance. Social critics of the 1950s, such as William Whyte, lamented the rise of the "Organization Man," who sacrificed his rugged individualism and drive for achievement to gain acceptance as a team player and enjoy the material rewards of a corporate salary. At the same time, cultural critics like Dwight Macdonald bemoaned the rise of mass culture, arguing that although democracy was desirable politically, it produced unfortunate results culturally by promoting the spread of "kitsch" rather than high culture.[2]

John Kenneth Galbraith and Arthur Schlesinger Jr. brought these strains of intellectual thought directly into national politics when they became advisers to President Kennedy and encouraged him to halt the potentially destructive downward spiral of American culture and to use government powers to extend the virtues and reward of American life to all U.S. citizens.[3] Extolling the artist as a quintessential American individual who worked diligently amid deprivation and loneliness to hone his skills and realize his vision, Kennedy promoted artistic individualism as a means of countering the deleterious affects of American mass culture and materialism. President Johnson was also encouraged by intellectuals to use his executive office to emphasize moral values rather than material ones. He maintained the hope that his administration would mark a new era of a postaffluent society that could overcome the problems of the 1950s. He asserted that the Great Society should be a "place where men are more concerned with the quality of their goals than the quantity of their goods."[4]

The perceived increase in American complacency was not only condemned for its decadence, however. On a broader scale, many intellectuals and consensus politicians feared that self-satisfaction and material indulgence would undermine American's ability to compete in a Cold War world. The Soviet launch of the satellite *Sputnik* contrasted with the initial failures of American space rockets, heightened such fear and produced an outpouring of literature, such as the famous tracts "Why Johnny Can't Read and Ivan Can" or "What Ivan Knows That Johnny Doesn't," each seeking to understand how Americans had lost their edge and explain what should be done about it.[5] Most agreed that material success meant little if education, creativity, and achievement failed to maintain American prestige and international leadership. In the early 1960s, arts policy was reevaluated as a Cold War measure, which would foster American ingenuity and display American devotion to humanism and free expression. Kennedy proclaimed that

the artist . . . becomes the last champion of the individual mind and sensibility against an intrusive society and an officious state. . . . I look forward to an America which will steadily raise the standards of artistic accomplishment and which will steadily enlarge cultural opportunities for all of our citizens, . . . an America which commands respect throughout the world not only for its strength but for its civilization as well.[6]

Kennedy had concluded that in the Cold War era the freedom of artists represented a fundamental American value posing an alternative to totalitarianism. He noted that "in Soviet Russia, Chairman Khrushchev has informed us, 'it is the highest duty of the Soviet writer, artist and composer . . . to be in the ranks of the builders of communism, . . . to fight for the triumph of the ideas of Marxism-Leninism.' "Americans were reminded of Soviet denunciations of

Figure 7.1. President Lyndon Baines Johnson swearing in the first members of the National Council on the Arts, Washington, April 9, 1965. Photograph courtesy of the Lyndon Baines Johnson Presidential Library.

abstract art exhibits in Moscow and were encouraged to draw the conclusion that American modern artists were to be praised for their style and that American citizens were to be congratulated for their tolerance and vision in accepting abstract modernism. Kennedy argued that the 1960s would be a new age for knowledge and pluralism, which would enable the United States to beat the communists and celebrate freedom and democracy. The arts would be a beautiful way to do so.

In the fall of 1963, President Kennedy established the National Advisory Council on the Arts by an executive order and was scheduled to announce the appointments of its first members in November when he was assassinated. Lyndon Johnson appointed the first council in 1965 just before the passage of legislation establishing the National Endowment for the Arts and the National Endowment for the Humanities. To show his support for the arts, Johnson held the first meeting of the National Council on the Arts in the White House (figure 7.1). Johnson and council chair Roger Stevens discussed their responsibility in "raising the cultural level" in America and using their leadership "to recognize the highest standards of excellence." Johnson cautioned the council that the stakes of their endeavors could well be the "survival of our entire society."[7]

The National Council on the Arts

By all accounts, the first National Council on the Arts was an illustrious assembly of prestigious artists representing numerous fields of artistic expression—including dance, theater, opera, music, literature, the visual arts, and museum development. Its members included the actor Gregory Peck, the author Ralph Ellison, the composer Leonard Bernstein, and the classical musician Isaac Stern; among the few female members were the choreographer Agnes de Mille and the actress Elizabeth Ashley. The notability of each member on this original council marks it as extraordinary, as did its mandate to organize the new arts endowment and set forth its goals. There is no question that it held a great deal more power and willingness to act than the present-day NEA councils, which are bound by increased regulations and decreased finances. In 1965, all were aware that they were embarking on a federal art policy experiment that would determine the future of federal support for the arts and that they hoped would encourage American appreciation for artistic achievement.

The council immediately set out to develop an official policy statement and structural outline for the new arts agency. With its first public breath, the council pronounced:

> With increased leisure, and widespread education, it is imperative that the federal government support the arts more actively, and provide leadership and resources to advance the arts to a point where our national inner life may be continuously expressed and defined. . . .
>
> In a society which has always been marked by that special disorder which comes of vast spaces, a highly diversified people, great natural and technical resources, and a rapid tempo of historical change, the arts are here of utmost importance—not only as a moral force, but as a celebration of the American experience which encourages, clarifies and points to the next direction in our struggle to achieve the promise of our democracy. . . .
>
> The Council is convinced that the arts, at the highest level of excellence, must become an enriching part of the daily life of the American people.[8]

The statement reflects both the ideological origins of the NEA and its future development. The council's insistence that the federal government provide leadership in the arts at a time of increasing leisure echoes ideological antecedents from the late 1950s and early 1960s. In addition, its call for mustering the federal government's resources to advance the promise of American democracy resounded Great Society aims. The council then went on to organize specific projects to accomplish its goals, one of which was the award of individual grants to artists under a visual arts program.

It is important to consider the backgrounds and aesthetic tastes of the council's visual arts leaders for two reasons. First, their work and reputations were critical in gaining the president's attention and contributing to their appointment to the council; thus, their selection reveals the aesthetic preferences of the White House and the president's vision for visual arts administration. Second, once chosen for the council, they set the tone for NEA visual arts program development and artistic grant selection. In both respects, the council members' specific interests and influence in American aesthetics (modernist painting and sculpture) were pivotal. Theirs became the standard by which political and cultural ideology was transformed into a tangible visual arts program.

The styles and interests of those rejected for council membership are also worth noting, because their rebuff reinforced the development of what would become the dominant high art (modernist) forms promoted by the NEA, often at the expense of other popular art forms. The Kennedy administration's recommendations for arts advisory council membership were initially more wide-ranging than the final form of the arts council would suggest. Original White House files reveal that Kennedy was considering the appointment of the artists Andrew Wyeth and Ben Shahn.[9] Each met the criterion of mastery in their fields of American painting and, significantly, both were primarily representational painters. Wyeth is perhaps best known for his figurative scenes and portraits and for being one of the more famous American painters who did not succumb to the abstract style that dominated the American scene after the 1940s. Likewise, Shahn is one of the notable social realist painters who gained attention during the 1930s for his figurative works, often depicting social scenes with an unmistakable political commentary. One example of his oeuvre would be *The Passion of Sacco and Vanzetti, 1931–32*, which presented sympathetic illustrations of the two executed anarchists in their coffins and implied a critique of the American legal system that had condemned them. Neither Wyeth nor Shahn produced work that would have been considered high art by culture brokers in the early 1960s, and neither was appointed to the council.

Another figure considered by the Johnson administration was the art critic and writer Susan Sontag. Sontag was young, bold, and rapidly making a name for herself in the art world, and she would certainly have added flair to the council and expanded its aesthetic sensibilities as a whole, because she might be classified as more forward looking and postmodernist than most. Moreover, she would have been highly desirable to expand the representation of women on the arts council, which turned out to be quite low. Nevertheless, she was ultimately discarded because of her position against the war in Vietnam, which became widely known and angered the president.[10]

The rejection of these artists signifies that political leaders ultimately did not want representational artists or controversial ones on the council. The bulk of those considered and those appointed reinforced the White House's and art institutions' preferences for modernism. Both the Kennedy and Johnson administrations proposed more abstract painters and sculptors, including Philip Guston, Willem de Kooning, Robert Motherwell, and Helen Frankenthaler, who eventually became a council member in 1984. As is the case for all these painters, Frankenthaler's work figures prominently in the abstract style. She uses multiple layers of paint stain washed on her canvases, usually with a central design motif. It is also completely abstract and focused on design and color.[11]

One of the most important artists appointed to the arts council was the renowned sculptor David Smith. His work centers on welded and polished metal sculpted in abstract designs generally on a monumental scale, as is true for his series titled *Cubi* (figure 7.2). These pieces are constructed of polished stainless steel and, like abstract paintings, concentrate on forms and linear relationships, in this case on a three-dimensional scale. Smith believed metal sculpture could best symbolize modern industrial society and represent American achievement.[12] Tragically, Smith died in an automobile accident in 1966 and was soon replaced by another abstract artist.

Smith's successor was the California painter Richard Diebenkorn. Although Diebenkorn experimented with both abstract and representational work, he demonstrated a greater interest in formalism and exploring fields of color and geometric design in relation to the flatness and shape of his canvases, which shows up even in his more representational work. Examples of his style include *Berkeley No. 22* (figure 7.3) and the *Ocean Park* series. These are oversized "monumental" canvases and very much in the abstract style favored by the art world in the late 1950s.

René d'Harnoncourt and Henry Geldzahler represented the museum world's point of view on the National Council on the Arts. D'Harnoncourt had been the director of the Museum of Modern Art in New York since the late 1950s. Thus, at the time of his appointment to the arts council, d'Harnoncourt headed an art institution containing what is considered one of the most comprehensive collections of modern art in the world and was dedicated to modern art forms.

Like d'Harnoncourt, Geldzahler also came to the council as a museum curator and contemporary art aficionado with an interest in federal government art sponsorship. He began his career as a curator of contemporary art at the Metropolitan Museum of Art. In his position at the Met, Geldzahler consistently promoted modernist, abstract art and aided in the rise of contemporary artists, such as Jules Olitski, Helen Frankenthaler, Kenneth Noland, Roy Lichtenstein, Frank Stella, and Jasper Johns. He himself participated in several of

Figure 7.2. David Smith, *Cubi XII*, Washington, 1963. Art © the Estate of David Smith / licensed by VAGA, New York. Hirshhorn Museum and Sculpture Garden, Smithsonian Institution; gift of the Joseph H. Hirshhorn Foundation, 1972.

Figure 7.3. Richard Diebenkorn, *Berkeley No. 22*, Washington, 1954. Courtesy the Estate of Richard Diebenkorn. Hirshhorn Museum and Sculpture Garden, Smithsonian Institution, Regents Collections Acquisition Program, 1986.

Claus Oldenburg's "happenings" and became the subject of an Andy Warhol film, which featured him smoking a cigar for ninety minutes. Despite this sometime affiliation with notable pop artists, Geldzahler ultimately concluded that pop art was "interesting" but not a major movement, whereas he remained committed to what he considered more timeless and generative movements, such as abstract expressionist, color field art, and monumental sculpture. In 1969, Geldzahler organized a major modernist exhibition called New York Painting and Sculpture:1940–1970, and he explained to *Newsweek* that he gave abstract expressionists special consideration because "no period, not even the Renaissance, has ever had forty-three major artists," as the American abstract expressionist period had. Geldzahler's argument placed him firmly in the company of established American art critics and museum directors.[13]

Eventually, in 1977, Geldzahler departed the Met in controversy when he participated in a secret trade of six traditional paintings, including a Renoir, for two contemporary works by David Smith and Richard Diebenkorn—who were both members of the National Council on the Arts along with Geldzahler. In addition, Geldzahler was further isolated from other Met officials after he refused to organize what later became a highly popular Andrew Wyeth exhibit. (He left in 1977 to become the New York City cultural affairs commissioner.) Of course, these controversies were long after he secured a position on the arts council and departed from it, though they do reveal something of his artistic taste. It was Geldzahler's recognized influence as a contemporary art curator and his well-known defense of those he considered the best representatives of modern American art that gained him notice as a confident voice in the field of visual arts. This earned him a position of influence on the National Council on the Arts.

The Visual Arts Program

The National Council on the Arts developed the original concept for the Visual Arts Program during a series of meetings between 1965 and 1967. Most significant among these was a gathering of a subcommittee on the visual arts in the spring of 1966. This subcommittee, of d'Harnoncourt, Geldzahler, Diebenkorn, and Motherwell, outlined a program of grants that would accomplish the following: (1) allow artists to work in schools to develop art programs and heighten student's awareness of the arts; (2) underwrite the production and distribution of modern art prints; (3) enable museums to purchase works by contemporary American artists; (4) fund individual painters, sculptors, and photographers to enable them to develop their talents; and (5) encourage cities to purchase and display sculptures on public property. While programs for artists in schools and the museum purchase plan eventually developed into larger entities warranting their own programs, the major thrust of the Visual Arts Program centered on the funding of individual artists, allowing them to advance their work as they wished.

In the earliest days of the program, the council itself had a great deal of influence over its grants. Council members solicited applications from artists and organizations they considered worthy of support. Indeed, during the first year it would not have been unheard of for artists to be considered for money for which they had not applied. At first, individual artist awards were made on the basis of "recognition of past contributions" to the field of visual arts. Thus, when Geldzahler initially conceptualized artists awards, he drew upon what he and the established art critics and culture brokers considered to be the best in American art in the early 1960s—primarily abstract expressionist and color field painting and abstract monumental and minimalist sculpture.

In one of the first actions to support the visual arts, the NEA organized a print workshop to reproduce modern art and distribute it to smaller museums and schools. The goal behind these grants was twofold: both to funnel money to contemporary American artists and to encourage the display of modern artwork for more of the American public. Among those whose works were reproduced were such modern artists as Robert Motherwell, Willem de Kooning, Louise Nevelson, Helen Frankenthaler, and Philip Guston.[14] Again, the dominance of a modernist abstract style is clear among these prints.

The first visual arts grant was given out under the NEA's Art in Public Places Program. This award stemmed from a visit Geldzahler paid to the Grand Rapids Art Museum in 1967. While giving a lecture there, he was introduced to the museum vice president, Nancy Mulnix, who then showed him through a large plaza that was to become the center of the city's urban renewal program. Geldzahler mentioned the newly formed Art in Public Places Program and encouraged the city to apply for a grant to secure a sculpture for the plaza. Only a month later, the NEA awarded city of Grand Rapids $45,000 for a public sculpture, provided the city could match the grant and would commission an American artist. A panel of NEA and city art consultants selected the sculptor Alexander Calder because of his excellent reputation and because the panel wished to commission a large-scale, colorful piece that would dominate the plaza. The result was the installation of *La Grande Vitesse* in 1969—a massive iron sculpture in the monumental abstract style preferred by arts administrators and painted a bright red to announce its presence in the plaza (figure 7.4). At the dedication ceremony, Representative Gerald Ford noted with pride, "This is a dramatic and significant moment in the life of our community because it illuminates our city in the eyes of all of us and . . . those of the State, of the Nation, of the World."[15]

The federal government, the NEA, the State of Michigan, and the City of Grand Rapids and its citizens celebrated the sculpture as a great achievement and testament to the successful marriage of policy and aesthetics. Initially, some residents complained that it was too abstract and unrecognizable and that they simply did not understand it. Although this controversy surrounding the Calder sculpture faded, similar arguments would be made regarding other NEA projects, which were primarily abstract and monumental.

The Art in Public Places Program became much larger and more formalized as the years progressed. From the National Council on the Arts' original conception of it as "Awards of Excellence" to major American sculptors, the program developed into one that was less controlled by NEA officials and more of a collaboration between NEA and city representatives. The Visual Arts Program initiated a joint panel system through which three NEA panel members and three city art professionals would review the site and select the artist for the commission. Initially, this new process changed little about the art se-

Figure 7.4. Alexander Calder, *La Grande Vitesse*, Grand Rapids, 1969. Courtesy of the artist and the City of Grand Rapids.

lection trends but gave local officials and the public a greater sense of participation in the grant process, even if they often deferred to NEA Visual Arts
representatives.

As it was originally conceived, the Art in Public Places Program was to focus on promoting three large-scale public sculptures a year. In its first three
years, the program actually funded only one large sculpture annually. However, from this humble beginning, it grew into a division of the Visual Arts Program that awarded a significant number of grants for public art—sculptures,
murals, and prints—twenty-two in 1973, thirty-one in 1974, and thirty-six in
1975. Overwhelmingly, the sculptures commissioned for public sites were abstract and monumental works. Among the public sculpture grants awarded between 1967 and 1975, 95 percent were abstract, while only 5 percent of the
pieces were figurative.[16]

The Art in Public Places Program also funded commissions for public mural projects, acquisitions of prints and paintings for public locations, and special projects for which cities applied for matching funds. These grants consisted
of 40 percent of the program funding, 86 percent of which went to mural projects. My research in this area has been limited due to incomplete records and
the frequent selection of lesser-known artists for many municipal mural projects. However, from the available sources, it is clear that mural projects included both abstract and figurative illustrations that reflected community life.

Unlike the large-scale public sculptures placed in one location, generally in a city center, mural projects often subdivided grants to several artists whose work could be spread out across a larger urban area. Such projects targeted inner cities with the dual aims of community development and urban renewal. These goals had been emphasized by political leaders, such as President Johnson, under the rubric of his War on Poverty and community action programs, and by the arts council. City planners and arts commissions reiterated them in their proposals to the NEA, indicating that local areas had taken up the ideals expressed on a national level. The Boston Foundation's Summerthing festival application for a mural grant argued that "art can make the city civilized again" by giving local minority artists means to express pent-up energy and to "resist the bleakness and blind walls of decaying parts of the city." It was hoped that murals would visually transform rundown areas and "help to catalyze social change."[17]

To this end, the NEA awarded the Boston Foundation a $5,000 grant in 1970 and another $20,000 in 1971 with the agreement that half the funds would be allocated to black artists in the Boston area. The foundation and the NEA also hoped that the abstract artist Frank Stella would be commissioned for a mural, but they were disappointed that details for a contract with him could not be arranged in time. Instead, in 1970 the foundation granted several awards of $500 to $600 to local artists for various community murals. These included funds to Sharon Dunn, a black teacher, who constructed a frieze of pregnant women in front of a low-cost housing project; an award to Keiko Prince, a Japanese artist, for executing a brilliantly colored abstract design in a North End Italian community area; and a grant to Maria Cordez to paint a mural in Fields Corner which, according to the foundation, "transformed a hideous Parks Department wall . . . [and provided] an alternative to outright destruction."[18]

The NEA awarded similar grants to the cities of New York, Chicago, and Los Angeles. Mural projects reached wider locations within municipal areas but received consistently smaller grants than those for large public works. On average, mural grants were for amounts between $5,000 and $10,000, while sculpture grants were between $25,000 and $50,000. In part, this was due to the less costly nature of mural art. Nonetheless, the thrust of public sculpture coincided more closely with NEA officials' aesthetic sensibilities and desires to promote modernist abstract art. Eventually, the public mural movement lost some momentum in the later 1970s as community activism waned, and the Visual Arts Program cut back its mural project grants.

Individual Fellowships

The NEA's modernist vision also influenced the development of the first awards to individual painters and sculptors in the form of visual arts fellowships. When the NEA was in its developmental phase, artists had already begun to request funds for their work by writing directly to the Johnson White House or to NEA chair Roger Stevens. At that point, procedures had not yet been established and funds could not yet be disbursed.[19]

By 1967, such requests were being forwarded to the new Visual Arts Program to handle. Despite outside interest by artists in possible visual arts awards, the program remained relatively unknown and loosely organized during its first two years of operation. Initially, fellowships were not awarded based upon letters and grant applications. Rather, selection was determined by nominations solicited from museum directors, art critics, art magazine editors, and artists.[20] Established art institution leaders who were approached by Geldzahler determined which aesthetic was best suited for recognition. The first visual arts fellowships were awarded to individual painters and sculptors in 1967 on the basis of such nominations. This inaugural group of fellowships consisted of sixty awards of $5,000 each. They were given to artists to develop their careers by setting aside time and purchasing materials for their work. The artists could spend the funds as they saw fit. Thus, the grants were not awards for commissions of particular art pieces but more resembled bonuses that affirmed the artists' achievement in the field.

An analysis of this group of fellowships indicates that the solicitation and nomination process had a significant influence on the award of funds to artists in certain fields of painting and sculpture who were deemed worthy of support among the small group of established arts leaders making the selections. The first group of grantees included such artists as Robert Goodnough, Donald Judd, Agnes Martin, Richard Stankiewicz, Theodoros Stamos, and George Sugarman, who were all well-known painters and sculptors. These and many of the other grantees also conformed to a modernist aesthetic. Of the awards granted in 1967 by the Visual Arts Program, 67 percent were given to abstract artists, 7 percent went to artists whose work contained both abstraction and figuration, and only 5 percent went to purely representational artists.[21]

Typical of the kinds of work awarded funds in this first group was that of Robert Goodnough. He had staked his claim in the world of abstract painting during the 1950s, developing works that incorporated analytical studies of form and color with expressions of motion. He drew on art historical traditions stemming from analytic cubism, like that of Piet Mondrian, to American abstract expressionism, but he added his own mark through his recognizable geometric shapes.[22] For example, his work *Movement of Horses* combines a gray-toned color field background with a flurry of geometric shapes in various color shades that signify motion in the central portion of the canvas (figure 7.5). In 1962, *Newsweek* magazine announced that Goodnough had "arrived" with the distinction of working in "two or three styles at once." Not long afterward, *Art News* proclaimed him as one of the more complex painterly artists of his day.[23] Thus, Goodnough was a critically acclaimed abstractionist well before receiving his NEA Visual Arts Program award in 1967.

Figure 7.5. Robert Goodnough, *Movement of Horses B*, Washington, 1961. Courtesy of the artist. Hirshhorn Museum and Sculpture Garden, Smithsonian Institution; gift of Joseph H. Hirshhorn, 1966.

Generally, the NEA and the art world as a whole considered the first individual visual artist awards a great accomplishment. *Art News* lauded Stevens and Geldzahler's leadership and announced that the NEA's first awards were the "best list of grants (or prizes, or honors, call them what you will) that we have ever seen in the field."[24] Yet some people outside the close-knit circle of abstract painters complained that the awards reflected too great an interest in abstract forms. Representative Theodore Kupferman brought to the attention of the House of Representatives the objections of Francis Vandeveer Kughler, a portrait painter and muralist, former president of the Salmagundi Club, and president of the Hotel des Artistes in New York. Kughler protested before Senator Claiborne Pell and the Senate Special Subcommittee on the Arts that the majority of NEA funds were unfairly given to modern artists rather than representational ones.[25] His call for a more equitable balance joined with others advocating more traditional forms.[26]

In one Senate hearing, the artist Michael Werboff captured congressional leaders' attention with his colorful objections to modern abstract art. He displayed a print of an abstract expressionist work done by Willem de Kooning as typical of modern art. Then he held up another canvas of indistinguishable forms and informed the committee that the second work had been done, not by a human artist, but by a monkey! This juxtaposition served as his proof that modernist forms were unworthy of federal support. Endowment officials reacted quickly to this attack, defending the intellectual and aesthetic validity of modernism. More tellingly, Deputy Chair Livingston Biddle quietly informed the committee that the artist who had spoken so disparagingly about modern art was in fact a Russian and, of course, Russians were known for their distaste of abstract art. This news checked any further questioning of the art grants by the congressional leaders, who wished to avoid being goaded by a "communist" into curtailing American artistic freedom.[27] Such a response would have been considered less than patriotic in the Cold War era while competition with the Soviet Union remained strong on all levels.

In the end, while leaders such as Senator Pell listened sympathetically to the complaints, they ultimately defended the NEA's policies and grants and upheld the congressional policy of noninterference in NEA procedures. Their actions confirmed that it was more politically acceptable to support freedom of expression than their personal tastes—even though, ironically, that meant supporting the high modernist tastes of cultural officials at the time.

Thereafter, Senator Pell would periodically ask the NEA for a list of artist awards by style, to indicate that he monitored the NEA's selections and encouraged it to maintain a balance of support for both modernist abstraction and more realist forms. The NEA complied fully to the request for a list. However, it prepared the list's content creatively. Officials defined as "representational" any art style that contained recognizable elements, so that the proportion of grants could be perceived as more equally distributed among the abstract and representational art forms.[28] A more objective analysis of the NEA Visual Arts Program grants reveals that such a balance was rarely achieved in the actual awards of grants to individual artists. NEA visual arts fellowships manifest the aesthetic ideals held by the National Council on the Arts and Visual Arts Program leaders and advisers who selected the painters and sculptors for awards. However, this became more subtle once the NEA developed formal application procedures and organized peer panels of "experts in the field" to select finalists for awards. Still, expert advice was solicited from among notable modernist-oriented artists, critics, and museum directors, who tended to select artists whose work complemented their own taste and definitions of aesthetic excellence.[29] Criticism of their choices from more avant-garde and left-wing artists and arts supporters drew little response.

As the number of panelists and amount of funding increased, NEA staff formalized program procedures and adjusted award policy. During its first year or two of administration, the Visual Arts Program had granted awards to artists primarily in recognition of past achievement. By 1969, individual fellowships were granted to artists for the production of future work. This policy marked a return to the original arts council ideal of granting funds to individual artists to use as they saw fit to advance their career. Artists still submitted portfolios of past work as part of their application résumé to be reviewed by the panels; however, individual painters and sculptors did not propose specific projects to which the award of funds would be applied. If chosen, they could use NEA funds however they wished.

Not only was this policy shift a reemphasis of Visual Arts Program goals to support artistic talent and individual creativity, it was also a coup for the program in protecting itself against criticism for funding modernist art that might not have pleased those with more traditional tastes—especially members of congressional committees such as the aforementioned Senate subcommittee that questioned the disproportionate funding of abstract artists. Wishing to avoid potential conflict over specific awards, NEA chair Nancy Hanks quietly advised the Visual Arts Program staff to delete proposals for projects from grant applications.[30] Thus, by having highly regarded artist panelists review an application and award funds based solely on an individual's noted talent, the Visual Arts Program fulfilled the NEA's mission of advancing the careers of excellent artists without the risk of funding a proposal that could be criticized. The new Visual Arts Program director, Brian O'Doherty, considered this a brilliant move by Hanks in defending individual artists' freedom.[31]

O'Doherty took over the reins as the director of the Visual Arts Program from Henry Geldzahler in 1969, and during the next five years he guided the expansion of the program while guarding its modernist vision. Like Geldzahler, he came to the NEA from New York and, while working for the endowment, retained a full time job in the art world as the editor of *Art in America* magazine from 1971 to 1974. He was also an artist, who practiced under the name Patrick Ireland. O'Doherty's work revealed an enchantment with abstract, color field, and minimalist art, but he also gravitated toward newer forms of conceptual art, which he encouraged the Visual Arts Program to fund.[32] Yet his somewhat more postmodern views developed toward the mid-1970s and did not sway the NEA to dramatically change directions in its art funding policies.

NEA grants to individual painters and sculptors between 1967 and 1975 reflected a distinctly modernist preference. Individual artists who displayed abstract expressionist, color field, and geometric abstractionist aesthetics received the majority of the funds allocated by the NEA for painters and sculptors, averaging 75 percent or more of each year's awards. Second to these in the number of awards received were those artists who practiced figurative or conceptual work—styles that remained primarily abstract in execution, while often incorporating recognizable elements into the overall scheme of the painting or sculpture. This second group received approximately 15 to 20 percent of the funds. Finally, realists and neorealists consistently received the smallest number of awards, amounting to less than 10 percent a year.[33]

Many of the artists who received grants were notable figures in the 1960s art scene, especially in the areas of abstract painting and minimalist sculpture. Edward Avedisian, Darby Bannard, Dan Christensen, Ron Davis, Friedel

Dzubas, Al Held, Richard Pousette-Dart, Dorothea Rockburne, and Mary Miss were among the individual painters recognized for the excellence displayed in their abstract works. Geldzahler had been following many of their careers and believed these young artists out of the abstract tradition were growing in stature and accomplishment.[34] Many of Christensen's paintings of the 1960s looked almost like minimalist versions of Jackson Pollock's work, with intersecting, colorful lines of paint swirled onto an otherwise barren canvas, although they also hint at other emerging artists' fascinations with neon. Bannard's work resembled more of a color field than gestural style of abstract expressionism. His paintings showed a concern with distinct and overlapping triangular constructions washed onto the canvas in muted colors. Davis, conversely, explored the cube form, and thus the formalism and construction of space on the canvas as well as in sculpture. Each of these artists emerged from the historical tradition of post–World War II American abstract painting, and each was rewarded for extending its life by some of the older generation's artistic figures who sat on the arts council and the visual arts panels.[35]

This is certainly true of Pousette-Dart, who became one of the most acclaimed among this group. He was influenced by abstract expressionism and studies of American myths and symbols in the 1940s and 1950s as he began working with modernist abstract designs and forms. In fact, Geldzahler considered him part of the abstract expressionist generation.[36] As Pousette-Dart's work matured, he synthesized his style into a purely abstract "sheer optical saturation," which provided "no forms, shapes, or images to serve as convenient points of reference."[37] His paintings concentrated his aesthetic vision into a focused area of space and demanded that the viewer consider it emotionally and subjectively, suspending comparisons of the art with material forms. Critics have described these works as spiritual and transcendental in the same way that Mark Rothko's works were considered expressions of an ageless and universal human understanding. Many cultural leaders, including NEA officials, believed such expressions perfectly represented universality and desires for beauty and truth rather than materialism and militarism in a nuclear age.[38] Pousette-Dart had his own full-scale retrospective at New York's Whitney Museum in 1963 and was acclaimed as a giant in color field painting with close ties to his contemporaries in abstract expressionism in the early 1960s. His stature and the obscure but positively interpreted aspects of his paintings made him an attractive Visual Arts Program awardee.

Individual sculptors who received NEA awards were an even more immediately recognizable group than the painters. These grantees included Dan Flavin, Donald Judd, Carl André, Mark di Suvero, Sol LeWitt, Robert Irwin, Charles Ginnever, Richard Serra, Tony Smith, Larry Bell, and Nancy Holt, among others. Almost all the sculptors selected by the NEA for awards worked with monumental abstract styles, often incorporating the use of new materials such as steel alloys, Plexiglas, environmental elements, and neon. By and large they were also minimalists, who streamlined the elements and concepts of their art into simple executions.

Di Suvero's work expressed many of the ideals that these NEA grantees offered both aesthetically and intellectually through their art. His sculptures presented large-scale combinations of welded metal and natural elements, such as wood, often painted brightly in reds or yellows. On occasion, he included recognizable human-made pieces such as a chair or a tire in his work, and he always strove to achieve a balance of natural, oppositional forces in his sculpture. His sculpture entitled *Isis* was a monumental steel piece architecturally employing long steel beams welded into a horselike structure that suspended another large metal panel from wires and hooks at its front. Similarly, *Are Years What? (For Marianne Moore)* (1967) used steel beams to form a tall, angular support structure from which a large V-shaped section dangled by wires and hooks (figure 7.6).

Di Suvero's work has been described by some as the sculptural equivalent to the bold linear strokes of a Franz Kline abstract expressionist painting.[39] More aptly, he realized an aesthetic akin to that of the arts council member David Smith, focusing on using a material that symbolized Western technology and power—steel. After receiving his award, di Suvero told the NEA that it helped him to effectively advance his career by allowing him to purchase a crane that he used like "a paintbrush . . . to do what every modern sculptor has dreamed of: to use industrial scale and size in sculpture."[40] Yet he also appreciated "the edge of irony in using [steel] . . . to provoke memory and emotion; to express universal, primordial forms . . . in a state of gently precarious equilibrium." He believed his art was a means of expressing modern human emotions in tangible form and, more important, connecting humankind across space and time in new possibilities of cooperation.[41] For di Suvero, such connections were meant to express not just American national unity but also a sense of international cooperation and understanding. He understood that these sensibilities and hopes were important in a modern, Cold War world. His hopeful expressions and abstract aesthetics were engaging to art critics and cultural leaders in the same way that abstract expressionism had been.

However, while di Suvero's aesthetic lineage stemmed directly from the abstract expressionism that politicians and culture brokers used as a Cold War weapon, he was also a member of a younger generation of artists who began to challenge Cold War rhetoric by the late 1960s. He so strongly advocated peace that he participated with other artists opposed to the Vietnam War in building the Peace Tower in Los Angeles in 1966, and he later left the United States between 1971 and 1975 after President Richard Nixon began bombing Cambodia.[42] Amid these activities, he received his first NEA grant as an individual artist in 1967 and was again awarded grants in 1971 and 1972 for commissions of sculptures under the Art in Public Places Program. Thus, his antiwar stance did not prevent his recognition by the federal arts agency. In fact,

Figure 7.6. Mark di Suvero, *Are Years What? (For Marianne Moore)*, Washington, 1967. Courtesy of the artist and Spacetime C. C. Hirshhorn Museum and Sculpture Garden, Smithsonian Institution; Joseph H. Hirshhorn Purchase Fund and gift of the Institute of Scrap Recycling Industries, by exchange, 1999. Photograph by Lee Stalsworth.

NEA officials struggled to maintain the principles of artistic freedom and non-political awards that had been established in its authorizing legislation.

The NEA was not so generous to nonmodernist or "postmodernist" artists, who were routinely overlooked or marginalized in the award process. Pop art, feminist, ethnic, folk, and performance art did not begin to garner individual visual arts awards until late in this period, although these genres were gaining increasing attention in the art world by the late 1960s and early 1970s.[43] The NEA began craft awards in 1973, and folk art was later recognized under its own program after 1978, which served not only the visual arts but also music, dance, literature, and performances.[44] A very small number of new representational arts were recognized, including neorealist or hyperrealist works by artists like Richard Estes and Philip Pearlstein. Nevertheless, these awards were not significant in number to signal any shift in Visual Arts Program trends.

Thus, NEA visual arts awards were not as pluralist as some have suggested. Ann Galligan and Elaine King have celebrated the NEA as a democratic and pluralist art institution.[45] And in his recent work *Visionaries and Outcasts,*

Michael Brenson has argued that the NEA focused on the "creative process," its fellowships "rewarded risk taking," and the "majority of panel members were attentive to the unfamiliar."[46] I have found the contrary. Far from being "outcasts," modernist artists and devotees were insiders at the NEA. In its first decade, the endowment was more conservative in its visual arts funding than it became in the late 1970s. Between 1967 and 1975, the Visual Arts Program awarded individual artists who carried on in the celebrated traditions of abstract expressionism, color field painting, and minimalist, monumental sculpture, which had been the proven champions both in the art world and in the successful cooperation between art and politics. Political leaders, cultural officials, and in many cases artists who belonged to the first generation of abstract expressionists believed that this genre best represented American freedom and used it to highlight the ideals of American democracy in international exhibitions.[47] Their outlook, which stemmed from the Cold War context of the 1950s, remained in place during the 1960s and 1970s. It became manifest in NEA policy as political leaders selected cultural leaders from the older generation for the National Council on the Arts, and they in turn chose likeminded artists and cultural leaders to head the Visual Arts Program. Evidence indicates that this program initially focused its attention on recognizing artists whose aesthetics continued to represent the tried-and-true marriage of abstract art and Cold War politics. Eventually, as Americans began to change their views and the Cold War consensus began to collapse, artists' styles also began to change and to increasingly incorporate figurative and sometimes controversial content. The NEA did little to keep apace with these transformations until well into the 1970s.

Conclusion

The Visual Arts Program accomplished much of what the National Council on the Arts and program directors organized it to achieve. Its leaders and expert consultants set a standard for excellence in the form of modernist painting and sculpture and rewarded hundreds of individual artists who met those standards. In contrast to the now widespread perception of the NEA, and the Visual Arts Program in particular, as a leader and radical supporter of an ultraliberal avant-garde, evidence demonstrates that the agency generally favored more conventional art forms. Just as in opera, music (classical), theater, and museums, which were its major funding programs, the NEA supported long-established arts.[48] The arts administration analyst Edward Arian has claimed that the "cultural preferences of elites . . . are the result of a self-perpetuating circle of conservatism wherein traditional organizations . . . continue to satisfy elite demands for the tried-and-true repertoire."[49]

For the NEA Visual Arts Program, such a repertoire was modernist. Visual arts trends change at a more rapid rate than that for classical music, opera, and theater. Museums purchasing Impressionist paintings support an art form that is 100 years old and has been the staple of fine painting for at least a half century, whereas classical music and opera remain focused on centuries-old standards. Seldom, and only very cautiously, do these arts accept newer genres. The Visual Arts Program clearly celebrated abstract expressionist and color field painting and monumental abstract sculpture—post–World War II modernist forms that by the 1960s had become "classical" and standard visual art forms.

By the time these modernist arts were supported by the NEA as the epitome of fine arts achievement, they no longer represented the most current and pathbreaking forms in the art world. Instead, the avant-garde genres of pop, postminimalism, performance, feminist, black, and ethnic arts, and even folk arts were at the pinnacle of fashion in the late 1960s and 1970s. These were marginalized by the NEA's focus on the more conservative abstract forms, which were considered symbolic of American individuality, risk taking, and free expression.

These qualities had been lauded in opposition to the conformity and control associated with totalitarianism during the 1950s, and American politicians continued to uphold them during the 1960s and early 1970s. Political and cultural leaders hoped that the NEA could use this standard of high culture to model American achievement internationally and to raise the level of American culture in the United States. Abstract art proved particularly desirable in this respect, not only because of its international acclaim but also because it lacked distinguishable—or politically controversial—content, allowing viewers to interpret canvases as they saw fit. At the same time that federal art support was extolling abstract modernism, American art forms returned to more figuration, much of which could be read as political protest during the late 1960s and 1970s, as more of the American public began to question the nation's policies during the Vietnam era.

Not surprisingly, the NEA did not rush to keep pace with awards for these styles. The agency proved only partly successful in attaining its mission to promote excellence and encourage the democratic enjoyment of art. It strove to educate the public in high art appreciation and thus promote a form of social uplift rather than to encourage public enjoyment of popular or mass culture. Its vision of excellence remained defined by modernist art, and the promise of democracy in arts funding remained elusive.

Notes

1. Jesse Helms's remarks were quoted on National Public Radio, *Morning Edition*, March 13, 1995.
2. David Riesman, *The Lonely Crowd* (New Haven, Conn.: Yale University Press, 1950); William Whyte, *The Organization Man* (New York: Simon & Schuster,

1956); Dwight Macdonald, "Masscult and Midcult," in *Against the American Grain,* by Dwight Macdonald (New York: Random House, 1952); Clement Greenberg, "Avante-Garde and Kitsch," *Partisan Review,* 6 (Fall 1939); and Clement Greenberg, "The Plight of Our Culture," *Commentary,* June 1953.

3. John Kenneth Galbraith, *The Affluent Society* (Boston: Houghton Mifflin, 1958); and Arthur Schlesinger Jr., *The Vital Center* (Boston: Houghton Mifflin, 1949) and "The Challenge of Abundance," *Reporter,* May 1956.

4. Lyndon B. Johnson, "Remarks at the University of Michigan," May 22, 1964, in *Public Papers of the President of the United States; Lyndon Baines Johnson* (Washington, D.C.: U.S. Government Printing Office, 1965), vol. 1, 704–7.

5. Arthur Trace, *What Ivan Knows That Johnny Doesn't* (New York: Random House, 1961).

6. John F. Kennedy, "Remarks at Amherst College," October 26, 1963, in *The Public Papers of the President of the United States: John F. Kennedy* (Washington, D.C.: U.S. Government Printing Office, 1964), 815.

7. Lyndon Johnson, "Remarks at the Swearing in of the National Council on the Arts," April 9, 1965, in Harry McPherson Papers, "Arts: The National Council on the Arts," box 4, Lyndon Baines Johnson Presidential Library, Austin (hereafter LBJ Library).

8. "Policy Statement of the National Council on the Arts," 1966, in Papers of the Chairman, Roger Stevens, box 15-21, National Endowment for the Arts (NEA), Washington.

9. White House Central Files, Schlesinger Papers, box 1, "Advisory Council on the Arts," John F. Kennedy Presidential Library, Boston (hereafter JFK Library).

10. John Macy Office Files, "National Endowment for the Arts," box 841–42, LBJ Library.

11. August Heckscher Papers, box 29, JFK Library; and White House Central Files, "National Council on the Arts," box 123, LBJ Library.

12. Garnett McCoy, ed., *David Smith* (New York: Praeger, 1973).

13. Henry Geldzahler, *New York Painting and Sculpture: 1940–1970* (New York: Museum of Modern Art, 1969).

14. The Museum Purchase Plan is discussed and the Gemini Print Workshop is listed as grant number A68-I-15 at $20,000 in "Meeting of the National Council on the Arts, May 12–14, 1967." The prints are also listed in the May 22–24, 1969, meeting, NEA Records, Washington.

15. Gerald Ford as quoted in John Beardsley, *Art in Public Places: A Survey of Community Art Sponsored Projects Supported by the National Endowment for the Arts* (Washington, D.C.: Partners for Livable Places, 1981), 17.

16. Figures were compiled from NEA annual reports, 1967–75; and Beardsley, *Art in Public Places.*

17. Boston Foundation grant applications and report, 1970, NEA, Visual Arts Program, Public Art Projects files, Washington.

18. "Report on Grant to Summerthing 1970 Mural Program," in NEA, Visual Arts Program, Public Art Projects files.

19. Roger Stevens' files and Johnson Presidential Papers contain numerous examples, such as Letter from William Phillips and reply by Roger Stevens, March 10, 1966, in box 3/21, Stevens Files, NEA Papers.

20. Michael Straight, *Nancy Hanks* (Durham, N.C.: Duke University Press, 1988), 285;

and author's interviews with former NEA chair Livingston Biddle and NEA program staff, 1993 and 1996.

21. These percentages are based conservatively on calculations from the database I compiled on visual artists awards. Other sources have determined that the percentage of grants to abstract artists were even higher. Frank Wright, president of the Council of American Artists Societies, complained to Congress that of all sixty awards, only eight went to representational painters. See Fannie Taylor and Anthony Barresi, *The Arts at a New Frontier* (New York: Plenum Press, 1984), 97.

22. For a more detailed account of Goodnough's work and career, see Martin H. Bush and Kenworth Moffett, *Goodnough*, McKnight Fine Arts Center Book (Wichita: University Art Museum, Wichita State University, 1973).

23. *Newsweek*, March 19, 1962; and Irving Sandler, *Art News*, April 1963.

24. *Art News*, February 1967.

25. Theodore R. Kupferman (R-N.Y.), speech in the House of Representatives, November 9, 1967, *Congressional Record: Proceedings and Debates of the 90th Congress, First Session, 1967*, 10415. The Salmagundi Club membership consisted of artists who were more traditionalist in style, and the Hotel des Artistes was a housing complex on the Upper West Side of Manhattan that housed recognized artists, many of whom were also representational and traditionalist painters.

26. E.g., Martin Hannon of the Salmagundi Club wrote to President Richard Nixon in October 1969 to complain about the dominance of modern abstract forms in NEA Visual Arts grants; White House Central Files: Subject Files AR: (Arts), box 1, Nixon Papers, National Archives.

27. Author's interview with Livingston Biddle, November 7, 1996.

28. Several NEA staff members and Livingston Biddle noted that this was a common practice, although I have not discovered any such lists.

29. "Panel Members," Memo from Devon Meade to Roger Stevens, October 4, 1966, Papers of the Chairman, Roger Stevens, National Endowment for the Arts, box 18/20, NEA Papers.

30. Several NEA staff members explained in interviews that when the individual grants were questioned by congressional members, Hanks devised this change to sidestep potential conflict over specific grants and to defend the artists' right to freedom of expression. Her plan worked quite well in preventing criticism while allowing the NEA to fund hundreds of artists for their future work. The individual awards were later brought into question again in the 1980s after the negative publicity over Mapplethorpe, Serano, and the NEA Four. With the downsizing of the NEA in 1995, the individual artists fellowships were eliminated. See "GOP Foes of Tax-Financed Arts Win Victory in House," *Los Angeles Times*, July 14, 1995; and "NEA Plans Nearly 50% Cut in Staff," *Los Angeles Times*, October 19, 1995.

31. Author's interview with Brian O'Doherty, January 4, 1993.

32. Ibid.

33. NEA annual reports, 1967–75.

34. Geldzahler singled out Richard Pousette-Dart, Robert Goodnough, Jack Youngerman, Al Held, Friedel Dzubas, Edward Avedisian, Walter Darby Bannard, and Ron Davis as such noteworthy artists. Henry Geldzahler, *Making It New: Essays, Interviews, and Talks* (New York: Turtle Point Press, 1994), 106.

35. See James N. Wood, *Six Painters: Edward Avedisian, Darby Bannard, Dan Chris-*

tensen, Ron Davis, Larry Poons, Peter Young (Buffalo: Buffalo Fine Arts Academy, 1971).

36. Geldzahler, *Making It New*, 106.

37. Edward F. Fry, "The Mind Behind the Art: Recent Painting of Richard Pousette-Dart," in *Richard Pousette-Dart: Recent Paintings* (New York: ACA Galleries, 1991), 6.

38. Fry calls his work transcendental; ibid., 7. Also see Carter Ratcliff, "Concerning the Spiritual in Pousette-Dart," *Art in America*, November–December 1974, 89–91; and for a discussion of the spiritual aspects of Mark Rothko, Robert Hughes, *The Shock of the New* (New York: Alfred A. Knopf, 1991), 320–23. Art critics hailed abstract expressionism for this ability to express universal human concerns in the Cold War era, as has been noted by Eva Cockcroft in "Abstract Expressionism: Weapon of the Cold War," *Artforum*, June 1974, 39–41; and Serge Guilbaut, *How New York Stole the Idea of Modern Art* (Chicago: University of Chicago Press, 1983).

39. Phyllis Tuchman, *Mark di Suvero: 25 Years of Sculpture and Drawing* (New York: Storm King Art Center, 1985), 1–2.

40. Mark di Suvero response to NEA questionnaire, August 1970, as quoted in NEA *Annual Report*, 1970, 51.

41. Ann Wilson Lloyd, "Gazed into like Crystal," and Gilbert Perlain, "Entretien Avec Mark di Suvero," in *Mark di Suvero: Retrospective 1959–1991* (Nice: Musée d'Art Moderne et d'Art Contemporain, 1991), 21, 24.

42. For a more comprehensive look at artists' participation in creating the Peace Tower, see Therese Schwartz, "The Politicalization of the Avant-Garde," *Art in America*, November–December 1971. At the time of this article's publication, Brian O'Doherty was both the head of the NEA's Visual Arts Program and the editor of *Art in America*. As did others at the NEA, he supported the antiwar movement while working under Richard Nixon.

43. See Barbara Haskell, *Blam! The Explosion of Pop, Mininalism, and Performance, 1958–1964* (New York: Whitney Museum, 1984); Eva Sperling Cockcroft and Holly Barnet-Sanchez, *Signs from the Heart: California Chicano Murals* (Los Angeles: Social and Political Art Resources Center, 1990); and Henry Geldzahler, *Making It New*.

44. See NEA *Annual Reports*, 1973–76.

45. Ann Mary Galligan, *The National Endowment for the Arts and Humanities: An Experiment in Cultural Democracy* (New York: Teachers College, Columbia University, 1989); Elaine King, *Pluralism in the Visual Arts in the United States, 1965–1978: The National Endowment for the Arts—an Influential Force* (Evanston, Ill.: University Microfilms International Dissertation Service, Northwestern University, 1986).

46. Michael Brenson, *Visionaries and Outcasts: The NEA, Congress, and the Place of the Visual Artist in America* (New York: New Press, 2001), 30–32.

47. Guilbaut has argued that even artists who might not have believed in this expression of their artwork allowed others to represent their art in this manner because it was beneficial to their careers. See Guilbaut, *How New York Stole the Idea of Modern Art*; and Cockcroft, "Abstract Expressionism."

48. The NEA's Music Program supported opera at a rate of two times that of classical music until 1970, when classical music surpassed opera. Opera became its own

program. Jazz and folk music were excluded from NEA support until 1969, when they began receiving very small proportions of Music Program funds. The rates at which classical forms outpaced jazz and folk music are astounding. Classical music was funded at rates approximately seventy-two times higher than jazz, and folk music was listed in its own category only once in 1969. Figures for 1969 are typical of the first years of Music Program funding: classical music, $259,770; opera, $525,000; jazz, $25,500, and folk, $15,700. In the 1970s, a new Jazz, Folk, and Ethnic Program was formed to fund not only music but also dance, literature, visual arts, and performances in these categories. This program was funded at rates significantly lower that those for the Music, Opera, Theater, and Dance programs.

Theater Program statistics are similar to those for Music. Classical theater works and Shakespeare plays received the bulk of NEA funds, while contemporary theater programs lagged behind. In 1969, Theater Program funds were broken down as follows: Shakespeare, $345,000; classical, $282,500, American classics, $314,000; and contemporary, $135,000.

Dance Program funding also follows the same pattern, with classical ballet receiving the highest level of funding. Again using 1969 as a typical year, dance grants were distributed in the following way: ballet, $400,000; modern, $200,000; and other, $35,000. There was no folk dancing category that year.

For further statistics on NEA funding by program, see the NEA *Annual Reports*, 1966–75.

49. Edward Arian, *The Unfulfilled Promise* (Philadelphia: Temple University Press, 1989), 8.

CHAPTER 8

Between Civics and Politics:
The Modernist Moment
in Federal Public Art

CASEY NELSON BLAKE

On June 14, 1969, a crowd of 2,000 people gathered in downtown Grand Rapids for the dedication of Alexander Calder's sculpture *La Grande Vitesse* (figure 8.1). Calder's abstract work was the focal point of a modernist plaza cleared by urban renewal and then named for Michigan's late senator, Arthur Vandenberg. The sculpture had a local constituency in the city's cultural and economic elites, who hoped that Vandenberg Plaza would give Grand Rapids a public square comparable to the Piazza San Marco in Venice or Saint Peter's in Rome. *La Grande Vitesse* also had a national constituency in the administrators at the National Endowment for the Arts (NEA), who had awarded Grand Rapids the first grant of its new program for Works of Art in Public Places. At the dedication, speakers pointed to the Calder sculpture as evidence that culture in Grand Rapids—and the United States generally—had finally come of age. "Well, it's here!" announced one local promoter. "And nobody is ever going to take it away. It belongs to us. It

A slightly different version of this chapter was first published in *A Modernist Mosaic: Art and Modernism in the United States*, ed. Townsend Luddington (Chapel Hill: University of North Carolina Press, 2000), 256–78; it is republished here by permission. Research for this chapter was supported by a fellowship from the Woodrow Wilson International Center for Scholars. The author is grateful to the late Charles Blitzer and Michael Lacey for their generous support and to his colleagues at the Woodrow Wilson Center in 1994 and 1995, who offered many helpful comments on an early version of the chapter. He is deeply indebted to many people at the embattled National Endowment for the Arts—above all Jennifer Dowley, Michael Faubion, and Bert Kubli—for allowing him to examine the records of the endowment's public art program. And he is equally indebted to William Caine, Merideth Fisher, Susan Harrison, Dale Lanzone, and Page Weiss at the Art-in-Architecture Program of the General Ser-

Figure 8.1. Dedication ceremonies for Alexander Calder's *La Grande Vitesse,* Grand Rapids, 1969. Courtesy of Nancy Mulnix Papers, Local History Department, Grand Rapids Public Library.

stands here with the buildings which are so straight and strong and which represent monuments to commerce and industry and to our standard of living. . . . It will belong to you and to your children and to your children's children. They will grow up with it—and they will grow up to it. So, enjoy it—it's yours."

Five years later, on October 25, 1974, the General Services Administration (GSA) dedicated a second Calder sculpture, *Flamingo,* in Chicago, outside the new federal buildings designed by Mies van der Rohe (figure 8.2). Because of the success of the Grand Rapids project, the GSA had chosen Calder to receive the first commission of its newly revived Art-in-Architecture Program, a percent-for-art public art initiative that had begun under the John F. Kennedy administration only to fall victim to political controversy and budget cuts. Chicago officials made sure they would not be outdone when it came to celebrating the arrival of *their* Calder, which was a good ten feet taller than the

vices Administration for granting him access to their files. He is grateful, too, for the criticisms and suggestions he received from Thomas Bender, Richard Wightman Fox, Peter Bacon Hales, Jane Kramer, Charles McGovern, Barbara Melosh, Leslie Prosterman, Arlene Shaner, Michael Smith, Lisa Steinman, and Ellen Todd, among other commentators. His thanks also go to audiences at Boston University, the Catholic University of America, Columbia University, George Mason University, the Historical Society of Washington, D.C., the New School, Rice University, Scripps College, the University of California–Irvine, Washington University, Wesleyan University, and Yale University for their responses to lectures on related subjects.

Figure 8.2. Alexander Calder, *Flamingo*, Chicago, 1974. Courtesy of Art-in-Architecture Program, Public Buildings Service, General Services Administration.

one in Grand Rapids. Mayor Richard J. Daley proclaimed "Alexander Calder Day in Chicago." The *Chicago Tribune* crowed "It's a Whatchama-Calder!" And the publicity circus surrounding the sculpture took the form of an actual circus parade, inspired by the circus motifs of Calder's early wire sculptures. Thirteen circus wagons, eight clowns, ten unicyclists, bands, elephants, and countless other marchers, including Ronald McDonald and a man in a gorilla suit, made their way down State Street to the sculpture. Among them was Calder himself, who rode to the dedication in an enormous Schlitz beer wagon pulled down State Street by forty horses. As the wagon approached the plaza, hundreds of helium balloons were released into the air, and a ringmaster announced, "Ladies and gentlemen, children of all ages, I present to the people the one and only Alexander the Great, Sandy Calder."[1]

Twenty years after the dedication of the Grand Rapids Calder, federal officials invoked the authority of the public in support of their decision to "take away" a work of public art—in this case, Richard Serra's minimalist steel sculpture *Tilted Arc*, in Lower Manhattan (figure 8.3). The GSA's installation of Serra's sculpture in Foley Square in 1981 touched off eight years of public hearings, lawsuits, petition drives, media commentary, and protests. Judges and office workers in the area complained that the work obstructed their access to Federal Plaza and deepened the inhumanity of an already unfriendly space. In March 1989, the GSA ordered the sculpture dismantled and stored in a Brooklyn warehouse. After the removal of *Tilted Arc*, the GSA's regional administrator announced the triumph of the public over "a group of elitists in Washington."[2] "This is a day for the people to rejoice," he said, "because now the plaza returns rightfully to the people."[3]

The two decades between the installation of Calder's Grand Rapids sculpture and the destruction of *Tilted Arc* mark the modernist moment in federally funded public art. During this period, the federal government's two major public art programs—the NEA's Art in Public Places Program and the GSA's Art-in-Architecture Program—embraced modernism as a national style and commissioned hundreds of abstract murals and sculptures for public spaces around the country. In the aftermath of the *Tilted Arc* affair, it is difficult to recapture the hopes that inspired the federal government's original modernist commitments. Yet even today, in our decidedly postmodern and pluralistic moment, arts administrators invoke the heady memory of the confident and unified cultural policy that gave birth to the NEA and GSA programs. The Grand Rapids Calder now serves as the foundation myth for federal arts administrators. The success of Calder's sculpture—which was incorporated into the logos for the City of Grand Rapids, its Chamber of Commerce, and even its sanitation department—is a recurrent refrain in NEA reminders that a skeptical public will eventually come around to embrace avant-garde art. Jane Alexander, then chair of the embattled endowment, returned to Grand Rapids in June 1994 for events celebrating the twenty-fifth anniversary of the 1969 dedication. A maquette of *La Grande Vitesse* sat in her

Figure 8.3. Richard Serra, *Tilted Arc*, Lower Manhattan, 1981–89. Courtesy of Art-in-Architecture Program, Public Buildings Service, General Services Administration.

office in Washington, a reminder of past glories at a time when the endowment's very survival was in doubt.

This chapter traces the rise and fall of the modernist project in American public art, beginning with its inception in the arts policy of the Kennedy administration and continuing with the prolonged crisis in popular support for public art that erupted in the mid-1970s and culminated in the removal of Serra's sculpture for lower Manhattan in 1989. The unraveling of that modernist project for public art, so soon after its inception, reminds us that the transition from artistic modernism to postmodernism was not simply a shift in taste or aesthetic style. Rather, the crisis of modernist art in public spaces was intimately related to the crisis of the Kennedy-era liberalism that inspired it. Controversies over public art reveal that the movement from modernism to postmodernism was a thoroughly political process, shaped by deep conflicts over power and the structure of public life. "At stake in every struggle over art," writes Pierre Bourdieu, "there is also an imposition of an art of living, that is the transmutation of an arbitrary way of living into the legitimate way of life which casts every other way of living into arbitrariness."[4] As the site where politics and aesthetics meet in the streets and plazas of our cities and towns, public art has become a flashpoint for conflicting ways of life in late-twenti-eth-century and early twenty-first-century America. Controversies over pub-lic art thus offer an important vantage point on the troubled recent history of our country's public imagination.[5]

Camelot Cultural Policy

The Grand Rapids Calder was the first public installation of the National En-dowment for the Arts, which had been established in 1965 as a result of pol-icy decisions that were already well under way by the time of John Kennedy's assassination in November 1963. As John Wetenhall has argued, those re-sponsible for cultural policy in the Kennedy White House—especially Arthur Schlesinger Jr. and August Heckscher—saw the arts as a way to raise popular tastes, improve national morale during the Cold War, and celebrate cultural freedom in the face of Soviet aggression. Schlesinger, Heckscher, and other New Frontiersmen urged the president to ensure that the highest standards of design guided federal architecture, public art, government posters, and even postage stamps. Meanwhile, public artists and architects would work closely with urban planners to rebuild downtowns shaken by the postwar exodus to the suburbs—a project that inevitably involved the demolition of historic buildings and traditional working-class neighborhoods.[6]

The New Frontiersmen recalled the classical republican tradition in their assertion that Americans' encounter with a program of major monuments and buildings would prove a resource for national renewal. Heckscher repeatedly cited Pericles's support for civic architecture and sculpture, the implication being that the United States stood poised on the brink of another Periclean age. As Heckscher put it in his 1963 report to the president on "the arts and the national government," "there has been a growing awareness that the United States will be judged—and its place in history ultimately assessed—not alone by its military or economic power, but by the quality of its civilization."[7] The arts, in his view, would serve the national purpose by inspiring in their view-ers a profound respect for the virtue of individual freedom.

Freedom was the central theme of Kennedy's most extended public remarks on the arts, delivered in October 1963 on the occasion of the dedication of the Robert Frost Memorial Library at Amherst College. Frost's appearance at Kennedy's inauguration had set the stage for a glamorous alliance of intellec-tuals, artists, and liberal politicians. And his memory inspired Kennedy's de-scription of "the great artist" as "the last champion of the individual mind and sensibility against an intrusive society and an officious state." The United States, Kennedy continued, should "set the artist free to follow his vision wherever it takes him."[8] By giving artists maximum freedom to do their work, the federal government would demonstrate the cultural superiority of the free world and instill in Americans an appreciation for the rights of the individual.

In light of recent threats to public funding for the arts, there is something very inspiring about the Kennedy administration's support for cultural creativity. It is a mark of the self-confidence of the country's political institutions in this period that government officials were not intimidated by the arts, that they were not afraid of the potentially disturbing and dissident work that artists might produce. The commitment by the White House to a common cosmopolitan style for public spaces now appears part and parcel of the generous and inclusive civic culture that won at least lip service from politicians in the age of Kennedy and Martin Luther King Jr.—a civic culture premised on overcoming local and parochial attachments in the name of racial integration and loyalty to the state during the Cold War.

That said, the tragedy of "Camelot" cultural policy lay precisely in its failure to define a larger public or civic function for the arts. In keeping with its celebration of individual freedom, the Kennedy administration made its case for the arts in largely negative terms—in opposition to the domination of culture by the state in the Soviet Union. The result was a highly privatized conception of aesthetic experience that held neither artists nor art audiences to a common set of artistic and moral standards. American arts policy freed the artist to pursue his or her individual vision; its ideal of elevating public taste was likewise defined as a personal matter. This was a recipe for public art without public purpose, an art created for a nation of private individuals.

Camelot art policy further undermined the public nature of its public art program by endorsing an openly elitist commissioning process. Heckscher's report proposed that panels of experts act to insulate artistic judgment from state interference. But the panel system that evolved at the NEA and GSA drastically limited who had the competence to make decisions about the aesthetics and function of public space. Its insistence on professional authority fit easily with the autonomous aesthetic of modernist formalism. Disdainful of local context and popular conventions, the Kennedy arts advisers articulated a cultural politics that had little use for democratic deliberation about the place of art in public life. Their legacy to the public art movement was an aesthetic ideology that lacked legitimacy either as a program for moral education by civic leaders or as the expression of popular will—in short, a public art caught between civics and politics.

The contradictions at the heart of this cultural policy became clear during the summer of 1966, in the uproar that followed the installation of Robert Motherwell's abstract mural *New England Elegy* in the new John F. Kennedy Federal Building in Boston. Initial reports mistakenly held that Motherwell's mural portrayed Kennedy's profile at the precise moment of his assassination in Dallas.[9] Office workers in the area and other Bostonians condemned the work as an "atrocity," a "monstrosity," and "a blasphemy to the memory of our late beloved President John F. Kennedy."[10] They questioned the appropriateness of federal funding for such a somber work, or for abstract art of any kind. The mural "is a horrible and frightening thing," one man in Cambridge wrote the GSA. "It has nothing to do with the spirit of the dead president."[11] A security guard in the new building—itself a modernist work designed by Walter Gropius—told a reporter, "We're common people. We've never been to art school and we can't figure out what it is."[12]

Once the controversy erupted, critics, art administrators, and their supporters in the press were quick to instruct such people exactly how to "figure out" what the painting was. Metropolitan Museum curator Henry Geldzahler, a frequent arts adviser to the NEA and the Lyndon B. Johnson administration, complained that "a lot of people who are not art experts" had been "widely quoted" in press accounts of the painting.[13] And the *Boston Globe* defended Motherwell's selection by reminding readers that "the overwhelming majority of museums, critics and experts" had endorsed abstract expressionist art. One of those experts told the paper that "the public protest over the painting should not be taken too seriously."[14]

The official response to criticisms of Motherwell's *New England Elegy* made it abundantly clear that a policy granting freedom of artistic production to artists did not entail full interpretive freedom for the public. When popular responses to public art questioned the validity of the enterprise, federal arts administrators and their allies rushed to set limits to interpretations of their work. Modernist public art should stimulate individual appreciation, in their view, but not public debate.

The Grand Rapids Debate

The political instability of the federal program of modernist public art was evident, in retrospect, at the very moment of its earliest triumph. Despite its current status as an icon of a golden age of public art, the Calder sculpture in Grand Rapids provoked a debate during the two years before its installation that prefigured the reaction against public art in the late 1970s and the 1980s.

The advocates of the Grand Rapids Calder saw its installation as the crowning achievement of a program of urban renewal that would put the city on the map as a cultural capital. Their rhetoric portrayed Grand Rapids as a city without a history or local cultural tradition worth remembering—a city whose very identity waited on the arrival of a cosmopolitan symbol. Getting such a symbol required the intervention of specialists unconstrained by the parochial standards of a particular place, or by the pressures of local constituencies. The painter Adolph Gottlieb visited the city with the other NEA panelists and admitted that "it's unlikely the public will have anything to say on selection of the proposed sculpture for Vandenberg Center." All one could hope for was that a commission by "a committee of knowledgeable men" would eventually "be accepted by a majority of the people."[15]

Calder himself told reporters that it was not necessary for him to visit Grand Rapids before designing its public symbol. "If the art is good," he said, "it will stand by itself anywhere."[16] The NEA's "knowledgeable men" had given Grand Rapids a formalist public symbol that, in the words of one supporter, "will transcend time and place."[17]

Once the selection of Calder was announced, however, the sculpture's advocates rushed to describe the artist and his sculpture as quintessentially American. The dedication pamphlet for Grand Rapids described Calder as "all American. Apple pie type."[18] Portraits of the artist in the Grand Rapids newspaper emphasized Calder's engineering skills and compared him to Gary Cooper. "This has been the mark of Calder," declared one reporter, "that he has always been sure enough of himself to express himself in his own way."[19]

These descriptions of Calder as the last rugged individualist were part of a campaign to overcome residents' uneasiness about the avant-garde culture of the gallery, salon, and museum. Even as the selection process limited aesthetic discrimination to a few trained professionals, selling La Grande Vitesse to the public required repeated reassurances that one viewer's interpretation of the work was as valid as another's. In fact, advocates claimed that the advantage of an abstract work lay precisely in its openness to multiple interpretations: Modernist aesthetics imposed no constraints on viewers' freedom.

Such claims had little success in winning over local critics, who watched the NEA panel's closed deliberations and questioned whether the Calder sculpture was a "public" object of any kind. Despite all the talk of the sculpture's accessibility to multiple interpretations, they believed that the NEA panelists and their local allies had in fact imposed very precise standards of art appreciation on the city. One leading opponent of La Grande Vitesse warned against a sculpture like the recently installed Chicago Picasso, which he believed "might not be beautiful to more than a few artists and art lovers."[20] Critics of the Calder piece also objected to its replacing a reflection pool that had been planned for the plaza—a move they condemned as the substitution of a private amenity for public works. "Who is the [sculpture] committee trying to impress?" one opponent asked. "Are they supposed to be representing the people of Grand Rapids in this project?"[21]

Critics of the Calder sculpture saw themselves as the defenders of memory, place, and tradition against reckless innovation by cosmopolitan modernizers. In their view, the sculpture's promoters were complicit in the urban renewal that had left the city with a modernist plaza in place of its traditional downtown. Opponents pointed out that the old City Hall clock tower that had long been the defining visual marker for Grand Rapids had been destroyed without a murmur of protest from the city's arts elite. Attempts to save the City Hall clock tower had failed, a critic wrote the newspaper, "because the moderns evidently were ashamed of the great heritage of the yesteryears in Grand Rapids."[22] It was no surprise that the city's "moderns" had selected an expatriate sculptor like Calder, who had spent most of his life in France. "He is as foreign to Grand Rapids as is Charles de Gaulle and certainly as foreign to Grand Rapids culture."[23]

In addition to the old City Hall clock tower, there was another memory that haunted the Calder debate: the public's memory of turn-of-the-century commemorative sculpture, which seemed to render Calder's abstract form illegitimate as public art. Letters to the editor repeatedly asked why no one had commissioned a sculpture of Senator Vandenberg for the central plaza named after him. Instead of "some foreign-fabricated abstraction," one writer suggested, it would have been more appropriate "to dedicate a heroic-size bronze or marble bust of the senator for all to see, children and grandchildren."[24] Another wrote, "Maybe I could understand if the people of Grand Rapids wanted a monument for our men who have given their lives in Vietnam."[25] For these writers, memorials exemplified both the appropriate form and content for public sculpture. In contrast to Calder's cosmopolitan modernism, such sculptures seemed to serve an identifiable civic function—the honoring of local heroes—while at the same time giving local residents a sense of place. *La Grande Vitesse*, however, failed on both counts.

Cultural traditionalists were not the only people in Grand Rapids to condemn Calder's abstract sculpture. Antiwar demonstrators tried to disrupt the dedication ceremony. One protester shouted, "You should drop bombs on that damned Calder instead of on the Vietnamese and use the scrap to buy food for the poor."[26] More playful dissenters used trash and scrap metal to create amateur parodies of *La Grande Vitesse*, which they spray-painted in bright red and offered for sale at a fraction of Calder's commission.[27] What linked these critics to advocates of traditional monuments was their understanding that the installation of Calder's work in downtown Grand Rapids was as much an assertion of power as it was an exercise in artistic taste.

Criticisms of this kind were largely ignored as federal administrators and their local allies celebrated the arrival of Calder's abstraction to Grand Rapids. Yet what stands out in retrospect is the extent to which even this early triumph drew criticisms that would reemerge in subsequent challenges to an official program of modernist art in public places. Haunted by the example of earlier forms of civic iconography, abstract public works of art never won the allegiance of traditionalists seeking an art resonant of national purpose and local memory. And at a time of war and mounting social crisis, the autonomous aesthetic of modernist public art outraged political radicals as a distraction from more pressing needs.

The Popular Revolt against Modernist Public Art

After the installation of the Grand Rapids Calder in 1969, most of the criticisms of federally funded modernist public art came initially from groups on the left. NEA public art grants in the early 1970s ran into opposition from environmentalists who protested the use of green space for public sculpture and from African-American activists who denounced modernist works as irrelevant to their cultural traditions and political aspirations. Meanwhile, leading artists and critics began to question the ethics of working with the NEA while the government was prosecuting the Vietnam War.

With pressure coming from leftist and black nationalist movements in American cities, and from deep within the ranks of the art community itself, the NEA made strategic concessions to political art even as it kept modernist, nonrepresentational work at the core of its mission. The endowment created a short-lived Inner City Murals Program in 1970, which gave out many small grants to openly political arts organizations and activist groups in black and Hispanic urban neighborhoods.[28] NEA administrators privately voiced reservations about the quality of the work produced by these initiatives, but they nonetheless agreed to fund murals that championed leftist, black-nationalist, and feminist causes in a realist style far removed from the endowment's original aesthetic commitments.[29]

Another NEA response to the politics of the early 1970s was to award grants to environmental artists like Robert Morris, whose work drew its inspiration from the ecological movement, and to pop and minimalist artists like Claes Oldenburg and Richard Serra, who had left the galleries in the late 1960s to create enormous public sculptures that challenged the authority of traditional civic and patriotic monuments. Though the early beneficiaries of the Murals Programs were often obscure minority artists and community activists, artists like Morris, Oldenburg, and Serra were products of elite art schools and the very New York–centered art market they now dismissed as hostile to political change. When the country's politics moved right in the mid-1970s, they—and not the muralists—were left standing as beneficiaries of federal subsidy. The Inner City Murals Program was folded back into the NEA's regular public art program after two years, and soon the endowment was funding apolitical, decorative work suitable for the gentrifying districts of American cities—abstract "supergraphics" to cover exposed brick walls or the "trompe l'oeil" realism of Richard Haas. As the leftist protests of the early 1970s subsided, explicitly political art by minority artists and radical activists was marginalized.[30]

As late as the mid-1970s, then, the commitment of the NEA and GSA to a modernist project remained largely unchanged. With escalating budgets under the Richard Nixon, Gerald Ford, and early Jimmy Carter administrations, both agencies funded major installations of abstract—and especially, minimalist—sculptures throughout the country. Major GSA commissions by Isamu Noguchi, Beverly Pepper, Clement Meadmore, Louise Nevelson, Tony Smith, and Joseph Konzal were among the many public sculptures that appeared outside federal buildings in the middle and late 1970s. The NEA also funded hundreds of nonrepresentational public installations in this period, including pieces by Alexander Lieberman, Ronald Bladen, Mark di Suvero, and

Michael Heizer. These works—now widely derided as "plop art" dropped into public spaces without regard for local context and culture—constitute an official style for the 1970s that had its origins in the cultural program of the Kennedy era.[31]

What finally undermined that program was neither the challenge from the left, nor the movement of the 1960s avant-garde out of the gallery and into the streets, but the wave of explosive protests in local communities, often endorsed by conservative politicians and pundits, that beset modernist installations beginning in the mid-1970s. These protests were prompted by many of the same grievances that critics of the Grand Rapids Calder had tried to articulate. But now the outcry against public art drew on popular fears of crime and urban decline. As the economic boom of the 1960s gave way to the fiscal crisis of American cities in the mid-1970s, the idea that public art could resurrect downtowns and boost Americans' "morale" became impossible to maintain. Public art invited attack as the most visible manifestation of the liberal state in urban spaces. The very presence of modernist public artworks politicized the aesthetics of public spaces, leading more and more Americans to reject the idea of leaving artistic decisions to a few "knowledgeable men"—and, with it, the notion of a timeless, transcendent art that could "stand by itself anywhere." The result was a political crisis of the liberal-modernist project in public art that has still not been resolved.

The most immediate change in the discourse surrounding public art objects from the mid-1970s through the early 1980s was the shift from a celebration of such objects as symbols and vehicles of urban renewal to their depiction in media coverage, and in political debate, as bearers of urban decay. In Baltimore, federal judges condemned George Sugarman's 1976 design for the city's federal building and courthouse, *Baltimore Federal*, as a security threat (figure 8.4). As one judge put it, "The artwork could be utilized as a platform for speaking or hurling objects by dissident groups demonstrating in front of the building. . . . The structure could well be used to secrete bombs or other explosive objects."[32] The judges' association of public art with crime was linked, very explicitly, to a desire to restrict the use of public space to predictable, private pursuits. When Sugarman tried to explain the "emotional impact" of his sculpture, one judge snapped, "There is quite enough 'emotional impact' inside the courthouse without attempting to artificially generate it on the outside."[33] *Baltimore Federal* was installed a year later, but only after Sugarman had modified the design to open its interior to outside view and after the GSA had agreed to install a television security system to monitor activities in the area surrounding the building.[34]

In the early 1980s, several years after the Baltimore debate, a Richard Serra sculpture designed for a bleak downtown area in Saint Louis prompted letters to the editor from citizens who, understandably, feared that its walled-in interior space would become a crime site. "Wait until a woman or child is pulled

Figure 8.4. George Sugarman, *Baltimore Federal*, Baltimore, 1977. Courtesy of Art-in-Architecture Program, Public Buildings Service, General Services Administration.

inside, away from the view of the public, and raped," one resident wrote the newspaper, "then decide if the $250,000 was well spent."[35]

Such arguments obviously played to popular fears of crime and terrorism, but they also touched a nerve in local residents appalled by the physical devastation of their cities by postwar urban renewal and deindustrialization. Critics held that public art installations and the government buildings they adorned were responsible for the destruction of their communities' civic culture. In Baltimore, a resident asked supporters of the Sugarman sculpture whether they "really admire[d] the penitentiary-like structure" that the GSA had constructed for the city's downtown.[36] From the symbol of a glorious urban modernity in Grand Rapids, modernist public art had become an unwelcome reminder of a modern project gone wrong.

During this same period, conservatives became more outspoken in their view that modernist public art should give way to more traditional monuments. The judges in Baltimore were among the most vocal leaders of a broad conservative campaign to restore patriotic iconography to official buildings and public spaces. In Saint Louis, the 1971 NEA grant that eventually supported Serra's sculpture provoked an angry response from conservative activists who preferred that the money go to a memorial to Tom Dooley, a local doctor known for his humanitarian work in Southeast Asia. The chairman of the city's arts agency ridiculed the group's proposal for a Dooley memorial as a "junk statue." "You don't go to great talents today and ask for a statue of Dooley," he responded. "They'd laugh at you."[37] But when one local newspaper, city council members, and even the mayor lined up in support of the memorial, NEA officials quickly found $15,000 for the Dooley group.

The arguments made in favor of a Tom Dooley memorial found an intellectual rationale in the early 1980s in the writings of conservative critics who argued that federally funded public art should "exemplify a common tradition and shared political, cultural, and aesthetic heritage."[38] In the spring of 1984, the Alaska state legislature apparently came to the same conclusion and voted to have Robert Murray's *Nimbus* replaced by a war memorial. Murray's turquoise steel abstraction had been installed in 1978, with NEA support, outside the new state courthouse in Juneau, directly opposite the Alaska state capitol building. The work immediately drew attack from local residents angry that the commission had not gone to an Alaskan, and from state legislators who saw it as a deliberate assault on their authority. Late in December 1984, the governor ordered the sculpture removed—an act that prefigured the destruction of Richard Serra's *Tilted Arc* five years later.[39]

The Political Crisis of Modernist Aesthetics

The controversies surrounding NEA-funded works in Saint Louis and Juneau suggest that the political crisis over the liberal-modernist project in public art resulted, ironically, from its successful expansion during the 1970s. The modernist center held so long as its insistence on a selection process closed to average citizens enjoyed at least the passive assent of the public. But as art administrators commissioned more and more works throughout the country, they found it difficult to navigate their way through multiplying constituencies and pressure groups and still stick to the modernist course set by the Calder installations. Under attack at the local and national levels, the federal program for a modernist aesthetic of freedom gave way to open political warfare.

The chief casualty of this politicization of aesthetics was the authority of the panels of artistic experts that had originally given the federal programs their legitimacy. In the heat of the controversy over the proposed Tom Dooley memorial in Saint Louis, one NEA administrator wrote the head of the local public art effort to criticize his politically insensitive dismissal of representational art as "junk sculpture":

Taking an adversary position to local opinion on the level of taste is . . . dangerous, and . . . is seen as a form of dictation to which local people don't take too kindly and I can't say I blame them. . . . One reason we do the Works of Art in Public Places projects through a selection panel is to direct these pressures towards experts who take responsibility for these decisions, decisions not made by you and me.[40]

But by the mid-1970s, panels of experts gave the public art movement very little cover. In fact, it was the imagined arrogance of expert outsiders that infuriated local opponents above all else. In case after case, critics of federally funded modernist public art disputed the competence of panelists and charged them with pursuing a cosmopolitan agenda at the expense of indigenous cultures and grassroots participation. Expert panelists, such critics charged, were interested in the colonization of public space by the culture of museums and galleries. The art they commissioned was a bid for public power by people who already controlled private cultural institutions.

The NEA initially tried to respond to such attacks by surrounding modernist installations with more accessible works. At Northern Kentucky State University, the response to Donald Judd's 1977 minimalist sculpture *Box* was so hostile that university and NEA panelists went out of their way two years later to commission a second piece that would be more popular. Their choice was Red Grooms's *Way Down East,* an homage to the Kentucky-born director D. W. Griffith and the actress Lillian Gish.

Likewise, when the City of Hartford planned in 1979 for public art for its rebuilt Civic Center Coliseum, local officials tried to head off the sort of controversy that had plagued the appearance of Carl Andre's *Stone Field Sculpture* two years earlier. Andre's piece had touched off extraordinary protests from the public and politicians alike. The national media pointed to the work as evidence that the government had succumbed to the 1970s' "pet rock" craze. Stung by the controversy, Hartford art administrators decided to canvass local opinion about the work of eight different finalists before announcing their selection of the conceptual artist Sol LeWitt for the Coliseum. But having opened the selection process to public debate, the panel found it impossible to retain LeWitt for the commission. Complaints that the city had bypassed African-American artists led LeWitt to suggest that he share the commission with Romare Bearden—a concession that failed to satisfy his critics. In the face of mounting criticisms of his proposal for two geometric pieces, LeWitt decided to withdraw altogether, leaving Bearden's far more accessible murals as the only public art for the Coliseum.[41] One Hartford resident spoke for the growing backlash against modernist works in public places in a response to the survey conducted about the Coliseum commission. "I think people are tired of New York arty-art. You can keep it in museums where it won't bother anybody."[42]

Conservatives then and now have applauded such criticisms as a reaction against the "adversary culture" of the "New Class" by a "silent majority" of "normal Americans"—to use the rhetoric of Richard Nixon and Newt Gingrich. Such arguments are the mirror image of the view prevalent among artists, art administrators, and their liberal defenders that opposition to informed artistic opinion comes inevitably from ignorant "Know-Nothings."[43]

Yet more often than not, the reaction against federally sponsored modernist art for public places in the late 1970s and early 1980s took a very different form from what one might imagine from the standard accounts by conservatives and liberals. As in the *Tilted Arc* debate, much of the opposition to the liberal-modernist project grew out of a respect for local context and functional design, and out of a longing for opportunities to deliberate in public about the use of public spaces. A commitment to public debate lay behind most of the protests against public art installations in this period.

The democratic impulse at the heart of many of these protests can be seen in the campaign against *Hoe Down*, Guy Dill's abstract sculpture for the Hubert H. Humphrey Building in Huron, South Dakota, where Humphrey spent his childhood (figure 8.5). The GSA installed *Hoe Down* in 1979, with the artist explaining that he had chosen its theme and imagery to evoke the "sense of order and dependency on the weather" on the Great Plains.[44] But Dill's efforts to explain the local references in the work (which, he joked, included the initials "HHH," stacked sideways) were unpersuasive. Local critics organized an "undedication ceremony" to protest his work and gathered 5,000 signatures on petitions for its removal, but the GSA stood its ground and left the sculpture in place. A spokesman for Huron ACORN, a grassroots activist group, let GSA administrators and South Dakota politicians know that residents expected more control over public art installations in the future:

We are concerned that during the whole process of selecting the *Hoe Down* the GSA gave little or no thought to involving the community in the selection. Huron is *our* community—the Federal Building was built to serve *us*. We feel that we have a right to some kind of say in the kind of art which is chosen to represent our community.[45]

By the middle of the 1980s, demands of this kind had shattered whatever fragile consensus had briefly existed in support of the liberal-modernist project in federally funded public art. Art administrators and politicians were faced with two choices. They could work to create more inclusive selection processes, in which case they ran the risk of losing control of the process or of prompting public debates that would spill over from aesthetics to other controversial issues. Or they could stem such debates with bureaucratic maneuvers or the outright use of force. Either way, the modernist moment in American public art had come to an end.

Figure 8.5. Guy Dill, *Hoe Down*, Huron, South Dakota, 1979. Courtesy of Art-in-Architecture Program, Public Buildings Service, General Services Administration.

The Liberal-Modernist Project in Ruins

It remains to be seen whether the collapse of modernism will result in a commitment to a truly democratic and participatory public art movement, assisted by public subsidy, or in the open imposition of aesthetic choices by political and economic elites. Recent artistic and political developments are not altogether encouraging.

In the past twenty years, artists and critics on the multiculturalist left have essentially withdrawn from the public art movement that began in the Kennedy era and declared their allegiance to what they now call a "community arts" movement. They condemn much of the work from the 1960s and 1970s as modernist "plop art" for public spaces and question the very notion of art for a cosmopolitan public, suggesting that "the public" and "the public sphere" are repressive fictions that marginalize difference and diversity. Advocates of this "community arts" movement point with pride to mural projects like Judy Baca's extraordinary *Great Wall of Los Angeles* (1976–83) and the remarkable *Village of Arts and Humanities* created in the late 1980s by Lily Yeh and her associates in North Philadelphia—a project that has transformed a large area of an otherwise bleak and hopeless ghetto into a local cultural oasis. Proponents of such work see these "community arts" projects as examples of a collaborative art rooted in struggles for justice and group identity.[46]

Despite its many achievements, however, the "community arts" movement of the last two decades has yet to generate explicit aesthetic criteria for judging its work as public art, as opposed to exercises in community organizing. Moreover, much of the new public art on the left betrays a deep pessimism about the prospects for cultural and political consensus in contemporary America—indeed, about the very possibility of a public of any kind. The best "community arts" projects proudly root themselves in a local aesthetic and in bids for power and justice by local groups. Their organizers imagine that the makers and viewers of such art will be members of the neighborhood in which it is placed, with little concern for the more diverse and heterogeneous audiences that might gather in downtown streets or plazas. Community art projects directly address the issue of local participation that the modernist movement ignored, but at the cost of any aspiration to a cosmopolitan, democratic culture for the nation as a whole.

For their part, conservatives have responded to the collapse of modernism by mobilizing the localistic reaction against modernism of the late 1970s and the 1980s in the service of a newly lean and mean nation-state. The critic and novelist Tom Wolfe is one of many conservatives who have applauded the work of neotraditionalist public artists like Raymond Kaskey, whose 1985 *Portlandia* graces the facade of Michael Graves's postmodernist Portland City Building. Kaskey's art asks us, with a wink and a nod, to suspend disbelief and imagine that we are again in the presence of the confident civic monuments of our grandparents' day, rooted in a culture of Protestant republicanism. It should come as no surprise that Kaskey subsequently received a GSA commission for the Ronald Reagan federal building in Santa Ana, California. Kaskey may enjoy more such federal commissions in the future, but it is hard to imagine how his brand of neotraditionalist public art can resurrect whatever imagined cultural consensus underwrote the civic monuments projects of the late nineteenth century. In the aftermath of the modernist moment, any consensus on what cultural heritage Americans share will require sustained, inclusive, democratic debate, not the wistful nostalgia that informs Kaskey's work. Without such debate, there is no reason to question Lawrence Alloway's judgment, made over twenty years ago, "that the resources of the tradition that made nineteenth-century sculpture legible cannot be revived as if nothing had happened."[47]

Or perhaps such public art *can* be revived after all, without public assent or participation, if the powerful use their authority to foreclose other options. A disturbing case in point is the history of a 1993 GSA commission for a federal building in Knoxville. The GSA had selected Nizette Brennan to create a sculpture for the building, but the regional GSA administrator in Atlanta objected to her proposal for an abstract work titled *Aquadrop*. In response, Brennan came up with a proposal for *Knoxville Flag*, a limestone Stars and Stripes, which was finally approved by the GSA over the unanimous objections of its panelists.[48] Brennan's *Knoxville Flag* signals the replacement of modernism as

Figure 8.6. Nizette Brennan, *Knoxville Flag*, Knoxville, 1993. Courtesy of the Art-in-Architecture Program, Public Buildings Service, General Services Administration.

an official style by a new patriotic realism, dressed up in the rhetoric of conservative identity politics (figure 8.6). The GSA dedication pamphlet defends the sculpture as "a monument to the patriotism of the citizens of Knoxville and of Tennessee" and "an enduring tribute to the traditional and contemporary ideals of the region."[49] *Knoxville Flag* makes it absolutely clear that the liberal-modernist project in public art is dead and buried, with both its aesthetic commitments and panel system discarded in the interests of state authority and civic peace.

The ascendancy of neotraditionalist public monuments should give pause to those cheering the demise of modernist public art. At its best, the modernist public art movement aspired to the democratization of beauty and the expansion of aesthetic experience. In the case of Brennan's sculpture, the celebration of state power and the creation of a coercive political consensus take precedence over any other aesthetic considerations. Brennan's sculpture fits nicely with a conservative ethic that imagines a public life with no surprises—no surprises from artists, no surprises from racial and ethnic minorities, no surprises from crime and violence, and no surprises, above all, from public protests and civil unrest. From this vantage point, the public art movement that began in the Kennedy era deserves our grudging respect, in spite of its elitist cultural politics. The liberal-modernist project of the 1960s contained an implicit commitment to public spaces and a common civic life that citizens seized upon in the controversies of the 1970s and 1980s. That commitment is still worth defending, as the United States retreats to a garrison society where gated communities and prisons take the place of parks and plazas, and limestone flags find favor as public art.

Notes

1. Carol Oppenheim, "It's a Whatchama-Calder!" *Chicago Tribune*, October 26, 1974.
2. Interview with William Diamond in *The Destruction of Tilted Arc: Documents*, ed. Clara Weyergraf-Serra and Martha Buskirk (Cambridge, Mass.: MIT Press, 1991), 271.
3. William Diamond, quoted in Richard Serra, "Introduction," in ibid., 3.
4. Pierre Bourdieu, *Distinction: A Social Critique of the Judgment of Taste*, trans. Richard Nice (Cambridge, Mass.: Harvard University Press, 1984), 57.
5. There is a growing scholarly literature on the politics of modern public art in the United States. Among the most useful recent works are Michele H. Bogart, *Public Sculpture and the Civic Ideal in New York City, 1890–1930* (Chicago: University of Chicago Press, 1989); Barbara Melosh, *Engendering Culture: Manhood and Womanhood in New Deal Public Art and Theater* (Washington, D.C.: Smithsonian Institution Press, 1991); W. J. T. Mitchell, ed., *Art and the Public Sphere* (Chicago: University of Chicago Press, 1992); Harriet Senie, *Contemporary Public Sculpture: Tradition, Transformation, and Controversy* (Oxford: Oxford University Press, 1992); Harriet Senie and Sally Webster, eds., *Critical Issues in Public Art: Content, Context, and Controversy* (New York: HarperCollins, 1992); Erika Doss, *Spirit Poles and Flying Pigs: Public Art and Cultural Democracy in American Communities* (Washington, D.C.: Smithsonian Institution Press, 1995); and Rosalyn Deutsche, *Evictions: Art and Spatial Politics* (Cambridge, Mass.: MIT Press, 1996).
6. For Kennedy-era cultural policy, see John Wetenhall, "Camelot's Legacy to Public Art: Aesthetic Ideology in the New Frontier," in *Critical Issues in Public Art*, ed. Senie and Webster, 142–57; and Wetenhall, "The Rise of Modern Public Sculpture in America" (Ph.D. dissertation, Stanford University, 1987), chap. 5. Wetenhall's work is an invaluable guide to the history of arts policy in the postwar period.
7. August Heckscher, *The Arts and the National Government: A Report to the President* (Washington, D.C.: U.S. Government Printing Office, 1963), 5, n. 6; found in White House Central Files, box 4 "AR Arts," John F. Kennedy Presidential Library, Boston.
8. Quoted in Wetenhall, "Camelot's Legacy," 152, 153.
9. See "Abstract Painting of JFK Death Scene Stirs Furor," *Boston Globe*, August 12, 1966.
10. Paul L. Scanlon, "An Abomination" (letter to the editor), *Boston Globe*, August 19, 1966.
11. John Gosfield to the General Services Administration, November 25, 1966, letter in GSA Art-in-Architecture file FA897.

12. "Abstract Painting of JFK Death Scene."
13. Cathleen Cohen, "Artist Says Mural Doesn't Depict Death of Kennedy," *Boston Globe*, August 13, 1966.
14. Herbert A. Kenny, "Art Furor," *Boston Globe*, August 12, 1966.
15. Bernice Mancewicz, "'Public Will Have No Sculpture Say,'" *Grand Rapids Press*, August 28, 1967.
16. Calder is quoted in William Schiffel, "Questions About Sculpture Project Here Are Answered," *Grand Rapids Press*, December 24, 1967.
17. Glenn T. Raymond, "Views Calder Sculpture as Symbol of Today" [letter to the editor], *Grand Rapids Press*, February 6, 1968. When Braniff Airlines hired Calder to paint one of its intercontinental jets in 1973, it took the characterization of Calder's art as unbounded by geographical limits to its logical conclusion. See the coverage of Braniff's commission to Calder in *Braniff Place International Inflight Magazine* 2, no. 4 (1973).
18. *In Commemoration*, dedication pamphlet for *La Grande Vitesse* (Grand Rapids: City of Grand Rapids and County of Kent, Mich., 1969), 5.
19. Bernice Mancewicz, "The Strong-Handed Loner Who Made *La Grande Vitesse*," *Grand Rapids Press Wonderland West Michigan Magazine*, April 20, 1969.
20. Maury de Jonge, "It's Sculpture Time Again," *Grand Rapids Press*, February 21, 1968.
21. Lowell Moore, "Writer Voices His Displeasure Over Choice of Sculptor, Fee" [letter to the editor], *Grand Rapids Press*, January 1, 1968.
22. Paul F. Brandel, letter to the editor, *Grand Rapids Press*, November 30, 1967.
23. Moore, "Writer Voices His Displeasure."
24. Charles H. Frantz, M.D., "Insists Bust of Sen. Vandenberg More Fitting for Civic Center" [letter to the editor], *Grand Rapids Press*, January 15, 1968.
25. Aubrie C. Welch, letter to the editor, *Grand Rapids Press*, July 12, 1967.
26. "Sculpture Steals Spotlight at Dedication," *Grand Rapids Press*, June 15, 1969.
27. " 'Mini-Calder' Is Fun, Whether Art or Spoof," *Grand Rapids Press*, December 20, 1968; and Hank Bornheimer, "Calder Spoof Draws 'Haul It Away' Plea in East," *Grand Rapids Press*, November 10, 1968. The history of junk sculptures spoofing or criticizing fine art objects commissioned by local and federal agencies is a fascinating story in its own right, to which I can only make brief reference here. The NEA and GSA files are filled with references to art of this kind, which creators have displayed both as playful commentary on official public art and as vehicles for vehement protest. These junk sculptures, made of pipes, hangers, and other found objects, have less in common with a Dada aesthetic than with what Pierre Bourdieu describes as "a deep-seated demand for participation" at the heart of popular hostility to abstract art—a demand that "formal experiment systematically disappoints," and that elite commissioning procedures specifically prohibit (Bourdieu, *Distinction*, 32).

Two of the more imaginative efforts of this kind in recent years involved efforts by dissenting artists to embellish public art commissions. In Saint Louis in the mid-1980s, pranksters affixed white Styrofoam circles to Richard Serra's *Twain*, a triangular array of Cor-ten steel plates, giving the piece the appearance of a stack of dominoes. In 1993, in Seattle, an anarchist artist and his friends attached an enormous ball and chain to one leg of Jonathan Borofsky's *Hammering Man* as a pointed commentary on the condition of labor and the political blandness of most public art. Saint Louis officials removed the domino design immediately from Serra's piece. After a newspaper referendum showed overwhelming popular support for *Hammering Man*'s new accessory, Borofsky asked that the ball-and-chain remain in place. These artistic embellishments are exceptional. Far more common are angry graffiti scrawled on public works and parodies set up in residents' front yards, with price tags calculated at a fraction of the commission to the artist.

28. See Michael Moore memo to Richard Andrews, Michael Faubion, and Bert Kubli, December 11, 1984, in "Art in Public Places: Brief Program History," folder in NEA library.

29. In one of many instances where NEA administrators expressed misgivings about the aesthetics of the early-1970s murals movement, Brian O'Doherty jotted on a letter from a Boston city official about the city's 1971 "Summerthing" program, "These murals look like they're kid stuff. Very poor. Aren't *artists* doing them anymore?" His assistant wrote to the official in question that the NEA could only continue to support future "Summerthings" if "reputable artists [were] involved to provide at least the initial mural designs and supervise their completion." See O'Doherty's note on letter from Katharine D. Kane to Starke Meyer, February 7, 1972, and Starke Meyer's letter to Kathy D. Kane, March 14, 1972, both in the NEA Art in Public Places files, grant A72-0-1094.

30. A review of the NEA's Art in Public Places Program in 1984 confirmed that "virtually none" of the local murals programs from the early 1970s "survived the withdrawal of federal support. The program was discontinued amidst growing concerns by council members, panelists, and staff over the quality of the artwork it placed. This is when the guidelines begin to emphasize . . . 'innovative explorations of new media, sites, and approaches to public art.' Numbers of applications begin to decline and more resources were applied per project. That seemingly subtle change, from having social content define art, to allowing art to define its own context has been the most far reaching development in the field." Michael Moore memo, December 11, 1984.

31. Two documents of the federal programs' achievements in the 1970s are Donald W. Thalacker, *The Place of Art in the World of Architecture* (New York: Chelsea House/Bowker, 1980); and Andy Leon Harney, ed., *Art in Public Places* (Washington, D.C.: Partners for Livable Places, 1981).

32. Jo Ann Lewis, "The 'People Sculpture': Overcoming a Judgment," *Washington Post*, October 13, 1976.

33. This is quoted in John Blair Mitchell, "Anatomy of a Sculpture Commission," *Art Workers News* 6, no. 3 (June–July 1976): 6.

34. Judges in Baltimore revived their campaign to remove the Sugarman sculpture in the spring of 1995, in the aftermath of the Oklahoma City bombing, again citing security concerns.

35. H. Barton, letter to the editor, *Saint Louis South Side Journal*, May 19, 1982.

36. Walker Lewis, letter to the editor, *Baltimore Sun*, May 30, 1975.

37. " 'Dr. Dooley Statue Is Trash,' " *Saint Louis Globe-Democrat*, February 23, 1973.

38. Douglas Stalker and Clark Glymour, "The Malignant Object: Thoughts on Public Sculpture," *The Public Interest*, Winter 1982, 19.

39. One NEA administrator plaintively lamented in a 1987 memo about the work's possible relocation that "the same people seem to be supporting 'Nimbus' over and

over. What about support for 'Nimbus' from the non-art elite?" See "Review" notes dated December 24, 1987, in NEA Art in Public Places files, grant R60-41-34.

40. Brian O'Doherty to Robert H. Orchard, March 12, 1973, letter in NEA Art in Public Places files, grant A72-0-232.

41. See NEA Art in Public Places files, grant R50-41-121 and grant 02-440-79.

42. Response to survey for the Hartford Civic Center Coliseum project by the Office of Cultural Affairs in NEA Art in Public Places files, grant 02-440-799.

43. See my essay, " 'An Atmosphere of Effrontery': Richard Serra, *Tilted Arc*, and the Crisis of Public Art," in *The Power of Culture: Critical Essays in American History* (Chicago: University of Chicago Press, 1993), 246–89, for a discussion of the convergence of liberal and conservative views of public art controversies.

44. "Federal Building Sculpture Installed," Huron *Daily Plainsman*, July 6, 1979.

45. Clifford Roth to Roland Freeman and Dennis Jensen, August 30, 1980, letter in GSA Art-in-Architecture file AA34.

46. See Nina Felshin, ed., *But Is It Art? The Spirit of Art as Activism* (Seattle: Bay Press, 1995); Mary Jane Jacob et al., *Culture in Action* (Seattle: Bay Press, 1995); Suzanne Lacy, ed., *Mapping the Terrain: New Genre Public Art* (Seattle: Bay Press, 1995); and Doss, *Spirit Poles and Flying Pigs*, for examples of recent developments in leftist and feminist public art. Another work sympathetic to the "community arts movement" that has emerged in the wake of the modernist collapse is Dolores Hayden, *The Power of Place: Urban Landscapes as Public History* (Cambridge, Mass.: MIT Press, 1995).

47. Lawrence Alloway, "The Public Sculpture Problem," in *Topics in American Art since 1945* (New York: W. W. Norton, 1975), 246.

48. Richard Powelson, "GSA Official Nixes Duncan Plaza Sculpture," *Knoxville News-Sentinel*, August 5, 1991.

49. GSA *Knoxville Flag* dedication pamphlet in GSA Art-in-Architecture file AA199. See also the panel minutes and letters by panel members in the file, which make evident their opposition to Brennan's second design. It is worth noting, in this regard, the changes that the GSA has instituted in its commissioning process in the aftermath of the *Tilted Arc* affair. On the one hand, the Art in Architecture Program's panels now include greater representation of local groups and tenants of federal buildings, which suggests a responsiveness to community needs that did not exist when NEA-sponsored panels of artists and critics controlled the process. On the other hand, the new process appears in practice to give unprecedented power to regional and national GSA administrators, because many local panel members defer to their knowledge and authority. The result is a procedure that permits GSA officials to make aesthetic choices with little interference from artists, critics, or other professionals outside the federal government.

PART THREE

The Arts and Civic
Culture after Modernism

CHAPTER 9

The Swirl of Image and Sound:
On the Latest Version of Antirealism

KENNETH CMIEL

The postmodern aesthetic of the 1990s challenged the authority of the everyday. The last decade's postmodern art was mannered, overstated, ironic, allegorical, and distinctly hostile to realism. At the same time, we heard over and over about the "unreality" of contemporary politics. Politicians were disconnected from average people. They dealt in images and sound bites remote from any real needs of real people. In both the postmodern aesthetic and political critique there was, in the last decade, a felt disconnect between media life and lived experience. Both the September 11, 2001, terrorist attacks and the war in Iraq have, for the moment, altered these perceptions and turned attention to some very "real" politics. But questions of realism and cynicism are recurring ones for both popular aesthetics and democratic politics. They have been with us for the past two hundred years and there is every reason to assume that they will return to center stage at some point in the future.

Although the postmodern aesthetic of the 1990s and the commentary on political cynicism both discussed the gap between everyday experience and media life, each took this commentary in very different directions. The postmodern aesthetic celebrated the media's distance from realism, reveling in the culture's remove from common sense. Conversely, commentary on political alienation bemoaned these gaps—politicians were "spin artists," not speaking to the real needs of real people. This chapter explores the relationship between these two commentaries. Postmodern efforts to move beyond worlds of common sense, as beautiful and playful as they often are, will not overcome political alienation. Good democratic politics cannot disregard the claims of everyday experience. In the end, the aesthetic palate is richer than the directly political, allowing for fantasy and whimsy in a way that serious politics should not. Democratic political discourse *should* respect the homely, everyday needs of citizens. It fails if it does not. Direct political discourse reaches for a better life via the imagination, which takes everyday concerns as a given and "imagines" new ways to fulfill them. It avoids fantasy, the creation of unreal worlds, which has been one of the more endearing features of recent postmodern art.

The Postmodern Aesthetic

The postmodern aesthetic begins with a challenge to realism.[1] It is by no means the only art hostile to realism. Nor is hostility to realism the sole defining feature of the postmodern aesthetic. Nor is all contemporary art postmodern. My claim is more modest: Important recent forms of art, though markedly different in many ways, nevertheless shared a common way of distrusting realism.

A hallmark of traditional realism is a presumed continuity between aesthetic product and everyday life. Sometimes realism is vaguely associated with "objectivity," but the realism that I am speaking of revolves around the practices of the ordinary. It is about the world of common sense. Realism exhibits a respectful attention to the diurnal with all its quirks and flaws, to the problems of judgment that arise from the conundrums of daily living. When George Eliot interrupted *Adam Bede* (1859) to define realism, she said she wanted her novel to avoid the spectacular, beautiful, or noble. Instead, she hoped to capture "those old women scraping carrots with their work-worn hands, those rounded backs and stupid weather-beaten faces that have bent over the spade and done the rough work of the world." Eliot was most interested in the rich texture of lived experience: "My everyday fellow men, especially for the few . . . whose faces I know, whose hands I touch, for whom I have to make my way with kindly courtesy."[2]

The postmodern aesthetic challenges the realist assumption that text can capture forms of life. The concern for the everyday, wrote Roland Barthes in a seminal 1968 essay, did not produce an accurate record; it was a writerly technique. According to Barthes, the telltale realist detail, the knock on the door or the furtive glance, did not fill in the texture of lived experience but was a way to make the claim "We are the real." To Barthes, this interest in "referential plenitude" was "regressive," to be set against his own goal of emptying out the text, of infinitely postponing the object so as to challenge the very idea of representation.[3]

That there is no verisimilitude between a text that is composed and the texture of our lives is a belief shared not only by critics but also by an important number of contemporary artists. Art with a postmodern sensibility revels in techniques that disrupt the continuity of cumulative experience, that challenge the very notion of common sense.

One way this happens is by yoking together wildly different cultural fragments to represent a world in chaos, a world post-progress, post-order, on the edge of the apocalypse. The mixture of pop culture clichés, high culture references, borrowings from cultures around the globe, and stylized, brutal violence is a mark of films like *Pulp Fiction, Natural-Born Killers, True Romance, Blue Velvet, Road Warrior,* and the latest version of *Romeo and Juliet.*

Consider the last. Baz Luhrmann's 1996 *Romeo + Juliet* uses sixteenth-century Elizabethan language but is set in modern Los Angeles (although place names are ambiguous plays on LA and Italy, as with Verona turning into Verona Beach). As is common in contemporary Shakespearean interpretation, place is rather arbitrarily shifted away from the original locale. Compare this with the Zeffirelli *Romeo and* Juliet from the mid-1960s. Zeffirelli used countless "reality effects" in his movie to try to get viewers to ignore the fact that the play, literally speaking, was a bunch of English speakers pretending to be Italians. He worked to make his characters seem normal, embedded in their immediate context.

Luhrmann's remake is littered with cultural stereotypes, allegory, and mannered touches that announce its distance from realist canons. Montagues and Capulets have been transformed largely into Latino and white skinhead gangs. Juliet's nurse, of course, apropos of the LA setting, has become the Mexican household help. Coolly ironic references to Shakespeare dot the film (in faded letters on the rundown pool hall Romeo hangs out at are the words "Globe Theater"). The picture is loaded with rich and bloody Catholic iconography: Father Laurence's whole back is covered with an elaborate tattoo of a crucifix, pictures of the Virgin Mary as Our Lady of the Sacred Heart adorn the handles of guns. Allegory surfaces throughout, as with Juliet appearing as an angel in the costume ball.

Most of all, however, there is the pitched, stylized violence of contemporary action movies. Montagues and Capulets spin their guns with sound and visual effects taken from spaghetti westerns and (more recently) from Hong Kong martial arts films. Authorities swoop menacingly through the skies in helicopters spraying Verona Beach with automatic gunfire. The helicopters are drawn from real-life Los Angeles, but the liberality of gunfire (and the capacity of police firepower) comes from action movie clichés.

The referential plenitude of Luhrmann's recent *Romeo + Juliet* derives from gestures to other texts more than to any supposed "reality." And unlike the Zeffirelli *Romeo and Juliet,* the recent version quite explicitly tries to break apart any sense of everyday continuity of experience. Sixteenth-century English, LA characters with Italian names, techniques borrowed from contemporary popular culture films, stereotyped references to contemporary Southern California racial tensions, ironic gestures to the Bard himself—they all mingle together. Zeffirelli worked in a "realist" idiom, using various "reality effects" to create the sense of an everyday life that gradually comes apart. The new *Romeo + Juliet* tries to tell us from the start that the world is out of control. The first images Luhrmann presents are of a city in chaos (Zeffirelli's first images are of a city calmly doing its day-to-day business). The first fight scene in the Zeffirelli version is presented as the gradual disintegration of an everyday order in a public square. Tension gradually intrudes, tempers get hotter, and violence finally erupts. In the Luhrmann film, however, this scene is now set in a gas station, and Montagues and Capulets are screaming at fever pitch from the start. A sense of madness defines the situation. The only question is whether it will erupt into gunplay. The new version is less the story of star-crossed lovers and more the story of a star-crossed world.

Similar sentiments and techniques turn up in other violent movies—the *Terminator* films for example, or Oliver Stone's *Natural-Born Killers*. Stone's film uses a variety of camera techniques to announce the chaos. Cameras twist and turn—what at one moment was looking you straight in the eye the next moment is tilted sideways. Stone constantly and randomly shifts back and forth from color to black and white. Sometimes the background is in color, the foreground black and white. In one scene a window, for no apparent reason, turns into a television screen. As the scene progresses, we see a conversation between characters while in the background, outside the window, instead of a landscape we see different channels flip by, often with videotape of gruesome violence. If the telltale detail of the realist aesthetic was meant to portray the continuity of everyday life, the rapid and jarring juxtapositions in these films convey the sense of a world out of control.

But this is not the only way that recent art challenges the integrity of the everyday. Postmodern pastiche can be playful as well as threatening. Some art is joyous about yoking together the radically disparate. Life, in this version, need no longer be a web of cumulative experience—we can invent ourselves as we go on without the suffocating continuity of common sense.

Perhaps the most famous purveyor of this sensibility is the architect Frank Gehry. Yet not all Gehry's buildings are so playful. Indeed, his first major postmodern work—his 1978 redone house in Santa Monica—has much in common with the darker postmodernism (figure 9.1). To his conventional suburban home, Gehry added, rather famously now, a chain-link-fence balcony, corrugated metal siding, unpainted plywood, and a crow's nest on the beach side—all references that created not only a sense of a house of fragments but, as Gehry knew at the time, a "threatening" texture as well (a chain-link fence being associated with urban crime prevention).[4]

Most of Gehry's work, however, has a very different feel. It is far more playful and lighthearted.[5] A variety of techniques build the tone. Color is one. Unusual and brilliant colors have so quickly become an architectural convention that it is worth underlining how novel they were in the early 1980s, especially in nondomestic architecture. When Gehry began splashing bright reds, yel-

Figure. 9.1. Frank Gehry, Gehry residence, Santa Monica, California, 1978. © Julie Mason/ GreatBuildings.com. Used by permission.

lows, and blues on his architecture they were quite unusual, evoking a lighter, happier feel than the more staid, and ponderous, public architecture of high modernism.

Another technique is Gehry's staggered facades. Parts of buildings swirl in motion or seem dangerously close to tipping over. Buildings like his Bilbao Guggenheim Museum, the Nationale-Nederlanden Office Building in Prague, the American Center in Paris, and the Aerospace Museum in LA all seem to toy with logic, daring the laws of gravity to assert themselves (figures 9.2, 9.3, and 9.4). Yet the disorientation of these buildings is a joke, hinting at cartoon culture rather than looming apocalypse. If these buildings fall over, Gehry seems to be saying, they will pick themselves up in the next scene and be back to normal—just like Wile E. Coyote.

Color and staggering combine with Gehry's celebrated pastiche. Buildings appear as a bunch of parts jammed together instead of as an integrated whole. In the Toledo Art Museum, Gehry has added a postmodern jumble on the back of the neoclassical original. In his Vitra Furniture Company, in Basel, the connection between the two parts, the sales offices and administrative headquarters, is "a series of bridges crossing an open atrium at different floor levels." This is more than a passage, it is spatial wit, for the bridges "characterize the trans-

Figure. 9.2. Frank Gehry, Nationale-Nederlanden Building, Prague, 1996. Richard Bryant/ arcaid.co.uk. Used by permission.

Fig. 9.3. Frank Gehry, American Center, Paris, 1994. John Edward Linden/arcaid.co.uk. Used by permission.

Fig. 9.4. Frank Gehry, California Aerospace Museum, Los Angeles, 1984. Photograph courtesy Mary Ann Sullivan, Bluffton University.

fer between two areas that are totally unlike in use, look, and feel."[6] A sense of unity is exactly what is *not* wanted.

Even buildings that retain some integrity, like the Nationale-Nederlanden Building in Prague, confront the surrounding context rather than integrate into it. The Nationale-Nederlanden Building is set in a turn-of-the-century Beaux Arts neighborhood. The Gehry structure does not blend in or "merge" with the environment but rather bursts the visual continuity surrounding it. Gehry, in other words, has not responded to the end of modernism with a version of neotraditionalism. He has been dismissive of Prince Charles's efforts to revive traditional monumental forms, and he calls neotraditionalist urbanism like Seaside, Florida—an architecture whose explicit goal is to reconnect aesthetic form to the texture of daily life—an "elitist fantasy." Gehry imagines the children who grew up in such a place will soon be telling their parents: "The 21st century doesn't work like that. Why did you lie to me?"[7]

Just as with the darker postmodernism, Gehry's jumble connotes a world where lived experience is discontinuous. Common sense is absent. Each piece is simply contiguous to the next. Gehry defies cumulative experience, but not by unveiling a world spinning into mad violence. Instead, in his optimistic work, he builds an environment happily without order, one where we pick up the pieces laying all around us and put them together in whatever way we want. It is a world that does not take itself too seriously. His buildings, with their drunken facades, brilliant colors, and incongruous jumbles of parts, respond to the exuberant and creative disorder all around us. Not surprisingly, such work encourages a lighthearted response. The two towers of the Prague building have been labeled "Fred" and "Ginger" by locals, referring to the Hollywood dancing of Astaire and Rogers. Sympathetic critics evoke the terms "quirky," "wit and fun," "controlled chaos," "energetic jumble," "wonderfully funny," and "wacky" to describe Gehry's work.[8]

For Gehry himself, words like "chaos," "democracy," and "Los Angeles" are related to each other and share the same positive valence. Los Angeles is a "messy town," he argues, combining the automobile and "a freewheeling democracy where everyone has their own rights." It is on "the front line of the kind of chaotic product of democracy." He never would have survived in his native Canada, he says elsewhere. "In California," though, "it was crazy but it was freer." One might well argue with Gehry's understanding of democracy, but that would not change his vision. What he finds attractive is the fantastic possibilities in a world without scripted order. Democracy is the evasion of cumulative experience in the name of exuberant, messy, and crazy invention. "Today we have a kind of free-for-all in architecture," he notes, "and that is wonderful."[9]

Apart from the tune town playfulness of Gehry or the apocalyptic fever of *Natural-Born Killers*, there is a third way for the postmodern aesthetic to challenge the integrity of ordinary experience: the evocation of magical realism. The novels of Salmon Rushdie, Gabriel García Márquez, Toni Morrison, and Milan Kundera often reveal a more tender, reflective version of postmodern art. Magical realism shares with other postmodernisms the belief that conventional common sense does not do justice to our lived experience. But unlike the dark or exuberant postmodernisms, magical realism does not break experience into pieces. Instead, at key moments, the everyday flows into the magical and then back again. Realism is not enough precisely because the transcendental once again matters. As Zygmunt Bauman notes, one dimension of the postmodern condition is "a *re-enchantment* of the world that modernity had tried hard to *dis-enchant*."[10]

Much of this turns up in the celebrated film version of *Like Water for Chocolate*. It is set in Mexico.[11] Tita, the heroine, is forbidden to marry by her mother, who argues that as the youngest, Tita must stay home and take care of her in her old age. Tita is thus consigned to the kitchen. One of her sisters winds up marrying Pedro, the love of Tita's life. (Pedro loves Tita as well and secretly tells her he is marrying the sister so he can remain close to Tita.) The night before the wedding, we see Tita's tears drop into the wedding cake batter. The next day, at the wedding reception, all proceeds normally until the cake comes out. Up to that point, it has been a "realistic" portrayal of a turn-of-the century Mexican wedding reception. But after the first bites of cake, and without clear warning, the action slides into the magical. Everyone who eats the cake comes down with a strange melancholy and sickness. There is uncontrollable weeping and vomiting. "Nobody escaped the magic spell," the voiceover explains as the camera pans over some twenty guests lined next to each other while throwing up into the river.

The first time you watch the movie (if you have not read the book or heard what the story is), it takes a few seconds to realize that the realm of common sense has been left behind. When the scene is over, action returns to standard realist storytelling. This same movement into and out of conventional realism occurs elsewhere in the film. Food is often at the heart of the magic. Tita consummates her love with Pedro after all had been strangely affected by a quail with rose petal sauce that Tita had prepared with roses Pedro had given her. A couple of bites and the sister is ill while Tita and Pedro are magically eroticized. The voiceover explains: "A strange alchemical phenomenon seems to have occurred. Not only Tita's blood but her whole being had dissolved into the rose sauce, into the quails, and into every aroma of the meal."

At various moments in *Like Water for Chocolate*, the magic is announced by filling the screen with flickering light. This has become a stock cinematic gesture. Sparks, hundreds of candles, a dancing flame—always set against a dark backdrop—mark the moment where common sense is lacking and the world is reenchanted. There is an important scene in *Natural-Born Killers* where Micky and Mallory, the serial killers, wander into a Native American hut in the Southwest desert. For a few minutes, the savagery of the film slips into a more reflective magical realism. The Indian, functioning once more as a stereotype of non-Western wisdom, can see what "normal" people cannot. He knows from the start, without any conventional knowledge, that Micky is a "demon." He also intuits that Micky will murder him. Throughout this strange scene, a fire flickers in the foreground while desert darkness is the backdrop. Dialogue and action takes place in between. Once Micky does kill the Indian, it is the end of any magical realist gestures in the movie.

Still another example of cinematic magical realism is the widely acclaimed 1995 children's movie *A Little Princess*. Sara Crewe is a twelve-year old who falls from riches to rags when her father becomes missing in action during World War I. She is in a New York boarding school for girls at the time. When her father disappears, and Sara suddenly has no money, she stays at the school but shifts from student to servant. The tension in the movie revolves around whether Sara will give up her belief in magic. She has spent most of her life in India and tells the other girls about the magical life there. These stories are full of monsters, princes, and princesses. As she tells them, the stories are portrayed on screen, sharply set off from the realism of the boarding house action by highly unrealistic colors and stylized settings. After Sara's downfall, the mean female authority figure tells her she must give up her magic, that "real life has nothing to do with your little fantasy games." Falling into despair, Sara does begin to doubt, tearfully telling a friend that her stories were just "make believe" and that there is "no magic." Yet she gradually wins back her confidence, in part thanks to Ram Dass, an Indian manservant who lives in the house next door. In a visually marvelous moment in the film, the key moment where Sara reaffirms her faith in magic, she stands at her window in the attic, and while music swells she locks eyes with Ram Dass standing at *his* window next door. She twirls around, he knowingly smiles, and rushing about them are thousands of swirling snowflakes that have blown into the room, providing the flickering light to mark the confirmation of the magical.

This is all quite different from the Shirley Temple *Little Princess* of the 1930s and from the 1905 novel by Frances Hodgson Burnett. In the earlier movie, there is no magic at all. India is not an exotic other. It is, in fact, barely mentioned. Shirley Temple as Sara Crewe is nothing if not down-to-earth and full of common sense. She has no crisis of faith in the film, which is a story of how cheery optimism and persistence will win out in the end. In the novel, Sara's "magic" is simply a belief in make-believe. There is no "real" magic. In the original novel, as in the recent film version, Sara does have a crisis of confidence. In the book, however, it is overcome not by magic but through a renewed resolve to push on.[12]

Magical realism serves as still one more way that contemporary storytelling challenges the sufficiency of the everyday, one more art warning that "mere" common sense is suspect. All three versions of postmodernism, despite their very different sensibilities, share this sense of disconnect from the ordinary. There are, of course, other forms of art that are not realist, art that does not try to embody the everyday. Various forms of cultural idealism champion "perfection" or "the best that has been thought or said." Whether the words of Shakespeare or God touching life into Adam in the Sistine Chapel, this aesthetic does not claim that common sense is incoherent but that it must be pushed to a higher level. Similarly, modernism, with its invocation of a "deeper reality" than the conventional, does not argue that common sense is a sham, just that it is tedious and evasive of more important realities. The art I have been describing, conversely, suggests that lived experience is not cumulative, that common sense is either nonsense or limiting. Whether the shocking violence of a world out of control, the playful anarchy of urban chaos, or the magical undermining of "reality effects"—all these sensibilities challenge realism's unproblematic characterization of the everyday and presumptions about the continuity of lived experience. Life is, indeed, now experienced in fragments.[13]

Postmodern Politics

In the 1990s, a very different commentary also described a gap between the media and everyday life. We were bombarded with news about the alienation of citizens from their government. This commentary has a long history but reached a new pitch in the middle of the last decade. Washington is out of touch with the heartland, the argument ran. Politicians are disconnected from the needs of average people. The anger directed against our politics is tied to the "unreality" of a politics driven to play the game of manipulating the mass media. Antirealism, in other words, is a theme running through this commentary.

One problem identified by the commentary is the phalanx of campaign consultants and handlers who have wormed their way into contemporary political life. With the collusion of elite media, they have created a politics devoted to spin control instead of substance, image instead of integrity. According to Michael Kelly, insider cadres of "pollsters, news-media consultants, campaign strategists, advertising producers, political scientists, reporters, columnists, [and] commentators" all share the same concern—the shaping of political image in Washington. It is a remarkably inbred culture. They argue with each other, dine with each other, marry each other, and send their children to the same schools. It is also a self-contained culture, cut off from extensive contact with people living other sorts of lives. And it is also, Kelly notes, a deeply cynical culture. "If the reality of an action is defined by the public presentation of the action," he asks, "then what is a television reporter but an actor?" And if "the truth of an idea is defined by its advertising campaign, who but a mug can seriously believe in one set of ideas or another?" The Lee Atwaters, David Gergens, and James Carvilles that pull politics in a more image-conscious direction have distanced politics from the public.[14]

Closely related is the complaint about our sound bite politics. The sound bite, in both news and advertising, is the political media's own form of postmodern pastiche. It blends short bursts of words taken out of context with images that can jump as quickly as MTV. Kiku Adatto, in her well-known research, has shown that the average uninterrupted block of a candidate speaking dropped from 42.3 seconds in 1968 to 9.8 seconds twenty years later.[15]

The sound bite, however, is very much a marriage of clipped bursts of speech and dramatic and quick-changing images. It owes its origins to the virtuosity of videotape editors in the late 1970s. These editors were able to use new computerized editing technologies to pull together disparate images and sounds quickly and cheaply. Before, cutting film had been a time-consuming process. Now, editing videotape became a breeze. The only question was how fancy and elaborate the editing could get in time for that day's evening news. Suddenly, continuity did not matter. A former executive producer of CBS News explains that producers now want "an exciting, enticing piece on the air, even if it means breaking up the candidate's train of thought." Nor, he notes, is it just politicians who must learn to speak in clipped phrases: Correspondents are "not allowed to talk more than twelve or fifteen seconds before there is some intermediate sound."[16]

Still another theme heard often is the refrain of Protestant iconoclasm— the image as idol; the word as holy. Powerful pictures, critics fear, overwhelm substance. One story gets repeated often in this literature. It is about a piece Leslie Stahl did for NBC News on Ronald Reagan in 1985. Stahl juxtaposed a dark commentary about Reagan's record on top of bright, heroic pictures of the president standing in front of the flag or speaking to schoolchildren. She was sure her piece was hard hitting, exposing the gap between the Reagan image and record. Yet when she next saw White House staffers, they were ecstatic, telling Stahl that she did not realize that what mattered were the images, not the words.[17]

As in the postmodern aesthetic, in all these political commentaries, the theme of media disconnect from the everyday is common. So, too, is the sense that a mass-mediated politics is no longer realistic. Politics, the historian David Thelen says, is no longer close to "everyday life." Professional opinion managers have wedged themselves between politicians and public and "created a world of make-believe in which people converse in polls, sound bites, photo ops, attack ads, and spin doctoring."[18]

Yet there are dimensions of this critique that are strikingly different from the postmodern aesthetic. The political critics are not content with a life in fragments. Instead, they call for ways to reconnect politics to the needs of everyday life. They hope to overcome the "unreality" of political life and communication. And pervasive throughout is the belief that a densely textured form of life, one where some stability and continuity of lived experience makes sense, remains a normal and good thing. Everyday life is necessarily not in fragments, and if it is it should be repaired.

Although the political critique and the postmodern aesthetic both point to a divide between lived experience and media presentation, the arts attack the coherence of common sense while political commentators hope to repair it. The continuity of lived experience, recent aesthetics proclaims, is nonsense, for we are surrounded by crazed violence, anarchic self-invention, or magical transformation. The critics of political media, conversely, remain supportive of cumulative experience. People do not want fragments. They want to put their lives together in a meaningful way. And these same lives are increasingly distant from mass-mediated politics.

The Disconnect and the Resources of Everyday Life

Although I like both these commentaries, it is important to sort out what each does best. In the following, I distinguish between aesthetic cultural commentary and direct political communication. The dark postmodern aesthetic encourages us to confront our condition. Gehry's playfulness and magical realism elicit joy or wonder. None of these arts, however, are meant to directly mobilize political action. Because of this, they can leap into fantasy, delve into allegory, and not worry too deeply about any distance from common sense.

Political leaders or activists, conversely, must be more straightforward in communicating to a public. Their talk is about women beaten by husbands, jobs that have disappeared, bureaucrats who have overreached, racism that still burns. And most important, their talk tries concretely to answer the question "What is to be done?" To get people to vote, write a member of Congress, sign a petition, organize politically, or perform any other civic act—all take words that speak to "real" life. This does not mean they must lack vision, only that this be related to citizens' real needs. To put the distinction another way: Our best politicians show imagination, but we do not want them telling us fantasies.[19]

Much of the art I have discussed here is commentary on the chaos of our public culture. We do live in a new sort of mass-mediated environment where images rush past us in a previously unknown frenzy. Revolutions in the technology of image production are central. The sound bite, as noted above, only became possible with the rise of videotape and the marketing of computerized video-editing equipment, both of which only date from the second half of the 1970s. Replacing film with videotape has made the production of images remarkably simple and quick. Film had to be carried back to a station and developed. Videotape can be transmitted instantaneously through airwaves. Thus we can watch a scene of scud missiles sailing toward Jerusalem as it is happening, whereas in the late 1960s it took about twenty-four hours to get film shot in Vietnam on the evening news in the United States. Editing videotape is also much simpler than editing film. Film editing used scissors and paste; you cut apart the film and spliced it together. Videotape, since the late 1970s, has been edited on a computer, with a mouse. There is no more cumbersome cutting of a real physical product. The process is much quicker and leaves far more room for experimentation. Only the final version need be put on magnetic tape. All this has contributed to the frantic motion of images that we now see on our evening news.[20]

Videotape and computerized video editing not only made the news sound bite a possibility. They also set the stage for music video culture, a cultural form driven by extraordinarily quick cutting. It is rare to see a videotape without a cut every couple of seconds. Moreover, narrative line is rare; allegory dominates this art form. The jumbled images of MTV, which first came on the air in 1981, make for some of the most important antirealism around today.

Other changes have helped rearrange the speed of our image mutation. The success of cable television has meant that an increasing number of images come into our homes. Also important, and often overlooked, was the emergence of the remote control. Though invented in the 1950s, the remote was only mass marketed in the 1980s. It was in the middle years of that decade that remotes became ubiquitous. This has had the impact of speeding up image changes and shattering continuity as much as anything else mentioned here. Viewers fondling these remotes now surf from picture to picture with a speed rivaling the pace of MTV.

Montage has existed since the early part of the twentieth century, of course. But whereas its production used to be costly and time consuming, it is now quick and cheap. In the age of film, these techniques were restricted to the movies. It took time to produce an Eisensteinian montage. But now these techniques are seen everywhere—in movies, TV shows, ads, news reporting, music videos, home videos. We live in a jumpier image environment.

The postmodern aesthetic both contributes to and takes part in this environment. The use of electronic news media in films such as *Natural-Born Killers* and Luhrmann's *Romeo + Juliet* hint at the self-consciousness of this aesthetic. These filmmakers have caught something about our time when they frantically play with images. The fragmentation does say something about how media life proceeds. Similarly, Gehry's architecture does help us see the disorder of our built environment, the inescapability of its heterogeneity.

Yet if we take artists like Stone, Gehry, and Luhrmann to be saying that this defines a postmodern form of life, as I think they are saying, then we should be suspicious. It is by no means clear that most people's daily life is as chaotic or crazy as our built environment or mass media. Similarly, when a prominent critic can liken postmodern life to Lacanian schizophrenia, an "experience of isolated, disconnected, discontinuous material signifiers which fail to link up into a coherent sequence," he has overreached.[21] Such statements map the disorder of public culture onto the rhythms of daily life. Though recent shifts in capitalism have made a dignified life harder for more people, there is very little to suggest that, in general, pastiche has overwhelmed the felt continuity of everyday life or that experience fails to link into a coherent sequence. Even more, there is little to suggest that such disorder is what people want in their lives.

People continue to maneuver the world of common sense all the time. They continue to share, to a considerable extent, forms of life, which, after all, are built on practices learned through cumulative experience. Media life is relatively unimportant for such practices. People of all different backgrounds board and exit buses, buy gasoline for their cars, get up and go to work, and find ways to purchase groceries. They learn these things through lived experience, not mass media. And when people come here from some place with radically different practices, most are able to adjust. That is called learning from experience.

A common mistake is to assume that the coherent practices of everyday life depend upon an ideological consensus. That is not true, however. People who wildly disagree about what life should be often still interact in meaningful ways. Students continue to know the conventions of the college classroom, although they might have very different politics. They will get there on time, speak at appropriate moments, know how to take exams and write papers. The continuity of everyday experience is embedded in forms of life, not ideology.

Most of us use cumulative experience to navigate everyday life. This is called judgment. You see John scream at Judy at work. What do you make of that? Perhaps we have watched John behave horribly toward women for years. The interpretation is clear: John is a misogynist. But suppose we have seen Judy for several days cruelly make fun of John. In that case, John's anger might be a justified response to some last straw. To make these, or other assessments, depends upon a background context that is not discontinuous and fractured but cumulative. This is not to say that everyone would make the same assessment (that is why it is called "judgment"), nor that anyone would necessarily be objectively correct (some people, we know, have poor judgment). It is to say that the realm of the everyday is not so fragmented or chaotic as it is sometimes claimed to be.

When we hear the voices of citizens disenchanted with the political realm, the failure of established elites to address everyday needs is central. Moreover, the belief that stability and continuity of experience are good things is taken for granted. "Our safety is in jeopardy each time we walk the streets," Helen Neuner, seventy-five, of Miami Beach says. A twenty-four-year old graduate student in Pennsylvania worries that a "healthy economy right now does not mean a healthy economy in 20 years." A thirty-four-year-old police officer worries about the future of his one-year old: "It's scary down the line. What can happen is not having money there for him, for education." All these people also blame politicians for their unwillingness to address these issues.[22] Living in poverty does not mean a life joyously given to pastiche, nor a life necessarily moored in violent chaos. What is most often expressed is a fear of unraveling, a sense of fading expectations that there will be some stability to everyday experience. A single mother making $5.25 an hour worries that her twelve-year-old daughter has pregnant friends and that her eleven-year-old son watches graphic violence on television. (She bans such material in her own home. Her son sees it at friends' homes.) Her father made $23 an hour in a steel mill that was shut down in the early 1980s. She thinks Bill Clinton was a "phony" and believes that politicians in general do not really care. "Why did they do this to my town?" she asks.[23]

The research of Roy Rosenzweig and David Thelen on how people use the past also tells us that people still create coherent narratives about the past. Rosenzweig and Thelen have interviewed hundreds of Americans—white, African American, Hispanic, and Native American—and have found that they have elaborate and complicated ideas about the past. Yet one looks in vain in their research for celebrations of hybridity, pastiche, or a life of stitched together with fragments (although certain people may live these in certain ways). Instead, the interviewees recited stories where lived experience fell into coherent narratives.[24]

Indeed, the interviewees did distance themselves from civic life. The whites Rosenzweig and Thelen spoke with tended to understand the past exclusively in terms of family experience; their sense of past was disconnected from any grand narrative about the nation. These interviewees' pasts were the immigration of grandparents, the success of an uncle, the alcoholism of a father, the business success of a sister, how a mother was abused by a man. Any larger connection of these family stories to a national or civic narrative was lost. The African Americans and Native Americans interviewed, conversely, continued to be aware of the story of a glorious American past. Yet they tended to reject it vigorously as racist mythology. Their sense of the past was framed in terms of a familial and racial struggle against a usually oppressive dominant culture.

All the respondents, however, failed to see contemporary life as inherently chaotic; nor was cumulative experience shattered. Contemporary elites might be unworthy of trust, but that did not translate into a life in fragments. Instead, the common sense of the everyday remained intact. Personal and family histories defined cumulative experience.

The postmodern aesthetic, particularly that which sees the world fallen into pieces, confuses the disorder of public life with all life. In general, it underestimates the resources of the everyday. Postmodern thinking has in general been too dismissive of lived experience. From its inception, it has fallen prey to the belief that, as Douglas Crimp put it in 1977, "we only experience reality through the pictures we make of it."[25]

Such thinking misses how, as William James once explained, "chaotic pure experience" is thrown at us all the time without our losing the "concatenated and continuous structure" of cumulative experience. The reason the unexpected does not subvert the assumptions we bring to daily life, according to James, is that people naturally adjust new sensations to old ideas. Common sense, while something we should always be suspicious of, nevertheless provides a frame that saves us from vertigo.[26] A chaotic media life might make civic life incomprehensible, but it will not necessarily destroy the provisional order we make in our daily lives.

Magical realism works differently, not confronting common sense with anarchy but asking why daily experience ignores the transcendental. Though I am skeptical of the tendency of magical realism to repeat to Westerners the story of the superior insight of "primitives," this art does call attention to a part of life missing from conventionally realistic accounts. And here, too, James has something to contribute. His own account of religious experience in *A Pluralistic Universe* foreshadows many of magical realism's concerns. He hopes to save some space for the sacred while not letting religious sensibilities subvert what he calls "the continuity of experience." He wants to escape the limits of both naturalism and those who believe the absolute is radically separate from human experience. Like the magical realists, he claims that the sacred merges into the everyday. He is an indigenous source for many of magical realism's assumptions.

Yet despite the real force of magical realism, it is not meant to mobilize direct political action. Some of it, such as Rushdie or Kundera novels, mix the magical and political rumination. Much magical realism, however, simply pushes politics to the periphery.[27] This is not necessarily bad. Politics is not everything. Yet it does mean that despite whatever recovery of the sacred this art might add to life, it does no more to end the current alienation from politics than any of the other postmodern arts.

Magical realism, like the other postmodern arts, has a large dose of fantasy in it. I like fantasy. To try to definitively quash it in the name of some more important and grittier "reality" is a bad idea intrinsically and a hopeless project anyway. Fantasy can tell us things about ourselves, as in our baroque meditations about cyborgs or natural-born killers. It can bring joy to life, as in a building playfully swirling on a Beaux Arts street in Prague. And as with magical realism, it helps us leap beyond the merely quotidian—a practice that, I think, makes for a richer and more satisfying life. Fantasy, in short, does many good things.

Fantasy will not, however, end the current disconnect between politics and citizens. It does not speak directly enough to everyday needs for that. Democratic politics, if it has any meaning, must address the needs of the everyday, help stitch together a form of life meaningful to citizens. It should produce dignity. The arts can engage in whimsy, touch the sacred, and play with our fancies. Yet when citizens and political actors communicate in a democracy, it must be about the ways to secure a safe and coherent life. Political actors might try to lift the common sense of a community, as I hope they will in the matter of lesbian and gay rights. But this is not the same as attacking common sense itself. Fantasy has many uses, but it is not the idiom of direct political action.

The postmodern aesthetic cannot reanimate the political realm without a different attitude toward experience. But as long as the disconnect between politics, the media, and everyday life continues, it serves many purposes. Our darker postmodern fantasies confront the gap. Work like Gehry's teaches us how to revel in the chaos. And magical realism's reenchantment recovers a sense of wonder in the sacred. Yet what makes this art an important form of commentary on the world we live in might at the same time perpetuate the felt disconnect between politics and citizens. That is what we have to work out.

Notes

1. See the seminal essay by Roland Barthes, "The Reality Effect," in *The Rustle of Language*, by Roland Barthes (New York: Hill & Wang, 1986), 141–48.
2. George Eliot, *Adam Bede* (New York: New American Library, 1961), 177, 178.
3. Barthes, "Reality Effect," 147–48.
4. On Gehry and the "threatening" nature of chain-link fence, see *The Architecture of Frank Gehry* (New York: Rizzoli International, 1986), 51. On the dark side of Gehry, also see "Today We Have a Kind of Free-for-All in Architecture," *U.S. News & World Report*, May 30, 1983, 54. Also see the useful comments of Frederic Jameson, *Postmodernism: Or, the Cultural Logic of Late Capitalism* (Durham, N.C.: Duke

University Press, 1991), 108–30. Jameson only talks about Gehry's Santa Monica house in these pages. None of Gehry's public architecture is discussed.

5. Indeed, the interior of his home is also playful and lighthearted.
6. Ada Louise Huxtable, "The New Architecture," *New York Review of Books*, April 6, 1995, 19.
7. "A Maverick Master," *Newsweek*, June 17, 1991, 52–57; the quotation here is on 56. On the new urbanism and efforts to blend aesthetic form into the texture of daily life, see James Howard Kunstler, "Home from Nowhere," *Atlantic Monthly*, September 1996, 43–66.
8. Frank Gehry, "Since I'm So Democratic I Accept Conformists: A Lecture on Recent Work," in *Frank O. Gehry: Individual Imagination and Cultural Criticism*, ed. Charles Jencks (London: Academy Editions, 1995), 48; the critical terms are drawn from "Maverick Master."
9. Gehry, "Since I'm So Democratic," 40; "Maverick Master," 55; "Today We Have a Kind of Free-for-All," 54.
10. Zygmunt Bauman, *Intimations of Postmodernity* (London: Routledge, 1992), x.
11. I have very ambivalent feelings about the popularity of magic realism in the United States. It is common for the supernatural to appear in the guise of either a non-Westerner or the child. In the examples I use below, Mexico, India, and Native America are the source of reanimation. I fear that the popularity of magic realism is just the latest version of Westerners finding the spiritual in "primitive" cultures. Yet it is also the case that much of this art is produced by men and women who come closest to living lives of hybridity (Rushdie), in between cultures (Kundera), or on the border (*Like Water for Chocolate* is set on the Mexico/Texas border.) A more thorough investigation might want to explore the tensions between producers of this art and how it is being used in different parts of the globe.
12. Another key scene marking the difference between the three versions is when Sara wakes up to find a magnificent feast spread out around her in the attic. In the novel and 1930s movie, we are led to believe that Ram Dass brings the feast over from the house next door while Sara sleeps. (This is city living and the windows are only a few feet away from each other.) In the recent version, the feast is far more elaborate. Moreover, the food is accompanied by new clothes and bedding and drapes. In fact, the gesture is so elaborate the hint is that it is magical. That is distinctly not the impression left in the earlier versions.
13. Zygmunt Bauman, *Life in Fragments: Essays in Postmodern Morality* (Oxford: Blackwell, 1995).
14. Michael Kelly, "David Gergen, Master of the Game," *New York Times Magazine*, October 31, 1993, 64.; also see Edwin Diamond and Stephen Bates, *The Spot: The Rise of Political Advertising on Television* (Cambridge, Mass.: MIT Press, 1988); Larry Sabato, *The Rise of Political Consultants* (New York: Basic Books, 1981); Robert Westbrook, "Politics as Consumption: Managing the Modern American Election," in *The Culture of Consumption: Critical Essays in American History, 1880–1980*, ed. Richard Wightman Fox and T. J. Jackson Lears (New York: Pantheon, 1983), 143–73; and David Thelen, *Becoming Citizens in the Age of Television* (Chicago: University of Chicago Press, 1996).
15. Kiku Adatto, *Picture Perfect: The Art and Artifice of Public Image Making* (New York: Basic Books, 1993), 2; also see Roderick P. Hart, *Seducing America: How Television Charms the Modern Voters* (New York: Oxford University Press, 1994).

16. Adatto, *Picture Perfect*, 63.
17. See James Fallows, *Breaking the News: How the Media Undermine American Democracy* (New York: Pantheon, 1996) 62.
18. Thelen, *Becoming Citizens*, 193.
19. The following also relies on Arjun Appadurai's very useful distinction between fantasy and imagination. Fantasy, Appardurai argues, tends to pull us into our own minds. It is private, carrying "with it the inescapable connotation of thought divorced from projects and actions." Imagination, conversely, projects outward. It creates "ideas of neighborhood and nationhood, of moral economies and unjust rule, of higher wages and foreign labor prospects." Collective imagination is the "staging ground for action, and not only escape." Appadurai, *Modernity at Large: Cultural Dimensions of Globalization* (Minneapolis: University of Minnesota Press, 1996), 7.
20. For some discussion of the shift from film to video, see "Film Can Become Thing of the Past for Television," *Broadcasting*, October 25, 1976, 47–48; "Schneider: One of These, Some of Those," *Broadcasting*, October 25, 1976, 48–50; "Advocates of Electronic TV Keep Up the Pressure on Film," *Broadcasting*, June 20, 1977, 61–62; "CBS Thinks It Has the Answer to Problems of Editing in Tape," *Broadcasting*, October 6, 1980, 62–63. For a short history of computerized video editing, see Gary Anderson, *Video Editing and Post-Production: A Professional Guide* (White Plains, N.Y.: Knowledge Industry Publications, 1993), 1–17.
21. Frederic Jameson, "Postmodernism and Consumer Society," in *The Anti-Aesthetic: Essays in Postmodern Culture*, ed. Hal Foster (Port Townsend, Wash.: Bay Press, 1983), 119.
22. "Anger and Cynicism Well Up in Voters as Hope Gives Way," *New York Times*, October 10, 1994.
23. "The Blue-Collar Blues," *U.S. News & World Report*, November 7, 1994, 32.
24. Roy Rosenzweig and David Thelen, "How Americans Use and Understand the Past" (unpublished manuscript in author's possession).
25. Douglas Crimp, *Pictures* (New York: Committee for the Visual Arts, 1977), 3. This is the catalogue from one of the first and most important exhibitions of postmodern photography in the United States. Crimp then went on to become the editor of the very important journal *October*. Crimp continued: "To an ever greater extent our experience is governed by pictures, pictures in newspapers and magazines, on television and in the cinema. Next to these pictures, firsthand experience begins to retreat, to seem more and more trivial" (p. 3). This last sentence is exactly what I think postmodern sensibilities get wrong. For some discussion of the importance of this exhibition, see Michael Starenko, "What's an Artist to Do? A Short History of Postmodernism and Photography," *Afterimage* 10 (1983): 4–5. For similar, postmodern ruminations on experience, see Joan Scott, "The Evidence of Experience," *Critical Inquiry* 17 (Summer 1991): 773–97; and Elizabeth J. Bellamy and Artemis Leontis, "A Genealogy of Experience: From Epistemology to Politics," *Yale Journal of Criticism* 6 (1993): 163–84.
26. William James, *Pragmatism and the Meaning of Truth* (Cleveland: Meridian Books, 1955), 236, 199. On the tendency to interpret new experience in terms of old, see 50–52; on the role of common sense, see 111–27.
27. E.g., in *Like Water for Chocolate*, there is a sister who runs off and becomes a Mexican revolutionary. Yet what is striking is there is no politics on screen. The moment she becomes a revolutionary, the sister essentially exits from the plot.

CHAPTER 10

Public Attitudes toward Cultural Authority and Cultural Diversity in Higher Education and the Arts

PAUL DIMAGGIO AND BETHANY BRYSON

For much of the late 1980s and 1990s, controversy rocked America's universities and cultural institutions. Within the arts, well-publicized battles over controversial photographs, installations, and performance pieces—from the Robert Mapplethorpe controversy to the Brooklyn Museum affair—pitted defenders of modernism and artistic freedom against champions of traditional values and public decorum.[1] Within higher education, universities were castigated as preserves of "political correctness," dominated by "tenured radicals" who sought to replace traditional Western culture with a curricular goulash reflecting preferences and identities of a broad array of ethnic, gender, and lifestyle interest groups.[2]

As this volume goes to press, the culture wars in the arts and higher education are relatively becalmed. The rate of publication of screeds attacking academic liberalism has slowed, and, for now at least, conservatives have abandoned their effort to eliminate the much-maligned National Endowment for the Arts. With the migration of cultural controversy to the bedroom and the

The authors are grateful to John Evans, Richard A. Peterson, Tom Smith, Lynn Smith-Lovin, Blair Wheaton, and the members of the Princeton Sociology Department Summer Workshop on Empirical Research on Culture for comments and suggestions on drafts of this chapter. They deeply appreciate research support from the Rockefeller Foundation and institutional support from the Princeton Center for Arts and Cultural Policy Studies (as well as grants to the center from the Andrew W. Mellon Foundation and the Pew Charitable Trusts).

laboratory at the new century's turn, we may need to remind ourselves that the "culture wars" began in the nation's museums and universities.

We should *not* forget, for two reasons. First, the present moment may represent the eye of the hurricane. The paucity of controversial art exhibitions probably reflects curatorial caution more than increased tolerance. And storm clouds are gathering over universities again, as state legislatures across the country consider legislation mandating that public universities embrace the disingenuously titled "Academic Bill of Rights," a conservative effort to influence curricular content and chill academic speech.[3]

Second, quite apart from the likelihood of resurgent conflict, we have much to learn from the battles of the 1980s and 1990s, for their lessons bear directly upon the nature of cultural authority, especially religious and professional authority, in American democracy; upon the receptivity of the native born to the new immigration of the late twentieth century; and upon the mode and manner of cultural reproduction during an era in which all signs indicate that traditional bases of cultural authority have weakened as cultural diversity has increased. How the still widely perceived tension between greater cultural diversity and weaker cultural authority is resolved—whether it produces a "twilight of common dreams" (as Todd Gitlin put it) illuminated only by the blaze of intergroup conflict, or an efflorescent democratic culture—will depend on the shape and strength of our institutions and on how well we master the "arts of democracy" with which this book is concerned.[4]

In this chapter, we review the results of a 1993 survey of a statistically representative cross-section of U.S. adults to see what those outside the theater of battle made of the issues around which controversy raged. We conclude that mass opinion is more moderate and in many ways more sophisticated than public rhetoric. If published accounts of controversy have often depicted a two-sided battle between radical multiculturalists and tradition-minded conservatives, the structure of public sentiments has been more nuanced in at least three ways. First, attitudes toward cultural authority and cultural diversity are *not* polarized: Most opinions hew to the center of the ideological spectrum. Second, attitudes toward cultural authority do *not* follow in lock step from attitudes toward cultural diversity: supporters of multiculturalism do not have much more or less faith in cultural elites than their opponents. Third, and most important, respect for the value of high culture—specifically modern art and the classics of Western literature—is *not* associated with the devaluation of cultural diversity; indeed, people who value high culture are somewhat more likely than others to endorse some multicultural educational reforms.

The Arts and Education as Battlegrounds

Many observers, including some social scientists, perceived the debates over education and the arts as part of a broader "culture war" that pits religious conservatives or "traditionalists," who believe in God-given moral imperatives, against secular progressivists, who espouse moral relativism and seek to exclude religion from public life.[5] In this view, hostility to modern art, a reluctance to open the traditional canon to new works, support for English-only language policies, and distrust of the judgment of the liberal professorate follow from the traditionalist worldview. By contrast, so this position's adherents argue, support for expanding the canon and bilingual education, appreciation of modern and postmodern art, and respect for the cultural authority of professors and curators reflect a progressivist world view.

Studies of public opinion on other issues (including our own research) have found little support for the proposition that the United States has been in the midst of a "culture war," if by that we mean that Americans have become more sharply divided on many issues along progressivist and traditionalist lines. Our political institutions, of course, are sites of harsh struggle, and citizens who self-identify as strong Democrats or Republicans have become more sharply divided. But on most social and cultural issues, the attitudes of the public as a whole gravitate to the center; most people derive their attitudes on most issues from experience or specific considerations rather than broad ideological postures; and attitudes on most social issues (abortion being the great exception) actually became less rather than more polarized during the last quarter of the twentieth century.[6]

Nonetheless, many journalists came to the opposite conclusion, convincing themselves by the mid-1990s that the United States was in the throes of a full-fledged culture war. Indeed, reporters employed the term "culture war," which appeared in the press only rarely during the 1980s, with escalating frequency between 1990 and 1995. Our review of newspapers on the Nexis database indicated that whereas the phrase appeared in two or three articles per month between January 1990 and late 1991, references rose steadily thereafter to approximately fifty (distinct) articles per month by late 1994 and early 1995.[7] Whether or not social and cultural conflict actually increased in the United States during this period, attentive newspaper readers would certainly have concluded that it had.

The arts and education, especially higher education, were among the most visible arenas in which the cultural contests of the 1980s and 1990s were fought. Indeed, these institutions were the central focus of the cultural politics that sprang into public consciousness with conservative attacks on campus "political correctness" and the National Endowment for the Arts in the late 1980s. More than one-third of all references to "culture war" in the U.S. press between 1990 and 1993 (as these were recorded in the Nexis system) were about higher education and the high culture arts. (Many more concerned the popular media.) No less a belligerent than William Bennett, President Ronald Reagan's chair of the National Endowment for the Humanities, described the "culture war" as a battle "about music, art, poetry, literature, television programming, and movies; the modes of expression and conversation, official and unofficial, that express who and what we are, what we believe, and how we act."[8]

Part of the visibility and salience of attacks on universities and arts institutions reflected their sponsorship: Several conservative foundations supported a network of academic associations, publishing houses, and student groups that promoted the attack on the universities.[9] Many conservative Christian social-movement groups, as well as some Republican politicians, found it convenient to highlight government grants to "obscene" or "sacrilegious" artists in fund-raising appeals and campaign speeches.[10] Part of the attention lavished upon conflicts in universities and the arts is explicable by their immediacy: Photographs with in-your-face sexual or religious imagery and lurid (if rarely entirely accurate) tales of innocent college students crucified at the altar of "political correctness" have the capacity to engender shock and dismay.

In any case, campus controversies and arts-funding scandals received attention disproportionate to their number or significance, as isolated events were taken as emblematic of broad cultural trends. With respect to the arts, the fact that only a dozen or so grants out of tens of thousands by public arts agencies were suitable for condemnation by those agencies' adversaries is at least as remarkable—and, if one takes it as a sign of timidity, at least as sobering—as the fact that those grants were made at all.

In the field of higher education, reports of the trashing of Western civilization turned out to represent fevered reactions to modest reforms. As Bethany Bryson concluded from case studies of four very different English departments, campuses themselves (with some well-publicized exceptions) were the calm eyes at the center of the canon-war hurricane. Elite departments turned disagreements into spirited intellectual contests among entrepreneurial professors who, whatever the outcome, remained free to teach what they pleased. In non-elite departments, curricular decisions were dictated by the realities of university distribution requirements, what textbook publishers offered, and student preferences—faculty are happy to teach nearly any decent book if only their students will read it—leaving little time or occasion for philosophical contention.[11]

Bryson's results were consistent with those of a 1990 survey of English Department faculty conducted by the Modern Language Association. That study found that although courses in modern literature included works by women and African American authors (courses on earlier periods were largely unchanged), such additions only modestly leavened syllabi dominated by canonical figures. And while just over half of the departments had introduced courses on women writers or writers of color, almost 80 percent offered specialized courses on Shakespeare, with the typical institution offering as many sections of the latter as sections in all courses on women and authors of color combined.[12]

Public Opinion and the Arts of Democracy

Even if the press exaggerated the magnitude of change and the severity of conflict, such reports might have markedly influenced Americans' perceptions. Our purpose here is to explore the extent to which the public battles over the arts and higher education of the early 1990s reflected (or shaped) the underlying structure of American sentiments, as captured by a sample survey of more than 1,400 noninstitutionalized Americans aged eighteen years and over. These men and women were interviewed in their homes in the spring of 1993, a period of relative calm before the escalation of culture war rhetoric that preceded the 1994 midterm elections.

It may be worth asking both why we should be interested in public opinion, and whether surveys are capable of measuring it. As to the first, measuring public opinion is a central ritual of American democracy. This reliance on attitude surveys to characterize the public mind is a relatively novel and highly consequential aspect of contemporary politics. Whereas "public opinion" in other epochs was constituted in salons, coffee shops, or public squares, today it reflects specific practices of survey design and implementation, the results of which insert themselves as social facts into political discourse. Quite apart from whether the percentage of the public that favors or opposes bilingual education or government grants to artists reflects "true" attitudes (insofar as such things can be said to exist), survey results, once reported in the press, structure and constrain public debate.[13]

Because of this, the results of attitude surveys have significant political implications for both cultural democrats and elitists. If one believes that the public has a legitimate claim on the policies of universities or nonprofit arts institutions, then the weight one gives critical voices will depend, to some extent at least, on whether their views represent those of the constituencies for whom they claim to speak. If one believes that universities and cultural institutions should be insulated from fashions that sway the broader culture, then one must understand public opinion in order to fend off the forces of philistinism.

But do surveys really tell us what people think? Most polls invite respondents to affirm or reject an opinion (declared or embedded in a question) that the survey's authors have constructed. Affirmation does not mean that a respondent fully embraces the position endorsed, only that his or her view is more affirmative than rejecting. Moreover, as survey experts are quick to point out, many people construct opinions on the spot to oblige pollsters. If people have not thought much about an issue, their responses may be driven by the details of question wording. If they have thought a lot about it, their opinions may be too complex and ambivalent to be captured in brief precoded responses.[14]

Even so, attitude surveys can teach us a lot about the direction and structure of people's views, albeit not the specifics of what they believe. For one thing, surveys are excellent inoculants against partisan claims to represent the masses and against the natural tendency to infer the distribution of public sentiments from their visible expression in collective action and talk show debate. Equally important, inspecting the relationship between different items in an attitude survey—the extent to which people who take a certain stand on one issue take a predictable position on a second—lets us draw inferences as to how people reason about matters of controversy. Analyzing the ways in which responses to opinion surveys fit together helps us recover the narratives that structure the opinions of the public or of particular groups within it. Such narratives are often different and less ideological than those that animate public speeches and newspaper editorials. In other words, attitude surveys cannot reveal the public mind in stark clarity, but they dispel illusions and offer intriguing hints about how people understand their world.

Specifically, we believe that data from the 1993 General Social Survey can help us understand Americans' views of cultural authority and cultural diversity. By "cultural diversity," we refer to heterogeneity with respect to racial and ethnic groups understood to be "minorities." In the United States, cultural diversity ordinarily refers to communities of color, including persons of Asian, African, Latin American, and Native American descent. Debates about cultural diversity address the inclusiveness of institutions as manifested by the backgrounds of persons (faculty or students, curators or actors), of cultural objects (books in a curriculum, paintings in galleries), or of languages (as in controversies over bilingual education in the schools).

By "cultural authority," we refer to the legitimate rights of specialized elites to evaluate objects, ideas, or actions in specific spheres of collective responsibility. Societies vary in the extent to which such authority is vested in anyone at all; in the degree of consensus about what kinds of people possess it; in the extent to which it is differentiated by domain or concentrated across them; and in the extent to which its exercise is embedded in the state, in private organizations, or in more general discursive formations.

In comparison with other wealthy nations, the United States' pattern of cultural authority has been unusual in at least two ways. First, in the domain of arts and letters, it has been relatively weak and strongly contested. Second, at least since the Progressive Era, cultural authority has been concentrated in densely connected networks based in universities and the professions.[15]

Conflicts over the arts and education often challenge established modes of cultural authority from several directions. Some proponents of "diversity" castigate those who hold cultural authority for maintaining cultural hierarchies that arbitrarily exclude work by nonwhite or female artists, authors, scholars, and musicians. At the same time, attacks on modernist (and postmodern) art, and on "political correctness" (sometimes a code word for attention to "cultural diversity") in the universities have often entailed a rejection of professional authority, an antinomian appeal to the "common sense" of the American public that works, insofar as it does, precisely because cultural authority (in the arts and humanities) has never been very effectively established.

Of course, the most influential of these critics (e.g., Hilton Kramer, Allan Bloom, William Bennett) are no strangers to universities themselves: Such critics often speak on behalf of the traditional canon and in the name of a no-longer-dominant view of the humanities, drawing upon their own professional credentials to underscore their arguments. Thus combatants in cultural conflict construct both protagonists and villains—culturally diverse groups, "great" art or literature, the academic "establishment," and so on—in multiple and often inconsistent registers. Indeed, debates over education and the arts are complicated by the fact that they present themselves both as conflicts *within* a professorial and intellectual elite, in which each side claims the mantle of professional expertise, *and* as populist uprisings against secular cultural authority of any kind.[16]

Our study had three objectives. We wanted to find out if attitudes toward cultural authority and cultural diversity in the arts and education were as *polarized* as the rhetoric suggested. We wanted to know if the general public's opinions on the various issues that had become implicated in public debates *cohered* into the clusters of interlinked opinions marked out by conservative critics and their liberal opponents. Finally, insofar as we identified lines of cleavage, we were eager to learn how Americans of different genders, races, ages, and levels of educational attainment differed in their views.

Are Attitudes Polarized?

The 1993 General Social Survey contained eight questions designed to tap respondents' views on these conflicts.[17] In each case, respondents were presented with a statement and asked to indicate whether they agreed, agreed strongly, disagreed, or disagreed strongly with the sentiments it expressed. The items tapped attitudes toward the role of the classics in high school and college curricula, the capacity of "great books" to transcend their cultural origins, bilingual education in the public schools, reform of the canon to include literature by women and people of color at the expense of traditional works by white men, whether excellence can be found in popular and folk culture as well as the fine arts, whether teachers and professors can be trusted to decide what students should read, and whether many people are capable of recognizing quality in the arts. In some cases, the statements were phrased tendentiously to provoke varied reactions.

Given that these topics are hardly dinner table staples in most American households, respondents were strikingly able to produce opinions. Just between 4 percent (on the issue of bilingual education, which had been in the news) and 11 percent (on replacing traditional literature with work by women and minorities) confessed that they did not know how what they thought about the issues in question. Just over 10 percent were unsure how they felt about the role of the classics, 8 percent were not sure if great books are universal, and 7 percent had no opinion about modern art. These percentages are high by the standards of such surveys; by comparison, just 4 percent said "don't know" when asked if a book advocating homosexuality should be removed from their local public library, 3 percent were unsure if government spent too little or too much money on assistance for poor people, and fewer than 2 percent failed to express an opinion on whether gun buyers should be required to obtain police permits. Nonetheless, most respondents were sufficiently comfortable with the issues to express themselves to interviewers.

For all those who did respond to each question, our findings indicate the percentage choosing each of four options: "strongly agree," "agree," "disagree," and "strongly disagree." In each case, we analyzed results separately for all respondents and for college graduates only. We looked separately at the latter because we assumed that controversies about higher education and the arts are typically more salient to college graduates than to other people. We wondered if college graduates' attitudes differed from those of other Americans and if their views were more polarized than those of the public at large.

The General Public

Responses to questions about education indicate that Americans are more uncertain than sharply divided with respect to the authority of the classics, the desirability of expanding the canon to admit works by authors from previously underrepresented groups, confidence in educators' stewardship of the curriculum, and even the contentious issue of English instruction in the public schools. Most respondents were willing to "trust the judgment of the teachers and professors who decide what . . . students should be reading," but very few said they felt strongly about this and more than one-third withheld their trust—again, however, with little passion. (When the General Social Survey asked this question again in 1998, the results were very similar.)[18]

When respondents were asked to respond to a provocatively worded assertion that students waste too much time reading the classics, just over one-third rose to the bait, with most disagreeing. Again, strong opinions were notable for their rarity. Indeed, other evidence points to the fact that Americans are divided in their views of the importance of the classics, but not rancorously so. A 1998 telephone survey of registered voters found a bare majority agreeing with the statement that "every college student should have to study the classics of Western civilization in order to graduate," with a large minority expressing disagreement and a similarly small number of "strong" opinions.[19]

Respondents were more willing to agree with a statement, also provocatively phrased, bemoaning the substitution of works "promoted because they are by women or by members of minority groups" for "traditional American literature." Yet, even though the wording seemed calculated to maximize the proportion of sympathetic responses, fewer than one in twelve strongly agreed, and more than one in three dissented.[20] Between 1993 and 1998, when the General Social Survey repeated the item, opinion shifted toward multiculturalism, with only 56 percent in 1998 (compared with 66 percent) of those who expressed opinions endorsing the statement, 44 percent disagreeing, and an unusually high proportion (15 percent of all those questioned) declining to answer.

Respondents appear more comfortable with the notion of literary universalism: More than three-quarters agreed that "there is no 'white literature,' 'black literature,' or 'Asian literature,' " but that "the greatest books are universal in their appeal." Just over one in ten endorsed this view "strongly," the largest percentage taking a "strong" position on any item. (It is not clear in what measure these responses reflected aversion to ethnic segmentation in literature, admiration for "great books," or perhaps other messages that respondents found in the complex proposition with which they were confronted.)

Responses to the question about the exclusive use of English in public schools were split almost evenly between those who favored at least some bilingual instruction and those who favored English only. Approximately 10 percent of respondents took strong positions on each side, more than for other questions, but still surprisingly few for an issue that had been hotly debated, is linked to feelings about immigration, and had appeared on ballots in state elections.

Questions dealing with the arts also revealed much diversity of opinion and relatively few strongly held positions. Respondents were about evenly split between those who agreed and disagreed with the classically elitist position that "only a few people have the knowledge and ability to judge excellence in the arts." Fewer than 6 percent were willing to endorse this statement strongly, however, and fewer than 10 percent strongly opposed it. Five years later, in 1998, opinion had shifted noticeably in the direction of populism, with 57 percent disagreeing, 17 percent of them "strongly."[21]

A majority of respondents disagreed with a statement denigrating the work of modern painters, although two of five agreed; fewer than 5 percent strongly endorsed the negative view, however.[22] By 1998, opinion had turned even more cosmopolitan, with just over 30 percent of respondents agreeing and 14 percent taking vigorous exception.[23]

Responses to the statement "Artistic excellence can be found in popular and folk culture just as much as in the fine arts" were the most lopsided, reflecting a nearly unanimous rejection of the aesthetic ideology that once sharply privileged high culture.[24] Fully 95 percent of respondents agreed with an assertion that most educated Americans would once have deemed philistine, and only 6 of the 1,463 respondents took vigorous exception to it. Nonetheless, even in this case, respondents were reluctant to express strong opinions, with just over 10 percent agreeing "strongly" with the popular stance.

Overall, the responses demonstrate that Americans endorse universalism and reject a narrowly highbrow definition of aesthetic merit by wide margins, but that they hold divergent opinions about virtually everything else. Large minorities of respondents do not trust educators to create curricula, think that students have to read too many "classics," want English to be the only language of instruction in the public schools, are sympathetic to the substitution of works by women and people of color for "traditional American literature," believe that one must have special skills or abilities to judge excellence in art, and agree that "even a child" could produce modern painting—with small majorities taking the opposite positions. The pattern of responses implies uncertainty and tentativeness more than polarization, however, because only the hot-button issue of English in the public schools causes even one in five respondents to take polar positions. For all other items, the ratio of moderate to extreme responses ranges from 5.5:1 (the greatest books are universal) to 7.2:1 (substituting works by women and minority group members for "traditional American literature"). Most Americans, it seems, have either thought too little about these issues to feel comfortable with extreme positions or, if they *have* considered them, see enough merit on each side to find the extremes unappealing.

College Graduates

It stands to reason that people who have graduated from colleges and universities are more likely to care about what goes on in them than are less educated Americans. And because college graduates participate more actively in the arts than others, it seems likely that arts-related topics will engage them more deeply as well.[25] Consequently, we looked separately at the opinions of respondents who reported having graduated from college. Perhaps, we thought, opinions have become polarized among the most highly educated, even if the rest of the public has been indifferent.

For the most part, the views endorsed by college graduates are similar to those of other Americans. This is especially true of confidence in faculty curricular judgment, the universality of the great books, and, to a lesser extent, bilingual education and the expansion of the curriculum. The primary difference between college graduates and respondents with fewer years of formal education is that the former are more willing to take strong stands in defense of traditionally defined high culture *and* in favor of cultural diversity and cultural democracy. Thus 40 percent of respondents with less than college degrees, but only 15 percent of college graduates, agreed that the classics receive too much emphasis in U.S. education; 20 percent of college graduates—but just 5 percent of other respondents—disagreed *strongly* with this assertion. Similarly, almost half the respondents without college degrees, but just over one in four college graduates, agreed that "modern painting is just slapped on";

and more than twice as many college graduates (18 percent compared with 8 percent) took *strong* exception to this view.

At the same time, college graduates evinced a more democratic perspective on taste than other respondents. Whereas well over half of the less schooled respondents endorsed the statement that "only a few people can really appreciate great art," only 35 percent of college graduates supported this view. By contrast, twice as many college graduates (15 percent as compared with 7 percent) disagreed with it strongly. And although nearly everyone endorsed the populist position that excellence can be found in popular and folk culture as easily as in high art, fully 20 percent of college graduates, as compared with fewer than half that many nongraduates, said that they "*strongly*" agreed.

Conclusions on Polarization

Three things about these patterns are worth noting. First, as expected, college graduates are great defenders, although not the only defenders, of both classical and modern high culture. This is consistent both with the conventional notion that universities inculcate respect for the arts *and* with arguments by such sociologists as Pierre Bourdieu and Randall Collins that college graduates represent a kind of status group committed to defending a high culture from their command of which—"cultural capital" in Bourdieu's terms—they derive much prestige.[26] Although this result seems overdetermined, it does suggest that we must not be too quick to believe the Cassandras who claim that higher education no longer instills respect for canonized art and literature.[27] We shall have more to say about this later in the chapter.

Second, college graduates as a group evince a more democratic view of culture than other Americans, expressing faith in the majority's ability to judge quality in the arts and refusing to draw strong qualitative boundaries between high culture and other forms. This is surprising for two reasons. If college graduates benefit from their command of prestigious forms of culture, it would seem to be in their interest to endorse, and to claim a privileged relationship with, the established cultural hierarchy. That they fail to do so is news. For another thing, many scholars and journalists have depicted the United States as engulfed in a war over the value of established culture, with populist philistines arrayed against the defenders of the classical faith. James Hunter, for example, has written that "multiculturalists wish to increase the recognition, power, and legitimacy of various minority groups, in part through a delegitimation of an 'oppressive' mainstream American culture."[28] For this and other reasons, he argues "multiculturalism undermines the authority of cultural norms and cultural institutions."[29] Similarly, Richard Merelman has referred to multiculturalism as "a form of subordinate resistance to dominant group power."[30] Yet it seems that we find the same kinds of people, especially college graduates, overrepresented on both sides of the trenches. This suggests that the opposition posited between high culture and multiculturalism is a false one. Again, we shall have more to say about this below.

Third, college graduates are more likely to give emphatic responses—to report not just that they "agree" or "disagree" but that they do so "strongly." This tendency is small—like other people, most college graduates hew to moderate positions—but it is statistically significant for all items but two (bilingual education and trusting professors to decide on curricular matters). Only attitudes toward bilingual education—where 10 percent strongly agree and 12 percent strongly disagree—show signs of polarization. In other cases, college graduates tend to choose only one of the two polar alternatives. Thus 20 percent of college-educated respondents disagree strongly with the proposition that students have to read too many classics (compared with the 3 percent who strongly agreed); and almost 20 percent strongly agree that excellence can be found in folk and popular culture, compared with the just over half of 1 percent who strongly demurred from this view. Consistent with the notion that these issues are more salient to them, college-educated respondents are more willing to take strong stands on these items, but (except on the subject of bilingual education) not in a way that indicates that opinions are polarized. In other words, these data suggest strongly that the cultural battles that have raged around academia and the arts have neither reflected sharp division in the views of Americans (either college graduates or the general public) nor have had much of an effect on those views.

Are Attitudes Ideologically Coherent?

Even if Americans' views on cultural authority and cultural diversity are far from polarized, it is still possible that, consistent with the "culture war" story, people's attitudes (strongly held or not) might cluster into coherent ideological packages. If so, such a structure could serve as a scaffold around which broad polarization might yet occur.

We explored this issue by looking at a matrix of correlation coefficients, statistics that range from –1 (if x, then not y) to 1 (if x, then always y), with 0 representing statistical independence (knowing x tells one nothing about y).[31] If the conservative culture critics are right about how the sides line up, we would anticipate the following:

Traditionalists	*Progressivists*
Not enough emphasis on classics	Too much emphasis on classics
Great books are universal	No universal literature
English only in the schools	Bilingual education
Do not revise the canon	Make the canon more inclusive
Only a few can recognize good art	Anyone can recognize good art

Traditionalists	Progressivists
Modern painting is just slapped on	Modern painting is serious art
Excellence in high culture	Excellent in all kinds of culture
Do not trust teachers and tenured radicals	Trust teachers and professors to decide what students read

The first headline is that there is little evidence of ideological coherence of any kind. Correlations among items, though often statistically significant, are also quite low: The highest for the general public is 0.24. (Where opinions are ideologically coherent, so that different items essentially measure the same underlying worldviews, coefficients of 0.50 or greater are common.) As it happens, the strongest positive correlation is between two items that are often portrayed as negatively associated: People who think that schools should continue to teach the classics also take modern painting seriously.

Indeed, of twenty-eight pairwise correlations, only ten were statistically significant and consistent with the conventional wisdom described above. Almost as many—eight statistically significant associations—*contradict* the conventional wisdom. (Another ten pairs of opinions are essentially unrelated to one another.) In other words, the notion that solid blocks of ideologically unified traditionalists and progressives vie for control of our universities and cultural institutions, although possibly correct as a characterization of mobilized interest groups, provides no purchase in understanding patterns of response among a cross-section of the U.S. population. If in 1993 there was a culture war in progress, clearly most of the population had not enlisted on either side.

One might argue that ideological coherence in attitudes toward these matters would be found only among those highly educated men and women for whom the issues are most salient.[32] Indeed, more responses *were* significantly associated for college graduates than for those with less education, and the number of correlations consistent with the conventional wisdom rose from ten to thirteen (with seven contradicting it and eight pairs not significantly associated). Correlations remain modest, but they do indicate somewhat greater ideological coherence in the opinions of more educated respondents.

Almost all of this coherence reflects significant associations among five of the eight items: bilingual instruction in the schools, expanding the canon to include works by women and authors of color, whether many people can judge excellence in art, whether excellence is as likely to be found in popular and folk culture as in high culture, and views of modern painting. College graduates who oppose bilingual education and opening up the canon are also somewhat more likely than others to deride modern painting, believe that few people can judge aesthetic quality, and agree that excellence is more easily found in high culture than in other forms. Cultural democrats—people who think that excellence can be found in any cultural form and that most people can identify good art—are also more likely to favor bilingual education and expanding the canon, and are more willing to defend modern art. None of these tendencies is very strong, but they are all sufficiently marked that one would not likely find them by chance.

In other respects, however, the polarity that conservative critics have constructed was not evident in the opinions of the college-educated public. Support for the role of the classics in schools is associated not with conservatism but with commitment to cultural democracy, including an expansive view of how many people are qualified to judge art, appreciation of the excellence of folk and popular cultures, and support for modern painting. Also inconsistent with the conventional wisdom is the fact that respondents who endorse two "traditionalist" views—a belief in literary universalism and the belief that only a few people can judge quality—also express more confidence in professional educators.[33]

If the structure of opinion among the college educated affords only partial and equivocal support for the conventional wisdom, patterns among respondents with high school diplomas or less provide none at all: Only eight of twenty-eight correlations are significantly consistent with the "culture wars" story; nine significant associations contradict it; and eleven pairs of opinions are unrelated.

Some differences between college graduates and those whose schooling ended with high school are instructive. Whereas college graduates who agree (and agree strongly) that excellence can be found in folk and popular art are *less likely* to deplore replacing traditional American works with multicultural fare and *more likely* to defend modern painting, the pattern for the least educated respondents is the reverse. These and other results suggest that for college graduates, equating the value of popular and folk culture reflects a democratic openness to art and culture of many kinds. By contrast, for the least well educated, the same equation appears to reflect a rejection of all cultural authority and a *devaluation* of many kinds of art. Put another way, the most educated respondents tend to reject hierarchy in order to elevate the bottom, whereas the least educated tend to reject hierarchy as a means of devaluing what has been at the top.

Beyond Binary Oppositions: A Multidimensional View

We have seen that no one-dimensional explanation suffices to capture the complexity of Americans' beliefs (even as these are expressed in responses to prefabricated survey questions) about cultural authority and cultural diversity. In particular, the notion that conservative traditionalism and multicultural liberalism exhaust the space of opinions on these matters turns out to be especially implausible.

What then *does* explain how people respond to these items? To pursue this question, we eliminated two of the items—whether excellence can be found in folk and popular culture (because there was so little disagreement about it), and whether the great books are universal (because the question was confusing)—and submitted the rest to a "factor analysis" (a statistical program that places items that are associated with one another into clusters and provides some statistical guidance in deciding how many are necessary to apprehend the complexity of people's responses).[34]

The results indicated that three distinct dimensions structure people's responses. These three dimensions are

1. *orientation to high culture*, measured by attitudes toward the literary classics and modern art;
2. *resistance to multiculturalism*, tapped by attitudes toward bilingual education and expanding the literary canon; and
3. *rejection of cultural authority*, reflected in distrust of educators and the view that most people can judge art.[35]

Far from representing binary oppositions, these three dimensions tapped distinct and largely independent points of view. In the statistical analyses that follow, each of these dimensions is measured by a scale summing each respondent's score on the two items on which each dimension is based.

Explaining Attitudes

Having identified the dimensions that appear to structure people's attitudes toward cultural diversity and cultural authority, we can now begin to explain why people vary along them. We use "explanation" in the special sense, limited but illuminating, common to this kind of research: the prediction by statistical means of a person's position on scales representing each of the three dimensions. To accomplish this, we looked at many other "variables" (aspects of identity, life experiences, or beliefs) on which people differ, and we asked how these differences are associated with people's positions on the dimensions of interest (attitudes toward high culture, multiculturalism, and cultural authority). To distinguish between the "effects" of different characteristics, we used a statistical method called "multiple regression analysis" to examine each variable while "holding constant" effects of all the rest. Thus we can interpret the results as representing the difference between people who differ with respect to any given variable but are similar with respect to other characteristics of which we have taken account. The characteristics we used to predict the attitude measures are age, race, gender, years of formal education, residence in the Southeast, income, membership in a conservative Protestant religious denomination, and political conservatism.[36]

In addition, we used four scales based on the addition of other separate measures. One combines three items tapping support for legally sustained racial separation into a measure of *racism* (of a particularly crude variety).[37] A second scale, *tolerance*, is based on responses to fifteen questions about whether advocates of various unpopular opinions should be permitted to speak in public, teach in a college, or have a book in the local library.[38] A third scale, *confidence in professional institutions*, sums measures of the respondent's confidence in education, the press, medicine, and the scientific community.[39] A final scale sums measures of attendance at several kinds of arts events and several related attitudes into a measure of *commitment to the arts*.[40]

We shall discuss the three dimensions (our three kinds of cultural attitudes) one at a time. In each case, we start by examining the way in which people's identities and experiences are associated with their cultural attitudes (without considering their attitudes in other domains); then we look at the relationship of cultural orientations to other attitudes; and finally we examine together the effects of those characteristics *and* attitudes that are associated with the perspective we are trying to explain, in order to see the effect of each with the others taken into account. We separate the measures in this way because a strong (if not unassailable) case can be made that personal characteristics are causally implicated in the development of the attitudes they predict. By contrast, the link between attitudes in one realm and attitudes in another is more logical than causal, representing affinity rather than sequence.[41] We put them together, in the end, in order to explain to what extent personal characteristics influence cultural attitudes by shaping other aspects of a person's worldview, and to what extent their influence is independent of the other attitudes measured here. We shall focus on major findings described in broad strokes. Readers who would like to see the statistical tables may request them from the authors.

Support for High Culture

Respondents who scored high on this dimension rejected both the notion that schools focus too heavily on classics *and* the dismissive characterization of modern art. We expected that more educated respondents would evince more allegiance to high culture, because many studies have found the number of years a person has gone to school to be the best predictor of his or her participation in and attitudes toward the arts.[42] As expected, educational attainment is by far the best predictor of positive attitudes toward high culture among the sociodemographic variables, with an effect three times as large as that of any other. Considerably smaller, but still statistically significant, differences exist in the views of women (more supportive) and men, between Euro-Americans (more supportive) and African Americans, and between people who live in rural areas (less supportive) and others.

Members of theologically conservative Protestant denominations are also significantly less supportive of high culture than others. We initially attributed this difference to the inclusion in the scale of a measure of attitudes toward modern art, government support for which had been the target of highly publicized attacks by some evangelical leaders. To see if this interpretation was correct, we separately examined predictors of the scale's two components—attitudes toward modern art and positions on the place of the classics in school curricula. To our surprise, members of theologically conservative denominations have more negative sentiments toward the classics as well as toward modern art, and the magnitude of the differences are almost identical. Apparently, religious and secular conservatives part company in their view of the importance of traditional works of high culture.[43]

It was no surprise that people who attend arts events, enjoy classical music, and like their friends to be "cultured" would rank high on this dimension, because both scales tap an underlying interest in high culture. Indeed, this is the case. What *was* surprising is that political tolerance is almost as strongly related to positive attitudes toward the classics and modern art as is high cultural participation and taste. Moreover, racist attitudes are *negatively* and significantly associated with support for traditional high culture.

When we look simultaneously at the effects of both personal characteristics and other attitudes on support for high culture, we find that differences related to gender, race, residence, and religion stem from the fact that these characteristics shape other attitudes and behaviors—especially *participation in* high culture—that are associated with attitudes toward the arts.[44] By contrast, fully 75 percent of the positive effect on attitudes toward high culture of educational attainment persists even after we take account of the fact that more educated people attend more arts events, are more politically tolerant, and are less likely to endorse racist views than those with less education. Apparently schooling succeeds in instilling respect for the value of high culture, even among people who do not personally participate in the arts. (Schooling also engenders support for the arts because it has such a strong effect on people's own arts participation, but that mechanism appears to be of secondary importance.)

Support for Multiculturalism

Respondents who scored high on this dimension do *not* regret the displacement of traditional male authors by women and authors of color in university curricula, and they support the use of languages other than English in public school classrooms. We expected that education would be associated with support for multiculturalism, because research has shown that the highly educated tend to be cultural "omnivores," enjoying many kinds of cultural forms; and because they ordinarily express lower levels of racial or ethnic prejudice.[45] In fact, the more educated *are* significantly more sympathetic to multiculturalism, as are women and African Americans.[46]

A few proponents of multiculturalism have implied that assertion of the value of traditional Western culture represents a thinly veiled rejection of multiculturalism, or even a distaste for the "cultural others" themselves.[47] We suspect that this is too simple, and that one can be partial to Euro-American high culture because one likes it, not because one dislikes people who are not Euro-American. At the same time, research on symbolic racism suggests that cultural attitudes *may* be extensions or displacements of intergroup antipathies, with cultural representations of a group bearing a burden of hostility otherwise directed to the group itself.[48] For this reason, we anticipated that the less racist the respondent, the more he or she would favor multiculturalism. Indeed, racism is indeed significantly and positively associated with opposition to multiculturalism.[49]

Curiously, however, self-described political conservatism is even *more* strongly associated with opposition to multiculturalism than is the endorsement of crudely racist positions. Students of racial attitudes disagree on how to interpret such results. Some would argue that positions on policy issues related to cultural diversity (e.g., bilingual education and curriculum reform) are structured by *both* racial views and matters of philosophical principle unrelated to race. These scholars might interpret our findings as indicating that philosophical considerations are even more important than racial views in determining opposition to multiculturalism. Other scholars contend that changes in the political landscape and social norms have led to a conflation of racism and conservatism—that is, a situation in which people define themselves as "conservative" partly on the basis of attitudes that reflect subtle forms of racial stereotyping and aversion. As declines in the proportion of Americans endorsing crudely racist positions have made the latter poor predictors of most policy preferences, more subtle correlates of racial intolerance have picked up the explanatory slack. In this view, then, the fact that conservatism and racism together explain about 15 percent of the variation in people's positions on the multiculturalism scale reinforces the suspicion that opposition to multicultural reforms is often a form of symbolic racism.[50]

Interestingly, the effect of conservatism is significant only for the more educated respondents, and the effect of education depends upon how respondents placed themselves on the scale of liberalism to conservatism. For self-described liberals, higher education is strongly associated with support for multiculturalism; for self-described conservatives, it is associated with opposition. Thus it seems that education polarizes opinion by increasing the salience of multiculturalism, and therefore the correlation between political ideology and attitudes, for conservatives and liberals alike.[51]

Rejection of Cultural Authority

Respondents who score high on this final dimension reject the proposition that only a few people are capable of judging excellence in art and are reluctant to trust educators to choose what students will read in school. One might expect that education would instill faith in the authority of cultural elites, by exposing people to such elites and also leading them to view themselves as possessing legitimate cultural authority by dint of their own training. This is not the case: Consistent with the notion that the highly educated participate in an antinomian "culture of critical discourse" and exhibit a chronic disposition to question authority, formal education is actually the strongest *positive* predictor of rejection of cultural authority.[52] Older people and those living in the South are less likely (respectively) to question cultural authority than the young and people in other parts of the United States. These effects are small, but sufficient to refute the claim that Middle America has rejected the authority of a cultural establishment it views as a left-wing "cultural elite."[53]

We expected attitudes toward cultural authority to be related to attitudes toward professional authority of other kinds. Specifically, we anticipated that people who expressed little confidence in physicians, scientists, journalists, and educators would also hold populist attitudes toward judgments about art and literature. Our expectation was confirmed by a modest but statistically significant association in the expected direction.

The most striking finding about attitudes toward cultural authority, however, is that they are very hard to predict: Even with both sociodemographic characteristics and attitudes included, the statistical model explained (i.e., rendered predictable) only about one sixteenth of the variation in responses. We suspect that different Americans reject authority for quite different reasons—some out of grudging resentment and others out of a Whitmanesque faith in the capacity of the common woman or man—and that these different motives are associated with very different antecedents, making them unlikely to be well predicted by a single statistical model.

Closed Minds and Tenured Radicals: Are Universities Responsible for Generational Differences in Cultural Attitudes?

In the late 1980s and early 1990s, a conservative critique of higher education asserted that there had been a generational trend toward civilizational decline (i.e., devaluation of high culture, rejection of cultural authority, and support for multiculturalism), and it laid the blame for this supposed trend at the gates of higher education. We evaluated this argument by dividing our sample into three age cohorts—pre–baby boomers (born before 1947), baby boomers (born 1947–60), and post–baby boomers (born between 1961 and 1975)—and examining differences among them, focusing especially on people exposed to the effects of higher education.

There are actually two versions of the conservative story. We refer to the first, articulated by Allan Bloom in *The Closing of the American Mind*, as the *theory of boomer exceptionalism*. In this view, things began to go wrong in the 1960s, when the baby boomer generation seized control of America's campuses, laying waste traditional educational values as cowardly liberal administrators capitulated to their demands. If this story were true, we would expect to see steep declines in support for high culture among the baby boomer generation, accompanied by sharp increases in support for multiculturalism and rejection of cultural authority.

We call the second approach the *tenured-radical theory*, because Roger Kimball set it forth in his book *Tenured Radicals*. Not all boomers were corrupted, Kimball argued, but the bad eggs went disproportionately into college teaching. The diffusion of barbarism awaited their elevation to the tenured professoriate, just in time to corrupt the values of subsequent student cohorts. If this is the case, we should see a particularly sharp decline in support for high culture, increases in support for multiculturalism, and greater rejection of cultural authority in the postboomer cohort. Moreover, in each case, the generational change should be greater for respondents who attended college than for those who were unexposed to the academic milieu.

Both these accounts prove inconsistent with the evidence. Support for high culture evinces no decline from one cohort to the next, and years of education predicts respect for high culture as well for younger as for older respondents. Support for multiculturalism *does* increase with the boomer cohort (and it stays higher among the postboomers); but the increase is visible at all levels of education, so it cannot be attributed to the effects of higher education. (It more likely reflects a decline in racism as the baby boomers came of age.) Similarly, both boomers and postboomers are less accepting of cultural authority than their elders but, contrary to conservative criticisms, the change is actually *less* pronounced among those exposed to higher education.[54]

Conclusions: Public Opinion's Democratic Vistas

In this final section, we return to the broader themes that animate this volume. Whereas up to this point we have been cautious in presenting and interpreting our data, here we take more liberties, exercise more interpretive license (even to the point of speculation), and address normative, as well as positive, concerns. Our normative stance is both conservative, in the sense that we wish to conserve the great art and culture of the past, and democratic, in that we hold an inclusive understanding of the arts and culture, favor widespread diffusion of many cultural forms, and are reasonably optimistic about people's capacity to make their own choices about culture and the arts.

From this normative standpoint, we find the results of this inquiry into public opinion encouraging for at least three reasons. First, our analyses refute the notion that Americans (at least any sizable number of them) are engaged in a clash of coherent ideologies between traditionalist conservative and secular progressivist forces. Neither the views of the general public as a whole nor of college graduates constitute the coherent packages that culture warriors of the right and (to a lesser extent) the left have attempted to construct. Cultural conflicts in our schools, universities, and arts institutions reflect not a struggle between two well-defined sets of values but rather a set of loosely related contests knit together more by strategy and convenience than by common ideology.

Second, the worst fears of both liberals and conservatives are largely imaginary (with respect to public opinion, if not necessarily with respect to organized social movements, of course). Liberals may take cheer in the fact that (after one controls for political conservatism and other factors) fundamentalists and evangelicals are no less sympathetic to multiculturalism than other Americans. And supporters of high culture (though not opponents of multiculturalism) are likely to be *less*, rather than more, racist in orientation than opponents of the classics and modern art. For their part, conservatives may be pleased to learn that a university education and generational change have not had the radicalizing impact attributed to them. Other things remaining equal, younger generations are no less oriented toward high culture than their elders.

Third, and perhaps most encouraging, whereas a conservative cultural critique presupposes and constructs an opposition between Euro-American high culture and the cultures of women and people of color—"a culture war over the value of traditional Western civilization versus the works of Third World authors and thinkers"—it appears that most Americans are not buying it.[55] Support for traditionally defined high culture is driven by formal education and cosmopolitan values: Far from representing a form of symbolic racism, belief in the value of high culture is *negatively* associated with racism and *positively* associated with political tolerance. By contrast, opposition to multiculturalism reflects, to some extent, symbolic racism, as well as more general political conservatism. Despite the efforts of critics of cultural diversity to construct an opposition between traditional high culture and cultural pluralism, support for both is associated with high levels of formal education and racial tolerance.

None of this is to deny that cultural conflict exists, that activists form alliances across many different issues, or that social-movement elites hold more coherent ideological understandings of disparate issues than ordinary noncombatants. Nor is it to deny that rhetoric about "culture wars," or the recitation of discourses that link previously disparate issues, may eventually contribute to creating the very conditions they purport to describe. Rather, it suggests that explanations for conflict over education and the arts must be sought not in the structure of public opinion but in the specific institutional features of these fields and in the strategies and tactics of mobilized social movements.

Indeed, given the energy that the right poured into struggles over education and the arts, it is surprising that Americans' attitudes are as *unpolarized* as they are. We suspect that our findings provide a clue as to why efforts to foment broad-based conflict over the arts and education have not been more successful. To erupt into a culture war, differences in opinion should both pit one form of culture against another at the symbolic level and be rooted in a structural cleavage (e.g., membership in identity groups or political organizations) that permit identities to crystallize around symbolic struggles. Instead, we find that the strongest supporters of the traditional canon *and* of the alternative to it both come from the same social location—that is, the ranks of the highly educated—and that those who support one are also likely to support the other.

Moreover, reflecting the victory of the celebrated American faith in cultural democracy with the rise of mass higher education, college-educated people steadfastly refuse to play the role of "cultural elite" into which some have tried to cast them. Instead, college degrees are associated with support for traditional culture and multiculturalism, *and* with democratic attitudes toward cultural authority and a broad definition of aesthetic value.

The absence of a large constituency for cultural hierarchy would seem to indicate a sea change in educated opinion, given the cultural and institutional dominance of hierarchy at least through the 1950s. It is difficult to pinpoint the timing of that change. It appears that at some point higher education stopped inculcating an exclusive version of cultural hierarchy and began instead to produce an openness to and appreciation of a wide range of cultural forms. This change coincided with a shift in the social meaning of the arts, such that interest and participation in high culture became attached to an attitude complex including tolerance, social liberalism, and skepticism toward authority.[56]

This change may also have marked a shift in the form of cultural reproduction from the intergenerational transmission of a fixed hierarchy to the transmission of a capacity for cultural adaptation and flexibility. Whereas in past generations, prestige was mapped hierarchically onto cultural forms in a manner that reflected the stratification of their audiences, contemporary education instead imparts a standardized ability to display "individualized" tastes that enact identity and defy categorization. If this interpretation is right, the ranks of the highly educated will yield few willing conscripts to culture wars in higher education and the arts; and, as the stakes of such wars ultimately matter the most to the highly educated, even the most bellicose generals will find it difficult to raise large armies.

We suspect that this augurs well for cultural democracy, albeit cultural democracy of a particular kind. However one defines it, cultural democratization first entails an expansion of cultural diversity, so that art forms or genres cannot be dismissed because they failed to be sacralized in the late nineteenth century or because of their association with non-Western or non-elite social groups. Second, cultural democracy entails a rejection of narrow conceptions of cultural authority, so that more voices can be heard in conversations about artistic quality.

The cultural hierarchy that reigned in the United States for most of the twentieth century—a system that associated artistic quality with nonprofit institutions created and governed by urban upper classes, supported by philanthropic contributions, and closely tied to university specialties—provided a neat but flawed solution to the problem of defining and expanding access to excellence in the arts: "neat" because it sustained a lot of good art in ways that the market could not; and "flawed" because it embedded definitions of excellence in the status culture and identities of the upper classes upon which high cultural institutions relied for leadership and support. The institutions of that system remain largely intact; but the system's ideological erosion can be witnessed in the near unanimity with which Americans refuse to view excellence as limited to—or even more easily found in—high culture than in popular or folk art; and in the large plurality of the most educated Americans who regard the ability to identify excellence as widespread. The challenge is to nurture institutions that are consistent with this more democratic ethos. The challenge is not to eliminate cultural distinction but to establish a basis for identifying and promulgating excellence that is independent of class, race, and gender—in other words, to liberate artistic hierarchies from social-structural constraints. Thus stated, this a utopian vision. The practical question is: How closely can an actually existing society approximate it?

In addressing this question, it is important to recognize that each of the constructs with which this chapter is concerned—cultural authority and cultural diversity—comes in two very different forms. As we have seen, some people reject cultural authority because they reject many kind of culture; this *nihilistic antinomianism* is associated with rejecting both traditional high culture *and* multiculturalism. By contrast, higher education appears to inculcate in many Americans an *expansive antinomianism*, an inclination to reject artificial distinctions in order to affirm the value of many genres and cultural traditions.

Likewise, there is more than one route to cultural diversity. One approach, favored by classical cultural democrats, is *collaborative and deliberative:* Communities come together to celebrate their many strands, schools expose children to the wealth of cultures to which they have access, and artists and writers from different traditions share their work and even collaborate around common projects. We see examples of this in French experiments with cultural animation, in community arts projects throughout urban and rural America, and in some programs in the schools.[57] The other route, theorized less but practiced much more, is through the market: As technological change permits "narrowcasting," commercial enterprises can bring to market many more types of culture, tailored to the tastes of ever smaller audiences, thus fostering both diversity and innovation. The classic example here is the field of music, where the massive changes engendered by digitalization transformed the economic logic of the music industry virtually overnight.

With respect to cultural authority, expansive antinomianism is clearly superior on normative grounds to its nihilistic alternative. With respect to cultural diversity, the normative conclusions are less clear. The collaborative approach to diversity is deeper and more inclusive: It permits a cultural critique in which many voices can be heard and underlying assumptions can be made explicit. But it is also very labor-intensive (and therefore expensive, either in contributed time or in philanthropic donations), and it is therefore unlikely to prevail except during periods in which broad-based change-oriented social movements are politically active.

By contrast, the market has provided an extraordinarily efficient means of implementing cultural diversity (and, indirectly, by sidestepping institutions congruent with the existing cultural hierarchy, in fostering democracy). But the market is a risky ally. For one thing, whether markets foster diversity and excellence or hierarchy and monoculture depends upon details of industry structure, technology, and the incentive structures the latter produce. In large part due to the enabling effects of the Internet and the digitalization of cultural products, the market is a source of abundance today—but we cannot count on it remaining so in the future. Typically, new technologies have unleashed innovation and diversity, which is ultimately limited by the efforts of oligopolistic competitors to control markets and maintain stable revenue flows, efforts that have typically limited diversity.[58] Moreover, market-fostered diversity presents a risk of fragmentation: Cultural democracy requires not just diversity but also mutual awareness and respect; by contrast, emerging marketing practices reinforce the segmentation of taste cultures.[59]

In considering the prospects, it may be useful to consider how the differing approaches to authority and diversity might intersect. Nihilistic antinomianism is clearly destructive. Tied to collaborative cultural action, it leads to repression rather than democracy. Articulated to market forces, it is conducive to the mass culture of which the Frankfurt School warned us.

By contrast, the expansive approach to authority—increased faith in the aesthetic capacity of regular men and women, a willingness to find excellence in many genres—is an indispensable ingredient in cultural democracy. Associated with a collaborative approach to diversity, it provides the ingredients for cultural animation—an integration of art and literature into ongoing efforts at community development and change.[60] Associated with the market version of diversity, it offers a means to overcome the danger of fragmentation: a faith in the active intelligence of consumers and in their willingness and ability to cross boundaries and exercise critical discrimination in many realms.

We believe that public sentiments provide a basis for realizing some of the promise of cultural democracy—"a program of culture, drawn out, not for a single class alone, or for the parlors or lecture rooms, but with an eye to practical life . . . a scope generous enough to include the widest human area . . . eligible to the uses of the high average of men—and not restricted to conditions ineligible to the masses," as Whitman described it at the moment that the United States' urban elites were actively constructing a hierarchical culture of limited permeability.[61] To be sure, nihilistic antinomianism, opposed to both high culture and multiculturalism, retains a constituency, but it would appear to be dwindling. Instead, the sentiments of typical educated Americans—the ones with the most to say about cultural policy and educational practice, and the ones whose consumer decisions drive the cultural marketplace—combine a persistent respect for high culture with a curiosity and openness to new forms; a belief in critical standards with skepticism about their application; and a cosmopolitan openness to the cultural other with a persistent inclination to invest in conventionally defined cultural capital.

Given these sentiments, the commercial marketplace can contribute to the emergence of cultural democracy, at least as long as low barriers to entry permit many producers to offer a wide range of materials. Indeed, given the persistent respect for high culture evinced by Americans who reject the ideology that privileges high culture and the judgments of critics and curators, it appears that conservative traditionalists have had too little faith in the inherent value and appeal of the objects of their veneration. At the same time, there are many types of culture—and, even more, ways of apprehending cultural objects—that could not persist, or would persist much less widely and effectively, without the existing framework of philanthropically supported nonprofit organizations, and without continued public and philanthropic investment in institutions of collaborative diversity and cultural animation. Moreover, without public policy to ensure that barriers to entry in cultural industries remain low, the liberating potential of the market will not be realized. The key is to find the mix of policies, both public and philanthropic, that can guide and manage the new cultural marketplace in ways consistent with the new sensibilities that structure the public's understanding of culture and relationship to it.

Notes

1. See, e.g., Richard Bolton, ed., *Culture Wars: Documents from the Recent Controversies in the Arts* (New York: New Press, 1992); Stephen Dubin, *Arresting Images: Impolitic Art and Uncivil Actions* (New York: Routledge, 1992); Marjorie Heins, *Sex, Sin and Blasphemy: A Guide to America's Censorship Wars* (New York: New Press, 1993); and Margaret Jane Wyszomirski, "From Accord to Discord: Arts Policy during and after the Culture Wars," in *America's Commitment to Culture: Government and the Arts*, ed. Kevin V. Mulcahy and Margaret Jane Wyszomirski (Boulder, Colo.: Westview Press, 1994), 1–46.
2. Influential screeds include Allan Bloom, *The Closing of the American Mind: How Higher Education Has Failed Democracy and Impoverished the Souls of Today's Students* (New York: Simon & Schuster, 1987); Roger Kimball, *Tenured Radicals: How Politics Has Corrupted Our Higher Education* (New York: Harper & Row, 1990); and Dinesh D'Souza, *Illiberal Education: The Politics of Race and Sex on Campus* (New York: Free Press, 1991).
3. For a summary and critique, see American Association of University Professors, "Academic Bill of Rights Legislation: Summary and Comments," http://www.aaup .org/Issues/ABOR/aborsummary3.htm.
4. Todd Gitlin, *The Twilight of Common Dreams: Why America Is Wracked by Culture Wars* (New York: Metropolitan, 1995).

5. James Davison Hunter, *Culture Wars: The Struggle to Define America* (New York: Basic Books, 1991); Os Guinness, *The American Hour: A Time of Reckoning and the Once and Future Role of Faith* (New York: Free Press, 1993).
6. Rhys H. Williams, ed., *Cultural Wars in American Politics: Critical Reviews of a Popular Myth* (New York: Aldine de Gruyter, 1997); Paul DiMaggio, John Evans, and Bethany Bryson, "Have Americans' Social Attitudes Become More Polarized?" *American Journal of Sociology* 102 (1996): 690–755; John Evans, "Have Americans' Attitudes Become More Polarized? An Update," *Social Science Quarterly* 84, no. 1 (2003): 71–90; Catherine Bolzendahl and Clem Brooks, "Polarization, Secularization, or Differences as Usual? The Denominational Cleavage in U.S. Social Attitudes since the 1970s," *Sociological Quarterly* 46 (2005): 47–78; Kara Lindaman and Donald P. Haider-Markel, "Issue Evolution, Political Parties, and the Culture Wars," *Political Research Quarterly* 55, no. 1 (2002): 91–110.
7. Paul DiMaggio, "The Myth of Culture War: The Disparity between Private Opinion and Public Politics," in *The Fractious Nation? Unity and Division in Contemporary American Life,* ed. Jonathan Rieder (Berkeley: University of California Press, 2006).
8. William J. Bennett, *The De-Valuing of America: The Fight for Our Culture and Our Children* (New York: Summit Books, 1992), 25.
9. Gerald Graff, *Beyond the Culture Wars: How Teaching the Conflicts Can Revitalized American Education* (New York: W. W. Norton, 1993); Robert Hughes, *The Culture of Complaint: The Fraying of America* (New York: Oxford University Press, 1993) ; Lawrence Levine, *Highbrow/Lowbrow: The Emergence of Cultural Hierarchy in America* (Cambridge, Mass.: Harvard University Press, 1988); Ellen Messer-Davidow, "Manufacturing the Attack on Liberalized Higher Education," *Social Text* 36 (1993): 40–80; Gitlin, *Twilight of Common Dreams,* chap. 6.
10. Bolton, *Culture Wars;* Paul DiMaggio and Becky Pettit, *Public Opinion and Political Vulnerability: Why Has the National Endowment for the Arts Been Such an Attractive Target?* Working Paper 7 (Princeton, N.J.: Princeton University Center for Arts and Cultural Policy Studies, 1998).
11. Bethany Bryson, *Making Multiculturalism: Boundaries and Meanings in U.S. English Departments* (Stanford, Calif.: Stanford University Press, 2005).
12. Bettina Huber, "Today's Literature Classroom: Findings from the MLA's 1990 Survey of Upper Division Courses," *ADE Bulletin,* no. 101 (Spring 1992): 36–60; Bettina Huber, "What's Being Read in Survey Courses? Findings from a 1990–91 MLA Survey of English Departments," *ADE Bulletin,* no. 100 (Spring 1995): 40–48. The figure cited is from table 2 (p. 41) of the latter.
13. Susan Herbst, *Numbered Voices: How Opinion Polling Has Shaped American Politics* (Chicago: University of Chicago Press, 1993); *Politics at the Margin: Historical Expressions Outside the Mainstream* (New York: Cambridge University Press, 1994); David Zaret, *Origins of Democratic Culture: Printing, Petitions and the Public Sphere in Early Modern England* (Princeton, N.J.: Princeton University Press, 2000).
14. Herbst, *Numbered Voices;* John R. Zaller, *The Nature and Origins of Mass Opinion* (New York: Cambridge University Press, 1992). Although public-opinion researchers know all this, they still usually describe results as representing that, e.g., "35 percent of Americans believe x" rather than writing "35 percent of respondents reported that they agreed with statement x." In effect, the terse form has become

a shorthand for more accurate but less graceful constructions. In this chapter, we compromise, using the terse form in most cases, but interjecting the long form frequently enough (we hope) to keep the reader on his or her toes.

15. Alexis de Tocqueville, *Democracy in America*, 2 vols. (New York: Vintage, 1945); Michèle Lamont, *Money, Morals, and Manners: The Culture of the French and the American Upper Middle Class* (Chicago: University of Chicago Press, 1992); Thomas L. Haskell, ed., *The Authority of Experts* (Bloomington: Indiana University Press, 1984); Ellen Condliffe Lagemann, *The Politics of Knowledge: The Carnegie Corporation, Philanthropy and Public Policy* (Middletown, Conn.: Wesleyan University Press, 1989); Steven Brint, *In an Age of Experts: The Changing Role of Professionals in Politics and Public Life* (Princeton, N.J.: Princeton University Press, 1994).

16. The most sophisticated chronicler of cultural conflict is Pierre Bourdieu, who has addressed the professional politics of both universities and the arts in France in a series of trailblazing works. The primary difference between the United States and France is that the boundaries of cultural and educational institutions are for many reasons more permeable in the United States than in France, and claims against established institutions are more likely to be placed on behalf of groups defined by racial or ethnic identity in the United States, and by groups defined on the basis of class or region in France. See Pierre Bourdieu, *Homo Academicus*, trans. P. Collier (Stanford, Calif.: Stanford University Press, 1988); and Pierre Bourdieu, *The Field of Cultural Production* (New York: Columbia University Press, 1993).

17. Data are from the 1993 NORC [National Opinion Research Center] General Social Survey, a regular personal-interview sample survey of U.S. households. For details, see James A. Davis and Tom W. Smith, *The NORC General Social Survey: A User's Guide* (Newbury Park, Calif.: Sage Publications, 1992). The 1606 respondents to the 1993 survey were representative of noninstitutionalized Americans aged eighteen years or older. The items on which this chapter focuses were part of a special "module" of questions germane to the interests of sociologists of culture, described in "Conceptualizing and Measuring Culture in Surveys: Values, Strategies, and Symbols," by Peter V. Marsden and Joseph F. Swingle, *Poetics* 22 (1994): 269–90.

18. National Opinion Research Center, *General Social Surveys, 1972–1998: Cumulative Codebook* (Chicago: National Opinion Research Center, 1999), 465.

19. Daniel Yankelovich Group for the Ford Foundation, Campus Diversity Initiative Survey, July–August 1998, Roper Center Public Opinion On-Line, Question ID: USDYG.98CULT,R11B.

20. Question phrasings were intended to maximize variation in response. Because of the novelty of the topic area, however, it was difficult to anticipate the phrasings that would do this most effectively. In the case of this item, a more even break— perhaps with a plurality in the opposite direction—might have been achieved by changing "is ignored while other works are promoted because they are" to "receive less attention in order to make room for works." A considerably cruder formulation—"Adding material about women and minorities to the college curriculum makes it less rigorous"—elicited the agreement of 33 percent of a 1998 national sample of voters, with 59 percent disagreeing (Daniel Yankelovich Group for the Ford Foundation, Campus Diversity Initiative Survey, July–August 1998, Roper Center Public Opinion On-Line, Question ID: USDYG.98CULT,R17B).

21. National Opinion Research Center, *General Social Surveys*, 464.

22. The item was taken from Pierre Bourdieu and Alain Darbel, with Dominique Schnapper, *The Love of Art: European Museums and Their Public*, trans. Caroline Beattie and Nick Merriman (Stanford, Calif.: Stanford University Press, 1990), which reports results of a survey of French respondents in the late 1960s. One might argue that the wording was more appropriate at a point when modern art was still often popularly identified with abstract expressionism; but agreement was sufficiently high to suggest that negative stereotypes from that era are alive in popular culture even if the styles on which they were based are no longer fashionable.

23. National Opinion Research Center, *General Social Surveys*, 465.

24. Ideologies distinguishing sharply between "high culture" and popular forms and privileging the latter rose to prominence in the United States in association with the emergence of urban upper classes in the Victorian era, and were quickly embraced by much of the middle class. On this point, see Paul DiMaggio, "Cultural Entrepreneurship in 19th Century Boston," parts 1 and 2, *Media Culture and Society* 4 (1982): 33–50, 303–21; and Levine, *Highbrow/Lowbrow*. Surveys consistently have reported that people from higher socioeconomic status backgrounds participate more actively in audiences for high culture art forms (they also participate more actively in other kinds of cultural audiences, in differences that are less pronounced), but this is the first study that asked people to evaluate broad genres in this way.

25. The tendency for college graduates to participate more than others in most kinds of arts activities has been established in dozens of studies going back to the 1960s. For a review, see Paul DiMaggio, "Social Stratification, Life-Style, Social Cognition & Social Participation," in *Social Stratification: Class, Race and Gender in Sociological Perspective (2nd edition)*, ed. David Grusky (Boulder, Colo.: Westview Press, 2000), 542–52. For a recent example, see Paul DiMaggio and Toqir Mukhtar, "Arts Participation as Cultural Capital in the United States, 1982–2002: Do Trends in Participation Augur Decline?" *Poetics* (Special Issue on Gender, Networks and Cultural Capital) 32, no. 2 (2004): 169–94.

26. Pierre Bourdieu and Jean-Claude Passeron, *Reproduction: In Education, Society, Culture*, trans. Richard Nice (London: Sage Publications, 1977); Randall Collins, *The Credential Society: An Historical Sociology of Education* (New York: Academic Press, 1979).

27. Bloom, *Closing of the American Mind*; Kimball, *Tenured Radicals*; Bennett, *Devaluing of America*.

28. Hunter, *Culture Wars*, 191.

29. Ibid., 208.

30. Richard M. Merelman, "Racial Conflict and Cultural Politics in the United States," *Journal of Politics* 56, no. 1 (1994): 1.

31. The measure of correlation is Kendall's tau-b statistic.

32. Philip E. Converse, "The Nature of Belief Systems in Mass Public," in *Ideology and Discontent*, ed. David E. Apter (New York: Free Press, 1964), 206–61.

33. One might ask whether we were correct to locate trust in professional educators on the "left" or "progressivist" side of the ideological spectrum in the first place. Doing so is certainly consistent with the assertions of the conservative critics of universities like the National Association of scholars, who tend to view academic professionalism and multiculturalism as wrapped in an unholy alliance; see, e.g., Bruce Robbins, "Othering the Academy: Professionalism and Multiculturalism,"

Social Research 58 (1991): 355–72. But we were somewhat skeptical, and initially assumed that the unexpectedly positive correlations of the "distrust-of-educators" item with these two liberal views might disguise different patterns of association for liberal and conservative respondents (such that those on the left who distrust the professorate are likely to be especially radical, while those on the right who distrust educators are likely to be more ideologically conservative). But when we analyzed patterns of correlation between distrust of educators and the other items separately for GSS subsamples who characterized themselves, respectively, as liberal and conservative, we found no systematic differences.

34. We used the SYSTAT/PC Statistics principal-components factor analysis with varimax rotation (replicated with oblique rotation to explore the possibility that the factors were correlated), and retained all factors with eigenvalues of greater than 1.0.

35. Factor loadings on orientation to high culture were 0.845 for the classics and 0.620 for modern art; on resistance to multiculturalism they were 0.802 for expanding the canon and 0.691 for bilingual education; and on rejection of cultural authority they were 0.834 for confidence in educators and 0.631 for the ability to judge art.

36. Race and ethnicity are based on two binary variables identifying respondents who are African American or who describe themselves as being of Hispanic origin. (Race was assigned by interviewers, except when interviewers were uncertain. Hispanic origin was assigned to respondents who described their national background as Spanish, Latin American—excepting Brazil—or Filipino.) Income is based on a twenty-one-category scale, coded at the midpoint of each range. Conservative Protestant denominations are coded by GSS from denominational affiliation. The method is described in Tom Smith, "Classifying Protestant Denominations," GSS Technical Report 67 (Chicago: National Opinion Research Center, 1986). "Political conservatism" is based on self-placement on a seven-point scale ranging from "extremely liberal" to "extremely conservative."

37. The three items involved the right of Euro-Americans to keep African Americans out of "their" neighborhoods, legal establishments of a homeowner's right to discriminate by race when selling or renting, and laws again racial intermarriage, each rescaled to range from 0 to 1, with racist views taking the higher value.

38. The categories of persons toward whom tolerance was measured were atheists, communists, gay men, militarists, and racists—a selection intended to ensure that the scale measured tolerance and not simply right- or left-wing political sentiments. Each item was recoded so that 1 represented an intolerant response and 2 represented a tolerant response, and they were summed so that scale values ranged from 15 (less tolerant) to 30 (more tolerant).

39. Items were recoded to range from 1 (less confident) to 3 (more confident), with the scale value ranging from 4 to 12.

40. Items included in this scale are attendance at classical music performance, dance concerts, and art museums (three separate items); attitudes toward classical music and opera, respectively; and the importance of being "cultured" as an attribute of one's friends. Each item was recoded to make a higher response indicative of a positive orientation to high culture and then rescaled from zero to one, yielding a scale ranging from 0 to 6.

41. Howard Schuman puts this problem well: "Attitudes are mental entities or constructs based on verbalizations, and they all swim round in the same heads, with

no temporal or other labels to conveniently indicate causal order." Howard Schuman, "The Perils of Correlation, the Lure of Labels and the Beauty of Negative Results," in *Racialized Politics: The Debate about Racism in America*, ed. David O. Sears, Jim Sidanius, and Lawrence Bobo (Chicago: University of Chicago Press, 2000), 302–23; the quotation cited here is on 304.

42. Paul DiMaggio and Francie Ostrower, "Participation in the Arts by Black and White Americans," *Social Forces* 68 (1990): 753–78; Becky Pettit and Paul DiMaggio, *Public Sentiments Towards the Arts: A Critical Reanalysis of 13 Opinion Surveys*, Working Paper 5 (Princeton, N.J.: Princeton University Center for Arts and Cultural Policy Studies, 1998).

43. To see if religious conservatives were less supportive of high culture because of messages they received from the pulpit, we undertook the same analyses for actively church-going members of conservative denominations only, but the results were unchanged. A more recent study using a wider range of measures of religious conservatism and a more extensive range of attitude measures has likewise found theologically conservative Protestants to exhibit less favorable attitudes toward the arts: Peter V. Marsden, "Religion, Cultural Participation, and Cultural Attitudes: Survey Data on the United States, 1998," report to the Henry Luce Foundation, Harvard University Department of Sociology, 1999. By the mid-1990s, religious conservatives were also far more likely than any other group except partisan Republicans to favor sharp reductions of federal spending on the arts. Pettit and DiMaggio, *Public Sentiments Towards the Arts*.

44. We infer this by first including only sociodemographic measures in the predictive model, and then investigating a second model to which attitude measures are added. We interpret the percentage decline in the size of the coefficients of the sociodemographic measures as reflecting the percentage of their influence that is the result of ("is mediated by") the attitudes. The remaining coefficient represents the portion of the original effect (in the first model) that remains even after differences in attitudes are taken into account: i.e., the difference one would expend to find between people with similar attitudes who differed on the sociodemographic variable in question. The assumption in this procedure is that people's attitudes are shaped by the life experiences of which variables like race, gender, or educational attainment serve as indices, rather than the other way around.

45. On omnivorousness, see Richard A. Peterson and Roger Kern, "Changing Highbrow Taste: From Snob to Omnivore," *American Sociological Review* 61 (1996): 900–7; on educational effects on racial attitudes, see Lawrence Bobo and Frederick C. Licari, "Education and Political Tolerance: Testing the Effects of Cognitive Sophistication and Target Group Affect," *Public Opinion Quarterly* 53 (1989): 285–308.

46. Surprisingly, the views of respondents of Hispanic descent are not significantly different from those of otherwise similar Americans. Higher family income is associated with declining support for multiculturalism, but the relationship is small.

47. Ishmael Reed, "America: The Multinational Society," in *Multicultural Literacy: Opening the American Mind*, ed. Rick Simonson and Scott Walker (Saint Paul: Grey Wolf Press, 1988), 155–60.

48. Bethany Bryson, "Anything but Heavy Metal: Symbolic Exclusion and Musical Dislikes," *American Sociological Review* 61 (1996): 884–99; David Halle, *Inside Culture:*

Art and Class in the American Home (Chicago: University of Chicago Press, 1993), 154; Donald R. Kinder and David O. Sears, "Prejudice and Politics: Symbolic Racism versus Racial Threats to the Good Life," *Journal of Personality and Social Psychology* 40 (1981): 414–31; David O. Sears and Leonie Huddy, "The Symbolic Politics of Opposition to Bilingual Education," in *Conflict between Peoples and Peoples*, ed. Jeffrey Simpson and Stephen Worchel (Chicago: Nelson-Hall, 1992), 145–69; Dennis J. Downey, "Situating Social Attitudes Toward Cultural Pluralism: Between Culture Wars and Contemporary Racism," *Social Problems* 47, no. 1 (2000): 90–111.

49. Somewhat surprisingly, a related value, political tolerance, is unrelated to attitudes toward multiculturalism. This suggests that political tolerance and social tolerance may be distinct dimensions.

50. To decide which of these two positions represented a more accurate interpretation of these results, we would need additional measures that are not available. For a useful discussion of these contrasting positions, see David O. Sears, John J. Hetts, Jim Sidenius, and Lawrence Bobo, "Race in American Politics: Framing the Debates," in *Racialized Politics*, ed. Sears, Sidanius, and Bobo, 1–43.

51. These results reflect the inclusion of a multiplicative interaction term (education x political conservatism) in the model predicting attitudes toward multiculturalism. The results are consistent with other research that has noted stronger effects of blatant racism on preferences toward policies related to race for less-educated than for more-educated persons, and stronger effects of political ideology on the views of the latter. It is also consistent with the view that educated respondents who reject (or realize that they are not supposed to express) crudely racialist views nonetheless harbor antiminority sentiments ("subtle prejudice") that may be expressed in the form of conservative or traditionalist views. See Donald R. Kinder and Lynn M. Sanders, *Divided by Color: Racial Politics and Democratic Ideals* (Chicago: University of Chicago Press, 1996); and Thomas F. Pettigrew and Roel W. Meertens, "Subtle and Blatant Prejudice in Western Europe," *European Journal of Social Psychology* 25 (1995): 57–75.

52. On the "culture of critical discourse," see Alvin W. Gouldner, *The Future of Intellectuals and the Rise of the New Class* (New York: Seabury Press, 1979)

53. Bennett, *De-Valuing of America*.

54. In models not presented in this chapter, we replaced "age" with dummy variables for the boomer and postboomer cohorts, and we included interaction effects between the cohorts and educational attainment to test for differences in trends related to extent of formal education.

55. Clarence Page, "Where Narrow Minds Stifle Debate," *Chicago Tribune*, September 23, 1990.

56. Levine, *Highbrow/Lowbrow*; Peterson and Kern, "Changing Highbrow Taste"; Paul DiMaggio, "Social Structure, Institutions and Cultural Goods: The Case of the United States," in *Social Theory for a Changing Society*, ed. Pierre Bourdieu and James S. Coleman (Boulder, Colo.: Westview Press, 1991), 133–55; Joan Shelley Rubin, *The Making of Middle Brow Culture* (Chapel Hill: University of North Carolina Press, 1992); Paul DiMaggio, "Are Art Museum Visitors Different from Other People? The Relationship between Attendance and Social and Political Attitudes in the United States," *Poetics* 24 (1996): 161–80.

57. Arlene Goldbard, "Better Late Than Never, or Confessions of a Premature Cultural-Policy Wonk," Ukiah, California, 1995, http://www.wwcd.org/issues/cp_

wonk.html; Don Adams and Arlene Goldbard, *Crossroads: Reflections on the Politics of Culture* (Talmage, Calif.: DNA Press, 1990).

58. Richard A. Peterson, "Cycles in Symbol Production: The Case of Popular Music," *American Sociological Review* 40 (1975): 158–73; Eszter Hargittai, "Radio's Lessons for the Internet," *Communications of the ACM* 43, no. 1 (2000): 50–56.

59. Joseph Turow, *Breaking Up America: Advertisers and the New Media World* (Chicago: University of Chicago Press, 1997). See also Douglas Hartmann and Joseph Gerteis, "Dealing with Diversity: Mapping Multiculturalism in Sociological Terms," *Sociological Theory* 23, no. 2 (2005): 218–40, for a useful typology of forms of multiculturalism that makes a similar distinction between "interactive" and "fragmented" or "cosmopolitan" forms of multiculturalism. Depending on how they are structured, markets can sustain "fragmented" or "cosmopolitan" forms, but are less effective, in themselves, in fostering "interactive" pluralism.

60. Don Adams and Arlene Goldbard, "Animation: What's in a Name," Washington, 1982, http://www.wwcd.org/action/animation.html.

61. Walt Whitman, *Democratic Vistas* (New York: Liberal Arts Press, 1949 [1871]), 38–39.

CHAPTER 11

"Subtle, Intangible, and Non-Quantifiable": Aesthetics, Law, and Speech in Public Space

LESLIE PROSTERMAN

The National Mall in Washington, D.C., offered the site for some of my most evocative experiences growing up in the Washington metropolitan area. Known to my friends and me as "the Mall," its sweeps of green with the Capitol at one end, the Washington Monument in the middle, and the Lincoln Memorial at the other end near the Potomac River awed us both consciously and subliminally. Twice-yearly school trips to the National Museum of Natural History and the National Gallery of Art introduced us to the Mall. We knew we were lucky to get out of school to raise a little hell. We hopped around on the bus and whooped through the marble halls, though we found the constant cultural enrichment somewhat tedious. At some less conscious level, we took in the age of the Capitol, the sheer size of the columns, doors, atriums, the quantity of stuff inside the museums and monuments, and the buildings' beyond-scale physical setting on the Mall, and we were impressed.

As television increased in popularity and decreased in price, and we became aware of the news, we watched representations of the Mall in our own or in

The research for this chapter was supported by a generous Faculty Designated Research Initiative Fund award from the University of Maryland, Baltimore County. The author offers rich appreciation to the following people and institutions for their readings, suggestions, and research assistance: research assistant and now attorney extraordinaire Sarah E. Josephson, Casey N. Blake, Paddy Bowman, Robert Cantwell, John Dorst, Peter Bacon Hales, Arthur McEvoy, Greg Metcalf, Franklin G. Miller, Ruth Olson, the late Albert M. Prosterman, the late Betryce G. Prosterman, Susan Stocker, and the Law, Culture, and Humanities Conference at Georgetown University Law Center.

friends' living rooms. Throughout the 1960s, more and more of those photographs represented crowds of demonstrators petitioning for redress of grievances and officials reacting to those crowds, demonstrators, and petitions. Soon, we were out there (and in Lafayette Park, in front of the White House) during the Poor People's Campaign, Resurrection City, the March on the Pentagon, and the rest of the anti–Vietnam War demonstrations. Starting in 1967, the Smithsonian Folklife Festival appeared on the Mall during the summers; we learned how to play hammer dulcimer in ten minutes and to eat Indian fry bread (figure 11.1). The Mall really was the nation's front yard, the site of what was happening, and we went there to be part of it.

After college, I came back to Washington to work at the U.S. Senate in 1975. In the winter, when the Senate was in recess, we would grab our ice skates, leave early, and head for the new skating rink among the monuments, now a sculpture garden. Since returning again after graduate school in the early 1980s, my friends and I often walk on the Mall at sunset, watch the shapes of the buildings against the sky, and hang with the crowds of tourists from Japan, Kansas, and southern Virginia, workers from the National Archives and the General Services Administration, skateboarders, Frisbee players, and Falun Gong practitioners cramming the public space. It is a big space, and there is room for a lot of action, for observation, and for reflection. It is the only space like it in the United States.

The Mall means a lot to me as memory, as a personal quiet refuge, and as a site of multiple civic discourses. My scholarship has focused on observation and analysis of symbolic expressions, aesthetics, and the public realm. During the past few years, my research has concentrated on art and politics, particularly art and law in America. As I searched cases concerning law, art, and First Amendment issues, my personal and professional interests converged in cases dealing with demonstrators and the National Mall and Lafayette Park, which formed a distinctive body of aesthetic and legal discussion.

These legal cases from the 1980s and 1990s feature the development of aesthetics as a substantial governmental interest (presumably acting in the public good). A substantial governmental interest can supersede freedom of expression in historical public forums such as national parks. The National Mall and Lafayette Park are examples of such national parks, administered by the National Park Service.

In their written opinions, judges accept aesthetics without a question as to the meaning or content of the term.[1] Courts thus legitimize aesthetics (and a particular kind of aesthetics) as a substantial governmental interest, whether ruling in favor or against demonstrators' activities. Interrogation of the degree to which these aesthetic determinations represent shared or contested ideals, beliefs, and values of different groups of people raises questions as to the nature of the "public" in the "public good" that those substantial governmental interests protect. Different publics exist in American culture, and, therefore different aesthetic concepts; we need at least to explore the tacit assumptions

Figure 11.1. The annual Smithsonian Folklife Festival on the National Mall, Washington, 1999. Photograph by Jeff Tinsley. Courtesy of the Center for Folklife and Cultural Heritage, Smithsonian Institution.

underpinning the law and governmental regulation to ensure equal access to public forums.

This chapter calls attention to this phenomenon and examines the history and use of aesthetics in antecedent legal cases. I scrutinize the specific aesthetic judgments implied in the contemporary cases and explore different groups' competing notions of the beautiful and the good. In our highly segmented society, many hear the term "aesthetic" and think of it as a concept marginal at best to supposedly basic political and social concerns. In fact, aesthetics constitutes a determining and underestimated factor in how demonstrators are or could be allowed to represent themselves in two of the most symbolically loaded public forums in the country: the National Mall and Lafayette Park. It is important to question the largely unconsidered but clear aesthetic assumptions stated in court cases relating to National Park Service regulations of a fourteen-year period that now constitute legal precedent; we may find their nature to be antithetical to the expression of plural or unorthodox opinions. Through exploration of the nature of the aesthetic judgments involved, we begin to question the universalist notion of this aesthetic and to look at the relationship between the unexamined universalist aesthetic and the unspecified notion of the "public" in the public good. Consider the U.S. Supreme Court's definitions of the National Mall and Lafayette Park:

[The National Mall] include[s] the Lincoln, Jefferson, and Vietnam Veterans Memorial. . . . [It]extends almost two miles from the United States Capitol on the east to the Lincoln Memorial on the west and includes the Washington Monument. This vast expanse serves a multiple of purposes, none of them commercial. It is a place where the public will relax and enjoy its landscaped vistas between visits to the eight museums and galleries which flank the eastern half of the Mall. . . . It is also the place where men and women from across the country will gather in the tens of thousands to voice their protests or support causes of every kind. It is here that the constitutional rights of speech and peaceful assembly find their fullest expression.

[Lafayette Park], [a]lthough originally part of the White House grounds, [was set aside by] President Jefferson . . . as a park for the use of residents and visitors. It is a "garden park with . . . formal landscaping." . . .

Missing from the majority's description is any inkling that Lafayette Park and the Mall have served as the sites for some of the most rousing political demonstrations in the Nation's history. . . . [T]hese areas constitute, in the Government's words, "a fitting and powerful forum for political expression and political protest."[2]

These alternating sets of descriptions of contested terrain highlight the competing yet complementary characteristics that the government, the courts, and citizens ascribe to the Mall and to Lafayette Park. By citing aesthetics in legal cases as a determinative factor in how citizens may use the National Mall and Lafayette Park as sites for demonstrations, the courts and the National Park Service invoke a concept that requires close attention. The National Park Service, which must administer and police the Mall and Lafayette Park for various publics, most often explicitly cites aesthetics in its regulations and in its briefs in its numerous court cases. The Park Service not only refers directly to aesthetics but also to values, beauty, appropriateness, attractiveness, and other code terms for aesthetics in both its briefs and testimony. Judicial opinions in attendant court cases have cited Park Service briefs and regulations, appropriating the aesthetic characterization. The unexamined aesthetic has become precedent, whether or not the courts rule in favor of access for the demonstrators. Because precedent serves as the basis for governmental regulation as well as for further court cases, it behooves citizens to examine the nature of the aesthetic and how it may affect speech in public spaces.

The National Mall and Lafayette Park are particularly charged with national symbolic meaning; demonstrators choose these monumental environments to communicate messages with maximum impact. The symbolic context for protesters, the National Park Service, and the media derives in part from the attractions of the Mall and Lafayette Park for one sector of the American public: the tourists or "visitors," as the National Park Service describes them. By their reverence and their multitudes, tourists validate the symbolic messages of these imposing spaces.

Tourists make pilgrimages to Washington in large numbers to view the political symbols constructed on a grand scale in larger-than-life surroundings. They celebrate their own patriotism and dedication to education, represented by their attendance at memorials and museums. By their very presence, visitors participate in their own possible future commemoration in a historical continuum signified by the nineteenth-century buildings and various twentieth- and twenty-first-century festivals on the Mall. They absorb impressions about the stability of American institutions and the development of the values of self-improvement, leadership, freedom, and equality symbolized by the Greek Revival architecture of the National Archives and the U.S. Capitol. The National Park Service designates this area (excluding the White House) as the "Memorial Core." The visitors' alacrity in absorbing these lessons is helped by the simultaneously grandiose sweep of the Mall and the quiet, parklike atmosphere of the greenswards and gardens surrounding the impressive buildings, which appeal to and soothe the senses.[3]

The symbolic importance of the White House and the Memorial Core to these members of the American public increases the value of these same spaces to other members of the American public: demonstrators or protestors. The Washington Monument, the Lincoln Memorial, the National Museum of American History, and the massive Roman squares of the Mall teach lessons of democracy and power to Americans and visitors from foreign countries; they likewise serve as stirring or ironic contexts for demonstrators to state their cases. Public forums such as parks, sidewalks, and streets in general constitute the most typical arenas open to members of the public for demonstrating political or religious concerns to the government and the rest of the American people (figures 11.2 and 11.3).

Historically, Americans have held freedom of expression without governmental interference to be one of the most important attributes of democratic life; it is stated in the Bill of Rights' First Amendment to the Constitution. But Congress and the courts may abridge this freedom of expression for a number of reasons. Municipal courts, appellate courts, and the Supreme Court have increasingly used aesthetics as a substantial or compelling governmental interest since the 1950s, with consequences for more recent freedom of expression cases. In cases involving the Park Service in its capacity as administrator of the National Mall and Lafayette Park from *Watt v. Community for Creative Non-Violence* (1983) onward, aesthetics figures as a substantial governmental interest affecting freedom of expression in public forums.[4]

The complexities of aesthetics as a substantial governmental interest shape freedom of expression in paradoxical ways. Aesthetics as a substantial governmental interest can interfere with freedom of expression in public forums. But without aesthetic legal protections, there will be no significant space in which to demonstrate. Because of the flourishing condition of the monuments and public buildings and the presence of tourists and media interest, the National Mall and Lafayette Park furnish the best theatrical stages in the nation for the presentation of national issues.

The Aesthetics Cases

Nine Supreme Court, District of Columbia Appellate Court, and District of Columbia Circuit Court cases from 1983 to 1997 deal with the question of aesthetics and political freedom of expression issues in the National Park region of the National Mall and Lafayette Park.[5] These cases cover a range of different kinds of symbolic speech on the National Mall and in Lafayette Park: sleeping overnight in the case of demonstrations concerning homeless people to gathering with signs on a sidewalk; beating a drum to protest a Desert Storm victory parade; selling message-bearing T-shirts, beads, and tapes; and setting up signs and distributing leaflets near a memorial.

Cases tacitly or explicitly using aesthetics as a substantial governmental interest overriding freedom of expression in public forums began in 1983 with the National Park Service desiring to restrict certain kinds of expression, "camping" in particular. The first mention of aesthetics in connection with

Figure 11.2. The 1963 Civil Rights March on Washington. Photograph by Warren K. Leffler. LC-U9-10363-5. Library of Congress, Prints and Photographs Division.

Figure 11.3. Demonstrators on the grounds of the Lincoln Memorial during the 1963 March on Washington. Two men in the foreground are reading a newspaper with the headline "They're Pouring in from All Over." Photograph by Warren K. Leffler. LC-U9-10359-15, Library of Congress, Prints and Photographs Division.

demonstrations on the National Mall comes in *Watt v. CCNV,* in which the dissent states "the governmental interest alleged, the protection of the parks in the Memorial Core area from physical and aesthetic damage caused by camping is clearly unrelated to the suppression of free expression."[6]

In 1984, all the Supreme Court justices, both those in the majority and dissenters, agreed in their opinions in *Clark v. Community for Creative Non-Violence* as to ". . . the government's substantial interest in maintaining the parks in the heart of the capital in an attractive and intact condition, readily available to the millions of people who wish to see and enjoy them by their presence."[7] Later in 1984, Judge Malcolm R. Wilkey wrote in an opinion for the District of Columbia Appellate Court that had earlier supported the striking down of National Park Service regulations restricting demonstrations on the sidewalk directly in front of the White House:

> The government's interest in preserving a relatively unobstructed view of the White House for tourists and passersby constitutes a legitimate aesthetic goal which is not outweighed by the insubstantial infringement on the demonstrators' ability to engage in expressive activities.[8]

Relying on the precedent-setting cases from *Berman v. Parker* (1954) to *Clark v. CCNV* and *City Council of Los Angeles v. Taxpayers for Vincent* (both 1984), Wilkey continues later in the opinion: "The government has a substantial interest in the preservation and enhancement of the human environment; aesthetics are a proper focus of governmental regulation."[9]

In *Henderson v. Lujan* (1992), the court had announced earlier:

> We found the Park Service interest in preserving the public's view of the White House from Pennsylvania Avenue and Lafayette Park enough to justify a ban on displaying signs in the center of the sidewalk in front of the White House. Values are no less significant for being *subtle, intangible, and non-quantifiable.*[10] (author's italics)

In *ISKON of Potomac, Inc. v. Kennedy* (1994), the court referred to Park Service regulations that deplored the "'degraded aesthetic values' resulting from discordant and excessive commercialism on federal land and 'the diminishment of the Park's aesthetic value if set upon by hordes of solicitors.'"[11] The same court also asserted its own opinion: "The Park Service's interest in limiting commercial activity and thereby maintaining the unique aesthetic character of the Mall is undoubtedly significant."[12]

Subtlety, intangibility, and nonquantifiability apart, analysts do investigate values.[13] The embedding of values within aesthetic characterizations simultaneously brings them to the surface and obscures their relationship to the interests of particular groups, because many Americans assume both beauty and values to be universal. The nature and implications of those aesthetic determinations carry significant weight in allowing access to an important symbolic context for demonstration. By "aesthetics," I mean here culturally based systems of judgments and evaluations relating to the senses (taste, sight, feeling) that are usually expressed in the arts, which determine beauty, pleasure, or appropriateness, otherwise known as values.[14]

That is to say, "aesthetics" refers to evaluations of the beautiful, the competent, the pleasing, and the good according to culturally assessed canons of value. It was in the eighteenth century that philosophers started to bring the concept of beauty, which is an evaluative function, into their attempts to create understandings of systems of the arts as a whole.[15] Although not all cultures conflate the beautiful and the good, Anglo-American society, as exemplified in its courts, often does so, having been profoundly influenced by the philosophy of Immanuel Kant, among others, in his *Critique of Judgment*. "Kant ultimately aligns the beautiful with the moral, not as a means thereto but as a symbol thereof."[16] Kant aligns only the *judgment* of the beautiful with the good, a universal category, not the *experience* of beauty itself, because that is subjective.[17] But the judgment that maps the good onto the beautiful invests aesthetic characterizations with a significance beyond subjective experience into the social and the political.[18]

A Brief Historical Review of Aesthetics
and Court Cases on Freedom of Expression

Before 1954, the courts' attitudes toward aesthetics could be summed up by the opinion that stated "aesthetic considerations are a matter of luxury and indulgence rather than of necessity, and it is necessity alone which justifies the exercise of the police power to take private property without compensation."[19] The courts' opinions of the relationship of aesthetics to freedom of expression remained consistent as of 1939, when the majority declared in *Schneider v. State*, a landmark public forum case, "The State's interest in keeping the streets clean and of good appearance is insufficient to justify an ordinance which prohibits a person rightfully on public streets from handing literature to one willing to receive it."[20]

By 1983, the courts had begun to designate aesthetics as an important social and governmental value, sufficient in principle at least to override public political expression. The change in attitude from that of 1939 to that of 1983 and beyond is evident in *Berman v. Parker* (1954), and in the overall shift in post–World War II social concerns. In 1954, the U.S. Congress, then the governing body for the District of Columbia, wanted to redevelop sections of the city. Local business owners protested the razing of their enterprises. The Supreme Court held that this was a public purpose for which Congress could exercise its police power and the power of eminent domain:

> Miserable and disreputable housing conditions . . . may . . . suffocate the spirit . . . [and] may also be an ugly sore, a blight on the community which robs it of charm which makes it a place from which men turn. . . . The concept of public welfare is broad and inclusive. The values it represents are spiritual as well as physical, aesthetic as well as monetary. It is within the power of the legislature to determine that the community should *be beautiful as well as healthy, spacious as well as clean, well-balanced as well as carefully patrolled.* . . . If Congress decides that the Nation's Capital shall be *beautiful as well as sanitary,* . . . there is nothing in the Fifth Amendment that stands in the way.[21] (author's italics)

This impetus came in part from the City Beautiful movement, inspired by the White City of the Chicago Columbian Exhibition of 1893:

> The aim of the progressive groups . . . was to spread middle-class values through the uplift of unfortunates and the physical improvement of urban areas that they considered to be eyesores. There was general agreement that the city could and should be made beautiful through public parks, landscaped streets, public art, and classical architecture. Those groups put pressure on their communities to achieve new aesthetic standards in domestic and community landscaping, which included setting houses back from the streets, removing fences, and planting trees and lawns along urban streets.[22]

In addition, white anxiety over the effects of desegregation in the wake of World War II also influenced *Berman v. Parker.* The racially coded designation of urban "blight" enfolded into aesthetic terms begins a half-century use of cultural phraseology to mandate a particular majoritarian cultural concept of beauty as an unquestioned civic or national good. The initial sweeping idea was promulgated by the Court's acceptance of research findings, which concluded "that if the community were to be healthy, if it were not to revert again to a blighted or slum area, as though possessed of a congenital disease, the area must *be planned as a whole. . . . [I]t was believed that the piecemeal approach . . . would be only a palliative. The entire area needed redesigning so that a balanced, integrated plan could be developed for the region."*[23]

In *Berman v. Parker,* aesthetics—or what any group determines to be beautiful and good in Kantian terms—helped the administrators of the mid-1950s to declare propriety combined with health as a powerful justification for asserting once again that the District of Columbia could not lay claim to political autonomy. *Berman* reaffirmed the nation's capital, with its substantial black population, as an entity to be governed under the symbolic and economic as well as political control of traditional power structures. This was the first instance in which the Supreme Court upheld aesthetics as a legitimate municipal or governmental interest, though not yet in the realm of freedom of expression.[24]

The subsequent line of cases develops from the acknowledgment in *Berman v. Parker* of the municipal government's interest in invoking the police power to improve a city's appearance. After *Berman,* not only did zoning officials and historic preservationists use aesthetics as justification for their social and political regulations and policies, but eventually the courts accepted aesthetics as a legitimate governmental concern that could justify regulation of the First Amendment in municipalities. *People v. Stover* (1963) required the Stover family to remove its symbolic clothesline full of tattered garments protesting the amount of its taxes. The Court said, "Once it be conceded that aesthetics is a valid subject of legislative concern, it seems inescapable that reasonable legislation designed to promote that end is a valid and permissible exercise of the police power."[25]

Berman v. Parker eventually allowed municipal and then state governments to summon aesthetics as a substantial governmental interest, overriding freedom of expression in municipalities in *Metromedia, Inc. v. City of San Diego* (1981), and *City Council of Los Angeles v. Taxpayers for Vincent* (1984). *Metromedia* led to the assertion in *Vincent* of the state or municipal government's interest in protecting one segment of the public's enjoyment of its environment from another segment of the public's desire to make a statement. In *Metromedia,* aesthetics was considered a valid municipal interest but did not leave room for ample alternatives so that city regulations concerning the use of billboards with noncommercial messages had to be struck down. However, the principle was accepted: "[There cannot] be substantial doubt that the twin goals . . .—traffic safety and the appearance of the city—are substantial governmental goals."[26] This decision set the precedent for the widely discussed *Vincent* case.[27]

City Council of Los Angeles v. Taxpayers for Vincent[28] maintained that posted political campaign signs on utility pole cross-pieces constituted a "visual assault on the citizens" of Los Angeles, and thus ". . . a significant substantive evil within the City's power to prohibit," upholding the District Court's conclusions "characterizing the esthetic and economic interests in improving the beauty of the City 'by eliminating clutter and visual blight' as 'legitimate and compelling.'"[29] Justice William J. Brennan wrote a dissent to this decision in which he pointed out that the ban on street signs disenfranchised a significant population, because these signs allowed a poorly financed candidate to reach a large number of people for relatively little cash outlay. The dissent also implied that content might be implicated, because different interests may be presumed for owners of private property (who *can* erect signs on their property), over those advocating the raising of a property tax.[30]

The same Court passed this judgment in October, just a few months after the March decision that used aesthetics as a substantial governmental interest in *Clark v. CCNV.* The District of Columbia Appellate Court and the Supreme Court have used all these cases as significant precedents in examining the relationship of aesthetics and freedom of expression in public forums.

Public Forum: A Parallel History

These federal and municipal cases show instances in which the use of two public forums, the streets and the parks, has been limited due to aesthetic considerations. Increasingly since the early 1980s, the courts have declared the federal interest in developing or protecting aesthetics to be legitimate, substantial, or compelling enough to supersede freedom of expression in public forums. Traditionally, advocates of freedom of speech in the twentieth century had considered public forums important venues for political protest because they are accessible to all. From the 1930s to the early 1980s, the Supreme Court's deference to the exercise of freedom of expression under the First Amendment had tended to influence lower courts' opinions in favor of access to those cheap, visible, and audible public venues through which ordinary people could reach a wide audience.

For instance, in *Hague v. CIO* (1939), the Supreme Court formally acknowledged that public streets and parks "have immemorially been held in trust for the use of the public, and time out of mind, have been used for purposes of assembly, communicating thoughts between citizens, and discussing public questions."[31] In 1983, the Court further stipulated sidewalks and other grounds that the government has opened to the public for expressive activity as part of the "traditional" system of public forums in *Perry Education Ass'n v. Perry Local Educators' Ass'n.*[32]

This opinion contrasts with the previously predominant opinion of 1897, written by Justice Oliver Wendell Holmes, in which the streets and parks were analogized to a private home, restricting public access to and behavior in these locations.[33] Justice Owen Josephus Roberts, writing for the Supreme Court in *Hague v. CIO*, followed Holmes in cautioning that use of public streets and parks "may be regulated in the interests of all; it [the use of the streets and parks] is not absolute, but relative, and must be exercised in subordination to the general comfort and convenience, and in consonance with peace and good order." But Justice Roberts's opinion in 1939 nonetheless followed that admonition with "but it [use of public space] must not, in the guise of regulation, be abridged or denied."[34]

Justice Roberts's initial caution stands as the justification for a good deal of subsequent governmental regulation of speech and conduct, which has been framed generally as the need to balance the First Amendment rights of speakers with those rights of other members of the public. When the government wanted or needed to regulate speech in public forums from the 1930s to the 1980s, the courts often subjected the regulations to what is known as "strict scrutiny," as stated in *Perry v. Perry*, following *U.S. v. O'Brien:*

> For the State to enforce a content-based exclusion it must show that its regulation is necessary to serve a compelling state interest and that it is narrowly drawn to achieve that end. The State may also enforce regulations of the time, place, and manner of expression which are content neutral, which are narrowly tailored to serve a significant government interest, and leave open ample alternative channels of communication.[35]

But Supreme Court justices can assert strict scrutiny—without necessarily favoring freedom of expression—so as to allow more governmental regulation. As case law has developed since 1983, the conditions have grown under which the government—supported by the courts and the Supreme Court, in particular—can limit freedom of expression. Though it appears that *Perry v. Perry* defends the rights of the public to gain access to forums for speech against the encroachments of the state, in fact *Perry* narrows both the concept and the availability of public forums. For instance, *Perry* creates the concepts of the "limited" and "nonpublic" forums, thus classifying and restricting public spaces for freedom of expression still further in order to get around the following circumscription of governmental power:

> In places where by long tradition or by government fiat have been devoted to assembly and debate, the rights of the State to limit expressive activity are sharply cir-

cumscribed. At one end of the spectrum are streets and parks which "have immemorially been held in trust for the use of the public . . ." [note: this is quoted in full above]. In these quintessential public forums, the government may not prohibit all communicative activity.[36]

The advantage of "long tradition" legitimizing the use of public space for assembly and debate lies in the appreciation of public usage as the primary factor in determining the boundaries of space for demonstration; tradition, however, also makes the creation of new public forums, such as airports and schools, problematic. "Public property which is not by tradition or designation a forum for public communication is governed by different standards," thus allowing one teacher's union and not another to use a public school's mail facilities for interschool communications on the grounds that the school has become a "limited public forum."[37] "This type of selective access does not transform government property into a public forum."[38]

In turn, governmental regulation suggests that the state, rather than public usage, may decide locations for public assembly and political speech. These locations may not necessarily be the best place from which to deliver an important message to the most important audience. But increasingly since the early 1980s, the Supreme Court has asserted that the Constitution does not guarantee access to the *best* time, place, and manner of delivering a message; instead, as the phrase "the government may not prohibit all communicative activity" implies, the state merely must allow demonstrators to speak something, somewhere.[39]

If the government can show a legitimate, significant, substantial, or compelling governmental or state interest, which now includes "interests" such as aesthetics; if it shows a reasonable time, place, or manner restriction; if the regulation is neutral with regard to the content and viewpoint of the message presented; if it is narrowly tailored to fit the need stated; and if it leaves open reasonable or ample alternative methods of communication—then the courts will allow circumscription of First Amendment rights in public forums and consequent possible chilling of expression.

National Parks as Public Forums

Public parks, in particular, are indisputable public forums, specifically the Mall in Washington and Lafayette Park, in front of the White House:

> The Mall and Lafayette Park are special places in the stockpile of American fora. They are at the very heart of the nation's capital where ideas are to be expressed and grievances are to be redressed. Thus, the focus of this case is the symbolic locus of the First Amendment. This explains the series of understandable difficulties that the Park Service has had in trying to fashion rules that meet the multifarious de-

mands put upon these unique public lands. It also rationalizes the number of times that this court has visited the problems of the Mall, Lafayette Park, and the First Amendment.[40]

These two parks have been the site of many temporary and ongoing political demonstrations. According to the National Park Service, applications for permits, granted on a first-come, first-served basis, rise yearly.[41] The Park Service itself, while not giving protest use of the Mall the highest priority, nonetheless acknowledges that

> the remainder of the Monumental Core [outside the Vietnam Veterans Memorial], including the Mall, has been described as "the Nation's front yard," and as such has traditionally been the focal point of demonstrations on a full range of issues and causes—both domestic and international.[42]

The location of the Mall and Lafayette Park in the heart of the Nation's Capital, their visibility, and the charged symbolism of the monuments heightens the use of these lands.

Another and different charge to the Park Service includes the need to contend with multiple value systems that the Park Service represents, both from its own early charters dating from the creation of the Park Service in 1916 and from those of varied other authorities such as the secretary of the interior. An early policy letter of 1918 from the secretary's office directed that "every activity of the Service is subordinate to the duties imposed upon it to faithfully preserve the parks for posterity in essentially their natural state." This policy letter also set out plans to attract and accommodate large numbers of visitors for a variety of purposes, mostly recreational and lucrative.[43] Not only does the Park Service have to accommodate multiple contemporary uses of the parks and its own multiple duties; it must adhere to its need to maintain the parks "intact" for future generations.

Since 1983, the acceptance of aesthetics as a compelling state or governmental interest has somewhat influenced the Park Service's balance of activities, with implications for the future. Arnold Goldstein, superintendent of the National Capital Region Parks, articulated the dilemma of multiple values: "We have special events and demonstrations on the Mall from mid-March to December. December to March is not prime grass-growing season here in Washington, D.C. But we are supposed to maintain the grass."[44]

The maintenance of green lawns is an aesthetic dimension of the Park Service's charter; prevalent notions of beauty in the United States today date back to late-eighteenth- and early-nineteenth-century Romantic canons developed by English and French philosophers, architects, and landscape designers.[45] Lawns reference the parklands of English country houses. The City Beautiful Movement from the turn of the twentieth century helped promulgate the ideal of the value of extensive parklands surrounding buildings. The Park Service's policies and First Amendment protections in public forums require opening these lawns to members of the public so that they may play Frisbee, hold homecomings (e.g., the Annual Black Family Reunion), celebrate the Fourth of July and Christmas (and Chanukah and Kwanzaa) and express dissenting views of American policies.

Protected Communication: Speech/Conduct Distinctions, or "Pure" and Symbolic Speech

In the United States, most judges and justices historically have given priority to political speech, especially political dissent, as being protected by the First Amendment. Even though the First Amendment itself is much more inclusive of all speech in its protective quality: "Congress shall make no law . . . abridging the freedom of speech, or of the press; or the right of the people peaceably to assemble, and to petition the Government for a redress of grievances." The judicial system concerns itself primarily with freedom of political and religious speech. Justices and lawyers argue, however, not only over whether specific kinds of speech are worthy of protection but also over what constitutes speech in the first place. Different categories of speech receive more or less protection, depending on how closely the speech resembles words.

If speech consists of actual words, it is called "pure" speech; attempts to circumscribe pure speech receive the closest scrutiny. Strict scrutiny means the governmental body has the burden of persuading the court that its action is constitutional. Once strict scrutiny is invoked, the Supreme Court in particular has tended more often to protect the speaker and strike down governmental ordinances that restrict speech in public forums. Moving away from words, the courts traditionally have recognized the communicative value of flags more quickly than they have other modes of symbolic expression:

> Symbolism is a primitive but effective way of communicating ideas. The use of an emblem or flag to symbolize some system, idea, institution, or personality, is a short cut from mind to mind. Causes and nations, political parties, lodges and ecclesiastical groups seek to knit the loyalty of their followings to a flag or banner, a color or design. The State announces rank, function, and authority through crowns and maces, uniforms and black robes; the Church speaks through the Cross, the Crucifix, the altar and shrine, and clerical raiment. Symbols of State often convey political ideas, just as religious symbols come to convey theological ones. Associated with many of these symbols are appropriate gestures of acceptance or respect: a salute, a bowed or bared head, a bended knee. A person gets from a symbol the meaning he puts into it, and what is one man's comfort and inspiration is another man's jest and scorn.[46]

"Expressive conduct" as speech, including what is known somewhat tauto-logically as symbolic speech, receives the lowest level of scrutiny in this context. That is to say, the courts evince less concern over whether the government is unconstitutionally abrogating rights to symbolic speech or expressive conduct. The speech/conduct distinction had first been broached in 1965, in a case involving a civil rights demonstration in Louisiana. Justice Arthur Goldberg asserted that marching was not speech, it was expressive conduct, and therefore did not receive the same First Amendment protections as "pure" speech.[47]

This logocentric attitude on the part of the courts has resulted in some interesting problems. In 1971, *Cohen v. California*—a case in which a young man named Cohen paraded through a courthouse with "Fuck the Draft" on his jacket—presented a rather diffuse category for the judges, being simultaneously pure speech, offensive language, and symbolic statement in its offensiveness. In this case, Cohen did receive First Amendment protection.[48] But other activities—such as marching, draft card burning to protest the Vietnam War, and sleeping in tents in January to protest homelessness—have received fewer protections.

The Courts may enforce governmental regulation of expression if it is found to be content-neutral and if it is a *reasonable* time, place, and *manner* restriction:

> [A]esthetic regulations usually specifically target the visual or aural aspects of the dissemination of speech—in other words, conduct. . . . [M]anner has several definitions applicable to aesthetic regulations. It may refer to the actual medium or method of communication. . . . It may refer to the person's expressive conduct while using a method of communication. . . . It also refers to the physical character of the medium.[49]

"Manner" relates most frequently to conduct, and it is most frequently restricted by the courts with the least amount of scrutiny because it constitutes symbolic rather than pure speech. In the context of my analysis, conduct or symbolic speech functions as a form of art. Art is a form of symbolic expression, in which something concrete represents something abstract, understood by convention or within a context. A symbol functions in a metaphorical sense, as a comparison, and thus a bringing together of several worlds to make richer statements and evoke powerful emotions. As most artists will avow, changing the form often changes the content. The presence of a "reasonable" alternative may not be reasonable to the speaker. Therefore a "content-neutral" restriction on the form or manner of delivery may not end by being content-neutral at all, though perhaps not intended as content-prejudiced by the courts. When the government and the courts summon aesthetics as a substantial or compelling governmental interest, superseding freedom of expression, they often alter manner, one of the richest forms of expression with the fewest protections. And because aesthetics is not only subjective but also tacit and accepted without question in these legal cases, symbolic speech that carries great impact, and that is speech available to those without access to expensive media, will often operate at a disadvantage in the court's asserted value system.

Conduct as speech became a clear issue in *Watt v. CCNV*, and its subsequent Supreme Court case, *Clark v. CCNV*. These cases show how the differing concepts of speech, genre, and aesthetics can affect the interplay of public policy and legal decisions. It was the symbolic sleeping in tents, construable as political theater, that fell under aesthetic review and was dismissed as aesthetically harmful. The National Park Service had hastily drafted new regulations against "camping" for the public good and preservation of the "Memorial Core" in 1983, after the first Community for Creative Non-Violence (CCNV) tent city demonstration in 1982. In essence, these regulations said that camping (sleeping for more than four hours, especially overnight, even in a permitted "symbolic structure" such as a tent) would deprive others of the use of nationally significant space and cause significant damage to park resources.

These regulations, and indeed the mandates of the Park Service, require the Park Service to put conservation of park resources for future generations at the head of its concerns. Stasis, rather than change, is at the center of its charter. The language of 1983 expresses concern for "others," presumably more familiar constituencies who would be deprived of nationally significant space and who, by implication, have a better right to use it than demonstrators, who by definition seek change.

Attorneys for the CCNV argued that rather than "camping," the demonstrators wished to engage in a symbolic statement showing the kinds of conditions homeless people endured in the worst weather. These conditions included having to sleep in unprotected circumstances, the CCNV having planned its demonstrations for January. They also argued that rangers and police continually run homeless people off public land; the homeless people would fear to participate unless the courts legally guarded their sleeping presence from harassment. In *Watt v. CCNV*, the Appellate Court (with several important dissents) affirmed the concept of symbolic sleeping and the First Amendment protection of conduct as speech. In his dissent, Justice Wilkey argued that "camping in the park . . . is not a traditional form of speech. It has expressive First Amendment value only in a very limited set of circumstances."[50]

In *Clark v. CCNV*, the Supreme Court overturned *Watt v. CCNV* in 1984, ruling that this "good" of public order and conservation supplanted the public good of freedom of expression or sleeping as "symbolic speech." This left the homeless with a strong disincentive to participate in an important aspect of the demonstration: demonstrating the lack of a place to sleep for a section of the population. Though the Mall and Lafayette Park are public parks, they are also admitted important public forums with strong symbolic meanings. The dissent in *Clark* pointed out that to disallow a form of symbolic speech within these contexts disallows an important set of meanings as well as a particular population from participating in political protest.

These and other cases show how hegemonic concepts of aesthetics (beautiful or "good" behavior), embedded in the regulations and cases, can determine access to public spaces and definitions of public good. As Judge Harry T. Edwards wrote in his concurrence to *Watt v. CCNV* in 1983:

> A nocturnal presence at Lafayette Park or on the Mall while the rest of us are comfortably couched at home, is part of the message to be conveyed. These destitute men and women can express with their bodies the poignancy of their plight. They can physically demonstrate the neglect from which they suffer with an articulateness even Dickens could not match.[51]

According to mid- and late-twentieth-century courts, ugly conditions, like being cold, hungry, or homeless, affect the public in the same way as does the reminder of death. For instance, in *Powell v. Taylor* (1954), the court banned a funeral home from a residential district to protect the aesthetic sensibilities and mental health of neighboring homeowners.[52] Death and homelessness are not aesthetically pleasing; they have ugly consequences, reminding us of mortality and hurting our equilibrium. The equation of aesthetics with physical and mental health in *Powell* and in *Berman v. Parker* provides an interesting corollary to Kantian aesthetics as political and moral health in the 1980s and 1990s. The ugliness of the symbolic demonstration and the ugliness of its results, disruption, tend to disqualify it from the public forum.

In a separate dissent to *Watt v. CCNV* (1983), then-Judge, now-Justice, Antonin Scalia wrote on the subject of "camping" or sleeping as symbolic speech:

> I write separately to express my willingness to grasp the nettle which the principal dissent leaves untouched, and which the opinions supporting the court's disposition consider untouchable—that is, flatly to deny that sleeping is or can ever be speech for First Amendment purposes. That this should seem a bold assertion is a commentary upon how far judicial and scholarly discussion of this basic constitutional guarantee has strayed from common and common-sense understanding.[53]

Scalia relies on what is known in jurisprudence as strict textualism. "Textualism avoids external sources and glosses, such as legislative history, that are often used by judges who interpret statutes by searching for legislative intent or purpose."[54] Instead, strict textualists refer back to "original intent," that is, the putative intentions of the framers of the Constitution. Justice Scalia not only practices "originalism" but also derides those who do not.[55] He collapses common understanding and common sense with his own opinions and presumably those of the framers. Who is left but the ordinary, the marginal, the fringe, the stupid, the crazy?[56]

What is most important about Justice Scalia in this context is that his jurisprudence bears a striking resemblance to the nature of the aesthetic assumptions promulgated by the courts. He does not believe in change, in context, in multiplicity of interpretations. There is only one interpretation and there is only one set of aesthetic assumptions, and they are not affected by time, shifts in meaning, populations, or circumstances. They are timeless, majestic, and universal. The eighteenth-century intentions of the framers of the Constitution, as interpreted by Scalia, match the essentially eighteenth-century Kantian aesthetics preferred by the courts and the National Park Service. "It bears repeating . . . that the Platonic-Kantian tradition performs class service, and that its invocation usually signals a defense of power."[57]

"Values Are No Less Significant for Being Subtle, Intangible, and Non-Quantifiable"

To assume that "everyone" knows something that is not clearly stated is to create a discrete group with superior status. That group with the most important knowledge tends to rise to the top of any given power structure. Mystifying art and aesthetics has functioned well in art museums and art galleries to reassure well-educated upper-middle-class professionals of their superior status, to assure "others" that they do not belong, and to make it harder to challenge actual beliefs.[58] Those not sharing common understandings often find themselves outside the power structure, as evidenced by Scalia's scorn.

The nature of the aesthetic choices in the cases, however, reveals remarkably coherent if unconscious values and then ideology on the part of government and law courts. The words found most often connected to beauty are revealing: serenity, tranquillity, calm, reverence, peace and quiet, the preservation and conservative of property, intact, order, maintenance, unimpaired views for future generations, and dignity. These values are not only coherent but also specific to particular ends shared by particular people.

In various court decisions, opinions assert that the "governmental interest in protecting the serenity of such places as the Lincoln and Jefferson Memorials."[59] Even though the court in *Henderson v. Lujan* (1992) found the ban on leafleting on the sidewalks impermissible because it is too far from the Vietnam Veterans Memorial wall, it approved of the basic regulation: "The regulation is intended to maintain an atmosphere of calm, tranquility, and reverence in the vicinity . . . of the Vietnam Veterans Memorial."[60] The court continues: "This interest in maintaining a tranquil mood at the Memorial wall is similar to ones that the Supreme Court and this court have recognized as substantial" and refers to the "tranquil, contemplative mood at the Memorial wall—perhaps 'awe' captures it better. . . ."[61] Peace and quiet accompany tranquillity, awe, and reverence as included in the aesthetic realm:

> The government asserts that it has a substantial interest in maintaining "the peaceful setting" in the nation's public parks. In the National Park Service's brief, "people turn to [public parks] for refreshment from the commotion and turmoil of every-

day life. Maintaining Lafayette Park as a place of quiet enjoyment, therefore, is a legitimate goal [of government]."[62]

The Park Service's regulatory framework is upheld in *ISKON of Potomac, Inc. v. Kennedy's* 1995 charge to "[c]onserve scenery and the national and historic objects . . . and to provide for the enjoyment of the same in such manner and by such means as will leave them unimpaired for the enjoyment of future generations."[63] Along with conservation and concern for the future, dignity emerges as an important value. In their assertion of governmental interest, the courts cited with approbation a statement in response to regulations banning T-shirt sales by National Park Service director James Rittenour supporting the regulation as a means to "eliminate the carnival atmosphere that erodes the dignity of our national capital parks and memorials."[64] Finally, the uninterrupted gaze, placid and eternal, becomes important: "The asserted governmental interest . . . is that of preserving unimpaired the public's view of the Presidential Mansion from Pennsylvania Avenue and Lafayette Park."[65]

The persistent verb used by the courts and the Park Service in this context is "maintain." The quasi-religious charge to the state of maintenance derives from the verbal alliance with reverence, and it sneers at the instability implicit in "the carnival atmosphere" raised disparagingly in the context of national. The maintenance, conservation, and preservation of property for history and for future generations lend a timeless quality to these aesthetic preferences.[66]

Through the equation of a universalist but not consensual aesthetics with the public good—and with the maintenance and stability of order—the government and the courts conflate pleasure and beauty with morality and thus characterize a generalized state out of a universalist aesthetic. Pierre Bourdieu, in *The Field of Cultural Production*, pointed out that while aesthetic judgments derive from specific interests and dispositions on the part of agents in the artistic field,

they nevertheless are formulated in the name of a claim to universality—to absolute judgment—which is the very negation of the relativity of points of view. "Essentialist thought" is at work in every social universe and especially in the field of cultural production—the religious, scientific and legal fields—where games in which the universal is at stake are played out.[67]

For whom are these legal aesthetic judgments valid? Are these aesthetic judgments those of all Americans? How did the government and courts ascertain these subtle, intangible, and nonquantifiable attributes? The court noted in *United States of America v. Jane Doe (aka Diane Nomad)* (1992)—a case involving a demonstrator who beat a drum in Lafayette Park to protest the victory parade for Desert Storm, the first U.S. war against Iraq—that there was "no evidence to indicate [by any standard] 60 decibels at 50 feet is unpleasant. . . . [T]he government offered no evidence of its own to show that anything above a 60-decibel sound volume would irritate or injure passersby or non-protesting users of the Park."[68]

What is the nature of the publics or the people who are being protected by the Park Service? There appears to be some competition in the formulations of the Park Service and the court system between the notion of a visitor and that of a demonstrator who upsets the visitors. Though the visitor appears to be valorized, in fact the very *idea* of the visitor matches the Romantic category of the primitive, the Noble Savage, one who is essentially without rights and must be protected by those moderns who are the hosts of the National Park Service.[69] The constant assertion of both the Park Service and the courts that they are holding the lands in trust for the American people implies that these people cannot make decisions about land use themselves. The demonstrators do not enjoy the "protected" status of visitors. They speak for themselves, independent of the hosts, merely occupying the hosts' ground. And they, as spectacle, compete with the memorials and landscape that are the true objects of protection here.

The abstracted, universalized, timeless notion of aesthetics is possible in part because the government and the courts evacuate the term "public" of specific people in these contexts. Pro–First Amendment cases use the terms "public" and "people" as well.

In demonstrations, however, protesters clearly identify themselves and the nature of their complaint. The courts quote affidavits of Larry Bice, Gregory Scharf, Swami B. V. Tripurari, John Holland, and Diane Nomad—real people with particular concerns. They are disruptive and definite, and they desire to change rather than maintain the status quo. They address grievances and cite specific historical circumstances instead of behaving themselves quietly and expressing themselves tastefully at timeless shrines. As a sympathetic court said in *Friends of Vietnam Memorial:*

> The court is not unaware that T-shirts have been characterized as "cheap, cheesy and commercial." But the message-bearing T-shirt is also a tribute to the creative spirit of poorly funded but inventive activists of every political persuasion who have discovered the expressive power and appeal of making an item of clothing serve also as a means of communication.[70]

Protesters remind us that not all have access to the same resources or share the same assumptions with those who created the monuments and parks or with those who administer them, yet still retain citizenship:

> Appellees are engaged in a political protest and a petition for redress of grievances. . . . Sleeping itself may express the message that these persons are homeless and have nowhere else to go. . . . The demonstration seeks to create an inescapable night-and-day reminder to the nation's political leadership that homeless persons exist.[71]

Cheesy, noisy, real people, fragmented instead of intact, create piercing and painful meanings that are contingent upon real social and historical circumstances and expressive forms. They use the memorials and memorial space to create unstable meanings instead of maintaining timeless and "unimpaired" visions of the monuments. As discussed above, the subject and manner of many of these protests appear unaesthetic in the terms used by the courts. Nonetheless, it remains the case that "[a]mong the functions of free speech are to invite dispute, to induce a condition of unrest, and to stir people to anger"—actions that of necessity produce the opposite of serenity, tranquillity, and contemplation.[72] The functions of free speech in these demonstrations operate according to a set of possible alternative aesthetic values. These are values of some "good" demonstrations: noisy, unruly, fragmented, multiple heterodox, specific to the moment, particular to individuals and groups, urgent. The very nature of protest, expression, and plural opinions and circumstances is opposed to the unification implied in the belief that "[t]he government has a significant interest in protecting unimpeded views of the monuments on the mall."[73] "Public," "American people," "visitors"—these are empty categories, never specified, that the government uses at its own discretion. The monuments take on a timeless quality, in the same way that justifying a public forum on the basis of immemorial, historic, traditional grounds does.

Because of these generalized categories of public and naturalized categories of aesthetics, certain kinds of speech, symbolic expression, art, and forums may be shut down for populations that do not have access to more expensive media and locations such as television. The court cited our

profound national commitment to the principle that debate on public issues should be uninhibited, robust, and wide-open. . . . . A . . . regulation that restricts an inexpensive mode of communication will fall most heavily upon relatively poor [poverty-stricken] speakers and the points of view that such speakers espouse . . . judicial administration of the First Amendment, in conjunction with a social order marked by large disparities in wealth and other sources of power, tends systematically to discriminate against efforts by the relatively disadvantaged to convey their political ideas.[74]

By accepting an unexamined set of aesthetic assumptions, we risk cutting off access to speech, to self-representation, to public demonstration, to art as communication through a kind of aesthetic disdain—or orthodoxy disguised as aesthetics—overruling our avowed principles of heterodoxy. As Deborah Root writes in *Cannibal Culture: Art, Appropriation, and the Commodification of Difference,* "When authority is organized around a rigidly predetermined scale of values, people cease to believe they belong to the world in which they live. The state engenders profound passivity in its citizens."[75]

On the Mall and in Lafayette Park, demonstrators create fragmented culture rather than consume whole assumptions. This makes them dangerous in the uncomfortable specificity of purpose and representation that engenders action. I suggest that the timeless and stable qualities of the accepted aesthetic and neutralized "public" militate against the specific, historicized, and unstable grievances of demonstrators:

> Because of their subjective nature, aesthetic concerns are easily manipulated, and not generally susceptible of objective proof. The danger is not just, as the majority suggests, that government might adopt an aesthetic rationale as a pretext for an impermissible motive, but rather that so many forms of robust expression are by their very nature boisterous, untidy, unsightly, and downright unpleasant for unsympathetic viewers. Distaste for the vigor with which a message is asserted can too easily be cast as an aesthetic interest in compelling others to be more moderate and decorous—and, in consequence, less effective—in conveying their message.[76]

This calls into question the state-related aesthetics by which we apparently live; the problem of judges making aesthetic determinations; the nature of the "government" whose interests can override interests of freedom of expression; and the nature of the public, which may eventually exclude demonstrators (figure 11.4).

And yet, and yet. Congress charged the Park Service with maintaining the parks in an attractive and intact condition. For the demonstrators' protests to have meaning, they require an intact and attractive environment to provide the appropriate civic frame. The locations of the Mall and of Lafayette Park—not only in the heart of the Nation's Capital but also in close proximity to other well-maintained lawns, visible buildings, and monuments—invests the protests with symbolic force. Remember that the earlier *Watt v. CCNV* quoted the National Park Service in its own Rules and Regulations, reminding us that "[t]he remainder of the Monumental Core [outside the Vietnam Veterans Memorial], including the Mall, has been described as 'the Nation's front yard.'" Without these aesthetic protections, the front yard would deteriorate and the force of demonstrators' points would be diminished significantly. Photographs in the National Park Service archives bear visual witness to the destruction caused by huge crowds at the Fourth of July celebrations, the Christmas Tree Pageant, the various festivals, and the many demonstrations held on the Mall and in Lafayette Park. The statue covered in graffiti (much resembling pigeon dung) in Lafayette Park after several demonstrations in the 1990s reinforces the Park Service's concern over the deterioration of parkland. And, for instance, the eroded grasslands (those "greenswards") of the Mall took months to replace after the Promise Keepers' demonstration in October 1997.

The protests draw substantial meaning from their surroundings, the symbolic nature of the Mall and the White House, including the serene and contemplative nature of this landscape of privilege. The very qualities of awe and "goodness" that are sustained by the regulations and the particular aesthetics endorsed by the courts are the qualities that endow protests with meaning. The national ethic embedded in this landscape reminds tourists of civic values. In turn, the landscape acts as a dramatic backdrop for the protesters, who

Figure 11.4. Middle Eastern students marching in Lafayette Park, in front of the White House, Washington, 1980. Photograph by Warren K. Leffler. LC-U9-39477-26A, Library of Congress, Prints and Photographs Division.

often bear a somewhat conflicted relationship to these ethics and values. And the operation on the edge of the aesthetic law supplies another dimension of publicity and public interest to the demonstrators' cases.[77]

In their capacity as public forums, the Mall and Lafayette Park represent not only literal stages for numerous public dramas of unified national significance but also figurative stages for the roles of negotiation, contention, and multiplicity in the United States. Ironically, it is possible that a unified aesthetic is even necessary as a context for particularistic political interventions. It is also possible that the heterogeneity of protest aesthetics reinforces the "norm" represented by the Park Service's mandate to care for the monumentalized green spaces of Washington. Acknowledging the interdependence of at least two aesthetic systems is crucial for negotiating civic life on public property.

Notes

1. Judges Wilkey and Wald of the District of Columbia Circuit Court of Appeals constitute exceptions because they alone have discussed the implications of aesthetics and aesthetic judgments in several cases.
2. *Clark, Secretary, Department of the Interior v. Community for Creative Non-Violence,* 468 U.S. 288 (1984), at 3.

3. See the essays in *Critical Issues in Public Art: Content, Context, and Controversy*, ed. Harriet F. Senie and Sally Webster (New York: HarperCollins, 1992), esp. Kirk Savage, "The Self-Made Monument: George Washington and the Fight to Erect a National Memorial," 5–32; and Charles L. Griswold, "The Vietnam Veteran's Memorial and the Washington Mall: Philosophical Thoughts on Political Iconography," 71–100.

4. *James Watt, Director, National Park Service v. Community for Creative Non-Violence*, 703 F2nd 586 (1983).

5. They include *James Watt, Director, National Park Service v. Community for Creative Non-Violence* (hereafter *Watt v. CCNV*); *Clark, Secretary, Department of the Interior v. Community for Creative Non-Violence*, 468 U.S. 288 (1984) (hereafter *Clark v. CCNV*); *White House Vigil for the ERA Committee, et al v. William P. Clark, Secretary of the Interior*, 742 F. 2nd 1518 (1984); *David Henderson v. Manuel Lujan, Secretary of the US Department of the Interior*, 964 F. 2nd 1179 (1992) (hereafter *Henderson v. Lujan*); *United States of America v. Jane Doe, aka Diane Nomad*, 968 F. 2nd 86 (1992) (hereafter *USA v. Jane Doe*); *ISKCON of Potomac, Inc v. James Ridenour, et al.*, 830 F. Supp. 1 (1993); *International Society of Krishna Consciousness of Potomac, Inc., et al. v. Roger Kennedy, Director, National Park Service*, 61 F. 3rd 949 (1994) (hereafter *ISKON of Potomac, Inc. v. Kennedy*); *Friends of the Vietnam Memorial et al v. Roger Kennedy, Director, National Park Service*, 899 F. Supp. 680 (1995); and *Friends of the Vietnam Veterans Memorial et al. v. Roger Kennedy, Director, National Park Service*, 116 F. 3rd 495 (1997). This constitutes the significant body of law cases involving aesthetics and the National Mall/Lafayette Park up to 1999. This analysis does not take into account any changes which may have occurred as a result of the September 11, 2001 terrorist attacks, or the effects of the erection of the World War II Memorial between the Lincoln Memorial and the Washington Monument.

6. *Watt v. CCNV* at 614.

7. *Clark v. CCNV*, 468 U.S. 288 (1984), at 296.

8. *White House Vigil for the ERA Committee, et al., v. William P. Clark, Secretary of the Interior, et al.*, 746 F. 2nd 1518, 241 U.S. App. D.C. 201 (1984), at 203.

9. Id. at 211.

10. *Henderson v. Lujan*, at 7.

11. *ISKON of Potomac, Inc. v. Kennedy*, at 5.

12. Id. at 29.

13. Leslie Prosterman, *Ordinary Life, Festival Days: Aesthetics in Midwestern County Fairs* (Washington, D.C.: Smithsonian Institution Press, 1995).

14. "Aesthetic experience is about our perceptual, sensory, sensuous, emotional, and bodily experience. Although nurtured by the culture into unconscious habits, unthinking reflexes, and expectations, this experience actively animates cultural forms with a sense of the agreeable, the beautiful, the sublime, or the ugly." Ban Wang, *The Sublime Figure of History: Aesthetics and Politics in Twentieth Century China* (Stanford, Calif.: Stanford University Press, 1997), 6–7.

15. Paul Oskar Kristeller, "The Modern System of the Arts: A Study in the History of Aesthetics (II), in *Essays in the History of Aesthetics*, ed. Peter Kivy (Rochester: University of Rochester Press, 1992), 35–64.

16. Robert E. Wood, *Placing Aesthetics: Reflections on the Philosophic Tradition* (Athens: Ohio University Press, 1999), 133.

17. Dabney Townsend, "From Shaftesbury to Kant: The Development of the Concept of Aesthetic Experience," in *Essays on the History of Aesthetics*, ed. Kivy, 220.

18. See Wang's discussion of Mao's deliberate use of Kant and aesthetic theory for the construction of his political and moral personae in Wang, *Sublime Figure of History.*

19. *Passaic v. Patterson Bill Posting, Adver. & Sign Co.* 62 A. 267, 268 (N.J. 1905), quoted in Randall J. Cude, "Beauty and the Well-Drawn Ordinance: Avoiding Vagueness and Overbreadth Challenges to Municipal Aesthetic Regulations," *Journal of Law and Policy* 6 (1998): n. 92.

20. *Schneider v. State*, 308 U.S. 147 at 161, quoted in Geoffrey R. Stone, "For a Americana: Speech in Public Places," *Supreme Court Review*, no. 233 (1974): 240.

21. *Berman v. Parker*, 75 S. CT. 98 (1954); 348 U.S. 26, at 32–33.

22. Virginia Scott Jenkins, *The Lawn: A History of an American Obsession* (Washington, D.C.: Smithsonian Institution Press, 1994), 36.

23. *Berman* at 34; author's italics.

24. This survey of *Berman* comes from Cude, "Beauty and the Well-Drawn Ordinance," a history of aesthetics in municipal regulation.

25. *People v. Stover*, 191 N.E. 2nd 272, 278 (N.Y.), appeal dismissed, 375 U.S. (1963), quoted in Cude, "Beauty and the Well-Drawn Ordinance," n. 95.

26. *Metromedia, Inc. v. City of San Diego*, 453 U.S. 490 (1981), at 507–8.

27. See Harold Quadres, "Content-Neutral Public Forum Regulations: The Rise of the Aesthetic State Interest, the Fall of Judicial Scrutiny," *Hastings Law Journal* 37 (1986): 439–97.

28. *City Council of Los Angeles v. Taxpayers for Vincent*, 466 U.S. 789 (1984), at 807.

29. Id. at 795.

30. Id. at 820.

31. *Hague v. CIO*, 307 U.S. 496 (1939), at 515.

32. *Perry Education Ass'n v. Perry Local Educators' Ass'n*, 460 U.S. 37 (1983) (hereafter *Perry v. Perry*), at 45–48.

33. *Commonwealth v. Davis*, 39 N.E. 113 (Mass. 1895), affirmed, *Davis v. Massachusetts*, 167 U.S. 43 (1897).

34. *Hague v. CIO* at 516. The discussion of Perry to this point belongs to Cude's research found in "Beauty and the Well-drawn Ordinance."

35. *Perry v. Perry* at 7, following the landmark case of *U.S. v. O'Brien*, 391 U.S. 367 (1968), in which several persons burned their draft cards in public as part of a protest against the war in Vietnam. The Court found that this conduct was not protected under the First Amendment and found the right to regulate their behavior here because (1) the regulation was within the constitutional power of the government, (2) it furthered an important or substantial governmental interest, (3) that interest was unrelated to the suppression of free expression, and (4) that interest was no greater than was essential to the furtherance of governmental interest.

36. Id. at 7.

37. Id. at 45.

38. Id. at 47.

39. Commentators believe that the Supreme Court, along with the Federal Bench, has changed the emphasis in decisions from the strongest possible protections for political speech and its effective delivery to merely allowing a forum somewhere, somehow, for citizens to speak: "As our cases have long noted, once a governmental regulation is shown to impinge upon basic First Amendment rights, the burden

falls upon the government to show the validity of its asserted interest." Brennan, dissent, *Heffron v. ISKON, Inc.*, 452 U.S. 640 (1981), in response to the *Heffron* majority which admonished that the *First Amendment does not guarantee a message being delivered in the most effective manner possible and the protection of governmental interests* (author's italics).

And in fact, now some National Park Service sites have created "separate but equal" sections for protest, roped off from the rest of the park: "Lt. Hay told Sister Bernie that the group would have to move to an area reserved for protesters known as the `First Amendment area' located 150 to 175 yards from the Visitor Center." Their permit to protest the planned destruction of housing was denied because they wished to demonstrate in front of the Presidio's Visitor's Center. The National Park Service included the "damage to a protected area's atmosphere of peace and tranquility" as a factor in the denial; *1999 WL 641940 (9th Cir. (CAL.)*, at 2–3.

40. Majority opinion (later overturned by the Supreme Court in *Clark v. CCNV*) in *Watt v. CCNV*, at 599.

41. "Through March 8, 1995, the National Capital Region received 3,092 applications for demonstrations and special events. . . . During this same period in 1994, the Region received 2,884 demonstration and special event permit requests, an increase of over 200 applications." *Federal Register* 60, no. 67, Rules and Regulations, Department of the Interior, National Park Service, 36 CFR Part 7, RIN 1024-AC14, National Capital Region Parks, Special Regulations, 60 FR 1764634, 60 FR 17639, 17646.

42. *Watt* at 617, quoted again in *Federal Register* 60, no. 67, 17646.

43. Barry Mackintosh, *The National Parks: Shaping the System* (Washington, D.C.: U.S. Department of the Interior, 1991), 19–20.

44. Superintendent Arnold Goldstein, personal communication, September 24, 1999.

45. See Raymond Williams, *The Country and the City* (Oxford: Oxford University Press, 1973), and Jenkins, *The Lawn.*

46. *West Virginia Board of Education v. Barnette*, 319 U.S. 624 (1943).

47. *Cox v. Louisiana*, 379 US 536 (1965), at 555.

48. *Cohen v. California*, 403 U.S. 15 (1971).

49. Cude, "Beauty and the Well-Drawn Ordinance," 14–18.

50. *Watt v. CCNV* at 618.

51. *Watt v. CCNV* at 593, 52 263 S.W. 2nd 906, 907 (Ark. 1954), quoted in Cude, "Beauty and the Well-Drawn Ordinance," n. 94.

53. *Watt v. CCNV* at 622.

54. Ellen P. Aprill, "The Law of the Word: Dictionary Shopping in the Supreme Court," *Arizona State Law Journal* 30, no. 275 (Summer 1998): 278.

55. See David Sosa, "The Unintentional Fallacy" (Review of *The Unintentional Fallacy: A Matter of Interpretation*, by Antonin Scalia), *California Law Review* 86, no. 919 (1998): 932–36; and Michael H. Koby, "The Supreme Court's Declining Reliance on Legislative History: The Impact of Justice Scalia's Critique," *Harvard Journal on Legislation* 36, no. 369 (Summer 1999): 369–95.

56. "This is what you shall do: Love the earth and sun and the animals, despise riches, give alms to everyone that asks, stand up for the stupid and the crazy, devote your income and labor to others, hate tyrants, argue not concerning God." Walt Whitman, *Leaves of Grass* (Philadelphia, 1891–92). I like to bring in Whitman here because he anticipates and enjoins us to embrace those whom Scalia implicitly leaves

out or dismisses, or seeks to discredit, i.e., those stupid or crazy people who disagree with his obviously correct interpretation of the Constitution.

57. Thomas McEvilley, *Art and Otherness: Crisis in Cultural Identity* (New York: McPherson and Company, 1992), 23.

58. See Leslie Prosterman, *Framing the Exhibition: Multiple Constructions* (Baltimore: Albin O. Kuhn Library Gallery at University of Maryland, Baltimore County, 2000), 9–36.

59. *Henderson v. Lujan* at 1184.

60. Final Rule, 49 *Fed. Reg.* at 39680, quoted in *Henderson v. Lujan*, 1184.

61. Id. at 1184.

62. *USA v. Jane Doe 1992*, 88; Judge Wald does not permit this conclusion because she points out that Lafayette Park is an "acknowledged public forum," at 87.

63. *ISKON of Potomac, Inc. v. Kennedy*, at 951.

64. *Friends of the Vietnam Memorial v. Roger Kennedy, Director, National Park Service*, 899 F. Supp. 680, at 8–9.

65. *White House Vigil* at 217.

66. These elements, especially "maintenance," bear a resemblance to the exemplary polis described by Aristotle in *The Politics* (New York: Penguin Press, 1984), which includes the ideal of stability, and not demonstrations of difference and instability: "Observation tells us that every state is an association and that every association is formed with a view toward some good purpose. . . . The task of all citizens, however different they may be, is the stability of the association" (pp. 54, 179).

In *The Politics*, Aristotle often characterizes the ways to define and acquire the good life as comparable to perception through the senses (*aesthesis*) and more particularly as comparable to various art forms (including speech) which articulate sensory perception. The good life is the life that is good for the largest number of people in the polis and which is in fact the goal of the polis. He suggests that without speech (deliberate articulation of perceptions of good and evil) we merely have voice which can indicate pleasure or pain. But *speech* (author's italics) is crucial to the construction of the most efficient state, i.e., the state that creates the good life for the largest number of its inhabitants by its citizenry: "While the state came about as a means of securing life itself, it continues in being able to secure the good life. . . . Speech serves to indicate what is useful and what is harmful, and so also what is just and what is unjust. . . . It is the sharing of a common view in *these* matters that makes a household and a state" (pp. 59–60).

Throughout *The Politics*, Aristotle rarely considers that notions of "the good" and the kinds speech that articulate them may vary, because he imagines a largely heterogeneous and fairly small citizenry. This has been, of course, a topic of much discussion since many contemporary democracies are built on the foundations of Aristotelian theories of democracy. Therefore the relationship between citizen and inhabitant, public as voice and public as consumer of landscape becomes again an important discussion point.

67. Pierre Bourdieu, *The Field of Cultural Production* (New York: Columbia University Press, 1993), 263.

68. *USA v. Jane Doe* at 87.

69. See Marianna Torgovnick, *Gone Primitive: Savage Intellects, Modern Lives* (Chicago: University of Chicago Press, 1991).

70. *Friends v. Kennedy* at 687.

71. *Watt v. CCNV* at 590, 594.
72. *Terminiello v. Chicago,* (1949) 337 U.S., at 1, 4.
73. *Friends v. Kennedy* at 687.
74. *Clark v. CCNV* at 14.
75. Deborah Root, *Cannibal Culture: Art, Appropriation, and the Commodification of Difference* (Boulder, Colo.: Westview Press, 1996), 11.
76. Judge Priscilla Wald, dissent, *White House Vigil v. Clark,* at 233.
77. Harry Philbrick, *Art at the Edge of the Law* (Ridgefield, Conn.: Aldrich Museum of Contemporary Art, 2001); and Ruth Olson, personal communication, 2002.

CHAPTER 12

The Public
Display of Religion

SALLY M. PROMEY

*Congress shall make no law respecting an establishment of
religion, or prohibiting the free exercise thereof. . . .*

—FIRST AMENDMENT, U.S. CONSTITUTION

This chapter, a revised version of an essay that first appeared
early in 2001, represents a small piece of a larger project on the same subject.
Though my larger project is a historical study, examining the eighteenth and
nineteenth centuries as well as the twentieth and twenty-first, in this volume
on the "arts of democracy" my goal is to make some preliminary observations
about the contemporary dynamics of public religious display in American visual culture. This chapter thus represents a wide-ranging romp through my

This chapter revises an essay that first appeared in *The Visual Culture of American Religions,* ed. David Morgan and Sally M. Promey (Berkeley: University of California Press,
2001), 27–48. I am grateful to the University of California Press for permission to re-
visit the piece for this volume and to Casey Blake for his invitation to do so. I am further indebted to the Woodrow Wilson International Center for Scholars and to the Center for Advanced Study in the Visual Arts for providing both mental space and
intellectual community for work on this subject. At the Wilson Center, I owe special
thanks to Michael Lacey, then director of United States Studies. At the Center for Advanced Study in the Visual Arts, Dean Elizabeth Cropper played a similarly substantial
role. I also wish to acknowledge the expert research assistance of two University of
Maryland doctoral candidates, Leslie Brice and Guy Jordan.

subject, a summary overview of terms in search of useful definitions and opportunities to open conversation.

In the years since I began this project, the public display of religion in the United States has become an especially volatile subject, a moving target difficult to bring into analytical and critical focus. Observers of American society, its behaviors, practices, and beliefs, cannot yet predict the degree to which—and in what ways—the terrorist attacks of September 11, 2001 (and the presidential campaigns of 2000 and 2004), marked a permanent or fundamental shift in American attitudes.[2] Certainly the wave of post-9/11 public art making described by Casey Blake in this book's introduction was also, and very often, public *religious* art making (figure 12.1). "God Bless America," in every conceivable visual and graphic medium, morphed from the character of spontaneous prayer on September 11 and 12 into a ubiquitous, and then aggressive, declarative political and commercial slogan in the weeks (and months and now years) after the terrorist attacks. One disturbingly adversarial variation on this theme manifested itself in a bumper sticker sighted on Capitol Hill in January 2004: "My God can beat up your God." In patriotic red, white, and blue, and in this time and place, the viewer was clearly being asked to imagine a street brawl between a triumphant (and triumphalist) Christian "my God" and a Muslim "your God" in defeat.

Since 2001, in other domains, too, we have seen new alliances form and old ones reconfigure themselves. Despite Mel Gibson's theological distance, along important dimensions, from both evangelical Protestants and most American Catholics, many among the two groups (their historically distinct religious aesthetics notwithstanding) joined ranks in offering accolades to Gibson's film *The Passion of the Christ*, released in the United States on Ash Wednesday (February 25) 2004. In the days immediately following, Holy Week that year witnessed a kind of conservative Christian occupation of major movie theaters, remaking as temporarily "sacred" space these secular commercial spaces, with screenings of a brutal, medievalizing, and anti-Semitic *Passion* attended by the invocations and benedictions of clergy.

"The public display of religion": The phrase itself generates a broad spectrum of value-laden responses. In many quarters of the secular academy and among the mainstream historically liberal religious traditions, my subject evokes frequent expressions of distaste; and for some it even seems to carry the implication of a breach in public decorum.[3] When it comes to religion, the academy, of which I count myself a part, is generally more comfortable with disestablishment than with free exercise, with the emphatic separation of church and state than with the appearance of religion in the civic arena. The insistent role played by conservative evangelical Christianity in the 2004 United States presidential elections amplified the level of concern.[4]

A number of factors contribute to reactions of ambivalence about the public display of religion. Prominent among these are, first, the recognition that

Figure 12.1. Memorial in Union Square by candlelight, New York City, September 17, 2001. Photograph by Margaret Wilkerson.

religion rarely happens "in general," that it usually occurs in some particular or sectarian manifestation (and often with an equally particular and sectarian set of truth claims); second, a historical and practical inclination to count religion as something people do or ought to do in private; and third, an understanding of "public" display that implicates images and objects in government or civic facilities, at the initiative of civic agencies, or making some use of public funds.[5] Though few assume that all public displays of religion are publicly funded, consideration of the "appropriate" display of (largely sectarian) religion gets conceptually and categorically drawn into conversations about government endorsement or complicity—set off, philosophically and legally, against cultural pluralism and the establishment clause of the First Amendment.

During the past two or three decades, an increasing number of public display cases have come before the courts, with a few reaching the U.S. Supreme Court.[6] In March 2005, for example, the Supreme Court heard two cases (*Van Orden v. Perry*, 03-1500; and *McCreary County v. ACLU of Kentucky*, 03-1693) concerning the display of the Ten Commandments on state property. In the months of contention surrounding adjudication, and in support of such displays, metal placards loosely resembling real estate signs and picturing the Ten Commandments sprouted in yards around the nation, initially appearing in the South and Midwest (figure 12.2). Decisions in past public display court

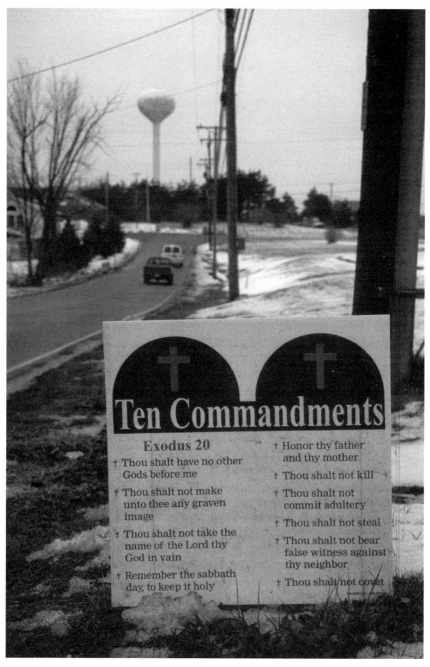

Figure 12.2. Ten Commandments yard sign, Louisville, Ohio, December 2004. Photograph by Sally M. Promey.

cases reflect the complicated histories and conceptual and categorical challenges presented by visual culture and religion in the American public domain. My research grants the critical importance of the establishment clause of the First Amendment. Here I more closely examine, however, the visible effects of disestablishment's constitutional sibling, the free exercise clause. For, as constitutional scholar Leonard W. Levy has pointed out, "religion saturates American public life," the establishment clause notwithstanding.[7] Here religion is not just something *some* people do but also something virtually *all* people see—daily—in public.[8]

This chapter is an exercise in reframing scholarly consideration of the public display of religion. Most important, perhaps, it proposes expanding along several dimensions the common notion of religion's public representation. The result is a shift toward "public" display that by definition is plural, particular, and accessible. My larger book project carefully scrutinizes issues of government funding, property, and supervision but it neither focuses nor stops there (though it does literally conclude with an epilogue on the visible resurgence of rightist Christianity in the years of the George W. Bush administration). Without minimizing the substantial importance of constitutionally bounded church-state relations in American religious expression, the accent in my study is equally on the nongovernmental operation of religious images and objects in the public arena—and this is where I place my emphasis in this chapter.

My purpose is twofold. First, I wish to define the public display of religion as a category of visual experience open to engaged academic and civic inquiry. To date, the scant literature on the subject addresses particular forms (e.g., John Beardsley's work on yard art); particular monuments (my own work on John Singer Sargent's Boston Public Library murals); particular functions (Edward T. Linenthal on public memory and sacred space); or particular aspects of public funding and legal history (Leonard Levy on the establishment clause and Wayne Swanson on the Supreme Court case *Lynch v. Donnelly*).[9] In addition, though there is a large body of writing on public art and on the 1990s culture wars,[10] scholarly acknowledgment of religion's significant presence in both those arenas has been thin. This is the case despite the frequency with which religious questions or phrasings have surfaced in recent contentions over art and public policy; witness Senator Jesse Helms's 1989 castigation of Andres Serrano's *Piss Christ* as "blasphemy" in a volley that initiated a particularly virulent set of attacks on public art funding in the United States and the more recent charges of similar trespass leveled in 1999 at Chris Ofili's *Holy Virgin Mary* by then–New York mayor Rudolph Giuliani in relation to the Brooklyn Museum's Sensation exhibition. My research aims to reorganize and reconfigure the subject of the public display of religion. I hope to account, in the process, for all three terms and some of their relations; and to treat in a more comprehensive fashion the materials usefully collected within this visual field of information. Ultimately, I want to understand more about how religion operates in the American visual landscape.

Second, beyond display's visual character, my book also considers the kinds of conversations that take place in a display's literal—and recollected—presence. Display assists in making social spaces available for negotiation about individual and collective identities. These exchanges, and their roles in shaping visual and mental landscapes over time, perhaps most fundamentally describe my subject. I am especially interested in the uses and roles of religious variety—and their implications for the construction and consolidation of human identity. Though it has functioned differently in the past, and clearly has other outcomes, too, today the public display of religion plays a key role in manifesting the nation's plural character. Religion's public display—especially in its current proliferation of forms—makes visible pluralism's fundamental relation to, as well as its complicated configuration within, American culture.[11]

The degree of ambiguity and complexity inherent in each of my terms ("public," "display," "religion") is greater than initial appearances might suggest. Each warrants its own discussion—and so I take up each term in turn, examining the intricacies inherent in each as well as some of the intersections among the three.

Public

Though art may be a private act in its origins, this is not what we can be expected to see as art becomes part of a system of public information. Art is a public system to which we, as spectators or consumers [or participants], have random access.

—Lawrence Alloway, "Network: The Art World Described as a System"

Jesse Treviño's nine-story hand-cut mosaic tile mural, *Spirit of Healing* (figure 12.3), is situated on the principal facade of the Santa Rosa Children's Hospital, a regional medical facility operated by the Sisters of the Incarnate Word, in San Antonio. This privately funded ninety-by-forty-foot mural is, nonetheless, among the largest works of "public art" in the city, easily visible to motorists on Interstate 10, a major San Antonio expressway. *Spirit of Healing* is part of what critic Lawrence Alloway calls a "system of public information" about the institution the mural adorns and about the people who inhabit the building, including the young patients and their parents as well as the medical personnel, the support staff, and the religious order that runs the hospital. Treviño indicates that publicness was a factor in the project's attraction for him: "It's not that I don't want my paintings in museums. I do. But the people are outside those museum walls. Public art, big pieces like this, brings the art out where everyone can see it."[12]

Despite the mural's public status, Treviño conceived aspects of its design in direct relation to his personal biography. Treviño, who was born in Mexico, be-

Figure 12.3. Jesse Treviño, *Spirit of Healing*, Santa Rosa Children's Hospital, San Antonio. © *San Antonio Express-News*. Photograph by Robert McLeroy.

came a United States citizen in 1970 and is now a resident of San Antonio. An artist by training and profession, he lost his right hand in military action during the Vietnam War. He subsequently retrained himself to paint left-handed. In the mural, the guardian angel's maimed left wing, while it also carries other meanings, surely alludes to Treviño's own injury as well as directing attention, in its orientation, to the large cross in the background.[13] In addition, and even more prominent than the angel's broken wing, Treviño's ten-year-old son, Jesse Jr., was the model for the child in *Spirit of Healing*. These rather intimate private associations, once known, become part of the mural's public significance, aspects of the work with which particular audiences (parents, children, Latinos, veterans) identify.

What I am suggesting here is that understandings of publicness occur in constant relation to and tension with notions of privacy.[14] In past and present practice, the public/private distinction has often been singled out as a way of approaching the problem of imagining religious action in a plural culture.[15] Though the word "public" has several possible meanings, from this historical perspective, public religion is oxymoronic; religion is a fundamentally private enterprise. A Gallup Poll conducted in 1988 reported that 80 percent of Americans agreed that religious beliefs belong to a voluntary and private domain, to be arrived at "independent of any church or synagogue."[16] (The percentages would undoubtedly have been even higher had government influence been considered along with that of religious institutions.) The origins of "public" and "private" are traceable to ancient Greece and Rome, but the early-twenty-first-century combination of privacy, individualism, and religious freedom has a specifically Euro-American lineage, including the early Puritan colonists and the Enlightenment thinkers whose works informed the founding of the republic. Assumptions of privacy reside at the very core of the historical construction of American religious liberty.[17] John Locke, for example, claimed in 1689 that the "true and saving Religion consists in the inward persuasion of the Mind."[18] Thomas Jefferson's famous 1802 letter to the Baptists of Danbury, Connecticut, the letter that introduced the phrase regarding the "wall of separation between Church and State," also asserted Jefferson's conviction that "religion is a matter which lies solely between man and his God."[19] By the later nineteenth century, there was widespread agreement that the "inner spiritual life" was the "domain of sovereign individuality."[20]

The definition of religious privacy assumed in these quotations is more or less consistent with the one I follow here. What is private, for purposes of this chapter, is that which is relatively inaccessible to others. As political and social theorist Jeff Weintraub suggests, privacy includes the "things we are able or entitled [or in some cases required] to keep hidden, sheltered, or withdrawn from others."[21] Historically, such a definition of religious privacy has generally been constructed in supposed opposition to "public" established or state-supported institutional religion.[22] I propose augmenting the definition of "public" in three ways. The modifications I recommend have to do with matters of visual accessibility, of dynamic relation, and of the constitution of audience.

First, my use of the word "public" is linked to degree of accessibility rather than to issues of official, state, or institutional administration. "Public" is thus, in the words of historian John F. Wilson, a "means of signifying that which is generally available for common inspection."[23] Wilson's recourse to the phrase "common inspection" with respect to "public" and Weintraub's understanding of "private" as that which is "hidden, sheltered, or withdrawn," suggest that it does not necessarily take an art historian to cast *accessibility* (in relation to the public display of religion) as *visibility*. Who can see it and when? Where is it and what is the level of exposure? What I am really writing about here, then, is *religion in plain view.*

In addition to accessibility, the question of collectivity (most simply, the numbers of people to whom a public display is visually available) is not irrelevant.[24] But the sense in which collectivity intersects with this definition of public is a very specific one. The issue is not whether something is seen by an individual or by a group, whether it is viewed alone or in company. It is rather that the viewer knows that others can and will see, too—and that they can and will do so with some facility. In other words, it is critical to this definition of public that many enjoy easy access to the object in question—but not necessarily that they do so at the same time. The viewing of a public display of religion can be a solitary experience without compromising its "publicness." Treviño's *Spirit of Healing* remains "public" whether there is one person or fifty people in the urban square in front of it.

Second, "public" is not rendered here as one term of a static, paired opposition (as in public vs. private), but rather as one direction along a conceptual, practical, and experiential continuum of accessibility. Public and private are relative and dynamic terms. Rather than simple binary opposites, they are, as Robert A. White has argued for the similarly associated pairing of "sacred" and "secular," interdependent "dualities that are the enabling conditions for each other."[25] The shared boundaries that define the two are mutable; public and private are constantly in the process of formation and reformation with respect to each other. Along the spectrum that charts the two, the advance and retreat of one is always relative to the other.

During the last century, in particular, technologies of mediation (e.g., halftone print technologies, film, television, and electronic imaging systems, including the Internet) have made "public" and "private" increasingly elastic terms. Much that was formerly private has now been articulated into public expression by the mass mediation of culture, with its tendency to subject human experience and production to the "persistent gaze of publicity."[26] As media artifacts, W. J. T. Mitchell has argued, all art objects become public art.[27] Even domestic religious objects and private devotional ones, when mediated by, for instance, the morning newspaper, take on a new "public" dimension for an expanded audience, though the objects simultaneously retain their "privacy" in the context of initial production and use.[28] In this sense, any given display might conceivably be public and private at the same time.

In the two modifications suggested above, the word "public" has its greatest applicability as an adjective—as in, for example, public space, public art, or public expression—where it now describes visual accessibility and where its relation to privacy is active and unstable. Third, and turning to the term's nominative usage, though I deem public spaces to be relatively more open and inclusive than private ones, no rhetorically all-inclusive "public" stands behind my argument. The public display of religion is observed not by a normative or representative public (singular) but by numerous *publics* (plural), multiple audiences, individuals and groups, who see religion around them as they conduct their daily lives and who approach the display of religion from many different perspectives. Though media exposure alters the equation, expanding the "geographical" referent and suggesting the advisability of attending to the macropolitics as well as the micropolitics of display, on the local level each example of display exists in its own "cultural space" and may be compared with but is not reducible to another.[29]

The publics for the display of religion are plural not only in any given place but also in the sense that each public changes over time and new publics emerge. In addition, any number of relatively discrete audiences may aggregate to constitute a larger public or disintegrate into smaller units. To discuss a display's publics is thus to deal with entities both kinetic and partial. Whenever something is set out for others to see, what they see depends on both who they are and on what is displayed. In its adjectival usage, and in relation to our purposes here, "public" describes the picture, object, monument, place, or performance seen. In its nominative usage, the emphasis shifts from the object to the spectator, from the thing that is visible to the person who sees it, from production and placement to reception. The most fruitful understandings of the public display of religion will involve the consideration neither simply of things nor of people but of the relations among things and people. The plurality of publics for the display of religion increases the contingency of the display's significance.

The public display of religion is thus fundamentally interactive, with the full range of interpretive responses being inherently unpredictable.[30] I offer as an example one of my own recent experiences photographing a display I took to be a statement of piety on the part of the owner of a vehicle decorated with a crucifix and a rosary hanging from the rearview mirror and a prominent "praying hands" window decal. A Montgomery County, Maryland, police officer observing me with my camera quickly "corrected" my initial impression. Whatever else I might think these items indicated, in the constellation in which they appeared in and on this sporty car, they were, he asserted, identifying insignia of gang members belonging to the Mara Salvatrucha, or MS-13.

Display

[Display] is not only endemic to human-being-in-the-world but fundamental to the process of constructing a human reality.

—EDWARD L. SCHIEFFELIN, "PROBLEMATIZING PERFORMANCE"

In observance of Hanukkah 1993, five-year-old-Isaac Schnitzer's parents placed a menorah in the front window of their home in Billings, Montana. Shortly after the arrangement of this domestic public display, someone launched a concrete block through the Schnitzers' window.[31] In response to this blatantly anti-Semitic crime, non-Jewish residents of Billings (a city of 85,000 with a Jewish population of approximately 100) put pictures of menorahs in their own front windows or on their doors to affirm their communal solidarity with the Schnitzers and with other local Jewish individuals and families. On December 11, 1993, in an editorial accompanied by a picture of a menorah (figure 12.4) to be clipped and used in this way, the *Billings Gazette* interpreted both the original family menorah and the city's visual and visible response to the crime as significant activities of public display:

> On December 2, 1993, someone twisted by hate threw a brick through the window of the home of one of our neighbors: a Jewish family who chose to celebrate the holiday season by displaying a symbol of faith—a menorah—for all to see. Today members of religious faiths throughout Billings are joining together to ask residents to display the menorah as a symbol of something else: our determination to live together in harmony, and our dedication to the principle of religious liberty embodied in the First Amendment to the Constitution of the United States of America. We urge all citizens to share in this message by displaying this menorah on a door or a window from now until Christmas. Let all the world know that the irrational hatred of a few cannot destroy what all of us in Billings, and in America, have worked together so long to build.[32]

The full shape of the display unintentionally initiated by the Schnitzer's menorah did not stop there. One year later, French photographer Frédéric Brenner assembled a deliberately diverse crowd of Billings residents ("cowboys, Indians, blacks, Latinos, ministers, priests, cops, you name it").[33] Directed by Brenner, this group staged a commemoration (figure 12.5) designed to reaffirm respect for the many different religious and ethnic groups represented in the city's population. Wearing vestments and "costumes" that visually accentuated their differences, each participant raised aloft a Hanukkah menorah. Crews provided electrical connections (note the wires on the ground in the photograph) to light the bulbs representing candle flames. Brenner signified the gathering's defiance of the initiating episode's specific violence by shooting his photograph of the assembly through a sheet of glass penetrated, but

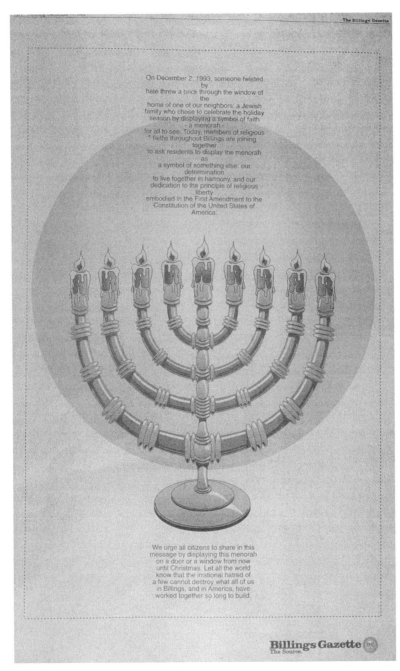

On December 2, 1993, someone twisted
by
hate threw a brick through the window of
the
home of one of our neighbors: a Jewish
family who chose to celebrate the holiday
season by displaying a symbol of faith
— a menorah —
for all to see. Today, members of religious
faiths throughout Billings are joining
together
to ask residents to display the menorah
as
a symbol of something else: our
determination
to live together in harmony, and our
dedication to the principle of religious
liberty
embodied in the First Amendment to the
Constitution of the United States of
America.

We urge all citizens to share in this
message by displaying this menorah
on a door or a window from now
until Christmas. Let all the world
know that the irrational hatred of
a few cannot destroy what all of us
in Billings, and in America, have
worked together so long to build.

Billings Gazette
The Source.

Figure 12.4. *Billings Gazette* menorah, Billings, Montana. December 11, 1993. Photograph by Henry Gregory. Reprinted with permission of the *Billings Gazette*.

Figure 12.5. Frédéric Brenner, *Citizens Protesting Anti-Semitic Acts, Billings, Montana, 1994.* © Frédéric Brenner. Courtesy Howard Greenberg Gallery, New York.

not shattered, presumably by a stone or rock. A two-story American flag draped (for the photo and, perhaps inadvertently, backwards) from a building in the right background asserted the perceived Americanness of this demonstration of plural and communal solidarity.

The photograph that resulted from the performance staged by Brenner was subsequently exhibited as part of a traveling show that began in September 1996 at the Howard Greenberg Gallery in SoHo, New York City. In the same month, the photograph was reproduced in *Life Magazine* with other images documenting American Jewish life and in a *New York Times* review of the SoHo exhibition. Brenner simultaneously published a book of his photographs, titled *Jews/America/A Representation*, which included the shot he now called *Citizens Protesting Anti-Semitic Acts, Billings, Montana, 1994*. In this case, one display expanded, layer upon layer, to include other displays that continued to bear a direct relation to the domestic ritual religious object in the Schnitzers' front window. With each added "layer," new publics and new sorts of publicness accrued to the event and its iterations. Brenner's work first provided the rationale for, and then recorded, the commemorative performance. Both the collaboration between the photographer and the city and the image that documented the collaboration asserted for the Billings community an identity and a human reality that were active alternatives to those presented by the hate crime.

When used in conjunction with the modifier "public," the word "display" maintains a rich and resonant redundancy: The verbal form "to display" includes "to make public" among its synonyms. Display sometimes carries with it connotations of ostentation, superficiality, or falseness. Often associated with these suspicions of ostentation, connections to commerce also make an appearance here. In a consumer culture like the early twenty-first-century United States, both the staging and the interpretation of display assume a commercial set of relations. It is not just the role of display in making its subject public, then, that seems ill suited to apparent preferences for religion "in private." The "taint" of commerce, too, sometimes preconditions initial negative reactions to religion's public display. Ironically (in this regard), the public display of American religion has enjoyed a long and even venerable acquaintance with commerce. As historian R. Laurence Moore points out, American religion itself played a critical and formative role in shaping modern consumerism.[34] American religious culture is thus an entity complicit and conversant in the mechanisms of commercial display; and public display is an important aspect of the "open market" of religion in the United States (figure 12.6).[35]

I have deliberately selected "display" (over some of the possible, but categorically more limited, alternatives) to be inclusive of the widest possible array of experiences while still emphasizing the explicitly *visual* character of my subject. "Art," for example, as one category of display, occupies an important and particular place in the public pictorial representation of religion. But from the perspective of my project, art is part of a larger whole constituted by the

Figure 12.6. Chimayo Holy Chiles, Chimayo, New Mexico, June 2002. Photograph by Sally M. Promey.

numerous modes of visual communication represented in religious display. If the operative question is where do we see religion in the visual practice of daily life, then the comprehensive response must be ventured, at least initially at any rate, without regard to the filtering mechanisms usually put into place by notions of aesthetic, intellectual, or economic hierarchy. We learn more about the way visual culture works when we look at a range of visual materials. The necessary second step, one that the prescribed length of this chapter precludes, is a return, with renewed understanding, to the various more tightly bounded categories of form and behavior.

Display, as a visual and material phenomenon, organizes space and experience.[36] The term accommodates two significant aspects of the public visual culture of religion in the United States: exhibition and performance. Exhibition is conceived here as the public presentation of objects and images (e.g., including such things as fine art, other pictures of various sorts, statues, bumper stickers, monuments and memorials, postage stamps, vanity license plates, billboards and signage, seasonal items like Nativity scenes or menorahs, and architectural facades). The category "exhibition" takes account of such specific displays of religion as Treviño's *Spirit of Healing* (see figure 12.3); John G. Chapman's *Baptism of Pocahontas* (1840) in the U.S. Capitol Rotunda; a sukkah in a Silver Spring, Maryland, neighborhood; and a sculpture at a Cambodian Buddhist temple (figure 12.7). The public exhibition of religion in the United States also includes the display of religious objects at one or more steps

Figure 12.7. Cambodian Buddhist temple, Colesville, Maryland, 2000. Photograph by Sally M. Promey.

removed from original use, as, for example, in a Tibetan Buddhist prayer wheel at the Smithsonian Folklife Festival in the summer of 2000. Just how far "removed" remains an open question, however, when the viewer becomes aware that Buddhist monks had filled the wheel with prayers for the dissipation of corruption in Washington, and that observant Buddhists left offerings at the adjacent "display."

This last example provides a natural segue from exhibition to performance. I use this second term to refer to the acting out in public of explicitly and visually religious behavior. It thus comprises such displays as the interaction with onlookers of the seemingly ubiquitous (in the late 1990s) rainbow-wigged figures at sports events with signs reading "John 3:16"; the outdoor consecration of, for example, the suburban Maryland Church of Our Lady of Vietnam (figure 12.8); the Sikh Vaisakhi Day Parade in New York City; and observances associated with the seasonal erection of Jewish, Muslim, and Christian symbols on the National Mall (e.g., the lighting of the "national" Christmas tree and Hanukkah menorah and the recent ritual placement of the Islamic star and crescent). Display can thus be considered to include public ritual as "a kind of performative behavior" with a visual component.[37] The Reverend George Stallings's ritualized destruction of pictures of a white Jesus, performed at Freedom Plaza on Pennsylvania Avenue a few blocks from the White House on Good Friday 1993, is an especially apt example (figure 12.9). Controversy and acts of iconoclasm themselves can be construed as cultural performances that serve to recall, foreground, and rework significant identity and boundary issues. Stallings intended his action, performed in clerical garb outdoors along a major thoroughfare, to constitute a proclamation about the visual appearance of Christianity's founder in relation to contemporary issues of race in the United States.

The Stallings event also demonstrates how performance, by comparison with exhibition, much more assertively introduces the elements of time and motion into religious display. Once again, however, mass mediation complicates this picture by re-presenting performances in still images (as in, again, figure 12.9, from the *Washington Post*) and re-presenting the exhibition of pictures or objects in video formats that include both time and motion (e.g., the appearance of a print version of Warner Sallman's 1940 *Head of Christ* in Spike Lee's 1991 film *Jungle Fever*).

Even before media intervention, however, exhibition and performance are less clearly distinguished from one another than some of the foregoing might be taken to imply. The Billings example (see figures 12.4 and 12.5) clearly includes elements of both exhibition and performance. So too does the woman worshiping at the Smithsonian's outdoor exhibition of Tibetan Buddhist objects and architecture; as well as the spontaneous construction of public memorials, often including explicitly religious symbols or messages, that has occurred with increasing frequency in response to acts of violence and death like the April 1999 shooting rampage at a public high school in Littleton, Col-

Figure 12.8. Consecration ceremony, Our Lady of Vietnam Catholic Church, Silver Spring, Maryland, 2000. Photograph by Sally M. Promey.

Figure 12.9. The Reverend George Stallings performing a Good Friday iconoclastic ritual, Washington, April 1993. © *The Washington Post*. Photograph by Bill O'Leary. Reprinted with permission.

orado, the 1995 bombing of the Alfred P. Murrah Building in Oklahoma City, or the terrorist attacks on New York and Washington of 9/11.

One might choose to see many seasonal exhibitions of religion—attending such holidays as Christmas, Hanukkah, Sukkoth, Ramadan, and Kwanzaa—as a kind of performance on the basis of their temporary, periodic, and repetitive usage. The evangelical Christian preacher who constructs giant and elaborate sand sculptures of religious figures on the beach at Ocean City, Maryland, and then leaves them for the tides and tourists, only to return and start over again every ten days during the summer season, stands with one foot in each of the two categories.[38] And in cases involving many sorts of religious decoration of the human body—such as yarmulkes, the hijab or head coverings worn by some Muslim women, T-shirts imprinted with religious pictures, crosses, crucifixes, or Stars of David worn as jewelry, and religious tattoos (figure 12.10)—exhibition and performance merge in the practice of display.

As the religious ornamentation of human bodies plainly suggests, within a given culture, display organizes not just space and experience but also identity and association. More specifically, display generates a discursive space, a social and political arena, where cultural negotiations about both individual and collective identities take place.[39] The varieties of public "aesthetics" of American belief have to do, then, not just with how a display looks on the landscape but also with the sorts of conversations evoked by its literal and recollected presence. Any given display is informed by the rules, conventions, and constraints deemed necessary to hold meaning in place in the specific discursive field the display occupies. Plural publics make prior discernment of "necessary" internal regulation an especially daunting task. Surely the fantastical architecture of the Mormon temple (figures 12.11) just off the outer loop of the Capital Beltway in suburban Maryland near Washington was intended by its designers to suggest a disjunction between sacred and profane, the disruption of ordinary activities and expectations. The desired disjunction from the ordinary, however, was not likely one that pursued the temple's conflation with secular fantasy lands. Nonetheless, over the years, the building's visual similarity (gleaming white and gold spires, strikingly surreal illumination, extreme verticality) to the fictional Land of Oz—along with the temple's unavoidable visibility from the Capital Beltway—has elicited a form of editorial vandalism. From time to time, someone enacts a kind of textual counterdisplay, inscribing the words "Surrender Dorothy!" on the exterior barrier of the overhead train crossing that Beltway traffic passes under on immediate approach to the Mormon structure (figure 12.12).

Different groups and individuals activate a particular display's meanings in different ways—or, as with the Mormon temple, they activate different meanings altogether. Attempts to deal with the inherent instability of meaning in public display contribute to the display's visual character. Religious displays often seek to exercise control of interpretive possibilities by the inclusion of easily legible and widely recognizable symbols and images pared down to their

Figure 12.10. "Only One Judge" tattoo, based on Albrecht Dürer's *Praying Hands*. Photograph by Sally M. Promey.

Figure 12.11. The
Washington Temple,
Church of Jesus Christ
of Latter-Day Saints
(Mormon), viewed from
the Capital Beltway,
December 1999.
Photograph by Sally
M. Promey.

Figure 12.12. "Surrender Dorthy" [*sic*] graffito on a railway overpass approaching the Washington Temple, Church of Jesus Christ of Latter-Day Saints (Mormon), viewed from the Capital Beltway, December 2002. Photograph by Sally M. Promey.

most basic elements. Display thus frequently and purposefully distances itself from the sorts of complexities often required of "art" in order to retain a higher degree of control over meaning. This phenomenon can be easily overstated, however. Even highly simplified images, symbols, and iconographies, achieving a substantial degree of cultural uniformity, may simultaneously retain a surprising variety, having to do with such things as pictorial style, rhetorical posture, location, context, and medium. Think, for example, of the visual and narrative dynamics of different Christmas displays of Nativity scenes. A very brief survey would need to take into account the handmade and the mass produced; a wide range of media including wood, plastic, paint, and fabric; both two-dimensional and three-dimensional forms; and displays in which the crèche stands alone as well as ensembles of decorations that include a Nativity scene.

Not infrequently, the activity of viewing display elicits an alternative exhibition or performance that seeks to supplant the meaning initially asserted. During the December holiday season in 1998 and 1999, for example, one manufacturer marketed specially designed cardboard-rimmed eyeglasses.[40] Their lenses turned every Christmas light in the wearer's line of sight into a Star of David. The "magic glasses" thus reconfigured the Christian landscape of Christmas and opposed the cultural imposition of a particular seasonal identity. Rather than merely neutralizing sectarian expression, the glasses wittingly and wittily transformed it.

This example points up a dynamic in which I am very much interested in my larger project: things *hidden in plain view*—things that are there—but not everyone sees them, not everyone attends to them: and here we might talk about the Orthodox Jewish *eruv*—and its virtually *invisible* transformation of public secular space into private sectarian space so that things can be carried through it on the Sabbath. My interest in what is hidden also extends to what is suppressed—to what does not appear in the public landscape—or what appears but only in the most out-of-the-way places.

Religion

There are, indeed, distinct alternatives to a coherent religious tradition as the common cultural core thought by many to be required at the center of our modern society.

—JOHN F. WILSON, "THE PUBLIC AS A PROBLEM"

Of the three terms I aim to discuss, about the third and final one it would seem that there might be a substantial degree of intuitive agreement with respect to when and where the term applies. The evidence suggests otherwise. Religion, it appears, resides most definitively in the eye of the beholder. What counts as religion in public display varies with the audience or audiences for a particular performance or exhibition. In February 1997, a coalition of sixteen Muslim groups wrote a letter of request to the justices of the Supreme Court; the coalition members understood their request to concern the public display of their own religious tradition. Specifically, they petitioned the court to remove the face from the figure of Muhammad in the courtroom's larger-than-life-scale frieze (figure 12.13) representing eighteen great historical law-givers, such as Hammurabi, Confucius, Moses, Charlemagne, Napoleon, and John Marshall. The lawgiver portions of the frieze occupy the north and south walls of the courtroom chamber, with Muhammad in the left front corner of the room as one enters. Allegorical figures representing various aspects or qualities of law (Wisdom, Truth, Justice, Divine Inspiration, Defender of Virtue) appear on the east and west walls. The courtroom frieze in its entirety was produced in the early 1930s by the Beaux-Arts sculptor Adolph A. Weinman.

In a letter dated March 11, 1997, Chief Justice William H. Rehnquist maintained that the representation of Muhammad would not be altered because it "was intended only to recognize him, among many other lawgivers, as an important figure in the history of law . . . [and not] as a form of idol worship" or sacrilege, as Nihad Awad, the director of the Council on American-Islamic Relations and the coalition's spokesperson, had contended. For Rehnquist and the Court, Muhammad's image on the frieze constituted a historical representation of legal development and innovation. For Awad and the coalition, it was an inappropriate depiction of a figure whose meaningful identity was undeniably religious. Though Muhammad's depiction remained unaltered, the Court did order changes in the educational brochures distributed to tourists and visitors. The brochures now specify that the image "bears no resemblance to Muhammad" and that "Muslims generally have a strong aversion to sculptured or pictured representations of their Prophet."[41]

An incident, now become anecdote, involving Sherman Minton, a Supreme Court justice from 1949 to 1956, suggests that the courtroom's aesthetics can be seen to complicate even further the issue at hand (the public perception of religious content). The justice's grandson, visiting the august chamber with Minton, was undeniably awed by the room's high, coffered ceilings, extravagant gilding, marble luminosity, and thirty-foot Ionic columns. Looking up at Weinman's friezes, the ten-year-old reportedly exclaimed, "Granddaddy! Where's God?"[42]

The city-funded Pawtucket, Rhode Island, Nativity scene that sparked the Supreme Court case *Lynch v. Donnelly* was, like the image of Muhammad in the Supreme Court building itself, viewed by some as inherently religious and by others as completely secularized and devoid of religious significance.[43] The decision on the case, delivered by then– (and until 1986) Chief Justice Warren E. Burger, indicates the degree of categorical slippage and blurring. Burger's lengthy written opinion included the observation that the display of artistic "masterpieces," such as Italian Renaissance paintings, with "explicit Christian

Figure 12.13. Adolph Weinman, east end of the north frieze (1931–32), including a figure of
Muhammad, Courtroom, U.S. Supreme Court, Washington. Collection of the Supreme Court of
the United States. Photograph by Franz Jantzen.

themes and messages" in the government-supported National Gallery of Art, constituted a plausible justification for toleration of the city-funded Pawtucket crèche.[44]

The categorical imprecision encountered with respect to the public display of religion accrues, in part, from the "location" of belief. Each display manifests at least three possible agents of belief: the artist, maker, or performer; the patron (institutional, group, or individual); and the various audiences or publics who may well disagree among themselves about the absence, presence, or degree of religion that is represented. In some instances, the most meaningful constituent unit of interpretation for a particular display is a single person, with public display thus becoming a medium of private meaning making. For example, passersby offered markedly different interpretations of a tree trunk carved into the shape of an upraised arm and hand near a residence in Silver Spring, Maryland. The educational executive and fundraiser who created the wood carving maintained that he understood this labor as "relaxing" and "therapeutic" and that he did not set out to make "a religious symbol." Among his neighbors, however, an Orthodox Jew saw in the work the Hand of Moses. And a Muslim woman identified the sculpture's subject as the Hand of Fatima, daughter of Muhammad.[45]

In social and historical analysis, where describing other peoples' understandings and perceptions of religion is paramount, psychologist of religion Roger Fallot makes a compelling case for adopting an expansive definition of the term, one that allows for the ambiguities and multivalences of use. Public displays of religion represent a subject that may manifest both experiential and institutional dimensions. Experientially, religion may include a sense of ultimate or existential meaning, values, order, or purpose; an awareness of the sacred or the holy; or a sense of relation to a transcendent being or higher power. Institutionally, religion generally involves an identifiable collective or community of adherents as well as a set of defined beliefs, ideas, practices, rituals, and symbols.[46]

In the late nineteenth century, intellectuals and liberal religious congregants on both sides of the Atlantic voiced the sometimes anxious opinion that modernity might necessarily be accompanied by a decline in both institutional and experiential religion. By the 1950s and 1960s, sociologists of religion had assumed and documented this decline, a phenomenon they called "secularization." In the last decade of the twentieth century, however, and countering this assumption, the scholarly literatures of the history and sociology of religion began effectively to overturn the notion that modernity—and especially modernity in the United States—would automatically defeat religious experience and expression. The "new paradigm" for the sociological study of religion in the United States, according to R. Stephen Warner's already classic article, "begins with theoretical reflection on a fact of U.S. religious history highly inconvenient to secularization theory: . . . In the experience of the United States, societal modernization went hand in hand with religious mobilization."[47]

Polls charting levels of religious belief and observance in the United States have consistently yielded figures substantially higher than intellectuals, especially, might have imagined. I single out intellectuals here because, outside departments of religious studies, the academy has long practiced a policy of containment, marginalization, and suspicion of the subject of religion, often conflating study with practice and assuming that the former opens the door to the latter.[48] During the past five decades, as Gallup Polls indicate, the number of respondents who claim "belief in God" has held remarkably steady, tallying 96 percent in 1997, for example, compared with 95 percent in 1947.[49] Though some suggest that respondents in such polls inflate their estimates of their own levels of commitment to religion, the fact that such a large percentage see theism as a desirable trait, and one with which they wish to identify, is surely significant.[50]

The polls indicate and almost all agree that what modernity *has* produced, rather than irreligion, is *pluralism* in belief and culture, especially in the United States, due largely to substantial immigrant populations and to political philosophies that rest on religious and social freedoms.[51] It is not just the plurality of audiences, of course, but also the pluralism of American religions that influences the interpretation of religious content and that affects the attachment of the adjective "religious" to display. Like "public," and in similar pursuit of greater accuracy and precision, "religion" becomes a plural term. It goes almost without saying that American religions are not organizationally or administratively monolithic. In discussions of the separation of church and state, the two variables are not parallel. Whereas "state" is a property of the whole society, "church" is not.[52] Numerous sociologists, historians, and journalists have commented on the increasing particularity of American religions, suggesting that religion in the United States not only is but has been all along the "vital expression of groups," a "refuge for cultural particularity."[53]

The historical conviction that religious variety in the United States could be navigated only by turning inward, by making religion private, is easily documented.[54] One outcome of this assertion has indeed been a high level of privatization in modern American religious experience. By 2000, however, rather than living in a culture in which religion had to become ever more private in order to tolerate pluralism, Americans occupied a place in time and space where pluralism (including religious pluralism) was becoming ever more public. The new visual accessibility of religious pluriformity could be attributed to several coincident phenomena. Chief among these were the social transformations attending changes in U.S. immigration law initiated in 1965. Between 1966 and 1990, nearly as many people immigrated to the United States as between 1890 and 1914. The situation in terms of numbers of newcomers in 2000, then, was similar to that in 1900. The new immigration, however, was much more heterogeneous in terms of race, ethnicity, religion, and language than any of its historical precedents.[55]

When historian Nathan Hatch argued that the prior existence of religious diversity in the American colonies accounted for the foundation of American religious liberty, the eighteenth-century pluriformity he had in mind was largely (though not exclusively) sectarian Protestantism.[56] By the mid–twentieth century, perceptions of religious pluralism in the United States had expanded to include Protestants, Catholics, and Jews. Half a century later, historian Diane Winston observed that

> we no longer live in a Christian nation, or even a Judeo-Christian one. As *The New York Times Magazine* reported in December, the United States is now home to 800,000 Hindus (compared with 70,000 in 1977) and to as many Muslims as Presbyterians. The numbers of Sikhs, Jains, Buddhists, Eastern Orthodox, and Baha'i in this country are also increasing.[57]

Notwithstanding the fact that some aspects of the statistical base upon which Winston based her assessment have come under scrutiny (and despite the current high political profile of conservative Protestantism), there is no question but that the number of belief systems to which Americans subscribe is expanding. The diversity of American religion is augmented, furthermore, by new compound religious ensembles. More and more people have adopted what Winston called "trans-religiosity," "blending . . . beliefs, mythologies, and practices from varying traditions . . . without feeling any contradictions."[58]

For historians and interpreters of American visual culture, it is especially significant that pluralism has become more public in terms of its *visual accessibility*. One outcome of the increasing visual accessibility of pluriformity is its tendency to challenge the "taken-for-grantedness" of individual values and beliefs, influencing—according to Peter Berger—"not so much what people believe as how they believe."[59] The concluding sections of my book project analyze the multiplication of plural religious signs subsequent to the relaxation of immigration regulations in 1965, positing for this public arithmetic of diversity a visual dilution that tempers Christian claims to normative civic status. This assertion does not imply real acceptance—or even necessarily tolerance—of difference (e.g., as continuing acts of anti-Semitism and desecration of Muslim religious architecture suggest); nor does it preclude the periodic reemergence of binary oppositions (as in the us-vs.-them mentality apparent in the "My God can beat up your God" bumper sticker text mentioned above). Still, religious pluralism in the United States is no longer something people practice, in large part, in private, hidden from (and sometimes even hidden in) plain view.

Granting significant local and regional variation in the extent and particularity of religious multiplicity, Warner argues that in the United States religion itself is nonetheless configured as a "social space for cultural pluralism."[60] The more and more frequent public expression of plural religions on television, in movies, in newspapers (with many major papers recently hiring religion reporters and establishing religion pages), and on the Internet supports his claim.[61] Though it is certainly the case that in most parts of the United States, Christianity retains clear precedence in the visual landscape, the prevalence of Christian displays in large areas of the country is nonetheless modulated by both the varieties of Christian expression and the display of wider multifaith religious pluralism in the mass media. Again, mediation enhances exposure and accessibility. It is one thing, for example, when Buddhists gather in Canton, Ohio, for private worship; another when a reporter for the *Canton Repository* publishes photographs of the worshipers; and still another when the story appears on the paper's Web site, accompanied by pictures of elaborate Buddhist religious sculptures and liturgical "performances."[62]

Recent religious architecture contributes perhaps most emphatically to the sense of multiformity and juxtaposition in the visual landscape of contemporary American religions (figure 12.14).[63] In Montgomery County, Maryland, on a principal commuter artery into Washington, a stretch of road less than ten miles long is home to almost three dozen religious congregations, including, among others, houses of worship for Hindus, Muslims, Buddhists, Jews, Catholics, and Protestants and liturgies spoken in Spanish, Chinese, Korean, Vietnamese, Arabic, and Ukrainian as well as English and Hebrew. A Cambodian Buddhist temple (see figure 12.7), for example, painted in lemon yellow with bright green and red, is sited for visual prominence. Nearby is the Vietnamese Catholic church mentioned above (see figure 12.8).

Especially striking, in terms of visual accessibility, is the constellation of buildings at the busy intersection of New Hampshire Avenue and Norwood Road.[64] Here, in a location passed daily not only by commuters but by hundreds of children and youth on their way to nearby elementary and high schools, adherents of three different religious groups have constructed buildings that express their different subcultures and beliefs. Appearing in immediate proximity to one another, the white, blue, and gold architecture of the Ukrainian Orthodox cathedral is set off against the minaret and copper dome of the Muslim Community Center's mosque; and both contrast with the understated modernism of the adjacent church of the Protestant Disciples of Christ. Not only is pluralism more insistently apparent in the visual stimuli of everyday life, but those who construct overtly religious public displays are thus increasingly conscious of the likelihood that religiously diverse audiences will see what they have produced. Like museums or shopping malls, in an increasingly plural culture and open market economy—and even within a single religious tradition—religious display elicits improvisation and accommodation to personal interpretations, expanding and reconfiguring, in the process, the boundaries of expectation.[65]

Figure 12.14. The intersection of New Hampshire Avenue and Norwood Road, Montgomery County, Maryland, August 1997. © *The Washington Post*. Photograph by Nancy Andrews. Reprinted with permission.

Visible Religion and the Cultural Practice of Pluralism

The reader will by now have gathered that I am casting a broad net with respect to the categories "religion," "display," and "public." I do so to direct attention to the ways American religions in the early twenty-first century alter our visual, and thus ultimately, our mental landscapes. The visual character of our surroundings shapes, supports, and transforms our conceptions of and assumptions about human experience.[66] Display is thus truly "fundamental to the process of constructing a human reality."[67] If, as Stephen Warner suggests, we view pluralism as "constitutive" rather than "degenerative" of American religion and culture, we begin to see that understanding this chapter's subject is not a purely academic exercise.[68] The objects and performances comprised in religious display claim a distinct place in the visual field of daily experience, and what we see contributes to our sense of who we are, collectively and individually.

Furthermore, although there is often something distinctly territorial about display, when "territory" is marked by a multiplicity of signs, a different mechanism is at work than when one sign dominates. To the extent that the public display of religion generates social spaces of conversation (and despite the fact that some of these conversations express or elicit conflict), it participates in exploring and defining the shape of religious and civic commonality as well as difference, clarifying a fabric of concordances and overlapping commitments in tandem with distinctions. That these concordances (and discordances) are fluid over time and space makes them no less significant. As American culture more publicly expresses its plural constituencies (*in plain view*), visible religion takes on an active cultural role: rehearsing diversity, practicing pluralism.[69] Especially in a period of political rhetoric to the contrary, the increasing visual pluriformity of religions encourages us to imagine and to reimagine, in public and in private, the permeable social boundaries of what it means to be "American."

Notes

1. My current book project on the public display of religion in the United States, *Religion in Plain View: The Public Aesthetics of American Belief*, explores attitudes and practices beginning with the founding of the American republic. Having once made this material from the past accessible, however, my goal is also to invite history to illuminate the contemporary situation of public religious display at the beginning of the twenty-first century.
2. At least one liberal, left-leaning denomination sought to respond: In 2004, the United Church of Christ launched an advertising campaign called "God Is Still Speaking" that allied the denomination with positions representing an expansive inclusivity. The denomination received even more publicity than it might have imagined when CBS and NBC refused to air the commercials; Alan Cooperman, "Two Networks Bar Religious Commercial: CBS, NBC Turn Down United Church of Christ's Ad Touting Its Inclusiveness," *Washington Post*, Thursday, December 2, 2004.
3. Historian of American church history Martin E. Marty had a similar sense of impropriety in mind when he titled his 1988 presidential address to the American Academy of Religion "Committing the Study of Religion in Public." The address, under the same title, subsequently appeared in *Journal of the American Academy of Religion* 57, no. 1 (Spring 1989): 1–22. Like the "public display of affection" (a behavior proscribed in the United States military—where it earns the acronym

PDA—and discouraged or regulated in public high schools), the public display of religion carries a trace of the illicit, the outcome of yoking the modifiers "public" and "display" with the topic "religion."

4. In 2004, the politics of religion in public registered as an almost surreal experience from an international perspective when observers measured George W. Bush's embrace of a so-called marriage amendment against the French legislature's endorsement of regulations banning personal religious symbols and garments from public life. I say "surreal" because Bush proposed to ensconce the "sacrament" (his term) of marriage in the U.S. Constitution, producing apparent attempts at a kind of Christian "establishment" on one side of the Atlantic ocean matched by the reassertion of secular "establishment" on the other.

5. Here the "sectarian" is not a less formalized, less-developed alternative to the "established church" but refers to any particularist expression of religious affiliation. For contemporary religion, especially, it is difficult to imagine the religious expression of a group or individual that would qualify as genuinely "nonsectarian." Furthermore, recent world events have brought to wider public attention the recognition that there is no more one Judaism or one Islam than there is one Christianity or even one Protestantism. The situation was differently perceived in the past. The development of both civil religion and liberal Protestantism in the United States were, in fact, predicated on the assumption that it was possible, and even desirable, to practice religion "in general."

    See W. J. T. Mitchell, "The Violence of Public Art: Do the Right Thing," in *Art and the Public Sphere*, ed. W. J. T. Mitchell (Chicago: University of Chicago Press, 1990), 38.

6. In 1868, the Fourteenth Amendment brought the states into conformity with national civil liberties standards; in 1940 Cantrell v. Connecticut asserted that the Free Exercise Clause imposed the same restraints on the states as on the nation; in 1947 *Everson v. Board of Education* ruled that the Establishment Clause extended in the same way. Since the 1940s, in part because of these decisions, establishment cases, most often concerned in some way with public school education, have appeared with increasing regularity on court dockets. Some cases have explicitly concerned the public display of religion as it is defined in this essay. See Wayne R. Swanson, *The Christ Child Goes to Court* (Philadelphia: Temple University Press, 1990), esp. 7, 12; see also John T. Noonan Jr., *The Lustre of Our Country: The American Experience of Religious Freedom* (Berkeley: University of California Press, 1998).

7. See Leonard W. Levy, *The Establishment Clause: Religion and the First Amendment* (Chapel Hill: University of North Carolina Press, 1994).

8. My larger project analyzes the visible contexts and attributes of this saturation over time. As an art historian, I am interested in the ways religion is visually articulated in the American landscape. As a historian of American culture, I am concerned with changing notions of plural religions in the United States, from the eighteenth century's competing sectarian Protestantisms to the twentieth century's global migration of world faiths to the reactionary reassertion of a rightist Christian "public" identity in presidential politics in the dawning years of the twenty-first.

9. See, e.g., John Beardsley, *Gardens of Revelation: Environments by Visionary Artists* (New York: Abbeville Press, 1995); Sally M. Promey, *Painting Religion in Public: John Singer Sargent's "Triumph of Religion" at the Boston Public Library* (Princeton,

N. J.: Princeton University Press, 1999); Edward T. Linenthal, "Locating Holocaust Memory: The United States Holocaust Memorial Museum," in *American Sacred Space*, ed. David Chidester and Edward T. Linenthal (Bloomington: Indiana University Press, 1995), 220–61; Levy, *Establishment Clause*; and Swanson, *Christ Child Goes to Court*.

10. See, e.g., Mitchell, ed., *Art and the Public Sphere*; Erika Doss, *Spirit Poles and Flying Pigs: Public Art and Cultural Democracy in American Communities* (Washington, D.C.: Smithsonian Institution Press, 1995); and Harriet F. Senie and Sally Webster, eds., *Critical Issues in Public Art: Content, Context, and Controversy* (New York: HarperCollins, 1992).

11. See R. Stephen Warner, "Work in Progress toward a New Paradigm for the Sociological Study of Religion in the United States," *American Journal of Sociology* 98, no. 5 (March 1993): 1044–93. Throughout this chapter, I use pluralism in the descriptive sense of pluriformity or diversity rather than the more ideologically laden sense of multiculturalism. For a recent history of the development, in the United States, of the notion of variety as a social good, see Carrie Tirado Bramen, *The Uses of Variety: Modern Americanism and the Quest for National Distinctiveness* (Cambridge, Mass.: Harvard University Press, 2000).

Historian of religion Diana Eck asserts the relationship to identity formation of pluralism and religious display when she describes the "culture wars" of the early 1990s as a "national identity crisis"; Diana L. Eck, "Challenge of Pluralism," *Nieman Reports* 47, no. 2 (Summer 1993): 7, as mounted on the Diana L. Eck "Pluralism Project" Web site, http://www.fas.harvard.edu/~pluralism/html/article-cop.html.

12. This quotation is taken from an unidentified newspaper clipping, "Mural to Provide Residents with Healing Image," September 28, 1997, Treviño archives, courtesy of Carolee Youngblood. Treviño describes himself as a "realist" painter; in 1994 he had a one-artist show at the National Museum of American Art, Smithsonian Institution; see http://www.jessetrevino.com.

13. The artist based his guardian angel on a local cemetery statue, also broken; the cross in the painting reiterates the large-scale cross on the adjacent hospital wing. The hospital itself is sited next to an urban park across from Market Square.

14. See, e.g., Jeff Weintraub, "The Theory and Politics of the Public/Private Distinction," in *Public and Private in Thought and Practice*, ed. Jeff Weintraub and Krishan Kumar (Chicago: University of Chicago Press, 1997), 1–3.

15. John F. Wilson, "The Public as a Problem," in *Caring for the Commonweal: Education for Religious and Public Life*, ed. Parker J. Palmer, Barbara G. Wheeler, and James W. Fowler (Macon, Ga.: Mercer University Press, 1990), 13. Nathan Hatch has suggested that the fact of colonial religious diversity (rather than the fulfillment of heroic aspirations for religious liberty) provided the basis for religious freedom in the United States; Nathan O. Hatch, "The Whirlwind of Religious Liberty in Early America," in *Freedom and Religion in the Nineteenth Century*, ed. Richard Helmstadter (Stanford, Calif.: Stanford University Press, 1997), 29–53.

16. Cited in Warner, "Work in Progress," 1075.

17. Richard Helmstadter, "Introduction," in *Freedom and Religion*, esp. 5–8.

18. Quoted in Robin Lovin, "Beyond the Pursuit of Happiness: Religion and Public Discourse in Liberalism's Fourth Century," in *Caring for the Commonweal*, ed. Palmer, Wheeler, and Fowler, 47.

19. Quoted by Robert T. Handy, "Changing Contexts of Church-State Relations in America, 1880–1920," in *Caring for the Commonweal*, ed. Palmer, Wheeler, and Fowler, 30, 34; the citation here is on 30.

20. Ibid., 37.

21. Weintraub, "Theory and Politics," 6; and Allan Silver, "Two Different Sorts of Commerce—Friendship and Strangership in Civil Society," in *Public and Private in Thought and Practice*, 45.

22. See Helmstadter, "Introduction."

23. Wilson, "Public as a Problem," 15; see also Stanley I. Benn and Gerald F. Gaus, "The Public and the Private: Concepts and Action," in *Public and Private in Social Life*, ed. Stanley I. Benn and Gerald F. Gaus (New York: St. Martin's Press, 1983), 20–21.

24. Weintraub, "Theory and Politics," 4-5.

25. Robert A. White, "Religion and Media in the Construction of Cultures," in *Rethinking Media, Religion, and Culture*, ed. Stewart M. Hoover and Knut Lundby (Thousand Oaks, Calif.: Sage Publications, 1997), 40, 45.

26. The quoted phrase belongs to Jean Bethke Elshtain, "The Displacement of Politics," in *Public and Private in Thought and Practice*, 167; see also Stewart M. Hoover, "Media and the Construction of the Religious Public Sphere," in *Rethinking Media, Religion, and Culture*, 283–97.

27. Mitchell, "Violence of Public Art," 30.

28. The Internet represents a particular challenge to conventional notions of privacy. See, e.g., artist John Snogren's Web site, "Heavenly Visions Byzantine Icon Studio," where he markets icons for contemplative use; http://www.heavenlyvisions.com; see also Mark A. Kellner, *God on the Internet: Your Complete Guide to Enhancing Your Spiritual Life via the Internet and Online Services* (Foster City, Calif.: IDG Books, 1996).

29. W. J. T. Mitchell, "Introduction: Utopia and Critique," in *Art and the Public Sphere*, 2.

30. On contingency of performance, see Edward L. Schieffelin, "Problematizing Performance," in *Ritual, Performance, Media*, ed. Felicia Hughes-Freeland (London: Routledge, 1998), 197–98.

31. Simply because it sets things out visibly for all to see, public display facilitates targeting and aggression.

32. Editorial from the *Billings Gazette*, December 11, 1993, as quoted in *Jews/America/A Representation*, essay by Simon Schama, photographs by Frédéric Brenner (New York: Harry N. Abrams, 1996), 58.

33. As quoted in Vicky Greenberg, "The American Chapter of the Jewish Saga," *New York Times*, September 22, 1996.

34. R. Laurence Moore, *Selling God: American Religion in the Marketplace of Culture* (New York: Oxford University Press, 1994), esp. 35, 43.

35. Warner, "Work in Progress," 1050–51. Curiously, as the face of global commerce has become more uniform in the late twentieth and early twenty-first centuries, the face of American religious display (both within a single religious tradition and among different religions) has become more various.

36. Karen-Edis Barzman's research on spectacle has informed my own thinking in this regard; see Barzman, "Ritual and Vision: Renaissance Spectacle and the Performance of Images," lecture delivered on March 11, 1999, University of Maryland, College Park.

37. Felicia Hughes-Freeland, "Introduction," in *Ritual, Performance, Media*, 3.

38. Minister and sand sculptor Randy Hofman sprays his creations with diluted Elmer's Glue to protect them from the wind; he illuminates them with colored lights at night. The groups of figures, about twelve feet high and as many wide, take about seven hours to complete and generally include one or more representations of Jesus. Hofman has been making them each summer since 1974. When a reporter asked about motivation for his figures, Hofman replied: "I'm just trying to remind people who may be away from home for the first time as young adults that God is still watching"; Lyndsey Layton, "Ocean City Sighs as Tide of Tourists Ebbs," *Washington Post*, August 30, 1998.

39. Warner, "Work in Progress," 1059; see Ananda Abeysekara, "Identity For and Against Itself: Religion, Criticism, and Pluralization," *Journal of the American Academy of Religion* 72 (December 2004): 973–1001.

40. See, e.g., Ivan Karp, "Introduction: Museums and Communities: The Politics of Public Culture," in *Museums and Communities: The Politics of Public Culture*, ed. Ivan Karp, Christine Mullen-Kreamer, and Steven D. Lavine (Washington, D.C.: Smithsonian Institution Press, 1992), 1–6, 14. I am grateful to Ellen Smith for bringing these eye-glasses to my attention. The manufacturer of these Gemini Holiday Specs is Gemini Kaleidoscopes of Zelienople, Pennsylvania.

41. For the quotation from Rehnquist's letter, see Tamara Jones, "Supreme Court Won't Alter Frieze Depicting Muhammad," *Washington Post*, March 13, 1997; for the quotation from tourist brochure, see "Courtroom Friezes: North and South Walls," Fact Sheet, Office of the Curator, Supreme Court of the United States, January 25, 1999.

42. Quoted in Joan Biskupic, "Lawgivers: From Two Friezes, Great Figures of Legal History Gaze Upon the Supreme Court Bench," *Washington Post*, March 11, 1998.

43. Wayne Swanson, *Christ Child Goes to Court*.

44. Ibid., 141.

45. Meredith Narcum, "A Hand That Grabs Attention: Different Meanings Evoked by Tree-Carving," *Silver Spring Gazette*, January 14, 1998.

46. Roger D. Fallot, "The Place of Spirituality and Religion in Mental Health Services," in *Spirituality and Religion in Recovery from Mental Illness*, ed. Roger D. Fallot (San Francisco: Jossy-Bass, 1998), 4–5; see also Robert Wuthnow, *Producing the Sacred: An Essay on Public Religion* (Urbana: University of Illinois Press, 1994), 3.

47. Warner, "Work in Progress," 1049. Roger Finke and Rodney Stark assign this phenomenon to disestablishment and to the rise of an open market in religion in the United States; Roger Finke and Rodney Stark, *The Churching of America, 1776–1990* (New Brunswick, N.J.: Rutgers University Press, 1992).

48. See Sally M. Promey, "The 'Return' of Religion in the Scholarship of American Art," *The Art Bulletin*, volume 85 (September 2003): 581–603; ; Henry F. May, "Religion and American Intellectual History, 1945–1985: Reflections on an Uneasy Relationship," in *Religion and Twentieth-Century American Intellectual Life*, ed. Michael J. Lacey (Cambridge: Cambridge University Press and Woodrow Wilson International Center for Scholars, 1989), 12–22; and Harry S. Stout and Robert M. Taylor Jr., "Studies of Religion in American Society: The State of the Art," in *New Directions in American Religious History*, ed. Harry S. Stout and D. G. Hart (New York: Oxford University Press, 1997), 15–47.

49. See, e.g., Bill Broadway, "Poll Finds Americans 'As Churched as Ever': Beliefs in God Have Changed Little Since 1947, but Faithful Sample More Forms of Spirituality," *Washington Post*, May 31, 1997.

50. See, e.g., Adam Walsh, "Church, Lies, and Polling Data," *Religion in the News* 1, no. 2 (Fall 1998): 9–11.

51. Peter L. Berger, "Protestantism and the Quest for Certainty," *Christian Century* 115, no. 23 (August 26–September 2, 1998): 782; and Peter L. Berger and Jonathan Sacks, eds., *The Desecularization of the World: Resurgent Religion and World Politics* (Grand Rapids: William B. Eerdmans, 1999). See also Hatch, "Whirlwind of Religious Liberty in Early America," on religious pluralism and the foundation of American religious liberty.

52. Warner, "Work in Progress," 1046–47. The terminology of the historical formulation, however, has always been slanted toward Christianity in the sense that "church" belongs to that domain.

53. Ibid., 1047, 1060. See also Diane Winston, "Campuses Are a Bellwether for Society's Religious Revival," *Chronicle of Higher Education*, January 16, 1998, A60; Richard Cimino and Don Lattin, *Shopping for Faith: American Religion in the New Millennium* (San Francisco: Jossey-Bass, 1998); and Mark Silk, "A New Establishment?" *Religion in the News* 1, no. 2 (Fall 1998): 3.

54. For a discussion of one prominent artist's expression of this conviction, see Promey, *Painting Religion in Public*.

55. Warner, "Work in Progress," 1061.

56. Hatch, "Whirlwind of Religious Liberty in Early America," 29–53.

57. Winston, "Campuses Are a Bellwether for Society's Religious Revival," A60.

58. Ibid.

59. Berger, "Protestantism and the Quest for Certainty," 782.

60. Warner, "Work in Progress," 1058.

61. See, e.g., Mark Silk, "Why *Religion in the News?*" *Religion in the News* 1, no. 1 (June 1998): 3. This increasing publicness of religion is not the result of religion in the United States entering the marketplace; it may be, rather, one result of its always having been there. See Moore, *Selling God*.

62. See Charita M. Goshay, "Buddhist Truth: Buddhist Monk Leads Local Group in Search," *Canton Repository*, February 13, 1999; and http://www.cantonrep.come/life.htm.

63. See Diana Eck, "Challenge of Pluralism," 2, 4–6, on religious architecture and the visibility of a "new multireligious reality."

64. Susan Levine, "A Place for Those Who Pray: Along Montgomery's 'Highway to Heaven,' Diverse Acts of Faith," *Washington Post*, August 3, 1997.

65. Simon Coleman and John Elsner, "Performing Pilgrimage: Walsingham and the Ritual Construction of Irony," in *Ritual, Performance, Media*, ed. Hughes-Freeland, 46–47.

66. W. J. T. Mitchell, "Introduction," in *Landscape and Power*, ed. W. J. T. Mitchell (Chicago: University of Chicago Press, 1994), 1.

67. Schieffelin, "Problematizing Performance," 205, where Schieffelin discusses the performance aspects of what I have called display. Ian Heywood and Barry Sandywell, too, understand visual culture as part of a "socio-historical realm of interpretive practices"; Heywood and Sandywell, "Introduction: Explorations in the

Hermeneutics of Vision," in *Interpreting Visual Culture: Explorations in the Hermeneutics of Vision*, ed. Ian Heywood and Barry Sandywell (London and New York: Routledge, 1999), xi.

68. Warner, "Work in Progress," 1052; Lawrence Alloway, *Network: Art and the Complex Present* (Ann Arbor, Michigan: UMI Research Press, 1984), 3, 8; and Bramen, *Uses of Variety.*

69. Pluralism can be understood as a cultural practice because it assumes some degree of social interaction. The visual expression of plural religion organizes varying degrees of engagement between individuals and the diversity of American culture. In the case of the United States, religion can be construed as a principal conceptual location for encountering difference, for the cultural practice of pluralism. See also Jesús Martín-Barbero, "Mass Media as a Site of Resacralization of Contemporary Cultures," in *Rethinking Media, Religion, and Culture*, 102. Martín-Barbero speaks, in particular, of mass-mediated forms of expression.

Contributors

Laura A. Belmonte is an associate professor of history at Oklahoma State University. Her publications include *Speaking of America: A Reader in U.S. History; Selling America: Propaganda, National Identity, and the Cold War;* and numerous articles on the intersections of cultural, social, and diplomatic history. She is currently at work on a study of U.S. foreign relations and AIDS.

Donna M. Binkiewicz is the author *of Federalizing the Muse: United States Arts Policy and the National Endowment for the Arts, 1965–1980.* She is currently a member of the History Department at California State University, Long Beach.

Casey Nelson Blake is a professor of history and American studies at Columbia University and the author of several studies of U.S. intellectual and cultural history, including *Beloved Community: The Cultural Criticism of Randolph Bourne, Van Wyck Brooks, Waldo Frank, and Lewis Mumford.* His essays and reviews have appeared in the *American Scholar, Commonweal, Dissent,* the *Nation,* and other journals of opinion.

Michele H. Bogart is a professor of art history at Stony Brook University. She is the author *of Public Sculpture and the Civic Ideal in New York City, 1890–1930; Artists, Advertising, and the Borders of Art;* and *The Politics of Urban Beauty: New York and Its Art Commission.* From 1999 through 2003, she was vice president of the Art Commission of the City of New York and presently serves on the commission's Conservation Advisory Group and on the Board of Directors of the Fine Arts Federation. She is pursuing research on New York as the place of art.

Bethany Bryson is an assistant professor of sociology at James Madison University and the author of *Making Multiculturalism: Boundaries and Meanings* *in U.S. English Departments.* Her current research with Matthew Hughey examines the survey responses of African Americans in order to explore the ethnocentric assumptions of public opinion research.

Kenneth Cmiel was a professor of history at the University of Iowa and the author of many works on the intellectual and cultural history of the United States, including *Democratic Eloquence: The Fight over Popular Speech in Nineteenth-Century America* and *A Home of Another Kind: One Chicago Orphanage and the Tangle of Child Welfare.* At the time of his death, he was at work on *The Human Rights Idea: The Ideological Origins of the Universal Declaration of Human Rights.*

Paul DiMaggio is a professor of sociology at Princeton University and the research director of the Princeton Center for Arts and Cultural Policy Studies. He has published widely on such topics as cultural participation and institutional change and is currently studying inequality in the access to and use of digital technology, cultural contention in the United States since 1965, the decline of the classical music public, and the economic career of Benjamin Franklin.

Neil Harris is Preston and Sterling Morton Professor of History at the University of Chicago, where he has taught since 1969. He has written many studies of American cultural history, including *The Artist in American Society: The Formative Years, 1790–1860; Cultural Excursions: Marketing Appetites and Cultural Tastes in Modern America;* and *Chicago Apartment Houses.* At present he is working on a study of J. Carter Brown and the National Gallery of Art.

Michael Kammen is the Newton C. Farr Professor of American History and Culture at Cornell University, where he has taught since 1965. His books include *People of Paradox: An Inquiry Concerning the Origins of American Civilization; A Machine That Would Go of Itself: The Constitution in American Culture; Mystic Chords of Memory: The Transformation of Tradition in American Culture; A Time to Every Purpose: The Four Seasons in American Culture;* and most recently, *Visual Shock: A History of Art Controversies in American Culture.*

Sally M. Promey has joined the faculty at Yale University as a professor of American studies and religion and visual culture. She was previously the chair of the Department of Art History and Archaeology at the University of Maryland. Her publications include *Painting Religion in Public: John Singer Sargent's Triumph of Religion at the Boston Public Library* and *Spiritual Spectacles: Vision and Image in Mid-Nineteenth-Century Shakerism,* as well as a volume of essays coedited with David Morgan, *The Visual Culture of American Religions.* She is at work on another book, *The Public Display of Religion in the United States.*

Leslie Prosterman, currently a senior fellow at the Vera List Center for Art and Politics at the New School University and a museum and exhibition consultant, was a tenured associate professor of American studies and folklore at the University of Maryland, Baltimore County, until 2003. She researches, writes, and teaches public policy on cultural institutions, the arts, aesthetics, and traditional culture. She. Her published work includes *Ordinary Life, Festival Days: Aesthetics in the Midwestern County Fair* and *Framing the Exhibition: Multiple Constructions.*

Penny M. Von Eschen is a professor of history and American culture at the University of Michigan. She is the author of *Satchmo Blows Up the World: Jazz Ambassadors Play the Cold War* and *Race against Empire: Black Americans and Anticolonialism.*

Vera L. Zolberg is a professor in the Sociology Department of the New School for Social Research, where she has taught for more than twenty years. Among her publications are *Constructing a Sociology of the Arts; Outsider Art: Contesting Boundaries in Contemporary Culture,* coedited with J. M. Cherbos; and a volume of essays, coedited with David Swartz, *The Sociology of Symbolic Power: On Pierre Bourdieu.*

Index

Page numbers in italics indicate illustrations.

A

Abstract Expressionism: and Cold War, 186, 195n38; and NEA, 185–86, 192; and Rockwell, Norman, 47, *48*, 49, 53, 60–61n20
"Academic Bill of Rights," 243
acculturation, performance festivals as instruments of, 26–27n5
Adam Bede (Eliot), 224
Adams, Henry, 89
Adams, John Quincy, 76, 79–80, 87
Adatto, Kiku, 234
adolescents and young adults, 40, 120n31, 122n54
advertising, effect of, 38, 40, 60n15
aesthetics, law, and speech in public space. *See* National Mall and Lafayette Park protest regulation
Africa. *See* Ellington State Department tours
African Americans, 104, 115, 119n11, 207, 239, 271n37. *See also* Ellington State Department tours
Ailey, Alvin, 156, 161
Air Bulletin, 132
Alaska, 210
Albert, John, 139
Alexander, Jane, 200
Alfred P. Murrah Building, 324
"alienation effect" in theater, 3
American aesthetic, 2–3
American art forms, 81
American Assembly, 78
American Center in Paris (Gehry), 227, *229*
American Council of Learned Societies, 80
American Labor Unions: Their Role in the Free World (USIS), 138

American Musical Institute, 28n17
"An American Worker's Family" (USIA), 138–39
Anderson, Cat, 153
André, Carl, 188, 211
animateurs, 112–13, 121n44
Anti-Intellectualism in American Life (Hofstadter), 90
antirealism, 5, 223–42; and disconnect and resources of everyday life, 235–40; and postmodern aesthetic, 224–33, 237, 239; and postmodern politics, 233–35
Appadurai, Arjun, 242n19
Apthorp, William Foster, 17
Aquadrop (Brennan), 214
architecture: Art-in-Architecture Program (GSA), 198, 200, 219n49; music festival buildings, 15–20, 28n20; for orchestras and museums, 20, 24, 105, 121n40; religious, 319, *320*, 321, *322*, 324, *326*, *327*, 334, *335*; U.S. Supreme Court building, 329, *330*. *See also* Gehry, Frank; Museums; *specific buildings*
Arendt, Hannah, 3
Are Years What? (For Marianne Moore) (di Suvero), 189, *190*
Argentina, 83
Arian, Edward, 191
Aristotle, 303n66
Armstrong, Louis, 152, 161
The Art Critic (Rockwell), 43, *45*, 47, 61n22
art critics, 55–56
Art-in-Architecture Program (GSA), 198, 200, 219n49
Art in Public Places Program (NEA), 181–83, 189, 198, 200, 218n30
Art Institute of Chicago, 103, 105, 119n19
Artist and His Muse (Vermeer), 38

arts and democracy, 2–3
Arts Council of Great Britain, 86
Ashley, Elizabeth, 175
Astatqé, Mulatu, 164
Atlanta, Georgia, 214
Auditorium Theatre (Boston), 105
Austro-Hungarian Empire, 85, 86
avant-garde of twentieth century, 3
Avedisian, Edward, 187
"Awards of Excellence," 181

B

baby boomer exceptionalism, theory of,
  261–62
Baca, Judy, 213
Bach Festival (Bethlehem, PA), 22
Baird, Spencer, 76
Balden, Ronald, 207
Baltimore Federal building (Sugarman), 208,
  209, *209*
Bannard, Darby, 187
Baptism of Pocahontas (Chapman), 319
Barnum, P.T., 15, 28*n*20, 103
Barthes, Roland, 224
Bauhaus, 3
Bauman, Zygmunt, 168*n*15, 231
Bayreuth, 22, 29–30*n*39
Bearden, Romare, 211
Beardsley, John, 309
Beatty, Tally, 156
Beijing's Museum of Fine Arts, 95*n*53
belief in religion, 331–32
Bell, Larry, 188
Bellingham, Helen, 138–39
Bellingham, Ray, 138–39
Belmonte, Laura A., 4, 123–50, 343
Bennett, William, 245–46, 249
Benton, Thomas Hart, 71
Benton, William B., 126
Berger, Peter, 333
Berkshire Music Festival, 22, 30*n*40
Berman, Ronald, 80, 81
Berman v. Parker (1954), 283, 284, 285,
  293
Bernstein, Leonard, 32, 175
Bethlehem, Pennsylvania Bach Festival, 22
Bibliothèque Nationale, 111
Biddle, Livingston, 73, 186
bilingual programming: education, 245–57,
  260; in museums, 107, 120*n*23
billboard and print advertising, 38, 40

Billings, Montana menorah display, 315,
  316, 317, 318, 321
Binkiewicz, Donna M., 4–5, 171–96, 343
Birmingham music festivals (England), 14,
  15, 18, 21
Blake, Casey Nelson, 5, 197–219, 306,
  343
Blake, Peter, 127
Blood Brothers (Rockwell), 66*n*48
Bloom, Allan, 249, 261
B-Minor Mass (Bach), 22
body decoration, religious, 324, *325*
Bogart, Michele H., 4, 31–66, 343
Borofsky, Jonathan, 217–18*n*27
Bosch, Albert H., 78
Boston, 15–17, 19, 103, 105, 119*n*17
Boston Foundation, 183
Boston Public Library, 309
Boston Symphony Orchestra, 24, 105
Botswana, 84
Bourdieu, Pierre, 100, 112–14, 201, 253,
  269*n*16, 295
Box (Judd), 211
Boy Gazing at Glamour Stars (Rockwell),
  40, *41*
Brackett, Thomas, 135
Brazil, 85
Brennan, Nizette, 214–16, *215*
Brenner, Frédéric, 315, *317,* 318
Brenson, Michael, 190–91
Breton regional culture, 99, 115, 121*n*37
Bridges, Ruby, 66*n*48
British Museum, 86
British Portrait Gallery, 78
Brooklyn Museum, 309
Brubeck, Dave, 152
Bryson, Bethany, 5, 243–74, 343–44
buildings. *See* architecture; *specific buildings*
Burger, Warren, 329, 330
Burnett, Frances Hodgson, 233
Bush, George W., 309, 337*n*4
Bushmen of Kalahari, 84

C

Cabanne, Pierre, 111
cabinet-level ministries of culture, 83
Cahill, Holger, 3
Calder, Alexander: in Chicago, 198–200,
  199; in Grand Rapids, Michigan, 89, 181,
  182, 197–98, *198,* 200–206, 208
Calhoun, John C., 76, 87

California Aerospace Museum, Los Angeles (Gehry), 227, *230*
Calvinism, 86
Cambodian Buddhist temple, Maryland, 319, *320*
campaign consultants, 234
"campaign of truth," 145*n*18
Canada, 71, 86
Cannibal Culture: Art, Appropriation, and the Commodification of Difference (Root), 297
Cantrell v. Connecticut (1940), 337*n*6
capitalism, 133–41
Capp, Al, 71
Capra, Frank, 32
Carnegie Hall (New York City), 20
Carney, Harry, 153
Carter, Jimmy, 73, 207
celebrity status, 50–51, 61–62*n*24, 62*n*27
Central Intelligence Agency (CIA), 75
Centre Beaubourg, 111–13
Centre Pompidou, 111
Chapin, Seldon, 131
Chapman, John G., 319
Charleston, South Carolina, 119*n*17
Chautauqua, New York, 22, 23, 29*n*37, 30*n*40
Cheever, John, 71
Chicago: Art Institute of, 103, 105, 119*n*19; Calder in, 198–200, *199;* Columbian Exhibition, 284; museum and orchestra in, 20, 103, 105; music festivals in, 18, 19, 20; NEA mural projects in, 183; Park District of, 105; Picasso in, 205
Chickering, Charles Francis, 27*n*16
China, 95*n*53
Christensen, Dan, 187, 188
Church of Our Lady of Vietnam, Maryland, 321, *322*
CIA (Central Intelligence Agency), 75
Cincinnati music festivals, 18–19, 28–29*n*25
Citizens Protesting Anti-Semitic Acts, Billings, Montana (Brenner), 315, *317*, 318
City Beautiful Movement, 284, 289
City Council of Los Angeles v. Taxpayers for Vincent (1984), 283, 285, 286
Civic Center Coliseum (Hartford, Connecticut), 211
civil rights movement, 65–66*n*48, 154, 156–58, 161. *See also* Ellington State Department tours
Civil War (U.S.), 119*n*11
Clark, William, 76

Clark v. Community for Creative Non-Violence (1984), 282, 283, 286, 292
Close Encounters of the Third Kind (Spielberg film), 58*n*5
The Closing of the American Mind (Bloom), 261–62
Cmiel, Kenneth, 5, 223–42, 344
"cocacolonization," 122*n*54
Cochran, Johnnie, 33, 58*n*5
Coffee-Pepper Bill, 70
Cohen v. California (1971), 291
Cold War: and abstract art, 186, 195*n*38; and cultural policy, 75, 89–90, 107; and Ellington State Department tours, 4, 5, 151–70; liberalism, 5, 154, 161; and NEA, 4–5, 171–96; and U.S. propaganda offensive (1945-1959), 4, 123–50
collectibles, requests for, 63*n*32
collective rituals, 3–14
Collins, Randall, 253
colonial religious diversity, 338*n*15
color, use of, 226–27
Columbian Exhibition, Chicago, 284
Columbine school shootings, 321, 324
comités d'entreprises, 120*n*33
commercial art, 34, 43, 47, 49, 57*n*3
Communism, 75, 78. *See also* Cold War; Soviet Union
community art, 213–14, 219*n*46
computerized video editing, 234, 236
Congress for Cultural Freedom, 75
Congressional Arts Caucus, 87
The Connoisseur (Rockwell), 47, *48*, 49, 53, 54, 55, 66*n*48
Constructivists, 3
consumerism, 136, 147*n*51
contemporary life, views of, 238–39
Contract with America, 87
Conway, Moncure D., 15
Cordez, Maria, 183
Corporation for Public Broadcasting, 69
"counterculture of modernity," 155–56, 168*n*15
court cases on aesthetics and political freedom. *See* National Mall and Lafayette Park protest regulation
crèches. *See* nativity scenes
Crimp, Douglas, 239
Critique of Judgment (Kant), 283
crucifix in urine images. *See* Serrano, Andres
Crystal Place (New York), 28*n*20
Cubi (Smith), 177, *178*

cultural authority. *See* public attitudes toward cultural authority and diversity in higher education and arts
"cultural cold wars," 34, 35, 59*n*8
cultural democratization, 101–8, 262–67. *See also* Franco-American comparisons in cultural democratization
cultural diversity. *See* diversity; public attitudes toward cultural authority and diversity in higher education and arts
cultural federalism, 90
"cultural imperialism," 125
culture and state in America, 4, 69–96; before 1965, 75–80; since 1965, 80–83, 101–2; complexities, ironies, and historical anomalies in, 70–72; and democratization in American high culture, 101–8; and failure to have national culture policy, 71–75, 85, 86, 89, 102; international comparisons and explanation, 83–87
culture of donation, 107
culture wars in arts and education. *See* public attitudes toward cultural authority and diversity in higher education and arts
Curtis, George William, 17
Czechoslovakia, 132

D

Dadaists, 3
Dana, John Cotton, 3
Dance Program of NEA, 196*n*48
Darbel, Alain, 113–14
Davis, Ron, 187, 188
Davis, Stuart, 3
The Deadline (Rockwell), 40, *42*
death, 293
De Gaulle, Charles, 110, 112
De Kooning, Willem, 177, 181, 185
Democratic Party, 154
democratization, 101–8, 262–67. *See also* Franco-American comparisons in cultural democratization
De Mott, Benjamin, 35
Denmark, 83
Department of National Heritage (Great Britain), 84
De Tocqueville, Alexis, 101
Dettingen Te Deum (Handel), 15
developing-world art, 122*n*55
Dewey, John, 3
D'Harnoncourt, René, 177, 180

Diebenkorn, Richard, 177, *179*, 180
Dill, Guy, 212, *213*
DiMaggio, Paul, 5, 105, 243–74, 344
disconnect of postmodern aesthetics. *See* antirealism
discrimination, 135. *See also* civil rights movement
Disney, Walt, 32, 77
"Display Democracy," 107
Di Suvero, Mark, 188, 189–90, *190*, 207
diversity, 99, 114–16, 117, 190. *See also* public attitudes toward cultural authority and diversity in higher education and arts
Dixiecrats, 130
Dixon, Ivan, 161
Dondero, George A., 71
Dooley, Tom, 209–11
Do the Right Thing (Lee film), 58*n*6
Double Take (Rockwell), 40
Downey, Thomas J., 73, 87–88
Dr. Seuss, 32
Duke Ellington. *See* Ellington State Department tours
"Duke Ellington and Civil Rights" (Monson), 156
Dulles, Allen W., 75
Dunn, Sharon, 183
Dzubas, Friedel, 187

E

Eames, Charles, 127
Eames, Ray, 127
Eck, Diana, 338*n*11
economic system of U.S., 133–41
Edinburgh festival, 24, 30*n*48
Edinburgh Fringe, 30*n*49
education. *See* public attitudes toward cultural authority and diversity in higher education and arts
Edwards, Brent, 170*n*76
Edwards, Harry T., 293
Eisenhower, Dwight D., 78
Elgin marbles, 86
Elijah (Mendelssohn), 15, 21, 27*n*16
Eliot, George, 224
elitism vs. populism, 114–18. *See also* public attitudes toward cultural authority and diversity in higher education and arts
Ellington, Edward Kennedy "Duke," 71. *See also* Ellington State Department tours
Ellington, Mercer, 159

Ellington State Department tours, 4, 5, 151–70; from Africa to Soviet Union, 161–65; and appropriation concerns, 165–67; and cultural cold war, 152–56; and playing for the people theme, 158–60; State Department agenda vs. artistic adventures in, 156–58

Ellison, Ralph, 175

Encounter (magazine), 75

English departments, case studies of, 246

English precursors of American festivals, 12–15

enlightened public sphere, 58n4

environmental artists, 207

Establishment Clause of First Amendment, 307, 309, 337n6

Estes, Richard, 190

Ethiopia, 163–64

European Economic Community, 84

European Mozart Foundation, 122n54

Evangelical Christians, 306

Evers, Medgar, 157

Everson v. Board of Education (1947), 337n6

everyday needs, 238

exceptionalism, 124, 144n11, 261–62

expansive antinomianism, 265

exploring expeditions, 76

expressive conduct as speech, 290–94

F

Facts about Communism series, 131

Fallot, Roger, 331

family life, 139–41

fan mail, 50–57, 61–62n24, 62nn26–27, 63n32, 63–64n33

fantasy and imagination, 236, 242n19

The Far East Suite (Ellington), 165, 166

Feather, Leonard, 162

Federal Council on the Arts and Humanities, 73, 80

federal public art, 35. *See also* modernist movement in federal public art

fellowships from NEA, 183–91

feminist art, 190, 219n46

festival culture in America, 4, 11–30; development of, 15–17; English precursors of American festivals, 12–15; German Americans' role in, 17–23; modern American festivals, 23–24

The Field of Cultural Production (Bourdieu), 295

Fifth Republic, 110, 112, 121n37

film industry, federal support for, 77

"Fireman's Quadrille" (Jullien), 17, 28n20

First Amendment protections. *See* National Mall and Lafayette Park protest regulation; public display of religion

First International Festival of Negro Arts, 161

Fiske, John, 63n32

flag "desecration," 101

Flamingo (Calder), 198–200, *199*

Flaubert, Gustave, 86–87

Flavin, Dan, 188

folk art and culture, 100, 190, 196n48. *See also* public attitudes toward cultural authority and diversity in higher education and arts

forced labor camps, 138, 139

Ford, Gerald, 181, 207

Forester, Clifton B., 136

Forester, Gail, 140–41

Forester, William, 140–41

Four Freedoms (Rockwell), 66n48

Fourteenth Amendment, 337n6

Fourth Republic, 109, 110

Fowles, Gib, 62n24

France, 83–86, 269n16, 270n22

Franco-American comparisons in cultural democratization, 4, 97–122; achievements and shortfalls, 112–14; contrasts in culture of cultural democratization, 100–112; cultural democratization à la Française, 108–12; democratization in American high culture, 101–8; elitism vs. populism controversy, 114–18

Frankel, Charles, 88–89, 94n40

Frankenthaler, Helen, 177, 181

Frankfurt School, 266

"Freedom Center" (New York), 2

freedom of expression. *See* National Mall and Lafayette Park protest regulation

Freedom Tower (New York), 2

French Ministry of Culture, 84

Front Populaire, 109, 120n33

Fulbright Scholarship Program, 75

Fuller, Buckminster, 127

G

Galbraith, John Kenneth, 173

Galligan, Anne, 190

Garment, Leonard, 74
Gehry, Frank, 5, 226–31, *227–30*, 235, 237, 240
Geisel, Theodore, 32
Geldzahler, Henry, 177, 179–81, 184–85, 187, 188, 204
gender and sexuality, 58*n*7, 119*n*11, 139–41. *See also* public attitudes toward cultural authority and diversity in higher education and arts
General Electric, 127
General Services Administration (GSA), 198–200, 207, 212, 214–15, 219*n*49
General Social Survey, 248, 249, 250–51
German Americans' role in festival culture in America, 17–23
Germany, 84, 89, 105, 136
Gibson, Ann, 60–61*n*20
Gibson, Mel, 306
Gil, Gilberto, 85
Gillespie, Dizzy, 152
Gilmore, Patrick, 16–17
Gingrich, Newt, 58*n*5, 70
Ginnever, Charles, 188
Gish, Lilian, 211
Gitlin, Todd, 244
Giuliani, Rudolph, 309
glamour girls, 38, *39*, 40, *41*
Glossary of Soviet Terms (USIS), 127–28
Goals for Americans: Programs for Action in the Sixties, Comprising the Report of the President's Commission on National Goals (Heckscher), 78
Goldberg, Arthur, 291
Goldstein, Arnold, 289
Gonsalves, Paul, 153, 159
Goodman, Benny, 161
Goodnough, Robert, 184, *185*
goodwill ambassadors, 75. *See also* Ellington State Department tours
Goodwin, Richard N., 93*n*30
Gottlieb, Adolph, 204
"Government and the Humanities" conference (1978), 93*n*34
La Grand Vitesse (Calder), 89, 181, *182*, 197–98, *198*, 200–206, 208
Grant, Ulysses, 16
Graves, Michael, 214
Great Britain, 84, 86, 101
Great Depression, 38, 40, 126
Great Society programs, 107, 173, 176
Great Wall of Los Angeles (Baca), 213

Greece, 83
Greenberg, Clement, 34, 47, 60*n*17
Grenoble, William L., 136
Griffith, D.W., 211
Grooms, Red, 211
Gross, H.R., 71
group identity, 213–14
GSA. *See* General Services Administration
Guggenheim Museum (Gehry), 227
Guston, Philip, 177, 181
Guthrie, Woody, 78

H

Haas, Richard, 207
Habermas, Jürgen, 3, 58*n*4
Hadju, David, 160
Hague v. CIO (1939), 286–87
Haiti, 83, 154
Haldeman, H.R., 74
Hamilton, Ann, 25
Hamilton, George Heard, 98
Hammering Man (Borofsky), 217–18*n*27
Hampton, Lionel, 153
Handel and Hayden Society of Boston, 15–16, 18, 19, 27*n*16
Handel festivals, 13–15
Hanks, Nancy: and artist grants, 194*n*30; as NEA chairperson, 73, 80, 81, 87; and Rockefeller, Nelson, 74; and Visual Arts Program, 187
"Happy Few," 98
Harris, Neil, 3, 4, 11–30, 344
Hartford, Connecticut, 20, 211
Hatch, Nathan, 333, 338*n*15
Hawaii State Foundation on Culture and the Arts, 72
Hayden, Ferdinand V., 76
Head of Christ (Sallman), 321
Heckscher, August, 74, 78–79, 202
Heffron v. ISKON, Inc. (1981), 301*n*39
Heinich, Nathalie, 112
Heizer, Michael, 208
Held, Al, 188
Hello Dolly (Armstrong), 161
Helms, Jesse, 171, 309
Henderson v. Lujan (1992), 294
Henry, Joseph, 76
high art and culture, 34, 35, 44, 55, 100–108, 172. *See also* public attitudes toward cultural authority and diversity in higher education and arts

higher education. *See* public attitudes toward cultural authority and diversity in higher education and arts

Hines, Earl, 161

Historic Preservation Act (1966), 71

Hodges, Johnny, 153

Hoe Down (Dill), 212, *213*

Hofman, Randy, 324, 340*n*38

Hofstadter, Richard, 90

Holder, Frank, 164

Holmes, Oliver Wendell, 287

Holt, Nancy, 188

Holy Virgin Mary (Ofili), 309

homelessness, 293

homoerotic images. *See* Mapplethorpe, Robert

Hopper, Edward, 71

Hosmer, Craig, 71

Hotel des Artistes, 185, 194*n*25

Howells, William Dean, 16–17, 28*n*19

Hubert H. Humphrey Building (South Dakota), 212, *213*

Hughes, Langston, 161

Hungary, 131

Hunter, James, 253

Huron ACORN, 212

hyperrealist art, 190

I

IBM, 127

iconoclasm, 321, *323*

imagination and fantasy, 236, 242*n*19

immigrants, 99, 104, 105, 332–33

India, 158, 169*n*29

Indigo Blue (Hamilton), 25–26

Inner City Murals Program, 207

Institute for Music and Acoustic Research and Coordination (IRCAM, France), 111

Institute of Museum Services (U.S.), 69, 83

Internal Revenue Service, 169–70*n*57

international art and culture policies, 83–87

international trade fairs, 135

Iowa Cultural Affairs Advisory Council, 72

Iowa Office of Cultural Affairs, 72

Ireland, Patrick, 187

Irwin, Robert, 188

ISKON of Potomac, Inc. v. Kennedy (1994), 283, 295

Israel in Egypt (Handel), 15

It's a Great Life, Comrades (USIS), 130

J

Jackson, Mahalia, 161

Jackson, Travis, 165

James, William, 239

Jane Doe (aka Diane Nomad); United States v. (1992), 295–96

Japan, 136, 145*n*17

jazz, 75, 81, 100, 116, 196*n*48. *See also* Ellington State Department tours

Jefferson, Thomas, 312

Jews, oppression in Soviet Union, 131

Jews/America/A Representation (Brenner), 318

John F. Kennedy Federal Building (Boston), 203

Johnson, H. Earle, 27*n*16

Johnson, Lyndon, 74, 107, 157, 171–77, 183, 204

Judas Maccabeus (Handel), 15

Judd, Donald, 184, 188, 211

Jullien, Louis, 16, 17, 28*n*20

Juneau, Alaska, 210

Jungle Fever (Lee), 321

junk sculptures, 206, 217–18*n*27

K

Kallen, Horace, 70

Kammen, Michael, 4, 69–96, 344

Kant, Immanuel, 283

Kaskey, Raymond, 214

Kelly, Michael, 234

Kennan, George, 75

Kennedy, John F.: and Art-in-Architecture program, 198; assassination of, 160; and cabinet-level arts position, 79; and "Camelot" cultural policy, 202–4; and campaign of 1960, 74; and civil rights movement, 154; and NEA, 171–77; and renaissance of cultural awareness, 78; support of arts by, 91*n*15

Kimball, Roger, 262

King, Elaine, 190

King, Julius, 30*n*40

"kitsch," 34, 172

Klosson, B.H., 162

Knoxville Flag (Brennan), 214–16, *215*, 219*n*49

Konzal, Joseph, 207

Korean War, 145*n*23

Kramer, Hilton, 249

Kughler, Francis Vandeveer, 185
Kulturstaat, 89
Kulturvolk, 89
Kundera, Milan, 231, 239, 241n11
Kupferman, Theodore, 185

L

Labor Air Bulletin, 139–40
labor laws, 139–40
labor unions, 138
Lafayette Park. *See* National Mall and
    Lafayette Park protest regulation
Lang, Jack, 114
Langley, Samuel P., 76–77
La Plus Belle Africaine (Ellington), 161
Larson, Arthur, 137–38
Larson, Gary, 32
Lasch, Christopher, 59n8
Lasky, Melvin, 75
Latin America. *See* Ellington State
    Department tours
Laurie, Clayton, 142n1
League of Women Voters, 131
Lebovics, Herman, 110, 120n35
Lee, Spike, 58n6, 321
Leftists public art, 219n46
"les arts premiers," 122n55
Levine, Lawrence, 20
Lévi-Strauss, Claude, 98, 113
Levy, Leonard W., 309
Lewis, Meriwether, 76
LeWitt, Sol, 188, 211
liberalist-modernist public art. *See* Ellington
    State Department tours; modernist
    movement in federal public art
Lieberman, Alexander, 207
Life Magazine, 49, 78, 318
Like Water for Chocolate (film), 231–32,
    241n11, 242n27
Lincoln, Abby, 161
Linenthal, Edward T., 309
Lippmann, Walter, 79
literalism of modern painting, 60n17
A Little Princess book and films, 232–33,
    241n12
Littleton, Colorado school shootings, 321,
    324
Live-Aid concerts, 122n54
local government support for arts, 102–3,
    104–6
Locke, John, 312

Lomax, Alan, 78
Look magazine, 33, 66n48
Los Angeles, 183, 213
Lovett, Robert, 131
Luhrmann, Baz, 224–25, 237
Lumiansky, Robert, 80
Lumumba, Patrice, 152–53
Lynch v. Donnelly (1984), 309, 329
Lynes, Russell, 71

M

MacDiarmid, Hugh, 30n48
Macdonald, Dwight, 75, 172
MacLeish, Archibald, 75
magical realism, 231–33, 239–40, 241n11
Maisons de Jeunes et de la Culture, 110,
    112, 121n37
Major, John, 84
Malraux, André, 75, 83, 84, 110–12,
    120n35
Mapplethorpe, Robert, 69, 95n53, 101, 243
Mara Salvatrucha gang, 314
Mardi Gras celebrations, 19
Mardsen, Peter V., 272n43
Mark, Charles C., 73
Márquez, Gabriel Garcia, 231
marriage amendment, 337n4
Martin, Agnes, 184
Martin, Randy, 170n75
Marty, Martin E., 336n3
mass culture, 34–36
mass media, effect of, 40, 43, 50, 51–52,
    56. *See also* U.S. propaganda offensive
    (1945–59)
matching grants, 86
McCarthy, Eugene, 35
McCarthyism, 125
McCracken, Grant, 63n32
McCreary v. ACLU of Kentucky (2005), 307
"McDonaldization," 122n54
McLuhan, Marshall, 114
Meadmore, Clement, 207
Meet Americans at Work (USIS), 135
Meiggs, Henry, 28n17
Mellon, Andrew, 78
Mendelssohn, Felix, 15, 21, 27n16
Las Meninas (Velasquez), 38
menorah display, 315, *316, 317,* 318, *321*
Menotti, Gian Carlo, 26
Mercouri, Melina, 83
Merelman, Richard, 253

Mesnard, André-Hubert, 108
The Messiah (Handel), 15, 21, 27*n*16
Metromedia, Inc. v. City of San Diego (1981), 285–86
Metropolitan Museum of Art (New York), 103, 106, 177, 179–80
Middle East. *See* Ellington State Department tours
Miller, J. Hillis, 63–64*n*33
Mills, Robert, 74–75
Mindszenty, Joszef Cardinal, 131
Minihan, Jane, 86
Minow, Newton N., 79
Minton, Sherman, 329
Mitchell, W.J.T., 58*n*6, 313–14
Mitterand, François, 111, 114
modern, defined, 168*n*16
modernist movement in federal public art, 8, 197–219; and Camelot cultural policy, 202–4; and Grand Rapids debate, 204–6; and liberal-modernist project in ruins, 212–16; and political crisis of modernist aesthetics, 210–12; and popular revolt against modernist art, 206–10
Modern Language Association, 246
modern music festivals. *See* festival culture in America
Mollard, Claude, 98, 111, 112
Mondale, Joan, 73, 80
Monson, Ingrid, 156
montage, 237
Moore, R. Laurence, 318
Morgan, Charles, Jr., 66*n*48
Morgan, J.P., 105–6
Mormon temple, Maryland, 324, *326, 327*
Morris, Robert, 207
Morris, Wright, 35, 47, 52
Morrison, Toni, 231
Motherwell, Robert, 177, 180, 181, 203
Movement of Horses (Goodnough), 184, *185*
MS-13 gang, 314
Muhammad figure, U.S. Supreme Court building, 329, *330*
Mulcahy, Kevin, 119*n*16
Mulnix, Nancy, 181
multiculturalism. *See* public attitudes toward cultural authority and diversity in higher education and arts
multilingual access to arts, 120*n*23
Mumford, Lewis, 3
murals movement, 207, 218*n*29
Murray, Robert, 210

Museum of Contemporary Art (Los Angeles), 120*n*23
Museum of Fine Arts (Boston), 103, 105
Museum of Natural History (New York), 104–5
museums: attendance at, 82, 104–5, 114–15; creation of, 103–07; in Netherlands, 113; in Nordic countries, 113; organization and collections in, 80, 114–17; tax deductions for cultural gifts to, 71–72, 106. *See also* Franco-American comparisons in cultural democratization; *specific museums*
"Musical Congress" of 1854, 16
music festivals. *See* festival culture in America
Music Is My Mistress (Ellington), 156–57, 161
Music Program of NEA, 195–96*n*48
My Adventures as an Illustrator (Rockwell), 55
My People (Ellington), 156

N

Nance, Ray, 153, 159–60
narrowcasting, 265
Nathan, George Jean, 71
National Advisory Council on the Arts (U.S.), 174–75
national and state partnership for arts, 88, 96*n*58
National Assembly of State Arts Agencies, 81
National Council on the Arts (U.S.), 81, 174–80, 181
National Endowment for the Arts (NEA), 4–5, 171–96; agenda and programming of, 81, 207–8; attacks on, 69–70, 211, 243, 245; campaign to save, 88; and cultural policy, 73–74; Dance Program of, 196*n*48; effect of, 83; and environmental art, 207; individual fellowships from, 183–91; Inner City Murals Program of, 207; leadership of, 87; Music Program of, 195–96*n*48; and National Council on the Arts, 81, 174–80, 181; and "new public art," 89; origins of, 71, 74, 172–75; and state agencies for arts, 81–82; Theater Program of, 196*n*48; Visual Arts Program of, 171–72, 180–87, 190–92

National Endowment for the Humanities (NEH), 69, 73, 81, 82, 83, 87, 88
Nationale-Nederlanden Office Building (Gehry), 227, *228*, 231
national identity, 116–17
National Jubilee, 16
National Lottery (Great Britain), 84
National Mall and Lafayette Park protest regulation, 5–6, 275–303, *277*, *281*, *282*, *299;* and aesthetics cases, 276, 278–79, 280–83; area defined, 278; and historical review court cases on freedom of expression, 284–86; and national parks as public forum, 288–99; and protected communication, 290–94; and public forum, 286–88; and speech/conduct distinction and protected communication, 290–94; and symbolic and "pure" speech, 290–94; and values as subtle, intangible, and non-quantifiable, 294–99
National Mall folk festivals, 25
National Museum of American Art (U.S.), 69
National Museum of Modern Art (France), 111
national parks as public forum, 288–99. *See also* National Mall and Lafayette Park protest regulation
National Park Service, 83. *See also* National Mall and Lafayette Park protest regulation
national portrait gallery, 77–78
National Science Foundation (U.S.), 79
National Trust for Historic Preservation (U.S.), 70, 83
Native Americans, 104, 115, 239
nativity scenes, 319, 328, 329–30. *See also* public display of religion
Natural Born Killers (Stone film), 226, 231, 232, 237, 240
NEA. *See* National Endowment for the Arts
NEH. *See* National Endowment for the Humanities
neorealist art, 190
Netherlands, 86, 113
Netzer, Dick, 107
Neuner, Helen, 238
Nevelson, Louise, 181, 207
New Deal, 77, 82, 83, 107
New England Elegy (Motherwell), 203–4
New Mexico Office of Cultural Affairs, 72
New Orleans, 119*n*17

Newport Jazz Festival, 26, 162–63
"new public art," 89
New York City, 1–2, 17–20, 28*n*17, 104–5, 119*n*17, 183. *See also Tilted Arc* (Serra); *specific institutions and museums*
Nichols, George Ward, 18
Nichols, Maria Longworth, 18
nihilistic antinomianism, 265, 266–67
Nimbus (Murray), 210, 218–19*n*39
Ninth Symphony (Beethoven), 21
Nitze, Paul H., 145*n*23
Nixon, Richard, 74, 157, 207
Noguchi, Isamu, 207
nonprofit cultural organizations, tax deductions for cultural gifts to, 71–72
Nordic countries, museums in, 113
North Carolina Department of Cultural Resources, 72
Northern Kentucky State University, 211
Norwich music festivals (Great Britain), 27*n*12
Nothing But a Man (Romer film), 161

O

O'Brien; United States v. (1968), 287, 301*n*35
Occitan regional culture, 99, 115, 121*n*37
Ocean Park (Diebenkorn), 177, *179*
O'Doherty, Brian, 187
Office of War Information (U.S.), 146*n*26
Ofili, Chris, 309
Oklahoma City Bombings, 324
Oldenburg, Claes, 179, 207
O'Meally, Robert, 159
opera, 195–96*n*48
Opéra (France), 108
Opéra Comique (France), 108
Orchestra Hall (Chicago), 20
orchestras. *See* symphony orchestras
"Organization Man," 172
"The other," 170*n*75

P

Panama-Pacific Exposition of 1915, 22
Paris Opera, 111–12
The Passion of Sacco and Vanzetti (Shahn), 176
The Passion of the Christ (Gibson), 306
past, narratives on, 238–39
Pataki, George, 2

Peace Tower (Los Angeles), 189
Peace under God (USIS), 133
Peale, Charles Willson, 77
Pearlstein, Philip, 190
Peck, Gregory, 175
Pell, Claiborne, 185, 186
Pepper, Beverly, 207
Perot, Ross, 58*n*5
Perry Education Ass'n v. Perry Local Educators Ass'n (1983), 287–88
Pershing, John J., 78
Peterson, Richard A., 116
Philadelphia, 119*n*17, 213
Philadelphia Centennial of 1876, 22
photography, postmodern, 242*n*25
Picasso, 205
A Picture Story of the United States (USIA), 128
Pipe and Bowl Sign Painter (Rockwell), 36, 37, 38, 40
Piss Christ (Serrano), 309. *See also* Serrano, Andres
"plop art," 208
pluralism, 307, 332–36, 338*n*11, 342*n*69
A Pluralistic Universe (James), 239
Poland, 83
political media, 234–35
political speech. *See* National Mall and Lafayette Park protest regulation
political tolerance, 273*n*49
politicians, 234, 236
politicization of endowments, 81
The Politics (Aristotle), 303*n*66
politics, postmodern, 233–35
Pollock, Jackson, 47, 53, 61*n*20
Pompidou, George, 111, 112
Pop Art, 119*n*11, 190
popular commercial culture, 122*n*54
Popular Front, 109, 120*n*33
populism vs. elitism controversy, 114–18. *See also* public attitudes toward cultural authority and diversity in higher education and arts
Portlandia (Kaskey), 214
postmodern aesthetics. *See* antirealism
Pousette-Dart, Richard, 188
poverty, 238
Powell, John Wesley, 76
Powell v. Taylor (1954), 293
Presel, Joseph A., 162
preservation of national heritage and environmental culture, 71–72

presidential campaign of 1948, 130–31
Price, Lucien, 23–24
primary schooling, 120*n*30
"primitive" art, 119*n*10, 122*n*55
Prince, Keiko, 183
print workshop of NEA, 181
privacy, 314, 339*n*28
private vs. public spheres, 33, 44–45, 58*n*6
The Problem We All Live With (Rockwell), 66*n*48
Procope, Russell, 153
Progressive Party, 130
Promey, Sally M., 6, 305–42, 344
propaganda, U.S. *See* U.S. propaganda offensive (1945–59)
Prosterman, Leslie, 5–6, 275–303, 345
Protestant Reformation, 86
protomuseums, 103
public art, 3, 31–32, 104, 197–219
public attitudes toward cultural authority and diversity in higher education and arts, 5, 243–74; battlegrounds of, 244–46; of college graduates, 252–64; explanation of, 257–62; and general public attitudes, 250–52; and ideologically coherence of attitudes, 254–56; multidimensional view of, 256–57; and polarization of attitudes, 249–54; and public opinion and arts of democracy, 247–49; and rejection of cultural authority, 260–61; and support for high culture, 258–59; and support of multiculturalism, 259–60; toward more inclusive democratic culture, 262–67; and traditionalists vs. progressivists, 254–55, 271*n*33; and universities and generational differences in cultural attitudes, 261–62
public display of religion, 6, 305–42; display, defined, 315–28; public, defined, 310–14; religion, defined, 328–34; and visible religion and cultural practice of pluralism, 335–36
public forums, 286–99
public monuments, 57*n*2
Punderson, Molly, 66*n*48
Putnam, Robert, 3

Q

Quadrille (Jullien), 17, 28*n*20
"The Quality of American Culture" (Heckscher), 78

quality vs. quantity in cultural programs, 80–81
quasi-autonomous nongovernmental organization (quango), 86
quotas for media and cultural production, 117

R

"The Race for Space" (Ellington), 154
racial diversity. *See* diversity; public attitudes toward cultural authority and diversity in higher education and arts
radio programs on arts, 94*n*41
Readymades, 119*n*11
Reagan, Ronald, 235
realism, 49, 207. *See also* antirealism; magical realism
Red Star over Islam (pamphlet), 133
religion: and culture wars, 244–45, 258–59, 272*n*43, 338*n*11; and modernity, 331–32; and U.S. propaganda offensive (1945–59), 131–33. *See also* public display of religion
religious architecture. *See* architecture
religious pluralism. *See* pluralism
representational art, 190
Republican Party, 153–54
Robert Frost Memorial Library, 202
Roberts, Owen Josephus, 287
Rockburne, Dorothea, 188
Rockefeller, Nelson, 74
Rockwell, Norman, 4, 31–66; *The Art Critic* (1955), 43, *45*, 47, 61*n*22; *Blood Brothers* (1968), 66*n*48; *Boy Gazing at Glamour Stars* (1934), 40, *41*; *The Connoisseur* (1962), 47, *48*, 49, 53, 54, 55, 66*n*48; and culture wars, 33–35; *The Deadline* (1938), 40, *42*; Double Take (1941), 40; fans of, 50–57, 61–62*n*24, 62*nn*26–27; *Four Freedoms* (1943), 66*n*48; and letter-writing publics, 50–56, 61–62*n*24, 62*nn*26–27, 63*n*32, 63–64*n*33; and people as public, 51–57; *Pipe and Bowl Sign Painter* (1926), 36, *37*, 38, 40; public art of, 36–50; *Shuffleton's Barber Shop* (1950), 40, 43, *44*; *Sign Painter, Billboard Painter* (1935), 38, *39*, 40, 53; *Triple Self-Portrait* (1960), 43–45, *46*, 47, 58*n*5
Rogers, William P., 161
Romeo + Juliet (Luhrmann film), 225, 237

Romeo and Juliet (Zeffirelli film), 225
Romer, Michael, 161
Ronald Reagan federal building (Santa Anna, California), 214
Roosevelt, Franklin Delano, 62*n*24, 70, 87
Root, Deborah, 297
Rosenzweig, Roy, 238–39
Ross, Edmundo, 164
Rothko, Mark, 188
Rushdie, Salmon, 231, 239, 241*n*11
"Russian Children to Throw Hand Grenades" (USIA), 140
Russia the Reactionary (State Department), 129–30

S

Sabato, Victor de, 24
Sacred Music Society, 28*n*17
Saengerfests, 18
Saint Louis, 208–11, 217–18*n*27
Sallman, Warner, 321
Salmagundi Club, 185, 194*n*25
Salzburg Festival, 22–23, 24
Santa Monica residence (Gehry), 226, *227*
Sargent, John Singer, 309
Saturday Evening Post. See Rockwell, Norman
Scalia, Antonin, 293–94
Schlesinger, Arthur, Jr., 79–80, 173, 202
Schneider v. State (1939), 284
Schuman, Howard, 271–72*n*41
Schuster, Mark, 113, 121*n*45–46
Seattle, 217–18*n*27
secondary schooling, 120*n*30
Secretariat of Fine Arts (France), 120*n*33
secularization, 331
segregation, 125, 154, 156
Selassie, Haile, 163
Seldes, Gilbert, 71, 79
"semiotic productivity," 63*n*32
Senegalese Suite (Ellington), 161
September 11, 2001 terrorist attacks: and aesthetics case law, 300*n*5; effect on art of, 1–2, 223, 306, 324; memorials to, 1–2, *307*; and world's view of U.S., 123, 124, 142
Serra, Richard, 89, 188, 200, 201, *201*, 207–11, 217–18*n*27
Serrano, Andres, 69, 171, 309
Shahn, Ben, 176

Shuffleton's Barber Shop (Rockwell), 40, 43, 44
Sign Painter, Billboard Painter (Rockwell), 38, *39*, 40, 53
Simkus, Albert, 116
Simons, Thomas W., 158, 159, 160
Simpson, O.J., 58n5
Situationists, 3
slave labor, 135, 138, 139
Sloan, John, 71
Smith, Cecil, 24
Smith, David, 177, *178*, 180, 189
Smith, Howard W., 71
Smith, Tony, 188, 207
Smithsonian Folklife Festival, 25, 321
Smithsonian Institution, 76–77, 83
Snogren, John, 339n28
social status and artistic preferences, 104–5, 116, 121n45–46, 270n22. *See also* public attitudes toward cultural authority and diversity in higher education and arts
Sontag, Susan, 176–77
Soul Call (Ellington), 161
sound bites, 234–35, 236
Soviet Communism Threatens Education (USIS), 130
Soviet Union: and American cultural policy, 78; and Constructivists, 3; goodwill tour to, 161–62, 169–70n57; oppression of Jews in, 131; standard of living in, 136–37, 139. *See also* Cold War
speech, freedom of. *See* National Mall and Lafayette Park protest regulation
Spellman, Francis Cardinal, 132
Spielberg, Stephen, 58n5
Spirit of Healing (Treviño), 310–12, *311*, 313, 319, 338n12, 338n13
Spoleto Festival (Charleston, South Carolina), 25–26
staggered facades, 227
Stahl, Leslie, 235
Stallings, George, 321, *323*
Stamos, Theodoros, 184
Stankiewicz, Richard, 184
state agencies for arts, 72, 81–82, 83, 87–88, 94n44, 102–3
State Department, U.S., 75, 123, 128, 129–30, 131, 136. *See also* Ellington State Department tours; U.S. propaganda offensive (1945-1959)
state humanities councils, 72, 81–82, 88–90, 94n44

Steichen, Edward, 127
Stella, Frank, 183
Stendhal, 98
Stern, Isaac, 175
Stevens, Roger, 73, 175, 184, 185
Stone, Oliver, 226. *See also Natural Born Killers*
Stone Field Sculpture (Andre), 211
Stover; People v. (1963), 285
Strauss, Johann, Jr., 16
Strayhorn, Billy, 153, 161
strict scrutiny, 287, 290
Such Sweet Thunder (Ellington & Strayhorn), 161
suffrage, 119n11
Sugarman, George, 184, 208, 209, *209*
Sullivan, Arthur, 15, 21
Supreme Court building (U.S.), 329, *330*
surrealists, 3
survey research on culture wars. *See* public attitudes toward cultural authority and diversity in higher education and arts
Swanson, Wayne, 309
symbolic speech, 290–94
symphony orchestras, 20, 24, 103, 105

T

Tanglewood, 22, 23–24
tariffs on artworks, 105–6, 117
tax deductions for cultural gifts, 71–72, 106
Taylor, Bill, 81
Taylor, Francis Henry, 98
Taylor, Joshua, 112
teenagers. *See* adolescents and young adults
television, 50, 79, 94n41
Temple, Shirley, 233
Ten Commandments, 307, *308*
Tenured Radicals (Kimball), 262
tenured-radical theory, 262
Terminator films, 226, 240
Thatcher, Margaret, 84
Thayer, Charles, 131
Theater Program of NEA, 196n48
Thelen, David, 235, 238–39
Third Republic, 108–9, 110
Thomas, Theodore, 18–20, 22
Thomas Brackett (USIS), 135
Three Choirs Festival (England), 13–14
Thyssen-Bornemisza, Hans Heinrich, 83
Tibetan Buddhist prayer wheel display, 321
Tilted Arc (Serra), 89, 188, 200, *201*, 212

time, place, and manner regulation of expression, 291–92
Toledo Art Museum (Gehry), 227
Treviño, Jesse, 310–12, *311*, 313, 319, 338nn12–13
Treviño, Jesse, Jr., 312
Triple Self-Portrait (Rockwell), 43–45, *46*, 47, 58n5
Truman, Harry S., 126–27, 132
Truman Doctrine, 145n23
The Truth Crushes Commie Lies (USIS), 135
Twain (Serra), 217–18n27

U

Undersecretariat for Sports and Leisure (France), 120n33
UNESCO (United Nations Educational, Scientific, and Cultural Organization), 72–73
unions, 138
Union Square (New York), 1–2
United Church of Christ, 336n2
United Nations Educational, Scientific, and Cultural Organization (UNESCO), 72–73
United States Information Agency (USIA), 75. *See also* U.S. propaganda offensive (1945–59)
United States Information Service (USIS), 163. *See also* U.S. propaganda offensive (1945–59)
university English departments, case studies of, 246
U.S. propaganda offensive (1945–59), 4, 123–50; and American response to Cold War, 124–26; capitalism and universal themes in, 133–41; and religious freedom, 131–33; snapshot of, 126–31
U.S. State Department. *See* State Department
USIA. *See* United States Information Agency
USIS. *See* United States Information Service

V

Van Buren, Martin, 76, 87
Vandenberg, Arthur, 197, 206
Van der Rohe, Mies, 198, *199*
Van Orden v. Perry (2005), 307

"Vast Wasteland" speech (Minow FCC head), 79
Velasquez, Diego, 38, 40
Vermeer, Johannes, 38, 40
Versailles peace treaty, 78
videotape, 234, 236
Vietnam Veterans Memorial, 294–95
Vietnam War, 66n48, 75, 207
Village of Arts and Humanities (Yeh), 213
Visionaries and Outcasts (Brenson), 190–91
Visual Arts Program of NEA. *See* National Endowment for the Arts (NEA)
Vitra Furniture Company building (Gehry), 227, 231
VOA. *See* Voice of America
Vogue magazine, 49
Voice of America (VOA), 125, 130–33
Von Eschen, Penny, 4, 5, 151–70, 345

W

Wagner festivals, 22
Warhol, Andy, 49, 179
Warner, R. Stephen, 331, 333–36
Washington, D.C., 74–75, 103
Watt v. Community for Creative Non-Violence(1983), 282, 292–93, 298
Way Down East (Grooms), 211
Weber, William, 14
Weinman, Adolph A., 329
Weintraub, Jeff, 312, 313
Werboff, Michael, 185
West Indian Pancake (Ellington), 161
West Virginia Division of Culture and History, 72
Wetenhall, John, 202
White, Robert A., 313
White City of Chicago Columbian Exhibition, 284
White House Festival of the Arts (1965), 74
Whitman, Walt, 302n56
Whyte, William, 172
Wiley, John C., 131
Wilkes, Charles, 76
Wilkey, Malcolm R., 282
Williams, Cootie, 153
Williams, Marion, 161
Williams, Raymond, 3
Williams, Roger, 128
Wilmer, Valerie, 165
Wilson, John F., 313

Wilson, Woodrow, 154
Winston, Diane, 333
Wireless Bulletin, 132
Wolfe, Tom, 214
women. *See* gender and sexuality
Woodrum, Clifton, 77
Woodstock music festival, 25
Woodyard, Sam, 153
World Jubilee, 16–17
World's Fair (New York), 28n20
World Trade Center site memorial, 1–2
World War II, 77, 78, 84, 126, 145n17
World War II Memorial (Washington, D.C.), 300n5
Wright, Russel, 127
Wyeth, Andrew, 176, 180

Wyoming Division of Cultural Resources, 72

Y

yard art, 309
Yates, Sidney R., 73
Yeh, Lily, 213
York music festivals (England), 27n12

Z

Zambia, 162–65
Zeffirelli, Franco, 224–25
Zenger, John Peter, 128
Zolberg, Vera L., 4, 97–122, 345